# Under Eastern Eyes
## A critical reading of Maritime fiction

A strong literary tradition has grown out of Canada's Maritime provinces, from the nineteenth-century narratives of Thomas Chandler Haliburton and Joseph Howe to the contemporary novels of Antonine Maillet and David Adams Richards. But Maritime fiction has never received the critical attention that writing in other parts of Canada has enjoyed. With this volume Janice Kulyk Keefer helps to bridge this gap.

Keefer has selected some of the best and most significant fiction produced in the Maritimes over the past century and offers readings that comprise both major works, including Charles Bruce's *The Channel Shore* and Richards' *Lives of Short Duration*, and such marginal texts as the historical fiction of Charles G.D. Roberts and Douglas Huyghue, in order to explore the defining characteristics of the Maritime experience and ethos. She offers new and provocative perspectives on such seminal but problematic figures as Hugh MacLennan and Ernest Buckler and places the work of more recent writers – Alistair MacLeod, Donna Smyth, Susan Kerslake – within the tradition of Maritime fiction, showing how they have expanded and, in some ways, subverted it. Special attention is given to the contributions of women writers such as Maillet, L.M. Montgomery, and Nancy Bauer, as well as to the attempts of such overtly political writers as Silver Donald Cameron to challenge the stereotype of Maritime conservatism.

Neither a thematic quest nor a historical survey, Keefer's analysis demonstrates that the literature of the Maritimes can hold its own with writing from any other region of the country. *Under Eastern Eyes* reveals the Maritimes as both a harsh and fertile ground, from which some of Canada's most challenging and rewarding fiction has sprung.

JANICE KULYK KEEFER has published a collection of short stories, *The Paris-Napoli Express*, and a book of poetry, *White of the Lesser Angels*. Her short stories won first prize in the annual CBC literary competition in two consecutive years. She lives in Annapolis Royal, Nova Scotia, and she has taught English literature at the University of Sussex and Université Sainte-Anne.

# Under Eastern Eyes

A critical reading
of Maritime fiction

Janice Kulyk Keefer

University of Toronto Press
Toronto Buffalo London

© University of Toronto Press 1987
Toronto Buffalo London
Printed in Canada

ISBN 0-8020-5747-0 (cloth)
ISBN 0-8020-6656-9 (paper)

Printed on acid-free paper

**Canadian Cataloguing in Publication Data**

Keefer, Janice Kulyk, 1953–
Under eastern eyes

Bibliography: p.
Includes index.
ISBN 0-8020-5747-0 (bound). – ISBN 0-8020-6656-9 (pbk)

1. Canadian fiction – Maritime Provinces – History
and criticism. I. Title.

PS8199.5.M37K43 1987     C813     C87-093992-0
PR9192.2.K43 1987

Front cover illustration:
*Trying to Figure the Human Factor in All of This*
by Nyna Cropas, 1985
charcoal on paper, 50 cm × 65 cm
Reproduced by kind permission of the artist

This book has been published with the help of a grant from the Canadian
Federation for the Humanities, using funds provided by the Social
Sciences and Humanities Research Council of Canada. Publication has
also been assisted by the Canada Council and the Ontario Arts Council
under their block grant programs.

*for Thomas and Christopher*

# Contents

# *Preface*

When New France was in its last agonies ... and when the rest of the present Dominion was wilderness or virgin forest, Halifax had its books and book sellers, its bookbinders and even its book auctions, its own newspapers and its own magazines. Thus Nova Scotia holds the position of primacy in the intellectual development of Canada.

ARCHIBALD MACMECHAN[1]

For many Canadians, the Atlantic region remains an anachronistic backwater of political, social, and cultural despair. Furthermore, according to the high priests of the so-called Upper Canadian historical and political tradition, the main thrust of Canadian development has owed little, if anything, to events or persons in the four Atlantic provinces.

GEORGE RAWLYK[2]

The course of Maritime literature can be interpreted not as a fall but a plunge from grace, as far as English-writing Canada is concerned. Perhaps the term 'plunge' is misleading, since it suggests something spectacular and implies that what's happened to Books in Atlantic Canada over the past 200 years has been considered worthy of notice. 'Very often the rest of Canada forgets that the Maritimes do exist, and when thinking of their writers cynically praises the work of Carman and Roberts and does not think of or remember anyone else.'[3] Donald Stephens's appraisal of the situation in 1960 remains not untrue today.

Margaret Laurence, for example, may have considered *The Mountain and the Valley* as 'probably one of the best novels in English in this century,' but in most discussions of the post-war or modern novel in Canada it tends to be slighted or totally ignored.[4]

To certain critics – those most opposed to 'regionalism' in its creeping or rampant forms – this is but just: what part, after all, has Maritime literature played in helping us develop an authentically Canadian sense of self, or cultural time and place? Lucy Maud Montgomery, Thomas Raddall, even David Adams Richards: are they not distinctly marginal in comparison with such figures as Sara Jeannette Duncan, Robertson Davies, Matt Cohen? And how do the Maritimes acquit themselves precisely as a region? Where British Columbia has inspired the mythopoeic exuberance of a Sheila Watson or Jack Hodgins; where the prairies have compelled profound explorations of moral landscape in the work of a Margaret Laurence or Rudy Wiebe; where Ontario fast-breeds sophisticated forms of urban, rural, and cosmopolitan consciousness in the writing of a Margaret Atwood, an Alice Munro, or a Timothy Findley, what paradigms do the Maritimes offer besides those of tidal bores or blowsy idylls? Surely the example of such a writer as Hugh MacLennan clinches the argument: not only did the most prominent of contemporary writers born and raised in the Maritimes end up settling in and writing about 'central' Canada – Quebec and Ontario – he also evicts his Maritime-born protagonists Jerome Martell, Archie MacNeil, and Daniel and Alan Ainslie from their native regions, as if to show that no man of any ambition or imagination could hope to prove or sustain his mettle there.

As a distinctive and vital literary region, the Maritimes has been virtually neglected by critics and scholars of Canadian literature. This study is an attempt to reduce, not bridge, an immense gap; it offers neither an historical survey nor a thematic plunder of Maritime writing, but rather an explorer's map of the primary features of a representative number of texts, considered in a variety of contexts.

By considering together works such as *The Old Judge* and *Barometer Rising*, *Rockbound* and *The Channel Shore*, *The Master's Wife* and *Lives of Short Duration*, the critic can begin to reveal the richness and often problematic diversity of Maritime fiction – and as well, the alternative values and vision this fiction realizes. For, if Canada's invisible or forgotten east has, as Rawlyk's Upper Canadians insist, contributed nothing to the Canadian mainstream – urbanized, industrial, conspicuously consumptive of all that technology and empire proffer – then perhaps the literature produced by the sidestream may possess an authenticity, even a subversive quality that could make the Maritimes the thought-provoking, if not the thought-control, centre of Canada.

Acquaintance with the scope and strength of Maritime writing is necessary not just because narratives by native-born Canadians actually began in the pens of Howe and Haliburton, and because Canadian poetry first took on imaginative authenticity in the verse of Roberts and Carman. As Thomas Raddall insists, Canada owes the Maritimes an incommensurable debt: 'the whole future of Canada hung on what happened in Nova Scotia during the American Revolution, because Nova Scotia then included what is now New Brunswick and the Gaspé. Had the fourteenth colony gone in with the other thirteen Canada would have had a fourteenth American state right on the mouth of the St Lawrence. And that would have finished her – if not in 1775 or 1783 ... in 1812.'[5]

Though the debate between advocates of nationalism as opposed to regionalism may persist as long as Canadians write and read it all, it would seem that the stranglehold of 'transcontinental' or 'Laurentian' criticism is being broken – that school which made imperative the focus on, or actual finding of, *the* Canadian imagination, *the* Canadian identity, *the* Canadian response to nature, at the expense of the manifold, obstinately heterogeneous forms of Canadian experience articulated on the west or east coasts, in the north, and on the prairies. The interest in prairie writing that has developed since Laurence Ricou's *Vertical Man / Horizontal World* signals the energy and importance of the regionalist new wave on which, as I hope to show, the literature of the Maritimes can securely ride.

The first chapter of this study consists of a polemical introduction to the prime issues and concepts involved in any exploration of Maritime literature. The nature, scope, and critical approach of this book will be outlined, and a preliminary version of the Maritime 'ethos' as expressed in the region's literature will be sketched. Finally, this introductory chapter will examine the reasons for the long-standing neglect of Maritime literature by Canadian critics, closing with a defence of regionalism by suggesting possible redefinitions of that problematic term.

Chapters 2 through 7 will treat the texts selected for study not in chronological order, but rather by contextual concerns, considering not themes or archetypes but instead topoi, genres, and concepts – for example, the interplay of conservative and radical forces in Maritime fiction, the opposing modes of idyllic and realistic fiction, and the complex mythos of that genre indigenous to the region, the historical romance. Chapter 8 will examine the evolution of creative paradigms established by and for Maritime writers. And the concluding chapter will concern itself with that desire for verbal expression and communication denied so long to women in the Maritimes, both writers and fictive characters.

Writing about Canadian fiction from 1940 to 1960, Hugo McPherson praised the few writers who have escaped 'the nets of nostalgia, parochialism and naïve nationalism' to begin to create an authentic and excellent Canadian literature.[6] Appropriately enough, given the metaphor, many of these fish derive from Maritime waters. The aim of this study is to bring an important area of Canadian writing to the attention of potential readers, and to provoke further critical discussion as to the nature, scope, and significance of Maritime literature.

I have taken liberties with Joseph Conrad's novel *Under Western Eyes* to give this study its title. Conrad wished, among other things, to present to his readers a unique way of seeing and being, to underscore the essential difference between the Russian and European traditions and temperaments. What I wish to emphasize is the fundamental coherence of the Maritime ethos and vision, and also its significant points of difference from other regional cultures and from what we have been taught to think of as 'the distinctively Canadian.' It is time for us to see ourselves under eastern eyes, in order to come to a better understanding of who we are, have been, and may become.

This book has been made possible by a Social Sciences and Humanities Research Council of Canada post-doctoral fellowship, the accommodation and services provided by Université Sainte-Anne, and the encouragement of a number of scholars of Maritime literature, among them Gwen Davies and Ken MacKinnon. I would like to thank Robert Kulyk and my parents, Natalie and Joseph Kulyk, for helping to look after my children so that I could have time to write; Mimi Stanfield and Murray Coolican, and Susan Kerslake for their hospitality during my raids on Halifax libraries; Mary Jo Anderson of Halifax's CBIC for giving me access to recent Maritime writing; Gerald Hallowell for his encouragement and editorial acumen; Alain Chabot for his patience and proficiency in making me computer literate. And to Michael Keefer I owe thanks beyond words.

# Under Eastern Eyes

# 1

# Polemical Introduction

We are a people, not because we have cleared the land, built roads and cities, thriven in trade, but because we have a voice. These printed pages tell how we think and feel, what we remember and what we desire. These dead leaves speak for the masses of us who otherwise were dumb.

ARCHIBALD MACMECHAN[1]

This study restricts itself to fiction because it is in novels, short stories, and narratives that the voice of Maritimers has most often and most compellingly been heard.[2] Second, it concerns itself with the fiction of the Maritimes and not of the Atlantic Provinces. That a comprehensive survey of Newfoundland literature, *The Rock Observed*, has recently been published is, of course, a better argument for the omission of Newfoundland from this study than the fact that, until 1949, literature produced in Newfoundland can't technically be considered Canadian at all. In *The Rock Observed* Patrick O'Flaherty proceeds according to a 'fundamental premise' stated by one of the writers he treats – the premise of Newfoundland's 'apartness' from the rest of British North America.[3] At the close of his study O'Flaherty observes: 'So little is known about the true history of Newfoundland, and indeed about the character and motivation of many of those who have tried to influence or describe it, that any writer who summarily reduces the complexity of Newfoundland's past or present to a ready formula must be regarded with great suspicion.'[4]

Indeed, it may be suggested that to reduce the varieties of fiction produced in New Brunswick, Prince Edward Island, Nova Scotia – and Cape Breton – to that conglomerate adjective 'Maritime,' is equally suspect. Yet it can be argued that these latter provinces do hold together in the way that Manitoba, Saskatchewan, and Alberta form the prairies – and that for a literary critic to slap on Newfoundland at their tail so as to create 'Atlantic Canada' would be as misguided as to tack British Columbia onto the prairies to make up that equally unmanageable fiction, 'the West.' In either case the rich and resistant particularity of the tag-along province would be betrayed.

The literature of Newfoundland, as Patrick O'Flaherty conceives it, relates 'the epic story of a people's struggle against overwhelming natural forces and economic adversity': 'the elements of wind, tide, and crag' compose a kind of canon which the writer may articulate but never alter.[5] As Sandra Djwa reveals, Newfoundlanders are attracted to such writers as Sinclair Ross partly because 'his concept of a prairie nature – hard, with overtones of fatalism' – corresponds to their own views of Newfoundland.[6] And, if there is a shibboleth which distinguishes Newfoundland from the Maritimes, it must surely be 'outport,' with its associations of an epic struggle against starvation and the sea. What gives to the outport its stark and final isolation is not only the intractable authority of the sea, but more importantly, the sheer lack of any alternative to it at one's back – there is no 'Happy Valley' rich in fruit and flower, nor is Newfoundland by any Herculean stretch of the imagination a 'Garden of the Gulf.'[7] Rarely has it sustained visions of imminent or actual Arcadia, as Nova Scotia, New Brunswick, and Prince Edward Island have done for writers as diverse as Joseph Howe and Thomas Haliburton, Charles G.D. Roberts and L.M. Montgomery. O'Flaherty's depiction of the outport ethos clinches the argument:

it would be hard to find a place in the world in which greater effort has been expended with so little remaining to show for it. In outport Newfoundland ... one generation could not tame the country for the benefit of the next, and thus all generations were really pioneers, in the sense that they had to confront the same wildness. While there was indeed what the geographers call 'a discontinuous strip of cultural fabric' along parts of the coast, such a strip was made by clearing away scrub and geological debris rather than by building any permanent structures, and many structures that were raised were built in the knowledge that they would not last. And so with so much effort directed at the sea, which shows no mark of human labour and savagely reduces the subtlest contrivances of man to garbage on beaches ... Newfoundland is a region, like Hardy's Egdon Heath, where human enterprise with 'pickaxe, plough, or spade' is less noticeable than 'the very finger-touches of the last geological change.'[8]

Contrarily, it is a sense of lasting structures raised by human effort, of continuous cultural and communal patterns as serviceable and enduring as a tightly woven rug, and finally, not of Hardyesque fatalism but instead of complex engagement, half-ironic, half-idyllic, with the reality of Maritime life that characterize this region's best literature.

A second question must now be broached: who, of all the writers born or born-again in the region, count as Maritime writers? For each MacLennan or Charles G.D. Roberts who has shipped out to such metropolises as Montreal or New York come such ex-Americans as Susan Kerslake or Nancy Bauer, or the H.R. Percys and David Walkers who have left Great Britain for Granville Ferry or Saint Andrews by the Sea: which kind of expatriate is to be seen as giving authentic voice to Maritime experience or sensibility? And what of those repatriated exiles, the Acadians, whose language and history would seem to form their true home ground: can Antonine Maillet, for example, be considered a Maritime writer or must what is known as the 'Two Solitudes syndrome' divide and impoverish the literature of this region?[9]

In attempting to define for Canadians their distinctive literary voice or mind, Ronald Sutherland made use of the term 'sphere of consciousness,' which he described as the result of a writer's 'total cultural conditioning and especially of the dominant influence' within his or her particular background. Thus, what roots any writer within a given country, region, city, is not his place of birth or upbringing or his adult choice of address, but rather his shaping vision of the worlds his texts create. Thus, argues Sutherland, someone like Brian Moore remains fixed within his northern Irish sphere of consciousness, whether his fictions are set in Belfast, Montreal, or Hollywood: '*Ginger Coffey* no more makes Brian Moore a Canadian writer than *For Whom the Bell Tolls* makes Hemingway Spanish.'[10] Mordecai Richler, on the other hand, remains for Sutherland obdurately Canadian, for all his protracted residence abroad.

If we transpose Sutherland's terms from a national to a regional context, certain preliminary points can be made. A description of the defining characteristics of the Maritime ethos I will leave for a later point in this chapter: the fiat I should here like to issue is that we consider as 'Maritime writers' those artists whose work reveals a strong imaginative involvement with and commitment to the region. The minds of such writers are either saturated (as in the case of Buckler, Raddall, Richards) or ironically gripped (as with MacLennan and MacLeod) by the Maritimes – their work reveals the kind of eyes the region gives to a writer; the kind of things those eyes are compelled to notice and to represent. Given this criterion, we can say that someone like H.R. Percy should be considered a generally Canadian rather than specifically Maritime writer: a work like *Painted Ladies* has more in common with *Lady Oracle* – or, of course, *The Horse's Mouth* – than with *The Mountain and the Valley*. Conversely, Hugh MacLennan, despite his having virtually abandoned consideration of the Maritimes in his fiction, has so influenced the way in which the region is perceived that any worthwhile study of Maritime literature must consider his oeuvre. Finally, as far as Antonine Maillet is concerned, her work is as indispensable to an understanding of the basic realities of Maritime life as Gabrielle Roy's has been to our conceptualizing of French-Canadian experience. This book, therefore, will draw such works as *La Sagouine* and *Pélagie-la-Charrette* firmly within *its* sphere of consciousness, on the assumption that, through the medium of translation at least, Maillet's works will become as influential in the English-speaking Maritimes as Roy's are in Anglophone Canada.

Such attempts as the foregoing to closely define or focus on a regional literature, rather than on national trends or on international literary movements must, of course, be underwritten by the premise that this literature possesses something of significant interest and enduring value; that, though it may have been long perceived as marginal to the development of Canadian writing, it is in no way sub- or pseudo-literary. The writers with whom I have chosen to deal have produced works which, however problematic or profoundly flawed many of them may be, yet possess a saving energy of imagination and observation. With the ephemera and effluvia which Nova Scotia, Prince Edward Island, and New Brunswick have thrown up, works which even the most conscientious archivist would find worthy, perhaps of preservation somewhere, but of public notice, never, I am not concerned. The texts which make up a Maritime canon, however, suffer from a double disadvantage within the context of contemporary criticism: many of the genres they favour are, paradoxically, both critically outmoded and commercially popular: the idyll, historical romance, and that current literary leper – the realist or representational novel.

Maritime writers would seem to share a confidence foreign to modernist and post-modernist alike, a belief in the reality and significance of the accessible world of human experience common to reader and writer. That which is actual, to hand, and meaningful by virtue of association with established patterns of thought and action; that which is richly particular – Sam Slick's clocks, Anne Shirley's red hair, Kezia Barnes's tinderbox, Ellen Canaan's rug – is the prime stuff of Maritime fiction. Absences, traces, *différance* usually possess a secondary status, how-

ever poignant or damning; they derive their power from the pre-
established authority of presence: 'Nova Scotia is a place where so
many inanimate things take on a living quality because of an intimacy
nearly personal with the man amongst them. His grasp on the imple-
ment. His way of life hewn to the shifting seasons ... Scarce anything
around him but touches, in some way closer than the mere retinal, on
his work and wonderment ...'[11]

As in Nova Scotia and for Ernest Buckler, so in Prince Edward Island
and New Brunswick for Montgomery and Macphail, Nowlan and
Richards. Maritime fiction is overwhelmingly representational in that its
producers engage in what Joseph Conrad called making us 'see' –
selecting, out of the welter of phenomena, impressions, actions, and
events, those things that have a peculiar resonance for the writer and
have been habitually overlooked by the reader. Representation in this
sense is no illusionist's substitution of cardboard words for elusive
realities but a matter of integrity and honesty, the arduousness of which
is suggested by that image of the stonebreaker with which Conrad
ends his celebrated preface to *The Nigger of the 'Narcissus.'* That such
work can be arduous is presupposed by the intractableness of reality,
of a phenomenally 'given' world which is not the pliable product of
perception, language, or cultural and social schemas, but against which
the truth of the meanings we have composed in language, and the various schemas we develop to structure our lives, may be tested. This is
the *sine qua non* of mimetic art which 'successfully conveys the real object
in a manner which deepens our experiential knowledge of that object
or like objects.'[12] It is with these concerns that the epilogue of that consummately representational and mimetic novel, *The Mountain and the
Valley,* is so tortuously involved.

Thus, while some of the most recently published writers in the Maritimes are busy fabulating self-reflexive, narcissistic, ludic, and diege-
tic narratives, the tradition of Maritime fiction, from Haliburton and
McCulloch down to Buckler and Richards, remains conservative, however much that tradition may be revivified, even radicalized, by the
different techniques and vision of individual writers. As the word vision
may suggest, the critical methodology which this study employs will
also be traditional in the sense that it will deploy what A.D. Nuttall has
termed the 'transparent' as opposed to the 'opaque' language of criticism. Given that the language and, by extension, the metaphysics of
literary criticism is now a central issue in Canadian letters, with writers like Robert Kroetsch demanding that post-modernist literary practice
be adopted in dealing not only with British and American but also

with Canadian literature, it will be necessary to clarify the terms which Nuttall has coined, and to indicate what my use of them will entail.

The opaque critic, according to Nuttall, practises a restrictive discipline, responding to any given work of literature exclusively in terms of what goes on in other literary works or within the chosen text itself. Refusing to submit to the 'mimetic enchantment' of the text, refusing to consider the fictive world as having any relation to or engagement with the world outside it, the opaque critic likewise refuses to talk of the text in ways which would compromise his and the work's autonomy. Restricting himself to formal analysis alone, to sifting the words of the text through the screens of self-reflexiveness or intertextuality, he may be displeased by the work but may never dissent from it. The transparent critic, on the other hand, 'can and will do all the things done by the opaque critic but is willing to do other things as well'[13] – that is, to explain the behaviour of fictitious characters by analogy with real-life equivalents; to enter the mimetic 'dream' or 'magic' in order to comprehend the work, but with the knowledge that it *is* magical and fictive. Whereas the opaque critic cannot move freely either 'into the proposed, hypothetical events of the book,' or else 'back from the public, manifest superficies of the work to the range of human activities and emotions which give force and meaning to fictions,'[14] the transparent critic, partly by his adoption of 'luminously normal' speech[15] (which makes sense both inside and outside the text, both when dealing with fictitious events and characters, and with real or ordinary experiences and people) can do both, and more. An opaque critic, for example, would be forced to discuss *The Mountain and the Valley* exclusively in terms of its image clusters, structural patterns and rhythms, and narrative narcissism, to use Linda Hutcheon's term – treating it thus as a novel about its author's procrastinations about writing a novel – and would have nothing to do with any discussion of, for example, how perceptively Buckler portrays male adolescence, how successful he is at giving profound meaning and dignity to the lives of inarticulate farming people. The transparent critic, on the other hand, would be able to do all of the above: would even be permitted, by her very conception of her task, to discuss the mimetic authenticity of Buckler's novels – his success in conveying to us exactly how things feel, look, seem – with relation to Buckler's highly abstract treatment of structure and his anxious awareness that objects themselves do not exist until the writer names them.

The simplified forms I have given to opaque and transparent critical practice, and my obvious preference for transparency, will make it appear that the opaque critic is a mere straw man to be blown down;

given a choice between all and very nearly next-to-nothing, who would plump for the latter? As Nuttall's *A New Mimesis* makes abundantly clear, however, behind these different critical positions lean complex and sophisticated sets of philosophical *données*, religious – or at least metaphysical – beliefs, arguments, and rationalizations; moreover opacity, as displayed in its fashionable and often dazzling post-structural dress, is very much in the ascendant. To choose to apply 'transparent' criticism to Maritime fiction is thus not to be old-fashioned, however much it may be out of fashion. Rather, it is to use certain perspectives and techniques developed by post-structuralist or post-modernist criticism which seem particularly suited to certain Maritime texts – the revaluation of the concept of marginality, and the notion of subtext, for example – without thereby vetoing the mimetic power and claims which those texts possess and press. Transparent criticism may even help us to test certain claims of opaque criticism: a look at a work like *Each Man's Son* for example, with its peculiar attitudes to labour and political activism, puts into intriguing context the 'opaque' claim that it is not a work's claim to truth, but only its internal coherence or lack of it, that merits the critic's attention.

Traditional forms of fiction and traditional methods of critical analysis and judgment, then, may be seen to have more than a nostalgic appeal and interest. Since tradition stands in opposition (as well as in inevitable relation) to that which is 'new,' 'avant-garde,' and 'post' everything, only from an awareness of traditional literary forms and practices can we gain the ground that will give us a critical perspective on what opposes them. To accept unresistingly the 'opaque' position would be a little like succumbing to Sam Slick's 'soft sawder' and finding ourselves landed with a Yankee tin clock at an exorbitant price. Thus the present vogue for metafiction, mythopoesis, fabulation which has led to a corresponding dismissal or actual ignorance of traditional narrative forms and approaches results not only in the continuing oblivion to which most of us have consigned Maritime literature, but also in an encroachment upon our freedom and our rights as readers. Works like *The Channel Shore, The Master's Wife,* and *Lives of Short Duration* demand to be encountered as forms of imaginative experience which give us ways of knowing our world, and perspectives which help us question and test the truth of inherited or imposed schemas and concepts. That these works are themselves informed by schemas and concepts is, of course, undeniable; that their substance is exhausted by them, is untenable. Through the active and interrogative reading of the full range of literary works – the representational and the self-reflexive, the

conventional and the experimental – we can master the techniques
and acquire the knowledge that will enable us to compare and select,
preserve or transform ourselves and our world. To this essential end
an awareness of Maritime literature will help us.

\*\*\*

the values of stability and rootedness, the sense of belonging to a well-
defined community, the gentler, domesticated beauty of farmstead and fishing
harbour. The sense that things are not altogether transient, that the idiosyncratic old home that has been there two hundred years will not have been tram-
pled by a high-rise developer tomorrow. The Maritimes have their own illusions, of course, but those illusions seem to me closer to the kind of thinking we
will all need as the Industrial Revolution transforms itself into something less
profligate, wasteful and greedy.

If I were a native Maritimer, probably I would not see it that way. Instead of
stability I would see stagnation; instead of tradition, I would see rigidity;
instead of durability, decay.

Silver Donald Cameron[16]

The twentieth century came very late to the rural Maritimes. In the 1930s my
native place couldn't have been much different from what it was in the 1880s,
except that the ships had vanished long ago and the lumbering was petering out,
so that most people were poorer than their grand-parents had been. We had
no telephone, no electricity, no central heating and no plumbing except a primitive kitchen sink.

Alden Nowlan[17]

For anyone born and bred outside the region, it is nearly impossible to
hear the word 'Maritimes' without being swept to sea on a wave of
memories and impressions formed by distant summer holidays or reful-
gent coffee table books whose pages frame the requisite romantic em-
blems: white clapboard church in scarlet autumn dale, dories in the very
shape of indolence nesting in placid harbours, the subtle rot of grey-
shingled shacks in dense spruce groves. The few picture books which do
include the unaesthetic images – senile, ruined faces, large families in
two-room shacks little less crude than those Nowlan describes – manage
to neutralize them. The poverty such images convey serves to authenticate the picturesque, saving it from kitsch and contributing to that
spirit of place intrinsic to the very notion of 'the regional.'

Yet these picture books which comprehend what Nowlan called the 'tourist' and the 'missionary' responses to the Maritimes have at least touched the two poles of this region's lived and written reality: a dry-eyed recognition of longstanding deprivation, and a sense of self-possession which privileges native values and truths opposed to the modern mainstream – habits of mind which, indeed, seem only able to survive in areas of chronic impoverishment.

If we look beyond recent photo-journalism to some of the region's earliest literary texts we will discover many of the most enduring and powerful characteristics of what we might call the Maritime ethos – which latter term the *Oxford English Dictionary* defines, after Aristotle, as 'the characteristic spirit, prevalent tone of sentiment, of a people or community ...' In choosing Joseph Howe's *Western and Eastern Rambles: Travel Sketches of Nova Scotia* as a prime example of an early Maritime text, however, an inevitable problem arises: Maritime literature runs the risk of appearing as, first and foremost, Nova Scotian literature. The only defence can be open acknowledgment of the fact that this province had a cultural and historical head start on its neighbours. New Brunswick, of course, was only carved out of the 'wild west' of Nova Scotia in 1784 at the insistence of the Loyalists; neither Fredericton nor Saint John ever received anything like the erratic but massive infusions of money and manpower which vitalized Halifax so that Nova Scotia could boast of having had 'the first newspaper, the first legislature, the first university, the first provincial history, the first famous writer, the first literary movement in what is now Canada.'[18] Prince Edward Island, on the other hand, remained so long embroiled in the abrasive politics of land ownership that not until the present century did creditable works of fiction appear, works that can hold their own against such pungent examples of that province's oral tradition as the ballad 'Farewell to Prince Edward Isle.' To begin at the beginning, then, is to confine ourselves to the work of native Nova Scotians.

The first thing to remark about Howe's *Rambles* is the way in which they invert the conventions of the travel book, as this genre took shape in Canada. Anna Jameson's *Winter Studies and Summer Rambles,* Susanna Moodie's *Roughing It in the Bush* and *The Backwoods of Canada,* and the exploration narratives of Thompson and Selkirk have one thing in common: they are outsiders' accounts of not merely a foreign, but more importantly, an alien land, and they were destined for readers who, by and large, would never set foot in what was to become Canada. As Janet Giltrow's aptly named essay, 'Painful Experience in a Distant Land' declares, standard travel narratives were structured by 'the idea of getting home,' and were largely undertaken to repair a sense of rupture with the writer's home community in the motherland. Should the writer, like Mrs Moodie, have retained on a one-way journey the ideal of round-trip travel, her art will be 'poignant with disappointment and unresolvable alienation.' In any case, 'the travel narrator is alone, detached from the scenes he describes, and unassimilated by the foreign community. At their most extreme, the conditions of travel lead to social disorientation, anomie, feelings of being *dépaysé.'*[19]

Nothing could be farther from the enthusiasm, confidence, and digressive brio of Howe's *Rambles*, the sheer at-homeness which is established in his prompt quotation of Haliburton's motto to his *Historical and Statistical Account of Nova Scotia*: 'this is my own, my native land.'[20] Nor is Howe content merely to express pride in his birthplace; he insists, indeed the whole project of the *Rambles* insists, on its readers – Howe's fellow Nova Scotians – sharing his pride-in-place: 'Aye, and indulge the feeling, man, and don't be ashamed of it; for it is a tower of strength to the country; 'tis that must adorn and beautify its bosom – 'tis that must enrich its literature and preserve the purity of its institutions.' Such patriotism, Howe concludes (some fifteen years after the War of 1812), will inspire Nova Scotians to defend their country from 'the tide of invasion' (WER 73).

Howe's *Rambles* set out to describe rural scenery and society in Nova Scotia, to both formulate and describe the 'common heritage' of reader and writer (WER 210) by contributing his own 'wise saws – economic, moral or political' (WER 64). This pressure of engagement with the social and economic realities of his time and place, which he shares with his contemporaries McCulloch and Haliburton, is to be found almost as a first principle in the work of later Maritime writers and forms one of the essential characteristics of Maritime writing. The precondition of this kind of engagement is a strong historical awareness which takes the form of 'the spirit of the past' in Howe's pages. Devotee as he was of Sir Walter Scott, Howe eagerly scans the landscape unrolling before him for traces of heroic exploit and romantic incident in his young country's past; at Bloody Creek and Malignant Cove he is able to relate properly thrilling anecdotes. Yet the 'spirit of the past' comes most tellingly to settle elsewhere: on that indispensable topos of Maritime literature, exploited by Buckler and Bruce, Macphail, MacLennan, and Maillet, among others – the graveyard. Howe has no use for gliding ghosts with which to titillate his readers; instead he labours to rouse emotions of admiration and gratitude for the 'privations and toils' of those pioneers who 'plunged into the forest, not as we do now, for a summer day's

ramble or an hour of tranquil musing, but to win a home from the rug-
gedness of uncultivated nature'; who transformed the wilderness into
a garden and 'bequeathed to their descendants the security of settled
government – the advantages of political freedom, the means of moral
and religious improvement, which they labored to secure, but never
lived to enjoy' (WER 134). If he invokes 'the muse of Gray' it is not with
any sense of the natural superiority of the 'sanctity and softened associations of an English churchyard' over the 'lowly beds' of those buried
behind the plain wooden Presbyterian Meeting House at Truro, but
contrarily, to plead the latter as an even worthier subject for 'deeper'
song (WER 133–4). At the close of the *Rambles* Howe comes to repeat his
panegyric to the dead while visiting the ruins of the old fortifications
at Guysborough. This sense of conscious connection with the past and
its heroes permeates the fiction of the Maritimes; not only Thomas
Raddall and Antonine Maillet have been gripped by it, but also Alden
Nowlan, who, quoting Edmund Burke's definition of a nation as 'a
communion between the dead, the living and the unborn,'[21] gives voice
to a peculiarly Maritime sense of shared community.

This sense of community conceived in the intimate terms of family or
village life and perceived as strongly influenced by religious and economic forces is a second aspect of that 'common heritage' Howe portrays. At Granville and Bridgetown, by the mills of Colchester and the
iron foundry at Albion Mines, Howe shows a keen appreciation of the
economic base of the various communities he encounters: almost like a
prototypical George Orwell, Howe descends into the coal pits at Albion
Mines to experience for himself the manner – and the dangers – of
their operation. And, though he admits to having chosen rose-tinted
spectacles through which to view the scenery and progress of his
native province, he finds ingenious means to voice censure and concern
over the tendency of prosperous farming settlements to slide into such
decadent customs and habits as Haliburton savages in *The Clockmaker*.
Yet Howe is disturbed not by mere social pretension – farmers' wives
and daughters putting on the airs of their urban 'betters' – but rather, by
the potentially doleful economic consequences to farmers of their refusal to work hard enough to discharge the mortgages on their exceptionally fertile lands.

The strengths as well as the inevitable thorns of community life on
which Howe discourses in his *Rambles* of 1828–31 will chequer the
literature of the Maritimes ever after; it is axiomatic that the region's
classics detail, not life in the city – however provincial – but in the
heart of the backwoods, the enclosed farming valley, the 'lost' island, or

the channel shore. Howe's travel sketches set up two archetypes: the community of Bridgetown, in which a spirit of solidarity triumphs over the niggling reticulations of social class, and that of Pictou, in which religious strife between Presbyterian sects has led the entire town into a slough of 'degrading and paltry bickers' (WER 149). Yet, since Howe finds the natives of Pictou as hospitable to strangers as they are quarrelsome with one another, it is clear that Pictou represents for him the tolerable exception to the rule of community. So imbued is Howe with this sense of solidarity that, even more so than McCulloch and Haliburton, he makes of his text a kind of personal conversation with the reader, whom he alternately teases and teaches in the course of his journeying. Howe's ideal reader is, of course, his fellow Nova Scotian; mere fact of birth in 'Acadia' makes one a member of the community. Thus it is not surprising to meet with what must strike a modern reader as an unusually accommodating attitude towards those who certainly struck Haliburton and McCulloch as natural inferiors and aliens. One of Howe's earliest digressions once out of Halifax stems from his encounter with a group of Black market-women. 'It has been the fashion,' Howe remarks, 'to revile these poor devils – man, woman and child, for lazyness, and for the heinous sin of not immediately accustoming themselves to a climate half a dozen degrees colder than it was where they were born' (WER 55). He then deftly turns the tables on the fashionable by asking: 'But suppose, good folks, that you were suddenly caught up and cast into Maryland – stripped to your trowsers, and a hoe put into your hand, do you think that hoeing Tobacco and Corn would come a bit more easy to you, under the burning rays of the sun, than cutting down trees and clearing land is to the negro where everything is opposed to his accustomed habits?' (WER 56–7).

There is nothing 'in their color,' Howe insists, to prevent the descendants of the present Black population of Nova Scotia from becoming 'as good farmers as your grandchildren would make hoers of corn ... on the Chesapeake' (WER 57). The point to remark here is not Howe's freedom from prejudice – several of his remarks are damning enough in this respect – but rather that driving impulse to make of Nova Scotia one powerful, prosperous, and patriotic community; he ends his address with the assertion that 'these gentlemen of color ... may one day or other be hard-working and independent landholders, and do good service to the Country' (WER 57).

The third aspect of that heritage of the Maritimes which Howe's text reveals is a peculiarly European response to nature. One looks in vain, through the pages of most Maritime fiction, for prints of Warren

Tallman's wolf in the snow – it turns out to be as exotic a species in the backwoods of New Brunswick, Nova Scotia, and Prince Edward Island as the flamingo. Nature, for the Maritime writer, is humanized, accessible, inexhaustibly rich or resistant, but never annihilating: this fact is reflected in the surprising rareness with which the sea makes any major appearance in works sprung from a region in which no writer can live more than a few hours' drive from salt water.

As D.C. Harvey remarked, 'Though the love of the sea is as natural to the Maritimer as the air he breathes, he himself, with few exceptions, does not give it literary expression.'[22] 'If the sea infixes some nameless and unslakeable yearning in a man's eyes, the farm yokes the facts of memory to his every breath. And more than the fisherman with his single-hearted gaze, he comes to be the sum, substance and museum of its thronging assembly.' This preference for land over sea to which the opening sentence of Ernest Buckler's story 'Man and Snowman' gives voice is implicit in Archibald MacMechan's Swinburnian swoon over Nova Scotia, *The Book of Ultima Thule*, as well as in its prototype, Howe's *Rambles*. At one point only in his travels does Howe pause from extolling the beauties of waterfalls, rolling meadows, sylvan scenes, and rustic cottages, and that is at 'Pictou Harbor.' Yet no sooner has Howe uttered a standard phrase about the 'Magic' of salt water for those 'who have been accustomed to seeing it making a portion of almost every prospect, from boyhood upwards' (WER 144) than he quits the harbour for the town, giving us a detailed picture of the people, buildings, and disputes which characterize it. Perhaps familiarity breeds ennui; at any rate, Howe's real raptures are reserved for the landlocked lake of Lochaber on which, he tells us, he spends a delightful evening paddling a canoe.

If Howe has little time for the sea, he has less for wilderness – again, it does not so much menace as bore him, as his frequent references to dreary patches of uncultivated land along the road reveal. Conversely, Howe's occasional complaints apropos of settlements encroaching upon wilderness, as in the case of Pictou, bear tribute to the securely civilized state of Nova Scotia, a colony in which wilderness has lost its menace and attained the status of a trope. Thanks to the toil of a previous generation, 'the wildness and primitive negligence of nature' have largely submitted to 'the cultivation and improvements of man' (WER 135) – a state of affairs that Susanna Moodie would have welcomed finding in Upper Canada's backwoods. The picturesque and pleasant state of nature that transports and soothes Howe during so much of his rambling finds ultimate expression in another topos of Maritime literature,

Arcadia, the notion of this region as the idyll's home ground. The 'little Paradise' (WER 76) through which Howe travels reappears in Montgomery's Avonlea, Raddall's Kingsbridge, Roberts's Ancient Wood, MacLennan's Margaree. It becomes the microcosmic Eden – fallen but all the same, as close as we may come to our true home – of Macphail and Buckler. Even for Nowlan and Richards the beauty and integrity of the natural world, as embodied in the Maritime countryside, is the inseparable counterpart to the brutishness of human society. Ironically, that very beauty has an almost metonymic relation to the poverty in which brutality and squalor flourish; if there is little industrial and urban blight in the Maritimes it is because there is no industry to provide the jobs that would help to alleviate the very definite rural and agrarian blight which remains either hidden or picturesque to the tourist's eye.

Thus the myth of Arcadia can be seen not merely as a spontaneous emanation of the scenery, but also as a defensive measure, an expression of wounded pride. For one of the most characteristic features of Maritime culture, especially in the years since Confederation, is the 'loser ethos' ingrained in the very history of a region which made exiles of much of its own population – the Acadians – and which offered refuge to defeated exiles from abroad – the Loyalists and Scots Highlanders. 'Nova Scarcity' is the dark side of Arcadia, and its shadows are to be found even in the resolutely sunny pages of Howe's *Rambles*. The 'shock of 1827' – when the entire Nova Scotian economy suffered badly from the repercussions of a financial crisis in England – leaves its mark on the towns of Merrigomish, Sherbrooke, and Bridgetown, as Howe duly notes (WER 196). As for the 'good times' which Howe prophesied throughout his travels, the celebrated golden age of timber and sail would prove a bubble pricked partly by Confederation and the economic policies it favoured. It is worth noting, in this context, that boom periods in the Maritimes have traditionally been chimerical, resulting most often from war and the artificial conditions it imposes, rather than from any indigenous cause.

The Siamese twins of beauty and poverty exhibited in the pages of Howe's *Rambles* are accompanied by one last component of the Maritime heritage – the alternative values or vision of life which this seemingly inseparable pair engenders. Throughout his journeying Howe calls down blessings on his native land. In one major respect, however, he goes badly wrong in his predictions: the protection from 'European horrors' which he saw as guaranteed by Nova Scotia's imperial connection later would be exploded, as MacLennan's *Barometer Rising* makes clear. The 'thousands of spirits as free as the air, who would unnerve the arm of faction by pointing to the blessings they enjoy, and who, if the minions of tyranny were to approach their dwellings, would drive them into the sea' (WER 108) are rendered in MacLennan's novel as helpless victims of a catastrophic accident brought about by the embroiling of Canada and, more immediately, Halifax, its strategic North Atlantic port city, in one of Britain's European wars. Yet other aspects of Howe's vision have proved accurate, or at least, enduring enough. His insistence on the 'moral as well as natural beauty' (WER 108) of his native province transcends even his fervid devotion to England; only in Nova Scotia, he implies, can true personal independence and real prosperity be achieved by individuals for the fair price of a lifetime's labour on the land.

Repeating the agrarian gospel preached by his confrères Haliburton, McCulloch, and 'Agricola' (John Young, the author of a widely praised series of letters on correct farming practice published in the *Acadian Recorder*), Howe locates the source of all the virtues in the countryside:

There is no moment of a man's life when he feels a more thorough contempt for Towns and Cities, than when he is going out of one to enjoy the free air of the country. He turns up his nose at the bustling and busy hive, toiling to and fro, although albeit but a few hours before he was among the number. He sees them piling pound upon pound – and laying stone upon stone, until Death comes quietly along, and carries them far away from their treasures; and anon old Time approaches – and levels their bricks and tiles, and throws their money bags to their heirs, who scatter them all abroad; again to be gathered by the thrifty, and dispersed by the thoughtless. (WER 53)

This conception of the city as a meaningless mill of profit and pleasure in which succeeding generations are ground will be echoed a century later by Archibald MacMechan; it will also direct the destiny of such archetypal characters of Maritime fiction as Buckler's David Canaan and Paul Creed, Raddall's Matthew Carney and Isabel Jardine; Montgomery's Anne Shirley and Richards's Packet Terri in *Lives of Short Duration*. Maritime 'city-bashing' is directed not so much against Halifax, Charlottetown, or Fredericton – which to visitors from Toronto or Montreal must seem as safe and tranquil as a country fair – as against that which 'city' has come to connote: an industrial, monopoly-capitalist ethos which is foreign to the economy of the Maritimes and increasingly destructive of its society, luring tens of thousands of 'spirits free as air' to anomie and wage-slavery in Boston or Toronto. The dichotomy Howe establishes in the *Rambles* between 'the dignity and character of the Farmer' and the 'pale cheeks of Tinkers, Tailors, Lawyers, Parsons, Cordwainers and Editors' (WER 185–6) is a recurrent feature of Maritime literature, whose farmers and fishermen must often choose whether to exchange 'the free air for some close cell, where sedentary labor might perhaps make [them] richer but could never make [them] so happy or healthy as [they are] now' (WER 86).

Traditionally, Maritime writers have been faced with as difficult a choice: whether to leave their native region in order to work in more varied and sophisticated cultural centres –Toronto, Montreal – as did Charles Bruce and Hugh MacLennan, Ray Smith and Antonine Maillet, for example – or whether, like Ernest Buckler, Alden Nowlan, and David Adams Richards, to 'stand by their land,' however problematic such fidelity might prove for their writing. Joseph Howe is one of the few Maritime writers not to have had to wrestle with this particular angel, not to have asked, but rather assumed, a blessing for his endeavours. As a later chapter of this book will show, the writer's dilemma over whether to go or stay often finds expression within his or her texts, becoming one of the major paradigms of Maritime literature.

The reader drawn into Howe's travels, urged to 'look abroad ... and let [his] mind take in other ideas of wealth' (WER 88) than the merchant or lawyer can comprehend, to recognize the value of a region in which, 'unless reduced by some deplorable stroke of Providence, no man should be poor' (WER 89), will soon encounter in the fictive worlds created by succeeding generations of Maritime writers a country which Providence would seem to have abandoned, in which the honest man cannot help but be poor, and in which 'other ideas of wealth' are inaccessible to the descendants of Howe's brawny farmers (though they may have been rediscovered by outsiders in self-imposed exile from cities well to the west of Fredericton). Yet belief in a redeeming vision of and response to reality persists, finding radical as well as disconsolate or ironic voice among the region's writers: the perception that some quality inherent in the history and conditions of Maritime life makes possible an authentic vision and expression of human experience continues to empower this region's literature. To the question of why this perception has been ignored by the makers of the Canadian literary mythos, we shall now turn.

\*\*\*

Canadians, even the most enlightened, do not know too much about their own country. The gentlemen who were lately promoting a better understanding between Quebec and Ontario would have done well to continue their labours even unto the bounds of either sea.

Archibald MacMechan[23]

There's always the problem for the hinterland, in bourgeois nations, of the centre. Always the centre thinks it is it. Isn't it ridiculous? Toronto – a city of immigrants, many of whom can hardly speak English – considering itself the centre, while the most ethnically Canadian part, the Maritimes, is considered sort of inferior. And then when the west gets up against this tendency, it directs its wrath against the whole east, so we get two walls of prejudice against us.

Milton Acorn[24]

Several years ago, I was interviewed by the chairman of a department in an Ontario community college ... The chairman said he had never visited the Maritimes, although he had been in Ethiopia. (Seemingly, he was under the impression that New Brunswick was located somewhere between Somalia and Eritrea.) Practically all his questions had to do with how well I was acquainted with Boston. He wanted to be sure, you see, that I was equipped to cope with life in the metropolis of Kitchener.

Alden Nowlan[25]

That many Canadian readers know little and care less about Maritime literature is not surprising – it is only recently that Canadians could be assumed to have any general acquaintance with their country's literature at all. It is equally understandable that a number of Canadian critics should have helped to consign Maritime literature to oblivion either by ignoring the corpus of literature the region has produced, or by 'centralizing' its most prominent writers, minimizing whatever in their text betrays local voice or focus and placing a premium on those elements that seem to confirm whatever myth or totem has been adopted as constitutive of the Canadian identity. The Maritime provinces, of course, have produced their share of trivial and tedious texts, yet there have been interesting, even 'classic' works – Frank Parker Day's *Rockbound*, for example, or Charles Bruce's *The Channel Shore* – which have only belatedly become available again to ordinary readers, and which have yet to receive their critical due. Most importantly, there seems to be a general ignorance about the imaginative worlds Maritime texts have created: the following remarks by Margaret Laurence continue, by and large, to be representative of the experience of those outside this region: 'the Maritimes existed in geography books but not in our imaginations, a sad lack in the teaching of Canadian Literature, I now think, being partly responsible.'[26]

The longstanding neglect of Maritime literature, contemporary as well as pre-Confederation, on the part of most Canadians outside the region can perhaps be related to the Maritimes' general economic and political decline after 1867. It must also be said that literary developments on the east coast haven't been as dramatic or frenetic as those on the west – there has been nothing like *Tish* out of Halifax, Fredericton, or Charlottetown, and the Maritimes' established literary journals, excellent though they may be, are not known for their experimental or innovative editorial policies. Traditionally, all has been quiet, even decorous on the eastern front, and even the departures from the norm – De Mille's fabulations, Buckler's explicit concern with sexuality, Nowlan's and Richards's focus on the working-class and poverty-stricken – might seem as colourful and conspicuous as waxed paper. So that if few people west of the New Brunswick border appear to know much about recent Maritime literature, the problem may lie partly with the region's low-key, low-profile literary scene. Yet what most outsiders, even the most informed and sympathetic, fail to comprehend is the frustration of Maritime writers and readers who open studies on Canadian literature and culture to find only the most glancing of references to their region's literary tradition, or worse, who receive the distinct impression that, as far as many critics outside the Maritimes are concerned, this region stopped having a significant literary culture around the time that Roberts and Carman laid down their pens.

To some extent, all the regions of Canada could voice similar complaints against the 'national' (ie, Toronto-based) critics. Prairie and west coast writers, however, recently have enjoyed a well-merited vogue, whereas Maritimers are only starting to scratch their initials on the consciousness of critics. Thus, in a recent article on the coming lights of CanLit William French did mention two Maritime writers – Susan Kerslake and Lesley Choyce – and moved David Adams Richards from rookie status to 'the first team' – but neglected to mention among the 'generation that has brought unprecedented lustre to Canadian fiction' the fine writer Alistair MacLeod.[27] One conclusion to be drawn from French's survey of current Canadian fiction is that there are not only fewer writers, but fewer fine writers in and from the Maritimes than in other parts of the country. Given the region's relatively small population, this doesn't seem surprising, yet what needs to be pointed out is that the Maritimes' lack of prominence on the modern

Canadian literary scene may be connected to a general perception of this region as a cultural has-been as well as an economic have-not, a perception rooted in the way the Maritimes has been reflected in, or excluded from, its own and other eyes.[28]

This perception has much to do with national ideology; from the pressing need to create for Canada a distinctive ethos that would tie its inhabitants together and fence out British and American interlopers, not the desired national identity so much as a restrictive hegemony resulted. That this hegemony has alienated many who happen to live outside Anglophone Canada's foremost region – metropolitan Toronto – Alden Nowlan bears witness: 'When I call myself a Canadian nationalist it's despite the fact that when I go to Toronto I sometimes feel like an Orkney Islander come down to London.'[29]

While it is true that certain regions of Canada are now vigorously contesting the hegemony of the centre, as the strength of literary movements in the prairies and British Columbia attests, the mystique of nationalism and its corollary, anti-regionalism, persist. Some twenty years ago, E.K. Brown made the following pronouncement in his seminal essay 'The Problem of a Canadian Literature': 'In the end ... regionalist art will fail because it stresses the superficial and the peculiar at the expense, at least, if not to the exclusion, of the fundamental and universal. The advent of regionalism may be welcomed with reservations as a stage through which it may be well for us to pass, as a discipline and a purgation. But if we are to pass through it, the coming of great books will be delayed beyond the lifetime of anyone now living.'[30]

Brown's position – a Carlylean Great Books theory of literary history – was bolstered by Hugo McPherson's astonishing reflection in the *Literary History of Canada*:

The regional nature of the bulk of Canadian fiction is rather a fact to be observed than a useful basis for critical classification. Unlike nineteenth-century America, in which genuinely regional idioms did develop, twentieth-century Canada is too close to articulate neighbours and too urgently pressed by international responsibilities to enjoy either the leisure or the isolation which produces distinct regional movements ... Canada's most gifted writers are in the throes of self-discovery; their struggle ... has been to reject the stolid provincial mask and, in Warren Tallman's phrase, 'come into presence' ... In any case, this common impulse towards self-discovery now transcends and obviates regional distinctions.[31]

As little as twelve years ago, Ronald Sutherland was to be found breathing new life into the centralist / nationalist bogey by asserting that literary works manifested a distinctively Canadian sphere of consciousness and formed part of the authentic Canadian mainstream in proportion to their authors' 'awareness of and sensitivity to fundamental aspects of both major language groups in Canada, and of the interrelationships between these two groups.'[32] In other words, for writers to qualify as 'Canadian' as well as 'mainstream,' they would have to write variations on *Two Solitudes* regardless of whether they were born, bred, and resident all their lives on the Canadian seaboards, in the north, or on the prairies. Not to do so, Sutherland implies, would be to espouse the view that 'Canada as a nation is not likely to survive. At least ... not ... as anything worthy of being called a nation.'[33]

Now that the menace of a 'Québec libre' would seem to have abated, Canadian literary criticism has taken a turn 'Beyond Nationalism' (as the title of a recent collection of essays has it) into the post-modernist melting pot. Yet the old prejudices persevere. In a recent essay entitled 'Seven Myths about Canadian Literature,' Don Precosky pits the myth that 'regionalism is a bad thing' against the myth that 'cosmopolitanism is a good thing,' stating that 'in a country that takes in 5.5 time zones, the most common national experience, the one that defines our national identity, is the regional nature of our country.'[34] The fact that Precosky feels compelled to raise these issues at all would seem to point to the fact that, at some basic level of our collective sense of self, anti-regionalism persists despite our best intentions to get rid of it.

Certain critics have announced that only the obtuse and ignorant continue to deplore regionalism as necessarily parochial and actively deleterious, but the following statement by John Metcalf, who, though elegantly opinionated, could scarcely be described as obtuse or ignorant, should give them pause: 'Everything seems to be splintering. Regional presses – a *disastrous* development. *Great Stories from Saskatoon.* Special Interest Presses. *Gay Maritime Stories ...*'[35] Metcalf's distaste for regional presses seems to be shared by Canada's major bookstores – if the Parent Company decrees that books published by regional or small presses are not worth selling, then those presses' products will rarely be stocked, even by chain stores operating in the home regions of the author. Lack of adequate distribution is the chief curse of the regional author's – and reader's – existence.

In both overt and subliminal ways, the Curse of the Hegemonic Article remains strong – *a* Canadian literature; *the* Canadian imagination – in spite of recent theoretical trends urging us to abandon notions of 'the centre,' and to rediscover the margins and subtexts of our literary canons. In order to fully understand the underprivileging of regional literature in general, and Maritime fiction in particular, it will be necessary to look briefly at the chief tenets of the nationalist hegemony-of-the-centre.

In his preface to *The Bush Garden*, Northrop Frye distinguishes in his usual lucid way between the concepts of identity and unity. The former, he asserts, is 'local and regional, rooted in the imagination and in works of culture'; the latter is 'national in reference, international in perspective, and rooted in a political feeling.'[36] 'The essential element in the national sense of unity,' he elaborates.

is the east-west feeling, developed historically along the St Lawrence-Great Lakes axis, and expressed in the national motto, *a mari usque ad mare*. The tension between this political sense of unity and the imaginative sense of locality is the essence of whatever the word 'Canadians' means. Once the tension is given up, and the two elements of unity and identity are confused or assimilated to each other, we get the two endemic diseases of Canadian life. Assimilating identity to unity produces the empty gestures of cultural nationalism; assimilating unity to identity produces the kind of provincial isolation which is now called separatism.[37]

It is an elegant, rational, and unworkable paradigm. Formulated at a moment when Quebec separatism was assuming alarming dimensions for those who had assumed that the 'Two Solitudes' approach would assuage French Canada's discontent within Confederation, Frye's ideal 'tension' between nationalism and regionalism could never be sustained in practice: at times of political crisis 'identity' would always be sacrificed to 'unity.' Moreover, Frye's contrast of a 'political sense of unity' with an 'imaginative sense of locality' allows political feeling to regionalism only as a kind of perversion (even if an 'endemic' one) of the proper state of affairs. Such a segregation of culture and politics may be possible in that looking-glass land of *The Anatomy of Criticism*, but hardly in Canada or any other nation on earth. Cultural expressions of regional 'spheres of consciousness' usually go hand in hand with demands for economic justice or a degree of autonomy. In the case of the Maritimes, the political dimension of regionalism is particularly strong. As Terry Whalen has observed, 'Regional character has a lot to do with climate and geography ... But it also has a great deal to do with the relative wealth of the region and how it is distributed; it has to do with the uniquely local variation that is spawned by the philosophy of greed and an economy of scarcity – as more than a few Atlantic writers well know.'[38]

Frye's unity-identity distinction, which permits him to discuss cultural nationalism as a form of imbalance, a disease, at the same time would appear to validate only those aspects of the regional world which can be safely universalized as imaginative (and, by implication, as apolitical). Thus it would appear that there is a powerful political as well as literary prejudice against regionalism. For to accept diversity is to recognize not only differing cultural patterns within one nation, but also the varied economic conditions out of which these patterns emerge. In 1937 the Rowell-Sirois report formally recognized the fact of regional disparities and the persistence of 'have-not' provinces within the Dominion; nearly fifty years later, economic historians must still insist that 'there can be no national unity in Canada until we attack the economic structure of regional inequality.'[39] In this context, the situation of the Maritimes becomes particularly grave, as a reviewer of Paul Phillips's *Regional Disparities* confirms: 'Atlantic Canada emerges clearly as one of the hinterlands: unemployment runs well above the national average and incomes below; the industrial base is weak and there is a heavy dependence on a few resource industries .. Much government policy has been designed merely to compensate the region for its difficulties, and the welfare state has tended to institutionalize the Atlantic region as a permanent dependency.'[40]

In the writing of Nowlan, Richards, and MacLeod this kind of political awareness has permeated the imaginative shaping of local reality, just as a comparable political sense had helped to structure the fictions of Haliburton and McCulloch. If nationalist literature mounts the case for Canada – as a work like *The Return of the Sphinx* attempts to do – then much regionalist literature may articulate one kind of case against Canada. Nowhere is this more evident than in the Maritimes.

The silencing of that subversive regional voice is a phenomenon of Canadian historiography as well as literary history. To date no comprehensive study of the post-Confederation Maritimes is to be had; while excellent studies of particular phenomena do exist – Ernest Forbes's *The Maritime Rights Movement*, for example – one must go to generalized histories of Canada in order to ascertain what the Maritimes' experience of Confederation has been. The effect of this is both exasperating and humiliating, for in most volumes on Canadian history any references to dates, names, and movements in the post-1867 Maritimes slip through the interstices of Quebec-Ontario politics like so many rats in the House that John A. built.[41]

William Kilbourn's essay on 'The Writing of Canadian History' makes readily apparent why the Maritimes – and other regions outside the

Quebec-Ontario axis – drop from sight after the fatal date of 1867. Noting that geographical determinants have shaped the prevailing interpretations of Canadian history since the 1930s, Kilbourn shows how partisans of the school named 'transcontinental' or 'Laurentian' ('after the continental shield and the great river they celebrated in their writing') ousted the 'vertical or continentalist' interpretation of Canadian history in the forties and fifties. The Laurentianists, he submits, 'believed that Canada was more than the artificial product of imperial policy and political circumstance. The acts of will and imagination which created and sustained the dominion were working with a transcontinental pattern inherent in the North American environment ... Canada was a creature of the early trade routes running east and west from the metropolitan centres of Europe and eastern Canada along the great river systems of the St Lawrence, the Saskatchewan, and the Mackenzie.'[42]

Not seaboard but inland water route is of importance here; not foggy beginnings or mountainous extremities of that route, but the home destination – the port cities of Montreal and Toronto – are worthy of attention. Thus in A.R.M. Lower's *From Colony to Nation*, for example, the recurring theme of 'the confrontation in Canadian history between the predominantly static, Catholic, and rural French-speaking community and the predominantly dynamic, Calvinist, and commercial English-speaking community'[43] squeezes out any extended consideration of, for example, that static, rural, Catholic / Calvinist, French- and English-speaking area, the Maritimes. For the other great interpreters of the Canadian mythos, Donald Creighton and Frank Underhill, this federalizing impulse also crowded out considerations of other issues and areas in Canada – with the result that to such historians of 'the outlying regions' as William Morton, 'this domination by central Canada has ... made Confederation seem an instrument of injustice.'[44]

Central Canada has also dominated our literary history, thanks largely to the magisterial myths set down by Northrop Frye. Invoking the Laurentian *Drang nach Westen* 'that makes the growth of Canada geographically credible,' Frye fashions his own paradigm of Canada as discovered by the literary imagination:

Canada began as an obstacle, blocking the way to the treasures of the East, to be explored only in the hope of finding a passage through it ... But Canada has, for all practical purposes, no Atlantic seaboard. The traveller from Europe edges into it like a tiny Jonah entering an inconceivably large whale, slipping past the Straits of Belle Isle into the Gulf of St Lawrence, where five Canadian provinces surround him, for the most part invisible. Then he goes up the St Lawrence and the inhabited country comes into view, mainly a French-speaking country, with its own cultural traditions. To enter the United States is a matter of crossing an ocean; to enter Canada is a matter of being silently swallowed by an alien continent.[45]

However persuasive this paradigm of Jonah and the whale may be as a reflection of the early explorers' initiation 'into that gigantic east-to-west thrust which historians regard as the axis of Canadian development,'[46] it is utterly skewed as any sort of schema whereby Canadians can continue to image and articulate the reality of their country. The implications vis-à-vis the Maritimes that can be drawn from Frye's paradigm are revealing: (1) there can be no good reason, in any imaginative quest for Canada, for beginning at the beginning with the Maritimes; (2) the Maritimes lack validity as an imaginative concept since they fail to meet the criteria for what Frye – presumably on a neo-colonialist basis – elects as a norm, namely a seaboard; (3) the Maritimes are not worth exploring since they are 'invisible,' uninhabited (the population of Canada beginning only as the St Lawrence narrows towards Quebec City) and presumably bereft of indigenous 'cultural traditions'; (4) since 'the Canadian experience' consists of being swallowed by an 'alien continent' one should not protest too much – if, indeed, one remembers to protest at all – the swallowing up of the Maritimes by the Laurentian whale; one should, instead, welcome the fait accompli as proof positive of the region's Canadianness.

To query the validity of these implications on the grounds that Frye never intended them is as misguided as it would be to argue that Frye is a Maritime writer – or at least committed to Maritime culture – because he spent part of his boyhood in Moncton. The Jonah paradigm betrays the strength of Frye's commitment to fictions of the centre, and hence his distrust of, or at least ambivalence towards, regions and margins. Though Frye's most recent remarks on regionalism in Canadian letters are collected under the heading 'From Nationalism to Regionalism: The Maturing of Canadian Culture,' he seems to have come to prize regionalism not as a good-in-itself, but as a means of depoliticizing culture: 'the conception of Canada doesn't really make all that much sense. "Canada" is a *political* entity; the cultural counterpart that we call "Canada" is really a federation not of provinces but of regions and communities.'[47] (In this case the idea of Canada's cultural sovereignty or independence wouldn't make all that much sense to Frye, either.) Similarly, in the essays collected in *Divisions on a Ground*, Frye presents regionalism as a means for circumventing nationalism in Canadian writing, in the interests of that 'single international style of which all existing literatures are regional developments.'[48] What Frye ends up talking about is a kind of metaregionalism which has little to do with the specific political, social, and economic realities which give to the various regions of Canada their significance and vitality; Frye's regionalism becomes, in fact, a kind of Star Wars of the Educated Imagination, shielding us from 'a world controlled by uniform patterns of technology'[49] and saving us from parochialism by linking us up with the Great Centres – Paris, New York, London.[50] Yet it would seem that he cannot do without a national mythos, as his essay 'National Consciousness in Canadian Culture' bears out. The components of this mythos are a numinous experience of Nature, acute awareness of the 'northern frontier,' a 'presbyopic sense' of 'vast distances of river and sky,' all of which confer fear and guilt upon us and give rise to recurring themes of 'individuals uncertain of their social context, of dark, repressed, oracular doubles concealed within each of us.'[51] While no one would deny that elements of this mythos are to be found in Canadian writing, it would be unfortunate to make this mythos a touchstone for what is truly Canadian in our literature. Maritime writing, for example, has very little to do with 'the blank world of white snow stained with the blood of murdered animals,'[52] much to do with a strong sense of community and a harmonious vision of the natural world. No wonder, then, that the theme-hunters have either by-passed Maritime texts or else performed Procrustean surgery on them in their search for a national literature.

Frye's Laurentian paradigm of Canada can, in fact, be seen as an incidental demolition of the Maritimes and that region's vision of the reality it constitutes. Yet anyone who reads much of the literature of this region becomes aware of how resistant the Maritime imagination is to such ideas as that of an 'alien continent' dominated by a terrifying wilderness which for Frye forms the *sine qua non* of the Canadian imagination. This resistance may be partially explained by looking at another of Frye's dicta: that Canada has had 'no enlightenment, and very little eighteenth century.'[53] This thesis holds no water when applied to a region like the Maritimes, for its earliest literature was indebted as much to eighteenth-century thought and style as to nineteenth-century Romanticism. Howe's *Rambles*, for example, make as many references to Sterne, Fielding, and Smollett as they do to Byron and Tom Moore; Haliburton's and McCulloch's satirical sketches have a firm base in the conservatism of Edmund Burke, who stressed the primacy of responsible community over romantic individualism – a belief which permeates a text like Douglas Huyghue's *Argimou*, making it, as we shall see later, the antithesis of a text such as Richardson's *Wacousta*. Moreover, Frye's assertion that 'Identity in Canada has always had something about it of a centrifugal movement into far distance'[54] is inaccurate as far as the Maritimes is concerned. Maritime writers have tended to view the region as a microcosm, or a self-contained, self-centred area – Hugh MacLennan has remarked on how, in his youth, Cape Bretoners talked of going to 'Nova Scotia,' as if their part of the province were a sovereign state.[55] Given this intense focus on the region itself, it would be surprising to find Maritimers constantly straining their eyes towards Ottawa, Toronto, Montreal, or to some illimitable, distant wilderness to receive the signals that would confer national identity on them – especially since they are prone to conceive of themselves as Maritimers and not as some distillation of 'far distance.'

How can the Maritimes fight back against the cultural and political hegemony asserted by a centre which, in paying lip service to the problems and rights of outlying regions, effectively refuses to recognize the importance of their contribution to 'anything worthy of being called a nation'? Ernest Forbes has documented the attempts of Maritimers to form a regional protest movement in the 1920s and 1930s in order to redress 'the decline in relative status and influence of the Maritimes which accompanied the rise of the West and the growing dominance of the Central Canadian metropolises.' This attempt, 'born amid a climate of optimism and progressive thinking' ended in the hands of the federal government as a 'program for political pacification,' helping to foster a new growth of the 'disillusionment, cynicism, and pessimism traditionally associated with the region.'[56] Culturally is the situation any less bleak? Archibald MacMechan's thesis in *Headwaters of Canadian Literature* that writing in this country developed in progressive stages and places would seem to imply that the muse which had inspired a burst of creativity in late eighteenth- and early nineteenth-century Nova Scotia soon absconded, practically without a trace, to other regions of Canada. Fortunately, the rumours of her disappearance have been exaggerated: Maritime texts, whether by forgotten masters such as Charles Bruce or by relative newcomers such as David Adams Richards are infiltrating the New Canadian Library series. University presses are reprinting 'lost' texts such as Huyghue's *Argimou* and Day's *Rockbound*, while small publishing houses are issuing a steady stream of books by new writers, some of whom are native, and some of whom are 'born-again' Maritimers, exiles from the cities of the centre. As the '"Laurentian orthodoxy" has ceased to dominate Canadian historiog-

raphy, interest has revived in the various regions of Canada.'[57] The
perception that regional disparities are not necessarily so many worms
gnawing away at the precarious confederacy we call Canada, that regional literature need not conform to, may indeed contest, the elected
archetypes of unity – Jonah-voyageur, wolf in snow, butterfly on rock,
cosmopolite in Cabbagetown – is bringing about a redefinition of the
very term regionalism.

Traditionally, the regionalist work has been held to refuse or ignore
those universal, timeless, transcendent qualities which, we have been
taught, imbue the World Classics. Great literature, we must assume,
never smacks of the local and particular, of the writer's own gusto for
or revulsion from her or his native environment, so that *Madame Bovary*,
for example, betrays not Flaubert's but rather Emma's frustrations
with village life in rural Normandy. This assumption would seem to
underlie Patricia Barclay's statement that the greatest artists somehow
stand free of their surroundings, using them as fodder for 'universal
statements, true not just for one man, region or nation, but for all
men.'[58] Yet surely the very particularities of time, place, and culture in
which universal truths are grounded save these truths from vacuity
and allow us to test their validity against our own particular experience.
As Margaret Laurence reminds us, no writer, however 'universal,'
can escape context: 'our perceptions and therefore our interpretations
are formed by the communities in which we grow up.' Great writers,
she insists, are those whose writings 'strike deep chords among their
own people and sometimes beyond their own people ...'; the task of
all writers is 'to write out of our own familiar idiom and out of our
deepest observations of our people and our place of belonging on this
planet.'[59]

Thus Barclay's definition of the regionalist writer as someone who
knows and describes for outsiders or nostalgic exiles 'a particular
corner' or district of the world is both patronizing and ultimately tauto-
logical. It is not the regionalist but the mediocre writer who articulates
her or his 'place of belonging' as souvenir album rather than microcosm;
conversely it is not the pro-regionalist but merely the incompetent
critic who skews his criteria for judging literary works so that allowances
are made or notice simply isn't taken of flaws, lapses, or dishonesties
in texts of whatever provenance or category. Thus, regionalism can be
taken as a *donnée* which, following Henry James's advice, we concede
to the writer outright, our business as readers and critics being to judge
what the writer makes of her or his choice of material and 'home
ground,' not to quarrel with that choice. We concede to Hugh Hood, for

example, his Toronto, as we concede to Lucy Maud Montgomery her Avonlea; as for the novels inspired by each locale, we respond to them according to their success as mimetic, aesthetic, and rhetorical structures.

The question may be asked that if all art is, in a sense, regional – owing its energy and authenticity to the particular physical, cultural, and social context which 'authors' it – doesn't the best art transcend, isn't it only hampered by considerations of region or context – who would wish to read *Faust* as an expression of the Weimar as opposed to the Berlin mentality? Yet surely our reading of Goethe's work can only be enriched and revitalized by an awareness of the particular contexts – geographical, social, historical, ideological – out of which his 'universal' insights sprang. Surely that 'quarrel with oneself' which Yeats saw as the essence of poetry has something to do with the time and place in which that particular quarrel arises.

Finally, the question must be asked as to whether regionalism is not too often put to illegitimate use as an umbrella under which flawed or (deservedly) forgotten works can shelter from a downpour of abuse or neglect. Should conscientious Canadians read regional writers in the same spirit in which they dutifully choose to holiday in some picturesque part of Canada rather than in California or Corfu? One attempt at an answer might be that any region's fledgling writers and readers must learn that a literary canon and tradition particular to their own experience do exist; they must come to recognize which texts within that canon are grossly inadequate or richly rewarding by comparing them not only with centralized Canadian classics, but also with the outstanding works their native region has produced.[60]

This said, it may then be permitted to the critic to group together texts which have been written in any given region of this country in order to come to as broad and profound a knowledge of a particular 'sphere of consciousness' as possible – not to obtain armchair experience of the region but to enlarge, deepen, and alter our understanding of what human life is and can be like, 'here' or 'over there.' Moreover, regionalism can be a doubly accommodating structure, permitting the growth and development of a native sensibility, and letting in 'outsiders' to form and play off impressions of the region against their experience of other places, as, for example, do Alice Munro in the short story 'Dulse' and Matt Cohen in 'Brothers.'[61]

Northrop Frye is one of this country's finest writers, and a significant literary theorist. Yet all theory is precisely that – not dogma, but hypothesis, to be tested against the rich and resistant reality it attempts to structure or systematize. What is missing in Frye's vision of Canadian culture is a recognition of the interpenetration of culture and politics, a sense of Canada as 'a mosaic of regions, each with its own sense of destiny,' composing a nation that 'exists in a dialectic of regional and ethnic tensions.'[62] Tensions, it might be added, whose political dimensions are reflected, articulated, and given imaginative form through the art of any given region. Without an active sense of the powerful divisions and disparities between the regions and that nation we have come to think of as 'Ottawa,' Canadian culture will be no more authentic or imposing than Canada's Wonderland, that mock-up Disneyworld north of Toronto. The country will not crack apart in consequence:

What is rare is a country which is a single cultural nation, or a nation without regions. It is not true of India, China, Mexico, Belgium, Spain, or Germany ... Yet it is a most common misapprehension that a country should be culturally united, notwithstanding the fact that such a state is the exception rather than the rule. And if the country need not be defined by the cultural nation, then the people of the nations should not assume that their only legitimate self-expression is through possession of their own country. There need not be conflict in having love for one's cultural nation, while offering allegiance to one's country.

It is obvious that Canada is not a single nation, and that within it there are more than two. [Confederation] ... was not warmly embraced throughout the Maritimes and Quebec, but, for its advocates, the fact that the colonies would not form a single cultural nation was not a reason to miss the opportunity to profit mutually as a country. A country is founded and persists, not because its people share common cultural bonds, but because they agree to common purposes, and accept that these can better be realized together.[63]

Given this multiplicity of cultural bonds, we must conceive of Canadian literature in a pluralist sense – not as the offshoot of one homogeneous mythos but as a variety of ways of experiencing and articulating a shared world. Cosmopolitan and regional forms of that literature should not be pitted against each other, or rated on some fixed critical scale. The one would be impoverished, etiolated, without the persistence of the other – they are equal and opposite reactions to reality, and there is no reason why a writer born and bred in Toronto could not create fictions about Sydney, Nova Scotia, or vice versa.

Alden Nowlan designated the Atlantic Provinces as 'the National Whipping Boy,' serving as the target of national jokes, swipes, indignation, or indifference. He went on to warn, however, that 'the worst thing about these simplistic attacks is that they provoke an equally simplistic defence.'[64] To detect, behind Northrop Frye's assertion that one of Canada's great lacks is an Atlantic seaboard, the accusation that the country lacks great seaboard writers is perhaps to succumb to the 'scapegoat syndrome' described by Nowlan. (Where is Canada's Melville, or even Marryat? If the Maritimes constitute the cradle of Canadian literature, couldn't the babies rocked therein have been a little lustier than McCulloch, Haliburton, or the luckless Julia Beckwith Hart?)[65]

And yet, it is necessary to go beyond simplistic attacks and defences to arrive at an accurate understanding of the strengths and weaknesses of Maritime fiction. The first step involves shaking ourselves free of rigid schemas. Thus, if we accept the fact that the historical, social, political, and economic inheritance of the Canadian Maritimes was distinctly different from that of the thirteen colonies of the Atlantic seaboard, and that accordingly, Nova Scotia, New Brunswick, and Prince Edward Island will differ as greatly from the seaboard states in their cultural as in their geographical configuration, we will be able to spend our critical time unwrapping and examining a gift, rather than resenting a hypothetical theft.[66] We might even arrive at a transvaluation of that generic term for Nova Scotian – and by extension, for all Maritimers: Bluenose. 'Its origin,' Archibald MacMechan has observed, 'is wrapped in mystery. Somewhere near the end of the eighteenth century, it was used to designate our potatoes and our people. It conveys a sneer at the cold pinched faces of our provincials, residing in a land of everlasting ice and snow.' Acquaintance with the literature of the Maritimes as a whole may lead us to read 'Bluenose' as an expression of a unique identity and worth. It may turn out to be 'like that mistaken curse, "Go to Halifax!" Whoever utters that malediction is like Balaam, the son of Beor; he desires to curse, but he blesses against his will.'[67]

# 2

# Community

You are a creature of habit ... you feel you have social duties to perform;
that grief is lessened when the burden is divided, and happiness
increased when it is imparted, that man was not made to live alone; and
that natural wants, individual weakness, and common protection require
that, though we live in families, our families must dwell in communities.

'THE LONE HOUSE,' *The Old Judge*[1]

Community is a Canadian paradigm. Citing E.R. Watters's generalization
that in contrast to his American counterpart, the hero of Canadian fiction
doesn't fulfil his destiny by heading 'west' to secure his individual
freedom, and recalling Northrop Frye's remarks on the cultural significance for Canada of the influx of United Empire Loyalists, Sandra Djwa
concludes that 'the Canadian hero is concerned basically with maintaining his own integrity within a chosen community.'[2] In what manner, then,
can Maritime literature be said to have cradled or perhaps contorted this
paradigm? How does the concept of community as presented and
explored in works of Maritime fiction significantly differ from concepts
articulated in Canadian fiction which stems from alternative experiences
of history, nature, and brute economics? Before we can begin to sketch a
reply to these questions, we might ask just what the notion of community
has come to signify.

The *Oxford English Dictionary* provides a succinct answer: the key word
is 'common,' with all its associations of unity and fellowship, and of
vulgarity or commonness as well. A community can be seen as an
extended family in which all is held by, or appertains to, all, and whose

members, through richer or poorer, share a common economic base, be it farming, fishing, or mining. Moreover, a community is a cohesive and inclusive body ruled more by recognition of what its members have in common than by awareness of what distinguishes and separates individuals, or groups of individuals, from one another. The concept of community thus can be contrasted with the term 'society,' with its meaning both of association – a large body of persons brought together 'for the purpose of harmonious co-existence or for mutual benefit' (thus inviting the notion of hierarchical groupings according to class) – and of coterie or 'Society': 'the aggregate of leisured, cultured or fashionable persons regarded as forming a distinct class or body ... especially those persons collectively who are regarded as taking part in fashionable life, social functions, entertainments, etc.'

Obviously, 'community' rather than 'Society' will be the imaginative base of any writer sprung from or engaged with rural or 'outpost' life, with pioneering ventures or with the attempts of post-industrial ex-urbanites to 'get back to the land.' Given the pattern of historical and economic development in Canada, it is equally obvious that a 'first wave' of significant novels dealing with life on or against the land would be followed by fiction centring on the modern city, in which the concept of community is either engulfed by that of society or restricted to a particular family, class unit, or ethnic group within society as a whole. Thus, after Frederick Philip Grove, Louis Hémon, Martha Ostenso, we have Gabrielle Roy, Mordecai Richler, and Adele Wiseman. More recently, however, writers such as Alice Munro, Jack Hodgins, and Matt Cohen have turned their attention to small rural communities, allowing the generally urban reader a voyeur's glimpse into the treasure chests and waste heaps of communal life.

The pattern of Maritime fiction is in this, as in most respects, stubbornly different. Because, with the problematic exceptions of steel mills and coal mines, the Maritime economy subsists on localized farming, fishing, and lumbering, and because the region is economically depressed, there are no burgeoning cities to lure immigrants, inspire authors, or provide alternatives to that imagination of community which has structured Maritime fiction from the work of Haliburton and McCulloch to that of Nowlan and Richards.[3] Yet though there has been no significant shift in Maritime writing from 'communal' to 'social' foci there has been a process of change in the imaginative portrayal of community – predictably, from that rockbound conviction of the primacy and solidarity of community one finds in nineteenth-century Maritime fiction to recent perceptions that crisis or decay is the bottom line of communal life. This chapter will examine the distinctive development of that sense of community which, according to Hugh MacLennan, is at the heart of the 'Maritime mystique';[4] it will proceed from a general analysis of the origins, components, and quality of 'community' in Maritime fiction to an examination of four texts which can be said to represent its seminal stages and possibilities: *The Stepsure Letters*, *The Old Judge*, *The Master's Wife*, and *The Channel Shore*.

\*\*\*

The three identifying marks on the body of Maritime fiction are an indelible historical sense, cultural homogeneity, and a social stability whose corollary is stasis or worse, stagnation. In comparison with the literature of the rest of English-speaking Canada, Maritime fiction can be said to have had a full century's extra seasoning. It has been suggested by editors eager to restore Maritime texts to prominence that McCulloch's *The Stepsure Letters* and Haliburton's *The Old Judge* bear comparison with Susanna Moodie's *Roughing It in the Bush*, with which they are roughly contemporaneous;[5] the suggestion, however, is an invidious one, in that it ignores the significant difference in context and mindset of these books and their authors. As Haliburton makes clear in the first pages of *The Old Judge*, he is writing of civilized and not barbarous life in Nova Scotia: 'Although extensive clearings are made yearly in the interior, principally by the children of old settlers, in which backwoods life is to be seen in all its simplicity, yet the country has passed the period of youth, and may now be called an old colony' (TOJ 4).

Both Haliburton and McCulloch were writing about a colony in which not primitivism but rather decadence was a prominent feature of communal life – the decadence which lured the sons of industrious farmers off the land into local taverns and shops, or into ballrooms and government offices in Halifax. Moreover, in their allegiance to the political and moral philosophy of eighteenth-century Torydom, the Nova Scotian authors could not be farther from that breathless belief in progress and rapid change characteristic of the Industrial Age's rapt daughter, Mrs Moodie. As late as the 1930s, Maritime historians such as D.C. Harvey could argue that the patterns of present-day Maritime society could be traced to eighteenth-century conservatism;[6] more recently, scholars such as Thomas Vincent have argued for the existence of an indigenous literary culture in the eighteenth-century Maritimes, one which articulated the moral, political, and religious values of the society which fostered it and whose poetry was, characteristically, 'community oriented, concentrating on public civility of one sort or another.'[7] Though with the rise of the

Fredericton school, Maritime poets left the drawing room to sketch wordscapes of Grand Pré or the Tantramar Marshes, fiction writers continued to engage with or redefine what Haliburton called 'civilized community' (TOJ 143), as the work of Andrew Macphail and Lucy Maud Montgomery, Thomas Raddall and Charles Bruce reveals.

If history has firmly rooted Maritime notions of community in an eighteenth-century mindset, then geography has contributed to preserving the relatively homogeneous nature of settlement in the Maritime provinces – or at least of settlement as it has been represented in the region's 'hegemonic' literature, which makes scant mention of Micmac or Milicete Indians, of dispossessed Acadians or dubiously liberated Blacks, and of the pre-assimilated Germans who settled Lunenburg County.[8] Those communal groups of which Raddall, McCulloch, MacLeod, and Will Bird write – the pre-revolutionary Yankees, the United Empire Loyalists, the dispossessed Scots Highlanders, Irish famine refugees, and Yorkshire settlers – shared a common language (with the exception of the Gaels and Celts) and were engaged in common pursuits. So quickly and completely did they work the land suitable for farming, the harbours attractive for fishing, and the forests fit for slashing down, that many of their sons and daughters were forced to emigrate south and west – a fact McCulloch laments as early as 1821.[9] Small wonder, then, that the massive wave of eastern European immigration in the late nineteenth century almost completely by-passed the cramped Maritimes for the promised infinitudes of arable prairie land:[10] small wonder, too, that Maritime fiction possesses almost no trace of what Margaret Atwood has pronounced as typically Canadian – the sense of forever being 'immigrants to this place, even if we were born here' – and little trace of any beleaguered garrison mentality.[11]

If, as Laurence Ricou has argued, prairie literature typically pits isolated protagonists against vast tracts of uncompromising land, then Maritime literature tends to set down its heroes and heroines within isolated communities which cleave to land or sea, however unproductive or grudging these may be; the struggle is not against any lupine wilderness, but often against the limitations and towards the strengths of communal life itself. Maritime communities are not primarily defensive in nature, nor do they demand unswerving loyalty to a common code – qualities essential to garrison life. Rather, it is the power to nurture, sustain, and preserve meaningful experience, as well as to cramp, choke off, or exclude new forms and expressions of being that makes of community an infinitely rich territory for Maritime writers.

What Robert Cockburn and Robert Gibbs observe of Maritime poets is true also of fiction writers: 'While we respond to cold and snow, or to distances, or to compelling scenery just as readily as do poets from other English-speaking parts of the country, we are more likely than they to people our landscapes with ghosts or with the living. Compared to the rest of the Dominion, ours is a small-scale region, and the memories and human intimacies of village and family, of valley and county, seem to be always in our consciousness.'[12]

The ghosts, it may be added, hold hands with the living; the sense of traditional values and rights as an inheritance to be preserved and guarded against outsiders is strong enough to lead to what some call 'birthplace bigotry' – the attitude that only Maritimers whose roots go back for the requisite number of generations have any right to speak about or for the region.[13] Silver Donald Cameron has contrasted the 'open' and 'closed' nature of community in west and east coast Canada, drawing attention to the fact that whereas only about 40 per cent of the present population of British Columbia was actually born in that province, in the Maritimes that figure is 97 per cent.[14] Moreover, as Alden Nowlan attests, Maritimers would seem to possess a talent for prolonging 'living memory' – an active and critical awareness of past traditions and habits of community life – for example, pride in self-sufficiency, that pre-consumer era virtue extolled by Howe, Haliburton, McCulloch, and Macphail, and passed on to Nowlan by his grandmother's stories of how she and her husband, an Annapolis Valley farmer, managed themselves to produce everything needful (excepting tobacco, rum, and sugar) for their family's consumption.[15] To the dirt-poor Nowlan these stories must have had a bitterly ironic resonance; to the majority of poor Maritimers, for whom the great leap forward into the twentieth century has meant the advent both of mod cons affordable on UIC – microwaves and VCRs – and of a standard of living qualitatively lower than their self-sufficient ancestors knew,[16] this gift of 'living memory' must bolster their conviction that any change is usually for the worse, and that stagnation is consonant with progress.[17]

The strength and continuity of community experience in the Maritimes have given the region's writers a great advantage in creating their fictive worlds: access to what Raymond Williams has termed 'knowable community.'[18] The narrators of *The Stepsure Letters* or *The Master's Wife*, protagonists such as David Canaan or Grant Marshall in *The Mountain and the Valley* and *The Channel Shore*, assume a representative as well as exemplary status; they speak and act out of a common pool of values, wisdom, and experience both positive and problematic. The fictional communities realized in these works can all be interrelated, and the mimetic resonance of each persuades the reader into a deeper, fuller knowledge of the limitations and possibilities of community as it exists outside the world of the text. And, as W.H. New has pointed out,[19] more than any other factor it is a shared consciousness of community which has shaped Maritime writing, distinguished as it is by social inclusiveness and a comprehensive vision of individual human life that has much to do with the seasonal patterns and natural cycles to which the community binds its living. For writers like Bruce and Buckler, community is a microcosm, not a festering backwater or dump of existential fragments. Buckler has reiterated his conviction of 'the great sustenance' afforded by small communities to the Maritime writer; it is the community's members who confer significance on his writing, and not vice versa. His neighbours, Buckler insisted, were 'the source of whatever talent or substance [he had] in [his] writing'; his attempt to articulate their lives would validate his very act of writing.[20]

The last word on the particular advantages to the Maritime writer of what we might call the cult of community, we can leave to Alden Nowlan. Relating an anecdote according to which, after a literary-cum-entertainment session, he found himself roaming the streets of Fredericton in the company of both Stompin' Tom Connors and the province's premier, Nowlan concludes 'there's no place on the continent where so broad a range of social and human relationships is so readily accessible.' Most Montreal or Toronto or Vancouver writers, he adds, 'have lived all their lives in one sub-caste of the bourgeoisie.' And, though he insists that 'being a Maritimer doesn't make it any more likely that you'll write well ... it sure as hell improves the chances of your having something to write about.'[21]

***

I didn't *feel* particularly poor, ignorant and isolated until I was about fifteen and the outside world, that until then had seemed half-mythical, began to be wholly real to me.

Alden Nowlan[22]

To Nowlan, too, we may turn for a trenchant awareness of the high price of that sense of communal belonging which seems so savoury to the 'outside world.' It is not so much the existence as the acceptance of impoverishment and entrapment that points to a painful stagnation: the overlooking of intolerable conditions because they have become part of the fabric of community life. It is this stagnation, spawned partly by the conservative ethos of community, which Nowlan lashed in the 'Note-book' he kept for *The Atlantic Advocate*: 'Back in the 1950s, New Brunswick was still in the era of the Parish Overseer of the Poor'; 'it was assumed that the children of the poor would grow up virtually illiterate.'[23]

While it is true that the narratives of such early extollers of community as McCulloch and Haliburton urge their readers to a change of economic heart in order to eradicate the 'vice' of poverty, it is self-help within the individual family unit they advocate, and not that extension of practical sympathy to outcasts which writers like George Eliot and Charles Dickens made the staple of their concept of community. When one considers, for example, the narrator's reaction in Haliburton's *The Old Judge* to the destitute Irish immigrants who flocked to Nova Scotia in the years of the potato famine, one finds not so much reactionary churlishness as moral ossification. To Judge Sandford these paupers are the champions of 'idleness, insubordination, and disloyalty' (TOJ 312) – vices which beget poverty, emigration, and disease in their turn. Why, he asks, should the deserving poor of old Nova Scotia be asked to maintain this walking 'Lazaretto' which will only consume them? Here, it may be argued, is 'birthplace bigotry' in its most noxious form. It can be observed as well in the fifth instalment of *The Stepsure Letters*, in which Mephibosheth Stepsure's neighbours cast an indigent but worthy traveller into debtors' prison: the sheriff so stuffs him with bad boiled cabbage that the unfortunate stranger literally expires of flatulence. It is such gallows — or gastric – humour as this which, perhaps, led one critic to lament the exhumation of McCulloch's chef d'oeuvre 'from [its] decent grave in *The Acadian Recorder*.'[24]

A refusal to shift perspectives, to take moral risks, to extend or alter boundaries – all these create the plague sore of community in Maritime writing. The homogeneity of community is achieved, as has been remarked, by excluding or considering as non-persons the most blatant outsiders.[25] It is revealing that the one 'established' writer who does use a Micmac Indian as the hero of a novel, Frank Parker Day in *John Paul's Rock*, also creates in *Rockbound* a community of fishermen whose common spite, greed, and infectious nastiness ultimately drive the declared 'outsider' among them to seek refuge on 'Barren Island.'

The hatred bred of community life which Day chronicles between the Jungs and Krauses of Rockbound Island is distilled in subtler form in novels like *The Mountain and the Valley* and *The Channel Shore*. There the tightness and closeness of communal life festers in gossip rather than in near-Sicilian feuding; the results, if less dramatic, are as destructive – Rachel's gossip about Bess Delahunt lodges the 'invisible worm' in

Martha's heartlong love for Joseph; Grant Marshall's exaggerated care not to rouse the suspicions of Mrs Wilmot, the doyenne of gossipers in Currie Head, is part of that 'gutlessness' on which his love for Anna founders and which, the logic of the narrative suggests, leads ultimately to Anna's death. And, though the gossips' easiest prey is that transgressor of sexual mores whom the community may banish to its outskirts, but without whom it cannot quite do – the Bess Delahunts, Vangie Murphys, or Fanny 'the potato girl' whom Day describes with such clear sympathy in *Rockbound* – their prize victim is the misfit whose vision, sympathies, and desires are too intense and wide-ranging to be constrained within the fixed circle of community. In *The Channel Shore*, Grant's first and formative battle is with the demon of 'what will people think – what will people say' if he were to follow his generous instincts and leave his adoptive father's house to live with the bereft Gordons, or to marry a 'fallen' woman.

Grant Marshall succeeds with the help of his adopted son in enlarging the hearts if not the minds of his neighbours; unlike George Eliot's Daniel Deronda, he does not have to quit a community which is incapable of allowing him to realize his own best potential within its bounds. Yet for many other characters in Maritime fiction, exile – through death or emigration – is the only possible response to the negative pressures of community, as David Canaan, MacLennan's Dan Ainslie, and Maillet's Mariaàgélas discover. And for some – the characters of David Adams Richards's novels, for example – the brute stagnation into which the old communal virtue of stability has decayed assures that the 'outside world' of alternatives to being poor, ignorant, and isolated will never become real.

\*\*\*

The concept of community is accepted as understood by McCulloch and Haliburton; *The Stepsure Letters* and *The Old Judge* are narratives and not novels perhaps because their authors felt no need to create and imaginatively empower autonomous fictive worlds for their readers. McCulloch's urgent desire was to alter his readers' relation to a given reality he shared with them; his narrative is an affective tool to prod, provoke and refashion its chosen product – not the text but, rather, its reader. Haliburton, on the other hand, wished to reveal to distant English eyes the pains and pleasures of established colonial life as experienced up and down the social ladder. His narrative is humorous, cynical, brusquely analytical, and mawkishly sentimental by turns. If neither narrative can honestly be described as a minor masterpiece, nor even as consistently engaging, it is not because they fail to be novels – the last twenty years of literary criticism ought to have disabused us of any lingering assumptions as to the novel's superiority over other forms of narrative. No more than Mrs Moodie are Haliburton and McCulloch worth reading for the literary pleasures to be found in a text by Munro or Laurence; if works such as *The Stepsure Letters* and *The Old Judge* bear examination and discussion, it is for their revelation of a set and structure of mind which, imaginatively transformed and critically developed, will inform the infinitely more rewarding work of later Maritime writers.

\*\*\*

Perhaps more vicious and desperate things have been said of *The Stepsure Letters* than of any other 'classic' of Canadian literature. It is simple to see why; the text's narrator (whose ungainly Christian name furnishes yet another reason to damn McCulloch's pen) is a prig and paragon to boot – anyone who likes Mephibosheth, or admires, as Northrop Frye professes to do, his moral 'good taste,' could reasonably be expected to plump for Fielding's Blifil over Tom Jones. To a non-Calvinist, Stepsure is the worst kind of snob – he is one of the Elect, and the virulence of his state of grace is manifest in the verse of Proverbs he alludes to in recounting the doom of a reprobate: 'I will laugh at your calamity; I will mock when your fear cometh' (SL vii).

It is debatable whether even Saunders Scantocreesh, that rags-to-riches Righteous Emigrant, with his fervent desire that the lazy and indigent be swept off the face of the earth so that there will be more room for Mephibosheth Stepsure and his like to prosper, is more villainously virtuous than Stepsure. One feels that McCulloch sets him up as Stepsure's straight man and also as a deflector for the queasy or revolted feelings that Stepsure's morality inspires in the average reader. Be that as it may, the very egregiousness of Mephibosheth Stepsure makes all the more vivid – and astonishing – the commitment to community McCulloch's text evinces. Like Howe and Haliburton, McCulloch was writing in a period of economic decline in the Maritimes: the bubble prosperity brought by the Napoleonic Wars had burst and now, more than ever, had it become imperative for the average Nova Scotian to embrace farming, the one form of labour which, if pursued with diligence and some intelligence, promised economic security if not great prosperity. The community McCulloch delineates in *The Stepsure Letters* can be divided between the economically elect – Squire Worthy, Stepsure (an auctioned orphan who limps his way to respectability as a farmer-writer), Scantocreesh – and the reprobate, those assorted Goslings, Ruffs, and Castups who have neglected once-thriving farms to join the 'idle, wandering, drinking, bundling part of the town' (SL 120). Significantly, the pre-eminent spokesman for the spurned values of 'homespun and homely fare ... labour and saving' (SL 13) is not the near-invisible Squire nor the windily ineffectual Parson Drone, but a true insider, Stepsure — that member of the farming community whose inherent virtue and indefatigable self-discipline give him that leg up to a position of moral superiority from which he can observe and judge the failings of his fellows.

As importantly for the notion of community, the generic affiliation of *The Stepsure Letters* would seem to be (*pace* the genealogists of Canadian humour) more with the sermon than the satire. Stepsure has his eyes and tongue on wordly things, to be sure, but his single-minded pursuit of economic security has communal implications to sanction it. As he argues, 'though a religious man cares nothing about worldly comforts, industry is an indispensable duty, as it affords the means of doing good to others' (SL 88). Religion, interestingly enough, is characterized as drawing the mind to 'social relations and social duties' (SL 85) rather than as providing a private key to the Pearly Gates. It is true that for Stepsure the all-important 'duties of the social life' (SL 65) are to be performed not in the tavern or at the frolic, but in the home; yet he stipulates that one man's folly (as abetted by too great a fondness for Society) is his entire family's misfortune. And since the community itself is an extended family, with black and white sheep part of the same fold, it should be the care of all to break the vicious cycle of improvidence and indigence – as illustrated by the case history of the aptly named Moses Slack – if only to ensure that the community's surplus wealth can be ploughed back into the land and not frittered on inexhaustible objects of needless charity.

To be sure, there are occasional scenes of burlesque and slapstick in *The Stepsure Letters* – the 'epic' battle between Shootem's soldiers and Snout's swine (SL 103–4), or Hodge's fearsome farting at Mrs M'Cackle's tea party (SL 125–7), but this is hardly 'superfine' satire. Rather, it is homespun humour, used by McCulloch to leaven his turgid sermons in order to keep his hold on the audience for which he aims. McCulloch reserves his satiric darts not for his humble readers but for his critics – Halifax's 'censor,' who upbraided the author of *The Stepsure Letters* for that lack of 'chaste imagination' (frogs in the broth pot, dogs in bed, and urine stains over shingled walls) which would prevent his letters from entering the 'drawing-room of polite life' (SL 135).

Mephibosheth is made to answer that the cottage chimney piece and not the demoralized drawing room is the proper place for his text – 'a plain

story to plain people in plain terms' (SL 137). By providing a series of
cautionary tales detailing the fall of those who start out with every chance
of success but who, through greed, laziness, and social climbing finish by
squandering wealth, neglecting duties, and mouldering in debtors'
prison while their families go begging in the streets, McCulloch hopes
to persuade his common readers to mend their ways and fortunes by
reverting to traditional habits of self-sufficient, home-based, communal
life. 'I was never satisfied that honour abroad would make my spouse and
me so happy as a snug farm affording us every means of domestic comfort'
(SL 105): there is a complacency in this vision of the good life which one
cannot imagine a Haliburton or a Leacock leaving unflayed, however
much they might agree with McCulloch's priorities. Even McCulloch's
dispute with 'Censor' is less a duel of wits than a slinging of mud – or in
this case, manure – pies. The pen he allots to his narrator is both blunt and
plodding, suggestive not of satire's sword, but duty's plough. The result
in *The Stepsure Letters* is a set of epistles to the community – repetitious,
instructive, as earnest as they are earthy – enjoining fidelity to old values
for the well-being of all. Anything more unlike the chicanery and op-
portunism of that verbal contortionist Sam Slick than the moralizing of
Mephibosheth Stepsure cannot be imagined.

'And thus the old man ran on for an hour, dilating on his own merits
and the sins of his neighbours': the description is not Censor's of
Stepsure, but Mrs Moodie's of a similarly self-righteous but less successful character in *Roughing It in the Bush*.[26] And a final impression of the
extent to which McCulloch's concern for community and the preservation
of its stability saturates his narrative can be gained by glancing at the
*Letters* in comparison with *Roughing It*. Where Moodie recounts an
isolated individual's struggle with the hardships of pioneering, McCulloch analyses an established community's experience of hard times; where
Moodie is preoccupied with preserving those distinctions of social caste
and class which assure her very sense of self in a foreign land, McCulloch
labours to preserve the moral character of a community in order to ensure
its economic survival. *Roughing It in the Bush* is in many ways a testy but
ingratiating address to Providence; *The Stepsure Letters* is a mammoth
sermon on Improvidence. And finally, where Moodie works to keep her
psychological and physical distance from her neighbours, McCulloch's
Stepsure knows his neighbours even as he loves himself – steeped as he is
within a common set of traditions, habits, and values he turns his
neighbours' best pretensions and illusions inside out for us without ever
presuming that anything other than superior moral fibre distinguishes his
identity and fortunes from theirs.

\*\*\*

The early Maritime writer whose hierarchical awareness of the social order bears comparison with Moodie's is, of course, Thomas Chandler Haliburton, author of *The Old Judge: Or Life in a Colony*. The cross-purposes in each writer's circumstances are worth noting. Moodie, the impoverished gentlewoman, writes from the bush or the clearing to those of her fellow Britons who, sharing her financial circumstances, must be dissuaded from engaging in the pioneer work for which, as Moodie repeatedly insists, gentlefolk are disastrously unfit. In so perceiving her mission, Moodie succeeds in securing her identity as gentlewoman – an identity threatened in England by the Moodies' comparative poverty, which prevented them from educating their children to keep their status among the gentry, and threatened in the Canadian wilderness by an unseemly conflation of social classes. Haliburton, on the other hand, was assured of the economic and professional base from which to cement his superior position in colonial society. By writing *The Old Judge*, Haliburton could reassure his British readers that he possessed those cosmopolitan tastes and professional accomplishments which should raise him from the rank of colonial, and thus second-class citizen to the role of English gentleman: a role he undoubtedly acted with consummate satisfaction at the end of his life as MP for Launceston in the British House of Commons.[27] It is this desire to show himself an English gentleman which animates Haliburton's exposure of the pretensions of Halifax society and the shortcomings of the British governors, their families and staffs. Yet if certain chapters of *The Old Judge* are at pains to establish the superior breeding, if not birth, of Judge Sandford and his urbanely cynical nephew Lawyer Barclay over a Sir Hercules Sampson or a Lord Edward Dumm-kopf, the preponderance of chapters set away from Halifax reveal that Haliburton's imaginative, if not ideological interests lay in the wealth of humorous anecdotes, tippler's yarns, fables, and ghost stories to be discovered among small communities in the Annapolis Valley and beyond.

Moodie, especially in *Life in the Clearings*, displays eventual enthusiasm for Upper Canada and shows herself dutifully committed to the fortunes of her adopted land; the nostalgic references she drops to England in *Clearings* are like a crocheted edging round a large, solid square of homespun. For Haliburton, who likewise wrote for Britons abroad or else newly resident in British North America, Nova Scotia was a native land into whose indigenous culture he could dip his pen without apologies, as chapters like 'The Witch of Inky Dell' or 'The Keeping Room of an Inn' reveal. And he was absolutely at home – as his travels as a court judge would have made him – in analysing the nature and psychology of settled communities, a subject which for Moodie always plays third fiddle to Nature-swooning and a preoccupation with the freakish characters chance has thrown in her path.

Reams have been written on *The Clockmaker*, and while it is, in linguistic terms alone, a more pleasurable text than *The Old Judge*, it is with the latter that I wish to deal in considering Haliburton's treatment of community. Though both books are 'disguised' as travel narratives so as to avoid 'the prolixity of a journal … and the egotism of an author, by making others speak for themselves in their own way' (TOJ xix), the predominant voice in *The Clockmaker* is, of course, that of Sam Slick, a carefully chosen outsider. Although a British traveller begins the narration of *The Old Judge* and takes nominal charge of the narrative reins, the most notable voices are native ones – those of Sandford and Barclay, among the gentry, and of Stephen Richardson, Sally Horn, Barkins the Bluenose fisherman, Zeb Hunt, and others among the country folk. In fact, only by the inclusion of such decorous rhetorical set pieces as 'The Tombstones,' 'The First Settlers,' or 'The Seasons' does Haliburton keep his narrative from throwing its decorous rider and bolting into the wilds of a popular, oral tradition of story-telling.

Haliburton and McCulloch have in common a conservatism which prizes the cult of individual initiative and industry, the stability of social rank and occupation, and the maintenance of strict controls as to who should be allowed to assume and initiate political office and action. Yet while McCulloch's interests are exclusively communal, Haliburton's are social as well, in that he introduces a supercilious sense of class distinctions whenever events seem to call for it. This can be seen by comparing two similar episodes in *The Stepsure Letters* and *The Old Judge*. In the sixteenth 'letter' of the former, the disastrous events of Miss Sippit's tea party and frolic are used to convict the whole community of vanity and sham; in the 'Merrimakings' chapter of the latter text, the droll speech and forthright manner of a representative country girl, Miss Sally Horn, prove as delicious to the two condescending gentlemen through whose eyes we view the scene as the pies and pickles which form the 'pickinick' fare; in other words, the knowingness of the gentry and the naïveté of Sally form the crux of the humour. The reader laughs with the gentlemen at Haliburton's rustics but is made to feel a part of McCulloch's country folk and the very follies this author exposes.

And yet, by endowing his rustic 'natives' with an engaging vitality and self-possession, Haliburton allows them to repossess the narrative.

Against the reality of community in this old colony, the accounts of
Halifax Society seem airily circumstantial and, in their concern to give
readers 'an accurate idea of the class to which [each character] belonged'
(TOJ 124), repellent.[28] Yet one must place such details as the narrator's
abhorrence of the indiscriminate mixing of social classes at the Governor's
gala receptions within the context of Haliburton's general philosophy,
according to which the stratification of classes, the jealous preservation of
barriers to position and power, could guarantee a harmonious and
prosperous society for all.[29]

   The Old Judge is an anomalous sort of narrative: designating itself a 'tour'
sketch, it yet insists on the traveller's becoming 'resident' if he ever wants
to comprehend the 'habits, manners and tastes' of the colonial population
(TOJ 162). The best way of doing this, we are told, is to give ear to the
stories people have to tell. In the course of The Old Judge it turns out that
the best of these stories are told by people whose imaginations are
embedded in the life of established communities, and that the best
story-tellers are those who favour 'homespun' to 'broadcloth' both in
dress and narrative style. Thus the affable farmer Stephen Richardson not
only mercilessly interrupts the bumbling anecdotes of the pretentious,
upward-sneaking Mr Layton, he actually refashions them according to his
own criteria of effective story-telling. In Judge Sandford's drawn-out
account of his dealings with the fisherman Barkins in 'How Many Fins
Has a Cod?', it is the near-Dickensian Barkins and not the harassed Judge
who grabs the narrative line and our attention. And Lawyer Barclay's
description of the patterns of settlement in Nova Scotia (Chapter 7)
scarcely holds a candle to Zeb the drover's tale of 'Old Daddy Hunt's
Garter Collection and How He Got It.'

   Thus as the nominal traveller-narrator goes back and forth between
Halifax and the county town of Ilinoo, hearing accounts of colonial
government from Judge Sandford and ghost stories from Stephen
Richardson, and, in the process, discovering the unique beauty and
inconvenience of a Nova Scotia winter, a composite portrait of a community is built up. The foundation of this community is our common
human lot, as Mr Barclay makes clear in the chapter entitled 'The Tombstones.' Using the graveyard as a topos from which to develop the idea
of man's double nature as social animal and possessor of an immortal
soul, he observes the gross differences between the tombstones of the
poor and rich ('the scale of colonial precedence survives mortality' [TOJ
59]) but ends with a 'transcendent' or at least levelling gesture to a child's
humble gravestone, watered by its mother's tears. Before our eyes are dry,
Barclay relates an anecdote of how a noble youth of Shelburne preferred

to drown rather than risk the life of a would-be rescuer who, unlike him, had a wife and family to support ashore.

This insistence on the common good over individual need, on the responsibilities and duties which bind us one to another, is the focus of Chapter 10 of *The Old Judge*, 'The Lone House,' from which I have drawn the epigraph to this chapter. 'The Lone House' can stand as a paradigmatic expression of community, pressing as it does for the transcendence of individual grief by communal feeling and insisting on that sense of continuity which is a feature of established communities. Moreover, the situation on which it focuses – how one accommodates the sudden, freakish death of a beloved person – is a recurrent one in Maritime fiction, as MacLeod's 'The Road to Rankin's Point' or 'The Turning of Perfection,' Bruce's *The Channel Shore*, Day's *Rockbound*, and Buckler's *The Mountain and the Valley* all show.

The plot of 'The Lone House' is straightforward: John Lent settles with his family on 'The Ridge,' a lonely stretch of coast. Caught in one of those winter blizzards that seem to be the Canadian equivalent of American apple pie, he freezes to death, leaving many children and an inconsolable widow who has hardly begun to pick up the pieces of her life when asked for help by a group of travellers even more miserable than she. The frame of the story is, however, fairly complex. The Judge begins his narrative by remarking on the extreme desolation of 'The Ridge.' Then, describing the usual pattern of settlement whereby the first lonely house erected in a clearing is soon joined by others until a community forms, he asks why anyone would have chosen to build a house in what would always remain 'the heart of a howling wilderness' (TOJ 143). The answer, as the story makes clear, is that John Lent did so precisely to bring 'the blessings of a civilized community' (TOJ 143) to travellers in need of shelter and direction in such a direly isolated spot. Upheld in the wilderness by the hand of God, Lent's widow decides to stay on at 'The Ridge' in order to carry out her husband's work. She has come to this courageous decision as a result of her experience with three shipwrecked sailors who, having dragged themselves to her door and received assistance from her, then learn of her husband's death and proceed to make his coffin and dig his grave – acts of practical charity which answer the widow's most pressing needs: 'There was a community of suffering, a similarity of situation, and a sympathy among them all, that for the time made them forget they were strangers, and feel towards each other like members of one family ... She had afforded them food, shelter, and a home. They had aided her in a most trying moment with their personal assistance, and comforted her with their sympathy and kindness' (TOJ 153).

This almost sacramental notion of community is complemented by Chapter 14, 'The Keeping-Room of an Inn; Or, the Cushion-Dance.' Here Mr Barclay and his companion, snowbound at a country inn, participate in an agreeable evening's feasting, story-telling, and dancing that comes to represent the apogee of community living – the open fellow-feeling to be had when a group of people, 'all neighbours and friends ... meet like one family and live with and towards each other as such. Each individual is dependent on the rest for mutual assistance and good offices, and they constitute themselves all the society they have. The protection that forms and ceremonies throw round the members of large communities is not here needed ... They are simple-minded, warm-hearted, hospitable and virtuous people' (TOJ 228–9).

The possibility of such an idyllic existence in a fallen world is gently queried not by the cynic Barclay, but by the life-of-the-party, Stephen Richardson, and yet this ideal of community is permitted to stand in *The Old Judge* both as a corrective to the false and fatuous pleasures of Society as it is found in the best Halifax drawing rooms, and perhaps, as a *memento mori*. For near the end of Haliburton's narrative comes a chapter entitled 'The Seasons; Or, Comers and Goers,' a chapter which details the migratory patterns to be observed among native Nova Scotians and visitors to the colony. Opening in spring with the influx of Yankee peddlers, circuses, and quack doctors, the chapter ends with winter and the freezing up of the ports, and thus, of people's comings and goings. Despite the fact that the factory-bound farmgirls who leave for New England are more than compensated for by the incoming boatloads of indigent Irish, a definite melancholy pervades the narrative, as though this balance cannot long last; as though the spectre of massive emigration from Nova Scotia and the blow this would strike to the very survival of knowable community were already haunting the air.

\*\*\*

By the time Andrew Macphail completed *The Master's Wife* in 1929, the solidity and solidarity of community life as experienced in rural Prince Edward Island had suffered the same fate as most elderly people's childhoods, limbo'd between an increasingly tenuous present, and an ever more tangible past. What immediately strikes the reader of Macphail's text is that community – which had functioned for McCulloch and Haliburton as an observable, exigent fact, as part of the hard currency of reality – has here become more a matter of dream and, to complete the analogy, frozen asset. 'The active man [who] occupied himself with carrying out a variety of agricultural experiments ... to demonstrate to interested Islanders how new crops could be developed, and how scientific methods could make farming viable once again'[30] simply doesn't figure in the pages of *The Master's Wife*. Instead – and we should be thankful, for it gives to this narrative its curious power – we have Macphail reinhabiting the mind of childhood, yet with the mobility which adult experience and understanding permit. The result is a memoir which, with the exception of its last few chapters, is one of the finest and oddest pieces of prose to be found in Maritime, or Canadian literature as a whole.

The opening chapter of Macphail's narrative is entitled 'In the Beginning,' but this genesis has little linear or chronological motion; rather, the thumbnail sketches of Macphail's family and neighbours in late nineteenth-century Orwell are twined together in the complex fashion of genealogical tables, so that the whole becomes a continuum difficult to grasp or place until the entire narrative has unfolded. Kinship structures and the awareness of conflicting traits inherited from one's parents' familial lines are as essential to *The Master's Wife* as they are to Maillet's *Pélagie*; moreover, the Macphail family comes to serve as a synecdoche for Orwell itself.

The family Macphail evokes in such curiously distanced fashion is a union of the Smiths – accused by Orwellians of 'paganism' because of their 'passionate' nature – and the arch-Calvinist Macphails, descendants of a line of gentlemen and scholars. The Macphails – the 'Master's' people – are native Orwellians, the Smiths 'foreign' since their 'native place was some miles away' (TMW 1). The incestuous nature of the community is a product of its policy of self-enclosure, its active embrace of that belief enunciated by Mephibosheth Stepsure that it is a man's duty to stay home and not to wander – even so far as the next town. The existence of a larger, outside world is discovered by the Master's children through the visits of their mother's uncle, a sea captain who brings brandy, profanity, and a sense of the sea into their lives: 'It was from this uncle we first learned that there were strange themes in the world, fresh words, and new rhythms, hitherto undiscovered in catechism, Bible or prayer' (TMW 3). And, as the sea captain uncle, bearing in his 'powerful, hairy hands' exotic gifts – 'a piece of silk, a box of spice, a parcel of strange green tea' (TMW 2) enters the lives of the children, he brings with him a force that threatens the entrenched power of the stable, static, closed community: the desire to get out and away.

Yet ships and the sea cannot dislodge the sheer gravity of community whose constitutive layers – the family, the house, the farm, Orwell, the Island – are laid down like bedrock, cemented by an ethic of duty and obedience, discipline and submission; sanctioned by Calvin's God and sealed by the observance of two cardinal rules, silence and secrecy on all family matters. Language itself becomes both an instrument and victim of conformity and repression:

Words too specific of certain fuctions were eschewed, and even those words were avoided which called up any image that was unpleasant ... Silence was decent; reticence was not hypocrisy. Exuberance of language was strictly checked ...

There was one absolute rule: anything that occurred in the house was not to be disclosed; anything unworthy heard outside was not to be brought in. If a child were pressed by a curious neighbour upon a doubtful matter, he was to answer, 'I cannot say,' leaving it to be impartially surmised whether his reticence was due to lack of knowledge or to an injunction not to say. (TMW 68)

And yet, as the narrative shows, the very terseness of speech which such discipline imposed comes to be more telling than the most effusive confessions: 'Apart from murder, there was no crime in that community except the crime of going in debt. A man who had stolen cattle was publicly whipped in the market place. A Negro sailor who stole bread was hanged at Gallows-point. His crime was wanton: it was proved that he had not eaten the crust' (TMW 36).

Exclusion of a peculiar sort is the principle on which the community of Orwell survived. Racial considerations were paramount: the purity of Highland stock must at all costs be preserved, so that discriminations were made between immigrants from different parts of Scotland itself: 'In every community there are conventions by which the status of the member is established, and the general safety preserved' (TMW 103); in Orwell, these conventions were rigidly observed:

A new arrival was fenced about with prejudice, rumour and convention, lest his children might corrupt the community in manners, morals or religion. It was only after rigid scrutiny he was adopted into the number, but for thirty years he would be described as 'an imported man.' One Englishman brought with him an Esquimau wife, and henceforth all English were regarded with grave suspicion. This woman would fashion a pair of mitts or a waistcoat for a boy from the skin of a grey seal he had caught in the bay. But after two generations of solitude the family disappeared to the States. (TMW 128–9)

Yet Catholics were treated with tolerance by the Presbyterian majority, and so, too, were certain kinds of sinners – Macphail relates his mother's laments regarding the 'decay of illegitimacy' in Orwell: as unwed mothers and their bastard children moved off to the States, they were consequently 'lost as servants in the settlement' (TMW 8).

For Macphail himself the most important exclusion decreed by community law would have been that of the arts: books, music, painting were either non-existent or barely tolerated. The Macphail children's sole acquaintance with music before their 'escape' from Orwell may have been the time they heard bagpipes playing in the dairy – at any rate, Macphail confesses that 'it was long before we learned that music is a thing to be enjoyed for itself and not for any ulterior purpose, such as freedom from rats' (TMW 33).[31] Moreover, anyone who had acquired aesthetic leanings during a period of residence outside the community immediately became suspect on his return; it is with more than wryness that Macphail observes, regarding the pleasures of walks in vernal woods: 'The conventions of that life were strict, and the place so thickly settled that any person who moved abroad was under a wide surveillance. Any such movement was a matter of comment, surmise and speculation. A grown woman wandering towards the woods might well be suspected of being "queer" ... A young man in that place who wears strange clothes, lets his hair grow long, or walks with his hat off is still in danger, even if he is a professor, of being put in the asylum' (TMW 111).

It is easy to see why Macphail and his numerous siblings, working on the small family farm whose produce the Master used to supplement his income as a school inspector, thought 'only of escape ... from the land and the ice' of Orwell (TMW 117–19). Yet this tightly knit community in which almost all shared a language, a religion, an understanding of the meaning of life and of man's proper use of it, and in which, therefore, all were roughly equal despite incidental differences in material possessions; this community in which a man would be known by his first name and the particular trade he plied in the community, acquires a sterling quality when contrasted with the 'completely civilized' town of Malpeque – the first example of 'Society' the narrator discovers (TMW 127). Only here does he come to clear consciousness of the facts of class distinctions and antagonisms: 'For the first time I learned, what I always suspected, that humanity is not one, but a congeries of families each with a unity of tradition, a similarity of interest, an equality of education, and identity of thought, manners and morals; a "society" in which the upper members could of their own free will penetrate to the bottom; in which the lower members could only by sheer merit and incredible difficulty rise to the top' (TMW 128).

'More instructive still,' Macphail continues, was the discovery in Malpeque of a 'segregated class which provided labour for the more menial tasks. They were admitted to the houses only on sufferance: they ate by themselves; they were treated with good-humoured toleration, their manners and morals a source of amusement' (TMW 129). In Orwell, he goes on to imply, these aforementioned distinctions of social class – if not racial group – would be considered as having sprung from 'false' as opposed to 'proper' pride.[32]

Yet if the farming world of Orwell was, for Macphail, an accursed place out of which one could escape either through the sea or else through the Eden of Education, it is a measure of the curious complexity and rich texture of *The Master's Wife* that the world of Orwell can be revealed with both proper pride and terror – as the foundation stone of Macphail's parents' generation and as the millstone of his own. The *odi et amo* which pervades Macphail's memoir is similar to that which percolates through Leacock's *Sunshine Sketches*, and yet the means by which this mood is achieved are entirely different. With Leacock it is the convention of the *faux naïf* narrator that permits the agreeable ironies and occasional sentimentalities of the *Sunshine Sketches*; with Macphail it is the decentring perspective of childhood that allows the peculiar honesty and almost total absence of nostalgia in *The Master's Wife*.[33]

The mind of a child is the mind of a dreamer by night. Things remembered, and unrelated, are joined in a fantastic sequence. He begins with a set of illusions from which fresh and logical illusions are developed, but the whole figment has the force of intense reality. (TMW 46)

The mind of Macphail's childhood is one ruled both by respect and curiosity regarding the adult world; the eloquence with which Macphail recreates family and community life reveals how successfully he transcended the absolute laws of his childhood: silence and secrecy regarding the contradictory or disabling facts of community life. In a sense, *The Master's Wife* is the subtext of Orwell's Book of Life, and this subtext is authored by the child / dreamer's mind. The narrative's very lack of chronological thrust, its eddying round of certain character traits or communal events which seem to acquire significance not through any pre-established order but in the very process of accretion, imitates the movement of dreams.

In fact, the effect upon the reader of the first chapter of *The Master's Wife* can be likened to the effect on the viewer of the opening dream sequence in Ingmar Bergman's *Wild Strawberries*; both free us from our rigid expectations of linear narrative and the logic it builds by. Instead of a conventional sequence of events and observations, Macphail gives us a teeming sea of perceptions, the acuity, starkness, or complexity of which derive from his refusal to categorize as good or evil any of the subjects he treats. While he may outline the 'secret hypocrisy' (TMW 46) which evangelical parents often sow in the minds of their children; while he may document, for example, the 'slow delight' with which his mother watched the distress and disintegration of the family that had poisoned her favourite dog (TMW 142), he does so with an uncanny detachment that permits us a perfectly dual vision – we see the people of Orwell as they saw themselves, and as they were there to be seen. If native Orillians came to cold-shoulder Leacock, Orwellians could have had little cause to do likewise, had *The Master's Wife* been published in Macphail's lifetime, for this text, though it articulates things Orwell decreed must be left unsaid, does so in Orwell's own idiom. The distancing effect Macphail achieves through his creation of a narrative patterned on the dreaming mind of childhood, and his use throughout of titles rather than names for the people to whom he was most closely related – 'The Master' instead of 'my father' – precludes any emotional skewing of his treatment of family or community. Macphail presents his need to escape Orwell as clinically as he does the fact of escape; though in superficial ways akin to MacLennan's Dr Daniel Ainslie, he is utterly different from that alienated, tormented character in the nature of the peace he has made with the place which made him.

On the fate of community, *The Master's Wife* is explicit and dispassionate. Sharing his literary predecessors' admiration for the ideal of self-sufficiency – 'a man who lives on his own land and owes no man anything develops all the dignity inherent in his nature' (TMW 13) – Macphail details both the structure and the breakdown of family self-sufficiency and its corollary, communal closure. His chapter 'The Economy of the House' is amazingly concrete in its explication of the psychology and 'aesthetic' of domestic economy[34] – here is Macphail's description of the devastating effects of industrialization on the 'well-established' fabric of domestic life: 'The apparent cheapness of articles which began to fill the shops, and the ease with which they could be obtained, destroyed the hardy spirit of economy; and when the old order was broken at one point it failed in all. Without the sanded floor there was now no means of restoring a rusty needle; a new one must be bought. When she found her needle rusted, she would place it on the floor, and roll it under her foot at an incredible speed. In a moment the needle was polished bright. This is an allegory' (TMW 76).

With the advent of factory-made convenience goods, and of general hard times on Prince Edward Island, not only individual families but also the community itself suffered grave losses: 'every year the surplus young men and women migrated to Boston as freely as the seabirds' (TMW 89). Joining them in the search for 'friends, work and money' were those ambitious few disaffected enough from the punishing life of the land to attempt to rise 'by sheer merit and incredible difficulty' to the top of the social ladder in Toronto or Montreal – almost never, we may observe, in Halifax.

\*\*\*

In the fiction published after *The Master's Wife*, awareness of the breakdown of community is coupled with an intense desire for the sustaining and validating powers of communal life. Even Frank Parker Day's *Rockbound*, published at roughly the same time at which Macphail completed *The Master's Wife*, and depicting the nadir of community in the violent, truly 'feud-al' kingdom of Rockbound Island, seems to be pleading for a regenerated vision of communal life by having its hero David found his own island kingdom with his new wife and his son from an earlier marriage to the daughter of his arch-enemy, Uriah Jung. MacLennan's *Each Man's Son*, though it presents the mining community of Broughton as demoralized, self-destructive, and actively harmful towards the interests of those with the courage or intelligence to escape it, also creates a 'composite' family – a farmer's son turned doctor, his Society wife, and their adopted son, child of a coal-miner's daughter, and a miner turned boxer – which, at least hypothetically, could serve as a microcosm of regenerated community. (As a later chapter will show, MacLennan rejects not so much the possibility of this regeneration as any interest in the project when he comes to pick up the loose ends of the MacNeil-Ainslie family in *The Return of the Sphinx*.)

Ernest Buckler's *The Mountain and the Valley* focuses on the struggle for self-realization of an individual within a chosen family inside a sustaining community. It presents to David Canaan the possibility of freeing himself as an individual precisely through his artistic articulation of the communal ethos. Yet the success of this project is enclosed within heavily ironic parentheses – those of David's premature death, of the novel's sabotaging of David's vision in the epilogue, and finally, those of the community's very fragility, the erosion of its rooted values and precepts by the technological changes which, by the novel's close, have penetrated Entremont.[35] And in Raddall's *The Nymph and the Lamp* the ideal of community (which, as Mrs Paradee's boarding house reveals, is extinct in Halifax) flourishes only on the island of Marina, due to its extreme isolation and the limitations imposed on the primitve islanders by history, nature, and a still infantile state of technology. Finally, a work such as David Adams Richards's *The Coming of Winter* would seem to be the logical end of the presentation of community in Maritime fiction: the people of his Miramichi seem to have lost even the memory of traditions and values which had imbued earlier community life with a native strength and dignity; now only the limitations and disadvantages of community remain to dog its inert members.

Yet what might seem to be an inevitable progression from a necessary solidarity to the fragmentation or dissipation of the ideal of community has been interrupted by a work of fiction which, in its critical exploration and redefinition of the nature of community, can stand as an apotheosis of the communal vision in Maritime literature. Charles Bruce's *The Channel Shore*, first published in 1954, and rescued more or less from oblivion thirty years later by its inclusion in McClelland and Stewart's New Canadian Library series, may not have inspired direct imitations, but bears articulate witness to the continuing validity and power of community as a workable ideal in Maritime experience, and in the fiction which recreates that experience.

\*\*\*

The paradigm which *The Channel Shore* creates is a dialectical one, in which the primacy of blood ties and the closed family unit is opposed by events and actions which reveal shared human desires, needs, and responsibilities as the only redeeming and enduring basis for communal life. The divisive forces of religion, of suspicion or envy of difference as manifested in the tidal power of malicious gossip are routed in various ways. The community simultaneously accepts a nominal 'outsider' – Bill Graham, the son of a self-exiled child of Currie Head – and rejects a tyranically disruptive native son, Anse Gordon. Most important, however, are the discoveries of Grant Marshall, the novel's hero, as he experientially redefines the roles of father and son for the community of the Channel Shore. Grant's most important discovery might stand as the novel's epigraph: 'Of body and spirit there is no right of blood possession, only the gentler ties of affection and respect.'[36] The deepening and widening of community loyalty and love which this lesson inspires come to vindicate the concept of community in the full face of its assailants and detractors.

*The Channel Shore* deals with the interwoven loves and hates of a small cast of characters within a tightly bound community. As with *The Mountain and the Valley*, the narrative of *The Channel Shore* is framed by a prologue and epilogue, both of which are set in the present. The novel opens in the present, immediately after World War II, with the meeting in England of the engaged observer, Bill Graham, and the novel's 'villain,' the quasi-Byronic Anse Gordon, neither of whom has set foot on the Shore for some twenty-five years. The memories this encounter raises prod both men to return for better or worse to the community they consider home.

While the first part of the novel deals with community events immediately after the close of World War I, Part Two describes life on the Channel Shore during 1933–4, long after Anse Gordon, having casually impregnated Hazel McKee, has as casually walked out on Hazel, his parents, and the community itself; and long before Bill Graham and Anse meet in London. It ends with another 'present' bridge over past waters: the train ride from Toronto to the Shore which carries the newly demobilized Bill Graham away from a sorry reunion with his difficult wife and the son he barely knows, and into the community whose struggle to survive will teach Graham the tolerance and respect for difference which might allow him to mend his marriage and truly father his son. Part Three, in which Anse tries and fails to stake his claim for the son Hazel bore him and who has been adopted as his own by Grant Marshall, is followed by a brief section entitled '1946 ...'. It finishes the novel in the same way a glaze does a painting, fixing and intensifying the colours of shapes which continue to move and relocate themselves in the viewer's eye. As Bill Graham takes his leave of the Shore with the intention of returning the next summer with his own son, we are given a sense of an ending but not of any termination. The dominant force is that of the passage of time and the process of change, both of which, we are made to feel, will insure the Channel Shore's survival as a living community.

Place is as integral a feature of *The Channel Shore* as time, and if the latter threatens the notion of community with the erosion of remembered bonds and promises, the former preserves communal memory by mapping it according to the prominent features of the Shore. Characters and plot are bonded to the distinctive geography of the place: the Gordons, for example, are 'downshore' people; the area in which they and the others who scrape a living as fishermen reside is known as 'The Rocks' and 'Catholic Country.' Anse and his sister Anna, with whom Grant Marshall is first in love, are 'Fishguts' – the name given to all downshore people by the Protestant farmers of 'The Head' – 'Bogtown' to Anse Gordon and his neighbours. One of the novel's symbolic poles is represented by 'the boat,' built by Anse's father just at the moment fishing ceases to be a viable enterprise on the Channel Shore, and restored by Anse who, on returning home, has plans to fish the Atlantic side of the channel with his new-found son, Alan.

The other pole is 'The Place,' the land Grant buys from his authoritarian uncle who has raised him and forbidden him, a Methodist from 'The Head,' to marry Anna Gordon, a Catholic from 'The Rocks.' It is on 'The Place,' a cradle of affection, peace, and well-being that Alan is raised, along with Margaret, Grant's daughter by his second wife, the outsider Renie Fraser. (Grant had previously married Hazel McKee, pregnant with Anse's child and dying of tuberculosis in Toronto. By restoring Hazel to the community and by legitimizing Alan, Grant secures for Hazel's parents their necessary role and rights as grandparents.)

The polarities of land and sea, 'The Head' and 'The Rocks' are bridged by two other distinctive features of the Channel Shore. One of these is Katen's store, at which members of both sexes, religions, and neighbour-hoods meet to gossip, talk politics, and to pair off for long walks home on hazy summer nights. Another is the beach and the fishing huts which dot it. It is in one of these huts that Hazel confides to her father, Richard McKee, the fact of her pregnancy by Anse; it is here, to Richard – who combines his skill as farmer with an instinctive love for boats and the sea – that young Margaret confides her love for Alan, a love she cannot publicly avow without shattering the fiction her father, Grant, has so carefully authored – the fiction that Grant is his natural son and hence, Margaret's brother. And it is in the hut, as well, that Anna Gordon was effectively betrayed by Grant, whose confusion between the blood loyalty he owes to his uncle and foster-father, and the love he feels for a girl whose religion and upbringing his uncle despises, becomes not just a personal crisis, but also a means of recognizing and healing the rifts within the entire community.

Place defines one's right to recognition within the community; even the town's 'loose woman,' Vangie Murphy, may not be excluded: 'A person's name might be entered on the books in hell, but as long as she was a neighbour, dealing with the same earth and weather and people as anyone else, she must be, in some sense, acknowledged' (cs 37). Only when a person physically leaves the community does his or her identity become forfeit, yet even then there is an immediate recognition of the rights of the wanderer on his or her return: Hazel McKee is given due recognition as Grant's wife when she comes back to end her pregnancy and her life at the Shore; Anse Gordon is welcomed back into the com-munity, and only his public insult against that community brings the people of the Channel Shore to acquiesce in Alan's blatant rejection of Anse. The 'pattern of place' incorporates all forms of human action and experience: 'Even sin and remorse, heresy and regret and failure were dark colours in the pattern' (CS 50). Bruce's tapestry motif becomes as integral to *The Channel Shore* as does the web motif to George Eliot's *Middlemarch*. The 'clan' structure of community, with its interweaving of families within a pattern of 'commonplace work and everyday good will' (CS 338) can, however, assume a destructive cast in the form of the 'shame culture' it breeds. Thus Eva McKee's 'bitter pride' (CS 131) delays the redemptive effects of Grant's act of solidarity in marrying her daughter. Similarly, Josie Gordon's shame at her son's 'enormous and furtive cruelty' (CS 111) to Hazel and to his own father casts her into a private hell of aloofness even after Grant has moved in with the Gordons to alleviate their sense of loss after Anna's death and Anse's abrupt departure. Moreover, the gossip which conveys the 'occasional meanness and cruelty ... intolerance and pride' which flourish alongside the 'generosity and courage and even kindness' (CS 197) members of the community show to one another, becomes the bitch goddess of this shame culture. It is only when Grant follows his own conscience and ceases to care about what other people will say about his unorthodox actions that he becomes free to act for the good of the community and according to the credo for which he seeks public recognition: 'Not a damn thing matters but what people can do for each other, when they're up against it' (CS 208).

Grant's defiance of his strict and emotionally dessicated uncle's code in leaving the Marshall home to live with the Gordons results in his discovery of a solidarity similar to that explored by writers such as Joseph Conrad and George Eliot: 'a kinship for all others isolated in their aloneness, stricken by circumstance ...' (CS 124). His wrestling with the concept of fatherhood, with the meaning and implications of his ties to Alan as opposed to Anse's blood right of paternity, brings about a public understanding of the roots of such solidarity, and with that understanding, the assurance that solidarity will endure and develop within the community as a whole. This becomes clear upon examining the roles played by Grant, Anse, and Alan in the novel.

It is illustrative of the subtle strength and strict integrity of Bruce's vision of community that he should have Grant triumphantly discover moral consciousness – the dues of 'fellow feeling' over the laws of propriety – in Part One of *The Channel Shore*, only to have him come a cropper in Parts Two and Three. The perfect husband and, more importantly, father, Grant flounders over his own conformity to the community's restrictive definition of fatherhood. Instead of recognizing the inadequacy of the law of blood ties, Grant submits to the tyranny of accepted opinion and as a result causes suffering to those he had most wanted to shelter – his wife and children. It becomes a point of personal pride with Grant, once Anse has returned to the Shore, to preserve the fiction of his own biological fathering of Alan; in so doing, however, he risks alienating Alan, who has already asked Josie Gordon to confirm his suspicions about his birth, and he plunges his daughter Margaret into a radical frustration of her love for Alan. Inadvertently, Grant contributes to that reality of stagnation which has forced many of the Shore's most promising sons to flee, and which he had previously struggled to explode. In an ironic inversion of the tapestry motif associated with the ideal of community, Margaret longs for some dramatic act on Alan's part 'to tear away this web of wrongs half-forgotten and sacrifice cherished in illusion' – and in which her happiness and Alan's have become impossibly entangled (cs 378). Yet any such act would involve what both lovers see as a betrayal of the man they regard as their father.

As for Anse, he is a kind of demonic *doppel-gänger* for Grant, manifesting the dark side of community, its acceptance of anyone who belongs 'by blood.' If Grant sins by omission in his treatment of Anna, how much more so does Anse in his abandonment of Hazel and his helpless parents. The law of Anse's being is 'a queer contemptuous malice, impulsive and yet deliberate' (cs 381) which makes of him an 'angel of devastation' along the Shore. His need for power over the community springs from his fear of being publicly rejected – as he has quietly been by Hazel before she even discovered her pregnancy, and as he will be by his own son in the presence of the entire community. Anse's contempt for the community, and particularly, for the 'respectable' people of 'The Head,' finds expression in his desire to smash the 'shell of protection' in which the community has enclosed Grant's fiction of fatherhood. We are made to feel that, in some insidious way, Anse nearly succeeds in claiming Alan – in whose best interests it would be to become Anse's son, free to marry Margaret Marshall. Anse, by skilfully and almost lovingly repairing the boat which his own father built, draws Alan into the smaller community of misfits and ne'er-do-wells at the Shore; a love of the sea and an inherent ability to manoeuvre rudder and sail attract Alan, against his will, to Anse's company.

As Anse encroaches upon the last third of the novel and Alan, now a twenty-six-year-old veteran of World War ii comes to grips with his knowledge of his origins, Grant Marshall diminishes in presence, though not in stature. It becomes Alan's task to prove to his adoptive father that 'kinship of the spirit [is] ... something warm, possessive and personal; as strong and as personal as kinship of the blood' (cs 259). And this he can do only by asserting it 'in the sight of all' (cs 262) – appropriately, at the annual picnic which has become a community institution on the Channel Shore, drawing together the people of 'The Rocks' and 'The Head.' When Anse openly insults 'The Head' and the values by which it lives, when he covertly asserts his fatherhood of Alan – by means of a sexual pun which deepens a previous insult against the farmers of 'Bogtown' – he is struck down by Alan, who had sparked off Anse's jeers by refusing his offer of a partnership in the boat Anse has resurrected. Yet it is not so much this open, dramatic act in which the slowly gathering violence of the narrative at last finds voice, as the cumulative process of Alan's self-realization which frees Grant from his obsession with Alan's supposed 'fealty' to Anse: 'In the face of his faith in Alan's stature as a man' – a stature in which Grant's example has played no little part – 'he could find in nothing else, not even fatherhood itself, a sense of urgency' (cs 383).

That ultimately the 'relationship ... of place and touch and word' (cs 225) proves stronger than blood ties between child and parent in both Alan's and Margaret's lives redeems the community, which has not only collaborated in preserving Grant's fiction of paternity regarding Alan, but which has also witnessed the explosion of that fiction and its replacement by the truth of general human kinship or solidarity. Publicly declared and received, this truth will endure as a transforming influence within the community. As the people of the Channel Shore are continually discovering, the things one generation says, does, feels, 'remain in the flesh of others' (cs 320), becoming something 'old and continuing, a blend of today, and the past and the future' (cs 83). As importantly, the discoveries made or epiphanies experienced are not restricted to individual characters locked away by superior sensibilities from community life. Whereas in *The Mountain and the Valley* only David Canaan climbs the mountain to find revealed the Truth of Time, in *The Channel Shore* a variety of characters – Grant, Margaret, Alan – are privileged with such revelations. A condition of their knowing, moreover, would seem to be that any transcendent awareness of rivers of time, rings of space must be firmly grounded within the commonplace experience of life with one's fellows (cs 243). Thus behind the exemplary figures in *The Channel Shore* stands a 'supporting cast' of characters – Richard McKee, Josie Gordon, Stan Currie, the Grahams – who are also shown to possess value and importance. Again, the strong contrast with *The Mountain and the Valley*, in which the villagers of Entremont seem shadowy, second-class figures in comparison with the members of the redolently drawn Canaan family, is clear.

Where Buckler seems modernist in his awareness of the alienation and isolation brought by full consciousness, Bruce seems positively nineteenth-century in his concern for knowable community, his belief that, no matter what an individual's private engagement with reality might be, 'there were still people you must meet and talk to, relationships you had to make, customs you had to follow' (cs 149). His conviction that evil or villainy consists of 'step[ping] free, not caring' what repercussions one's actions have on others (cs 149) is at one with the moral vision of a George Eliot or a Jane Austen. Indeed, the minuteness of scale and intimacy of detail with which *The Channel Shore* is plotted, and the resonance with which action finally does occur make one think of a novel like *Emma* – Anse's insult to Stan Freeman at the holiday picnic has something of the same force as Emma's insult to Miss Bates at the Box Hill picnic. Yet the innovativeness of Bruce's project in *The Channel Shore* – his impassioned attempt to transform, redeem and, for coming generations, validate the concept of community – can be seen in his definition and showing forth of community as a kind of human narrative, of human lives as endlessly interwoven, living fictions.

Thus Grant, when told by the keenly suffering Josie of Hazel's pregnancy and consequent disgrace, is conscious of a fundamental altering of his perceptions: 'He had seen it as something on the screen of a motion picture, in the plot of a story. Now the heart of it was clear, a thing of flesh and blood, as much a part of life as the people who faced it ...' (cs 250).

The ability to see 'the story' as written by 'flesh and blood, moved by its rooted hungers' (cs 3), to recognize the dead as part of that story, living 'in the separate memories of men and women on the Channel Shore' (cs 257), leads to a curious kind of intertextuality. Thus Bruce's fiction of Grant Marshall's creating and living out his own fiction of fatherhood becomes a text within the larger text which community authors: 'In a hundred years the tale would be part of that long hearsay, a thread in dim forgotten fabric ... linked through tenuous bloodlines to the moving Now' (cs 394). In the living out of their changed lives Alan, Margaret, Grant – even the observer, Bill Graham – will, as the novel closes, 'begin the new design, woven of the old ... in the memory and imagination and knowledge of the Shore' (cs 394).

Bruce ultimately presents a particular Maritime community as a microcosm of possible human relationships, and a given place, the Channel Shore, as human life itself. Thus *The Channel Shore*, following in its very representation of community that slow ebb and 'undulant curling roar' (cs 127) perpetually in the ears of its characters, becomes what D.H. Lawrence demanded the novel be: the book of life.

# 3

# The Book of Nature

Nature becomes significant to man when ... passed through the alembic
of his heart ... It acts either by interpreting, recalling, suggesting,
or symbolizing some phase of human feeling ... Whatever it be that is
brought to the alembic – naked hill, or barren sand-reach, sea or meadow, weed or star – it comes out charged with a new force, imperishable and active wherever it finds sympathies to vibrate under its
currents.

CHARLES G.D. ROBERTS[1]

In a chapter of the *Literary History of Canada*, Hugo McPherson defines
the 'transcontinental sweep' of post-war fiction by deferring to 'critics
from Northrop Frye to Warren Tallmann [who] have seen its development as a struggle against the violence, or the snowy indifference of
nature – as an effort to humanize and give articulate shape to this vast
landscape; to encompass it in imaginative terms and, in so doing, to
discover the self.'[2]

What I wish to show in this chapter is that Maritime fiction has traditionally perceived the natural world as a challenge rather than a menace – as accessible book, rather than metaphysical mirror. In order to
fully appreciate the relationship between human and natural worlds
as developed in Maritime texts, we have first to strip off the thick fur coat
and seven-league boots with which partisans of the transcontinental
school have burdened Canadian readers attempting to understand their
literature's representation of nature. Given that the elements of wind
and water, though capable of great destructiveness, were also prime
means of communication, commercial prosperity, and sheer mobility in

the Maritimes; given that the region's tempered climate and landscape contrast dramatically with the blasted climes and boundless wastes our mythmakers offer us as 'Mother Canada,' the paradigms and very particulars of the natural world given us by a Buckler, Roberts, or Raddall should be recognized as authentic and significant alternatives to the established Canadian tropes – Tallman's wolf and Frye's snow-fort garrison.

Frye's general convictions that we respond most profoundly and humanly to our fallen world and nature by imposing imaginative shapes and patterns on our environment receives heightened – almost hysterical – colouring in the context of Canadian literature. Such is our country's climate and terrain, Frye suggests, that we conceive a 'deep terror' of the soul in the face of that 'vast unconsciousness of nature' which threatens to annul our moral values.[3] In defence, we erect a material and psychological barrier against primal nature and whatever can be associated with it. The garrison is a corollary of the concept of frontier, a border imposed between civilized territory and the 'no-man's-land with huge rivers, lakes, and islands' that, Frye concedes, 'very few Canadians ha[ve] ever seen'[4] but which, presumably, continues to infect our consciousness with fear and trembling. As Canadians we should know ourselves to be irredeemable aliens in an eternal wilderness which our very humanness demands that we turn into a peaceable kingdom, a green and pleasant land.

From Canada as No-Man's land we leap to Tallman's Old Mother North America with 'her snow hair, her mountain forehead, her prairie eyes and her wolf teeth.' Tallman transforms Frye's fallen man struggling against a fallen world into a myth of existential man recognizing his oneness with a crude, violent, and vital world which annihilates the frippery of civilized European existence. Thus while for Frye we realize our true human selves in striving to impose form and meaning on the chaos of wilderness, for Tallman we wear our true faces only when we have sloughed off that European 'culture ... cultivation ... civilization' which conceal the bright blood of life.[5] These two myths – that of redeeming the natural world by transforming it into a 'city of splendid light,'[6] and that of razing this city and affirming the raw earth and stones out of which it was raised – may separate the sheep from the wolves in Canadian letters, but in doing so they distract us from the host of alternative conceptions of nature which our literature offers – alternatives which a few critics, at least, have attempted to sketch out.

In *Patterns of Isolation* – a work which swallows whole most Frygian absolutes, even if it does spit up a few bones and hairs – John Moss ventures to argue that Canadian literature presents nature as 'amoral, impassive, indifferent' – that is, neither as kindly Mother nor as Big Bad Wolf. Indeed, Moss discovers in most Canadian writing 'a fundamental correspondence between the worlds of nature and of man'[7] and does his utmost to demystify that *ne plus ultra* of Canadian imagining, death in the snow. He argues that while such a fate is a 'fundamental possibility of the Canadian experience' it is neither as prevalent nor as metaphysical as some critics would make it out to be.[8] And D.O. Spettigue has attempted to give a certain flexibility to the 'conceptual framework' erected by Frye, Tallman, and their followers by conceding that our natural environment can be legitimately conceived not merely as threat, but also as haven, or even as a brave new world a-making.[9] Yet the problem remains – the old conceptual framework doesn't require just to have a few more pigeonholes bored into it; rather, it needs to be toppled if our literature is to begin to be freed from its Procrustean bed.

Let us begin by questioning the framework's foundation. Frye's deep terror before Canadian nature seems inextricably bound up with his notion of frontier – that which marks the boundary between the seized, settled, and civilized, and the barbarous wastes beyond. And it is here, as we have previously seen, that the Maritimes is found wanting. For while Americans could choose either to embrace the wilderness beyond the Appalachians, or else ignore it by digging in the length of the Atlantic seaboard, Canadians, thanks to the scattered layout of the Maritime provinces, possessed no shield against the terrible unknown, but had resistlessly to sail into the jaws of the St Lawrence. Once again, geography is destiny, and destiny here is some primal *angst* at the thought of the vast outdoors, an *angst* inspired by our irreparable lack of what our neighbours to the south so obviously possess. Frye's famous Atlantic Seaboard Theory begins to seem a geographical version of Freudian Penis Envy.

A different, but related charge can be brought against Tallman, whose wolf in the snow would seem to derive from William Carlos Williams's *In the American Grain*.[10] It is true that some parts of the North American landscape admirably fit Tallman's conception of the continent, namely the north and the prairies. Other parts, however, do not – the lushly fertile west coast and the more spartan, but historically richer, east. Moreover, the Canadian part of North America has had a significantly different economic, cultural, and political reaction to that 'old world' whose civilization Tallman rejects, from that of the United States. If, as D.H. Lawrence argued, the genesis of 'the American Imagination' lay in its immigrants' desire to slam the door on post-Renaissance Europe and to articulate a radically new experience on a virgin continent, then something very like the opposite holds true for 'the Canadian Imagination,' dominated as it has so long been by protracted experience as a colony. In fact, one of the most pernicious effects of defining Canada as or in relation to 'the land' is the resulting mystification of those political and economic forces which structure our identity or lack of it.

Thus if we can shake off our habit of cloning or forever deferring to American conceptual models, we will be better able to understand the authentic possibilities of our literature's response to nature – that 'given' world we have marred but not made. Such an understanding would have to be pluralist and decentred, acknowledging that landscape, climatic conditions, flora and fauna, the very elements themselves may differ significantly, not only from one part of Canada to another, but within any one region as well. Consideration would also have to be given to our economic relation to our environment – not just to the guilt Frye discerns in our trans- or deformations of landscape in deference to the imperatives of industrialism, but also to the ways in which any region's prime economic activities inform its inhabitants' relation to and sense of place. In Maritime literature, for example, the complex emotional and economic ties of people to the land they farm or dig coal from, and the seas they fish, is a dominant feature: for the narrators of Alistair MacLeod's 'The Boat' or 'In the Fall,' for Frank Parker Day's David Jung or MacLennan's Archie MacNeil, and for the protagonists of David Adams Richards's or Alden Nowlan's fiction, economic pressures and realities, not terror or delight in wilderness, determine their relation to the natural world under their feet. What the critic and reader of Canadian literature need to become familiar with, then, is not any consecrated 'conceptual framework' but rather what Rudy Wiebe has called 'the way a man feels with and lives with that living earth with which he is always laboring to live. Farmer or Writer ...'[11]

The remainder of this chapter will first sketch out the general notion of 'nature' indigenous to Maritime fiction, and will then attempt to show how four representative writers, in responding to various features of their natural world – sea, barren sand-reach, meadow, snowy barren – have powerfully articulated in their fictions 'phases of human feeling' more complex and more varied than established paradigms allow.

\*\*\*

Here, starker than anywhere else, are the reminders of how inexorably one's address shifts from the letter to the tombstone; of what useless armour is the scarecrow, Thought, against the crows of Time ... Here too is where so much that seems like the stifled shriek of loneliness to an outsider is, to the native eye, through whatever storm or toil, merely the inmost and uttermost composure of things abiding by their own laws.

Ernest Buckler[12]


The origins of Maritime culture, I have argued, are distinctly eighteenth-century; certainly the 'obvious and immediate' sense of nature in this region is not 'the late Romantic one, increasingly affected by Darwinism, of nature red in tooth and claw' and inspired by a 'terrifying cold, empty and vast' environment[13] but rather a neoclassical one, in which such concepts as the 'book' of nature and an applied pastoral ideal feature prominently. The eighteenth-century heritage of the Maritimes is a reminder of the region's comparatively long history, a fact which makes it more sensible to speak of the region's topography than its geography: 'The very face of the landscape has been altered by the hand of man. The clearings, and embankments, and planting of fruit-trees have changed the whole aspect ... Another outcome of the long human usage of this land is a plentiful growth of place-names, which are unchanged by time. Such names both fix and make history.'[14]

Thus nature, as represented in Maritime literature, might emerge as much less monolithic, much more complex or subtle than expected. The sea that drowns so many of Uriah Jung's sons in *Rockbound*, that batters the father's corpse in MacLeod's 'The Boat,' is also a route out 'to all the world, a promise of adventure, a source of wonder and mystery, a perpetual prospect of liberation'[15] for the Dan Ainslies, Anse Gordons, and Toby Richmonds of Maritime fiction. The storm winds which set the aerials shrieking on the wireless station at Marina accompany and in some sense permit the liberating sexual passion of Isabel Jardine and Matthew Carney in Raddall's *The Nymph and the Lamp*. And if, in Charles G.D. Roberts's fiction, nature flaunts red tooth and claw, it is the animals and rarely the humans who get the worst of it; indeed, Roberts's New Brunswick backwoodsmen and women derive dignity and even moral stature from their mastery of elemental forces in the wilds.

'Have you ever studied the philosophy of nature?' Joseph Howe asks the readers of his *Western and Eastern Rambles* – 'Have you ever learned to gather wisdom from the expanded leaves of creation ... The artist who can copy a print, but cannot sketch a landscape, is not more deficient than is he who cannot learn a lesson out of a book – who heeds not the wisdom which is taught by the hills, and which a wise man may gather in the vallies. Every flower you see hath its instruction ...' (WER 54)

The Nova Scotia through which Howe rambled was one in which 'deep solitudes, the unbroken wilds of nature' were fast being invaded by 'the stroke of an axe, the bark of a dog, the bell of a cow, or some equally significant hint of neighbouring cultivation' (WER 153). And all to the good, Howe implies. The forest primeval inspired him with deep boredom rather than terror – Howe's real satisfaction comes when the road he travels takes him by softly luxuriant rural scenery, allows him a view of properly cultivated land, or discloses a suitably picturesque waterfall. Howe does not, however, subject the Nova Scotian landscape to the restrictive anglicization it is made to undergo in Oliver Goldsmith's *The Rising Village*, in which a hasty outline of pioneer hardships in gloomy wastes quickly gives way to hilltop views of 'verdant meads,' bumper crops of grain, 'smiling orchards,' and zephyr-kissed lakes.[16] Both in his narrative poem *Acadia* and in his travel sketches, Howe extols moose and mayflower in order to give his rural scene a distinctively New World stamp. And, though the *Rambles* ultimately applauds the triumph of settlement, and thus prosperity, over wilderness and privation, Howe's greatest pleasure in the course of his narrative is to take a leisurely paddle round Lake Lochaber, where 'the scene is essentially the same as it was a hundred, or perhaps a thousand years ago; except that the wild deer bounds not across the path, and the birds fly somewhat nearer Heaven' (WER 190). This is an interlude that could have come out the pages of a book written a good century after Howe's – Ernest Buckler's *The Cruelest Month*.

In *The Clockmaker* and *The Stepsure Letters* nature is a matter of profit or loss. Sam Slick and Mephibosheth Stepsure have little time to admire the beauties of Colchester or Pictou County – they are too busy suggesting improvements in agricultural methods or envisioning the benefits a railway line between Halifax and Windsor might bring. Nature is not so much a book as something to be used according to the book, in this case 'Agricola's' letters to farmers, or perhaps some forerunner of *The Philosophy of Railroads*.[17] The instrumentalism of this approach may well be preferable to the soft-centred mysticism of Susanna Moodie before the Glories of Creation. Haliburton and McCulloch are intent on turning grudging earth into profitable soil which will secure and enlarge the primary economic base of their province. Not surprisingly, *The Stepsure Letters* abounds in examples of this severely practical attitude towards nature: 'Summer had now fled, and with it, all that variety of prospects which charms and cheers ... But none of the harbingers of winter took me by surprise. I have always considered these as the preparations of nature for a returning crop, and, as the exertions of nature are made for the benefit of man, it appeared to me foolish, that, in the midst of so much activity, he alone should be idle' (SL 76–7). Accordingly, Stepsure occupies the short winter days with fashioning wooden tools that can profitably be sold, come spring, at Mr Ledger's store.

In *The Old Judge*, Haliburton does justice to the beauties of the Nova Scotian landscape – silver thaws and haunted woods among them – and, like Howe, expresses a sense of nature closer to the eighteenth-century taste for calm, order, and permanence than the Romantic delight in turbulence. The visible objects of nature, Haliburton tells us, 'are our early, our constant, and our sole surviving friends, the same to-day and tomorrow as they were of old. They are typical of Him who knoweth no change' (TOJ 63).

The great exception to these reasoned, equable views of nature is to be found in Huyghue's *Argimou* (1847), a romance at least as good, if not so grotesquely funny as Richardson's *Wacousta* – and a quarter the length. *Argimou* is half adventure story (Micmac chief and English officer team up to free their respective betrotheds from a barbarous band of Milicete Indians) and half elegy for the vanishing dignity and decaying way of life of the Micmacs. Not only does Huyghue lay on spectacular scenery – raging rivers, ragged cliffs, mammoth tides – firmly tied to New Brunswick, and not some composite Gothic locale, but he also laments the mutilation of that beneficent wilderness that had always been the Micmacs' source of life and virtue. Not until Roberts begins to set his fictions in the Tantramar marshes or the Miramichi will the kind of wilderness idyll Huyghue first paints in *Argimou* re-emerge in Maritime writing.

Island writers create a different sort of idyll. Avonlea in *Anne of Green Gables* is a conflation of bucolic and quasi-Arthurian bliss, as such chapters as 'An Unfortunate Lily Maid' reveal. All in all, the charms and beauties of nature play a much more important role in helping Anne to 'ope[n] the gates of her soul'[18] than does any trysting with Avonlea's Arthur, Gilbert White. And in *The Master's Wife*, as well, the Island is 'filled with the material of romance, with which a boy could fabricate a richer world of his own' (TMW 108). The worlds of fantasy and superstition, of 'bridges ... quiver[ing] in sign of an approaching funeral,' or of *bocans* which 'might leap upon a boy in the dark at any moment'

(TMW 108) are, however, complemented by 'the living world of growth' (TMW 109) – animals, indulgently tended gardens and, in winter, phalanxes of house plants laboriously nurtured. One of the most poignant passages of *The Master's Wife* describes the mother's springtime excursions into the woods to look for mayflowers – an excursion whose hedonism she disguises under the pretext of looking for the fine white sand with which any self-respecting housewife would scour her kitchen floors.

The mentality behind such furtiveness Macphail reveals in his description of man's necessary subordination to, and possible profit from, nature. The desirable condition of 'inner discipline' arises, he argues,

from a systematic obedience to the laws imposed by nature, against which it was useless to contend by force. But the powers of nature could be subdued and directed to human needs by a continuous effort of the mind and will. The boy learned ... how and within what limits he could bring into service the hardness of metal, the weight of stone, the lightness of wood, the buoyancy of water ... and the hidden riches of the soil. By obedience to those inevitable laws he acquired a morality; by developing the feeling of submission and dependence ... he acquired the rudiments of religion.
(TMW 33)

The 'inner discipline' and 'inevitable laws' to which Macphail makes reference can be related, however obliquely, to that notion of 'woodcraft' which Charles G.D. Roberts exalts in his backwoods fiction – that ability to 'read' the wilderness, registering the signs it flashes and interpreting its silence: that skill which permits man not only to survive in the wilderness but more importantly, to master nature and assert his title to lordship over the earth.

I will end this outline of nature as portrayed in Maritime fiction with the observation that in tragic works, nature usually features as hapless instrument or mute witness, rather than as angel of devastation.[19] The tree which fells Joseph Canaan in *The Mountain and the Valley* is a natural correlation for those metaphysical enemies which so obsess Buckler – Time and Fate. The snow at the novel's end does not kill, only decently buries the novel's self-defeating hero, and it is not the damp ground on which, for Toby's benefit, David 'has' Effie, but rather leukemia that kills the girl. Finally, if we consider such a story as Alistair MacLeod's 'The Boat,' we find that it is not the sea which 'gets' man, but rather, the reverse. To hold his son to his promise of quitting the sea and the labour of fishing – a labour for which the father, though not his son, is outrageously unfitted – the father commits suicide: never having learned to swim, he lets himself fall off the boat his son pilots in a choppy winter sea. And though the son is not destroyed by his father's action, he is psychologically riven, for fidelity to his father's command that he quit the sea and acquire an education entails betrayal of his mother, for whom the sea is the one thing of constancy in her world, the only thing on which she can look with unmixed love.

In Maritime fiction, the natural world with its earthbound pattern of seasonal change and renewal, its ambivalent elemental forces of wind and water, its small-scale and accessible landscapes, appears to exist in a complementary relation to the human world. Nature does not possess the implacable hostility that seems to rain or hail from the skies of Sinclair Ross's fictions, for example; neither is it stonily indifferent to those whose lives are, in Buckler's words, 'hewn to the shifting seasons' so that 'scarce anything around [them] but touches, in some way closer than the mere retinal, on [their] work and wonderment.'[20] Maritime writers, inhabiting a region in which heavy industry has made comparatively minor inroads,[21] and in which a considerable number of people still make their living off land or sea, have acquired what Charles G.D. Roberts called a 'habit of openness to nature,' a habit created by the special qualities of the Maritime 'landscape, earth, and sea and sky' (SPCP 261). To the forms assumed by this natural 'openness' in the work of four major Maritime writers, I will now turn.

\*\*\*

Thomas D'Arcy McGee ... in advocating Confederation, told his fellow Canadians that in uniting with the Maritimes they were about to recover one of their lost senses – the sense that comprehends the sea.

D.C. Harvey[22]

up on the beach, half-buried in the sand, lies the wreck of a schooner that drove ashore and drowned three men last winter. Empty, disembowelled, its spine broken, it still witnesses to the strength of man's hand and brain which formed it, but more terribly to the Titanic hand and brainless fury which destroyed it.

Archibald MacMechan[23]

One grievance which might be held against Maritime fiction is that it has not restored to us 'the sense that comprehends the sea'; our fiction boasts no equivalent to Moby Dick;[24] no *Typhoon* or *Nigger of the 'Narcissus'*; not even, except perhaps in Raddall's less inspired efforts such as *Pride's Fancy*, equivalents to Marryat's tales of the sea. The reason lies not in any lack of material – if the Maritimes' coastal fishing fleets did not provide the stuff of Odyssean adventure, then the schooners that regularly shipped from Maritime ports to the West Indies did.[25] Historical circumstance (the gradual eclipse of the sailing ship and with it, the Maritimes' privileged position and reputation in international trade) and economic factors (the shift of capital, and interest, from docks and shipyards to the factories of central Canada) have obviously played their parts. Yet even if we comb Maritime fiction for traces of that spirit which long acquaintance with the 'Titanic hand and brainless fury' of the sea must have bred, we come up with almost nothing. Where Joseph Conrad's best writing discovers an appalling metaphysics in the annihilating power of the sea, where his vision teeter-totters between nihilism and a barely redemptive stoicism, Maritime writers embrace a practical realism that all but shuns metaphysical inquiry.[26]

This 'practical realism' is best expressed in a passage from Raddall's novel *The Nymph and the Lamp*:

The people who most loudly profess a love of the sea are seldom the ones who live at grips with it. Even romantic young men who go to sea ... in a few years ... have discovered that all the romance lies ashore, and that every voyage is a travail to be endured between one port and the next. The people of the North Atlantic coasts and islands, where the winds are strong and the waters cold, have no illusions about the sea. It is their enemy. Their lives are fixed in its grasp, they must battle for an existence, each day's survival is a little victory; but like all wars their eternal struggle is in great part a monotony, an eternal waiting for tides to rise, for storms to subside.[27]

The best Maritime fiction, with few exceptions, makes only incidental or secondary reference to the sea and those who live by it. Of the Bluenoses who storm the narrative line in Haliburton's *Old Judge* only one, the egregious Barkins of 'How Many Fins Has a Cod?', is a fisherman, eager to instruct Lawyer Sandford on 'how to spear shad, and how to strike the fattest salmon that ever was ... and ... how to smoke herrings without dryin' them hard' (TOJ 26). Not until Frank Parker Day's *Rockbound* will as lively and detailed a sense of fishermen's work surface in Maritime fiction. Andrew Macphail gives, as we have seen, a peripheral yet suggestive role to the sea captain uncle in *The Master's Wife*; he even begins his chapter 'The Spar Maker' by comparing the making of spars in the craft of shipbuilding to 'making a sonnet in the craft of letters' (TMW 5), but he devotes the rest of the chapter to the landlocked history of the sparmaker's descendants. Of Alistair Mac-Leod's collection of short fiction, *The Lost Salt Gift of Blood*, only 'The Boat' and the title story have to do with the sea – the rest of the collection is concerned with the histories of miners' or farmers' families.

Antonine Maillet's Pélagie resists, though with difficulty, the chance of boarding Broussard Beausoleil's ship, preferring to take her straggling exiles back by land to the Acadie from which they were forced by New England vessels. *The Mountain and the Valley* makes only the most tenuous and symbolic connection with the sea through the mysterious sailor whom Ellen harbours without her husband's knowledge, and through the rather lumpish Toby, who is killed off on the high seas in wartime. And of Thomas Raddall's novels which have to do with the sea only *Tidefall*, which traces the irresistible rise and predictable fall of the ape-like latter-day privateer, Sax Nolan, makes significant use of salt water – to drown Nolan so that his wronged wife and her lover can continue the tryst they have begun on an idyllic offshore island.

The one Maritime text which significantly comprehends – and demystifies – a 'sense of the sea' is *Rockbound*. Despite its haphazard structure and narrative insouciance, it manages to embed in a solid fictive world the most fairy-tale of plots – a dispossessed orphan, having gone to seek his fortune and reclaim his possessions from his wicked Uncle-King, ends by winning fair maid and founding his own kingdom. Through a skilful use of dialect and descriptive prose, Day conveys to us the very taste and grain of a fisherman's life. The natural world and our relation to it are given dramatic definition in *Rockbound*: if, as Allan Bevan observes in his introduction to the novel, Day affirms 'the basic goodness of the natural man who lives in tune with his environment,'[28] then that environment is a stark one of brutal sea and a land which inflicted 'cold' and 'hardship' to defeat its first settlers (R 70).

The novel opens with its hero, David Jung, rowing the dory he has salvaged from the sea and which, along with his ragged shirt and trousers, forms his only other material possession. On the 'troubled' yet 'rich kingdom' of Rockbound (R 6, 69) he is met by his suspicious Uncle Uriah, who is appropriately clad in oilskins 'spotted with blood and glistening with sequins of herring scales' (R 4). From this old man of the sea, David is grudgingly given the chance to reclaim his dead mother's house and to serve a backbreaking term of apprenticeship in order to establish his claim to a tenth part of the island. The key to David's fortunes is the sea itself, of which he has intimate knowledge and on which alone he can become 'a free man and his own master' (R 29).

David performs the impossible task he is set, gradually acquires the equipment and materials which secure his independence, shotgun-weds his uncle's daughter and, after various misadventures, marries the woman he truly loves. A relatively wealthy and much-respected man, he ultimately escapes the enmity and slavish toil to which he was bound on his uncle's island by becoming keeper of the light on Barren Island. But the best parts of the novel depict not David's adventures in life and love but rather the labour he performs – the comparatively joyful task of fishing from his own boat on the open waters, the hauling up of endless herring nets with the other sharesmen and, worst of all, twelve hours straight of gutting and salting down herring in Uriah's loft. In the midst of 'a strange mixture of odours from gurry tubs, ancient fish heads, lobster shells, wetted salt, and gore-drenched floor' (R 52) the 'oilskin-clad, blood-bespattered figures' flash their knives 'in and out ... the hateful piles of fish that seemed never to diminish' (R 62). They sustain themselves with ballads, hymns, theological disputations, and amorous banter with the girl who sleeps in the sharesmen's loft and whom Uriah has hired to work his garden plots. This second chapter of the novel is a tour de force of realism, almost surreal in its clarity of focus and certainty of detail. Nothing else in the novel, except per-haps the tempest and shipwreck of Chapter 9, quite matches it. One of its most important effects is to eradicate romantic notions of the fisher-man's life by setting out the corollaries of that 'calling' – the 'hell of driving work' in the midst of 'dirt and confusion and stench' after the boat comes in (R 65, 63).

In the fictive world *Rockbound* creates it is not the shore which stands as antithesis to the 'wearisome argument of the sea' (R 46), but the lighthouse, on whose steady, faithful guidance the fisherman's very life depends. For, as Day makes clear, the sea is the devil's work and abode: 'you had to watch him, for he sprang at you treacherously out of a fog bank, or in a dead calm sent a sudden roller against you to swamp your boat, low down with fish' (R 72). On a rare holiday, David lies on a cliff top, looking down at the sea snorting and spraying over the rocks below, and speculates on how one day the island of Rock-bound will be cleft in two by the titanic force of the waves. His thoughts lead him to question the Christianity by which his uncle so hypocritically lives and prospers, and to recognize the senseless co-existence of destructive and creative forces in nature[29] – a fact which is brought home hard to him when his first wife dies in childbirth. Later, when a hurricane destroys the schooner on which he has been fishing and he battles for survival against the engulfing sea, David perceives 'reality stripped bare [to] the heart of things' (R 203). The wisdom he learns from the sea teaches him that as far as the ferocity of elemental forces is concerned, one can only acknowledge, endure, or simply submit to it. But against human hatred and greed, against the men who were 'as cold and cruel as the winter sea that crashed the ice against the cliffs and roared into the cannon rock to send up mocking cries' (R 170), one is morally bound to struggle. Accordingly, David does what he can to quell the absurd rivalries between Jungs and Krauses on the island, and finally makes the crucial decision to quit Rockbound with its perpetual feuds and 'endless labour but no ... goal that seemed worthy of attainment' (R 170).[30]

The feud which has made Rockbound 'an island of hatred' (R 136) has its origins in Uriah Jung's overwhelming greed – his family holds eight-tenths of the island, his Kraus cousins hold the remainder, and Uriah covets all. Though nature has given the island fitting means of fertility – 'from land loaded with sea dung and fish entrails, hay, potatoes, strawberries, and vegetables of all kinds grew in profusion' (R 69) – human viciousness and exploitation have poisoned the land. Poverty and greed, not wind and water, are man's worst enemies, Day seems to argue: the manic greed which has led Uriah's wife to lose eight of her fourteen children at birth because she has been made to toil on the fields or in the fish house to the last possible moment, or which has forced Mary Dauphiny (one of Maritime fiction's near-inexhaustible tribe of schoolteacher heroines)[31] into a repellent marriage with Uriah's unprepossessing son Joseph. Perhaps this is why Day permits the rhythmic sea to strike up a 'grand wedding march' (R 291) when David at last weds Mary on the little island he has transformed from a 'slatty rock protruding from the sea' (R 105) into a garden reminiscent of the flower-jewelled paradises of medieval painters (R 292). If not to deny nature's potential for destructive cruelty, then at least to oppose it, Day eclipses sea by land in the final chapter of his novel. He makes David keeper of the light and lord of his own land – earth being that part of nature in the angels' keeping.

***

If *Rockbound* can be described as a novel of the sea in which that demonic element is ultimately displaced by land, then Thomas Raddall's *The Nymph and the Lamp* is a novel in which 'wilderness' holds its own against the suasions of modern city and Edenic countryside alike. Day's

and Raddall's fictions are curiously similar in certain ways; whereas the
former exploits fairy-tale motifs, the latter sets up mythic structures
with Matthew Carney and Isabel Jardine taking on the roles of Adam
and Eve, Wounded King and Fertility Goddess, *Heimskringla* Warrior
and Underwater Nymph. The settings of each work are unusually isolated islands on which frustrated love affairs make life unendurable for
the protagonists; the heroes of each book, Matthew and David, share
epic stature, each having been orphaned as a child and having made
his way in the exacting world of ships and the sea. Finally, both novels
have the happy endings requisite for a certain kind of romance, with
each hero coming to possess the woman whom adversity and misunderstanding originally had denied them.

At first glance the island of Marina created by Raddall in *The Nymph
and the Lamp* seems neatly to fit the hostile wilderness paradigm. Modelled after Sable Island, Marina is referred to as 'the graveyard of the
Atlantic' (NL 316). Its sand dunes, which by moonlight have 'the look
of dead mountains on the moon' (NL 141), alternately reveal and conceal
not only the hulks of wrecked schooners, but the skeletons of mari-
ners as well. The island is surrounded by a sea which literally 'assaults'
it during fierce gales. That same sea which, when Isabel regarded it
from a Halifax park bench, had seemed prettily placid, comes to 'sicken
and humiliate' her once she arrives at this 'end of the world' (NL 108).

Isabel's first impression of Marina is one of 'small dwellings with-
drawn from one another amongst the miles of dunes, and in each a
little group of humans leading secret lives as if afraid of this immensity of
sea and sky' (NL 98). A 'beleagured garrison' bored to the edge of
insanity (NL 153), the islanders resort to absurd atrocities – slaughtering
the ill-tasting migratory ducks, shooting ponies, or keeping skull collections in their back sheds, all 'for something to do.' Altogether, Marina
seems a natural prison, even a 'sepulchre' (NL 192), and Isabel's first
response to this environment is to immure herself in the 'little citadel' of
her bedroom at the wireless station (NL 115), shutting herself off sexuality and psychologically from the husband who comes to seem 'the spirit
incarnate of the wilderness' (NL 100) and as much a part of the place as
'the wild ponies on the dunes' (NL 11). Since even Matthew concedes
that 'the devil made Marina' (NL 31), Isabel's defensive tactics are
understandable enough, and the sacrifices she makes in leaving the
mainland for Marina are emphasized by the novel's loving descriptions both of the Halifax Public Gardens in which Carney first proposes
to Isabel, and of the Annapolis Valley in all the beauty of spring,
summer, and autumn. It is to the Valley in which she was born that

Isabel comes to heal the physical and psychic scars left by her brief sojourn on Marina, finding in 'the massive calm of the land itself' (NL 248) peace after the self-betrayal, rejection, and violence she has experienced on her desert island.

Although the New Canadian Library blurb proclaims *The Nymph and the Lamp* to be a love story 'as powerful as the surging sea that is so much a part of it,' it is not the tired triangle formed on Marina between Matthew, Isabel, and the darkly handsome second officer Skane which empowers this novel. In terms of plot, *Nymph* is a retreading of *Jane Eyre* with the plain (but 'nicely made') schoolteacher-turned-typist heroine thrown in the path of a bearded, bronzed, Byronic giant of a man whom she forsakes in fear of some frightful 'mystery' and 'secret' (NL 308) that poison their life together. Isabel nearly submits to the suasions of Skane (a sexed and cynical St John Rivers) but ultimately returns to succour and sustain the near-blind, weakened hero. What *is* striking about Isabel's encounters with Matthew Carney and the wilderness of Marina is the way in which Raddall uses these to realign our perception of and relation to our natural and human worlds.

Nature in *Nymph* is Janus-faced. Not only is the lush fertility of the Valley contrasted with the utter barrenness of Marina, but Marina itself wears two distinct profiles – that of witless desolation and destruction, and that of endurance, courage, solidarity – heroic qualities without which human life on this island could not continue. These contradictory profiles are imaged by two houses on Marina. One is the MacBain house, its parlour an 'astonishing' replica of 'every village parlour on the mainland from Cape Sable to Cape Breton.' Raddall lovingly details its contents – hooked rugs, black horsehair sofa, rosewood piano, brass spittoon, and obligatory local curiosities: 'a rusty flintlock pistol found somewhere among the dunes, sea shells, a pony's hoof polished and mounted on a small block of varnished wood, a walrus tooth, a lobster claw ...' (NL 130). The very replication of an 'ordinary' interior in this fiercely minimal environment is, Raddall seems to suggest, indicative of extraordinary human qualities.

The other house is 'Old Number Two,' the station house which has, over the years, been repossessed by shifting sands. Isabel and Skane explore the part of the house which is still accessible – four small bedrooms whose floral wallpaper is 'stained with damp and peeling away in rotten strips' (NL 206). Claustrophobic, Isabel turns faint and needs to be carried out: 'Under the mass of sand, in the sinister darkness of the house, she seemed to feel the cold clutch of Marina itself, the evil sea-monster with its belly full of wrecks and dead men's bones still unsatisfied' (NL 207). These two profiles of Marina –mindless destruction of human lives and structures, and the opposing stability, faith, and energy needed to go on creating lives and building houses, to 'beat the Devil' – can never be made to merge, but may be brought about to face each other. And this they do through the agency of Isabel Jardine.

On Marina, for the first time, the romantically disillusioned and professionally jaded Isabel is able to experience life and the world in their elemental simplicity. Shortly after her arrival on the island she gazes up at 'a sky afire with stars' (NL 120), a sky whose boundlessness she contrasts with the prison of her days as Matthew's wife. Yet she recalls how, in the city, the stars which so delight her on Marina would be 'dimmed by smoke and the upflung glare of the streets.' 'Here the sky had no limit but the round edge of the sea; it was enormous, and she found a joy in being alone beneath it ...' (NL 120).

The complexity of Isabel's response foreshadows the change which will be brought about in her conception of the wilderness that is Marina. By the novel's close, after her stay in the blossomy, fruity 'Happy Valley,' Isabel has learned to use Marina as a ruler to take the measure of the human and natural worlds around her. On her way back to Matthew she recoils from the 'obscene' hustle of Halifax (NL 313), in which daily existence is summed up by the small, shut-in, and litter-strewn back court onto which her window at Mrs Paradee's boarding house had faced. And previously, while sunbathing in a lush glade more evocative of D.H. Lawrence's Mediterranean than the Baptist-ruled Valley, Marina had insisted itself on her perceptions: 'She tried to imagine Mr Markham on Marina, where, whatever riches might be stored in Heaven, there was no hard money to be made or lost. She tried to picture the Reverend Palliser there with his bald white dome and his trombone voice, preaching his fiery gospel to a people who fully believed in hell and damnation but who believed no less devoutly in a ghostly Frenchman who roamed the dunes by night ...' (NL 259). More imprisoning than any desert island, as Isabel comes to see, is the existence of many Valley women, cloistered within the four walls of home and 'having no outlet for their emotions but the religious ecstasies of the Sabbath' (NL 258).

In returning to live out the rest of her life on Marina with Matthew, Isabel accomplishes two things. First, she acknowledges that if Marina is a desolate wilderness, then in its absolute integrity and miraculous endurance (made as it is 'utterly of sand, without a rock, without even a pebble in its composition' [NL 200]) it utterly eclipses both the tangible fruits and flowers of the valley, and the pell-mell illusions bred by the city – 'The scrabble for cash that could not buy security, the frantic pleasures that could not give content, the pulpit-thumpings that could not summon virtue ... the whole brave new world ... that was only the old evil with a mad new face' (NL 321–2).

The novel's last page has Isabel embracing, in Matthew Carney, the spirit of pure wilderness; what she does not do, however, is 'to abandon defence, let down the walls and let the wilderness in, even to the wolves.'[32] Rather, she inaugurates the second phase of what is very much a mission. For Isabel Jardine, as her last name and the allusions to her as Rossetti's Monna Pomona suggest, brings to Marina a fertility essential for the symbolic and spiritual greening of an island on which only turnips, cabbages, and cranberries have grown. She and Matthew will have children, the novel implies (NL 318); as importantly, Isabel will set up a school for the island children to protect them against the perilous inertia of a life 'in which nothing ever happens but a duck shoot or a pony ride' (NL 317). Isabel returns not to embrace the darkness, but to be a lamp for her near-blind husband, who must face the fact that his role as a wireless operator on Marina has become hopelessly outmoded, that the technological advances of the 'brave new world' have already infiltrated and doomed the wilderness he loves. Raddall suggests that Matthew will, nevertheless, be able to stay on as lighthousekeeper for Marina, his lonely life gardened by Isabel's love, however unpalatable the modern reader may perceive that love to be.[33] The life which Raddall envisions for the Carneys is not made vital or meaningful by any acknowledgement of desolation, bleakness, and barrenness as 'true realities,' but by the affirmation of traditional 'Old World' virtues – 'watchfulness ... faith and duty' (NL 118) – in the face of those other, destructive realities. In his novel, Raddall implies that possibilities for human joy, growth, and renewal may be brought to fruition by enlarging our conception of the natural world to comprehend the wild, even the demonic as well as the idyllic. As importantly, he insists that we recognize Marina not just as wilderness but also as those human values of fidelity and solidarity which such wilderness compells.

\*\*\*

The pre-eminence of the 'natural over the romantic' in *The Nymph and the Lamp* is evinced by the sheer excellence of Raddall's prose in those passages of the novel describing the changing seasons on Marina, the peculiar formation of the island, and the periods of brief calm and brute storm which redefine its very layout. In lamentable contrast stands the language –flaccidly clichéd or coyly peekaboo – which depicts Isabel's voluptuousness or describes her sexual encounters with Matthew and Skane. The natural world can be said to subsume the emotional in this novel, so that the very plot of *Nymph* depends on the impersonal forces and patterns of nature as one season succeeds another, as calms are shattered unpredictably by storms. In Ernest Buckler's writing, however, nature is infused and irradiated by those perceptions of phenomena which to Buckler are the finest form of feeling and which turn description into consecration.

To point out the difference between Raddall's masterful descriptive skills and Buckler's sentient revelations, one need only contrast Chapters 31 and 32 of *Nymph* with Chapter 7 of *The Mountain and the Valley*, all of which evoke the change of seasons in the Annapolis Valley. To use Charles G.D. Roberts's terms, Raddall tends to produce 'mere description of landscape' while Buckler expresses 'vital relationships between external nature and "the deep heart of man"' (SPCP 281). Of course Raddall's descriptions of the natural world comprehend or even cue emotional developments among his characters, but what is lacking, what makes Raddall less important, though in some ways a more felicitous writer than Buckler, is the existential charge, the almost shocked intensity that characterizes Buckler's descriptions of the natural world.

What is remarkable about a novel like *The Cruelest Month* is the way in which 'vital relationships' between people and the natural world are realized almost in spite of Buckler's tendentious handling of character and plot. As with the equally ambitious and infinitely more readable *The Nymph and the Lamp*, the novel's love stories collapse under their own rhetoric while setting is realized in language of great power and assurance. Yet this irritating discrepancy between the characters' otiose speech and the vernal freshness of their surroundings allows us to perceive Buckler's conception of nature much more clearly than we can do in works like *The Mountain and the Valley* or *Oxbells and Fireflies*, works in which character and setting are so intricately bonded, and the tropes which reveal the immanence of the natural world so profuse and intertwined, that attempts to analyse them might bring on the same phenomenological dementia that besets David Canaan in the final pages of *Mountain*.

*The Cruelest Month* records the reflections, nightmares, conversations, and significant perceptions of some half dozen characters, losers in life and love, who have fled various cities and flocked to 'the very domicile of peace,'[34] hero Paul Creed's country estate, Endlaw. Here they expose and lick their psychic wounds while conversing with Paul (a mystery man whose reputed charm inspires everyone but the reader with a heightened kind of 'gee, golly, isn't he *swell*' admiration). As importantly, they have their bellies filled and laundry washed by Paul's just-plain-folks housekeeper Letty, the consummate faithful retainer. Thankfully, Buckler also creates the 'steeping primacy of woods, lake and fields' that is Endlaw (CM 110), a world, however, in which people and nature are usually at cross-purposes. For Morse, the blocked writer, Kate the fretful spinster cum lilac girl, Sheila the society dame with the heart of gold, Rex the wounded Adonis, and even Bruce, the country boy turned wounded king cum Dr Kildare, nature is just an Arcadian backdrop against which they carry out intercourse – mainly verbal. With a profligate benevolence, nature rolls out the green carpet for her tenants, providing halcyon weather and, to cap all, a vision of transcendent if transient grace in the shape of a deer which passes each character's path at the novel's close. Not surprisingly, it is Bruce, who has grown up on a valley farm, and Paul, who has definitely rejected the gritty sophistication of the city for the 'pristine cleanliness' of the country (CM 147), who are able to take the revelation of the deer for what it is and enter into a relation with the natural order that is based not on ignorance, indifference, or hostility but on a kind of illumined acceptance.

The subtext of *The Cruelest Month* can be summarized as *et in Arcadia ego*[35] – the transition from an ignorantly innocent sense of nature to an experienced awareness that the natural world comprehends the 'diagrams of life and death' (CM 262). Thus the warming sun and 'rain-green freshness' of the woods are shown to have their natural complement in the destructive energies of fire, which can turn the most tranquil treetop 'wild and blasphemous like a woman with her hair on fire' (CM 182, 278). Similarly, the wind that parachutes flames over the brook towards Paul's house is matched by the rain that not only quenches the fire, but also brings about 'the grass's second blading, greener on the scorched field than it would be in any other spot' (CM 295).

Arcadian innocence as self-consciously contrived by the characters of *The Cruelest Month* seems to be encoded in the very anagram of *Walden* Paul uses to name his house. In its grounds, guests are somehow freed 'to fit together the pure, unalloyed fabrics of Time, Place and Sentience as never before' (CM 110). Here even the emotions are spring-cleaned, as the sun 'open[s] up the closets of the heart and mind to the fresh linen air' (CM 132). Endlaw is directly linked to the Edenic childhood of the one strong character, Bruce – a childhood in which trees, fields, and people are said to have lived 'in a kind of eternal and unaging present' (CM 266). Now, in Paul Creed's hands, Endlaw has become a bower of bliss: 'The ferns uncurled their tips like a long green breath. The water in the brook ceaselessly chased its own sequins of laughter. And ... the first white butterflies [were] blurting and stuttering their immaculate diagrams over the benisoned road' (CM 182–3).

Appropriately, the woods in which the overarticulate Kate and Morse come together release a 'gentle acid wash' in which the would-be lovers' 'simple animacies' are at last allowed to 'tingl[e] in them as entities' (CM 147). And, as appropriately, just as Morse gets Kate supine on the floor of a narrow canoe, bullets come whistling through the leaves, so that the frustrated lovers are forced to beat a retreat back to the safety of the house. Yet long before this, death had given subtle warning of its presence: at the moment when Rex and Sheila drive their car down the road into Endlaw, a snail 'with the perfect spiral of Archimedes' on its shell (CM 87) inches towards their wheels and is crushed. Rex and Sheila, who have been quarrelling listlessly, appear to patch things up and drive on towards the house – the only one to have noticed the snail is a bird, 'immaculate as sunshine' (CM 90), dropping from its branch to peck at the shell. According to that natural law by which one creature devours another, and death is the end of all things, the snail's fate is unexceptionable. For Buckler, it becomes emblematic of the way in which human beings blunder into relation with the natural world, and of the selectiveness of our perceptions: we gladly hear the bird sing, but neglect to observe it consuming the snail.

The extinction of a snail is, of course, too trivial an event to be registered by anyone other than the narrator who, in his omniscience, forces our attention to it while we are still caught up in the bickering of Rex and Sheila. For we will be required to connect this small death with the others – the stroke which incapacitates, humiliates, and inchingly kills Kate's father, old Dr Fennison, near the novel's beginning, and the heart attack which will strike down Paul Creed, perhaps a moment, perhaps a year after the narrative closes. There is a kind of Blakean purpose in Buckler's narrative strategy vis-à-vis the snail: we are made to see beauty and mortality in a snail's shell as well as in a human brain or heart. In the process we come to an awareness of death as a natural, and not as a spiritual phenomenon, as part of the same law and cycle to which we are subject. Just as the snail's death means the bird's continued life, so Dr Fennison's demise and Paul's imminent death are balanced by the forthcoming birth of Rex's and Sheila's baby, and the projected birth of Kate's and Morse's. And finally, as the novel's ending shows, it is not any external force of nature –fire, flood, or storm – that most menaces us, but the nature of our own bodies, 'that could strike you for no reason whatsoever, like an animal you'd trusted to be entirely tamed ... suddenly baring its wild streak' (CM 175).

Buckler shows us Paul's ultimate understanding of his place in nature through his confrontation of one of nature's most destructive forces – the fire that threatens to destroy both woods and house at Endlaw. Paul must return from the city hospital which has given him the facts of his fate in x-rays and graphs, in order to learn the reality of death – what it will be and feel *like* – always, for Buckler, the epistemological heart of the matter. Decidedly anti-Byzantine, Paul recoils from any refuge 'out of nature' and rushes instead back to Endlaw. But there, of course, 'the stintless sunlight' (CM 198) only shows Death's face clearer than could any city rain – though at Endlaw an hour is said to go as far as a month anywhere else, the clock still ticks away at whatever is begotten, born, and dies. This realization panics Paul even further from the knowledge he is seeking; it is only when faced with the immediate threat of the forest fire that he quits fumbling with schemes to outwit death and is rekindled into life. Fighting the flames with Letty, Paul experiences 'a glorious intoxication' and 'rampant freedom' (CM 289) which, in making him know what it is like to be fully alive, give him also, by inversion, his only knowledge of what the state of death will be like – absolutely other than this full freedom of act, perception, and response.

For it is the fact that death annihilates sentience as well as consciousness that has so enraged Paul: immediately before the fire he had had the dubious inspiration of donating his eyes and indeed his entire body to organ banks if in so doing he might prolong the life of his senses. By the time he and Letty have put out the fire and lain down to sleep, Paul has come to know all he needs. Waking in the middle of the night in a house mercifully free of guests, he couples with Letty, whose gift lies not in thinking or talking, but in simple being: 'And in the moment when his flesh was exquisitely pitted of its stone, he had a glimpse of death's losing face dissolving far behind ...' (CM 296).

Thus for all the viciousness of the fire which turns the road out of Endlaw into 'a valley of hell [a]blaze at every ... exploding ... angle ... burning even in its own hissing, frying, crackling roar' (CM 280), it never assumes any concerted malevolence. It is started by human carelessness – Rex's throwing a lighted cigarette out the car window in his excitement at hearing Sheila's news of her pregnancy. The violence of this forest fire is, like the death of the snail, unexceptionable within the natural order – interpretable, even. For the flames are portrayed as speaking a common language, as spreading a 'message' from 'dryness to dryness' and 'speak[ing] with fire's *voice*' (CM 268) to whatever can hear and spread its word. It threatens the lives of Kate and Morse, Paul and Letty; it threatens to devastate Endlaw itself; but in the end it acts to 'temper' Kate, strengthening her in her resolve to marry Morse. It purges Morse of his cynicism, revivifies Paul, and transforms Letty in his eyes from a comical illiterate in bloomers to, if not Shakespeare's Rosalind, then his Phebe, desirable with all the wholeness, soundness, cleanness of the country-born and bred.

Finally, Buckler can even be chided for having tipped the scales in his portrayal of this intrinsic balance and rhythm of nature. Where 'the hodgepodge of reality [takes] no sides at all between green and grime, butterflies and phlegm, spring and death' (CM 183), nature appears to, if only this once. The 'gentleness' of rain, 'so much stronger than the fire's spite, conquer[s] the fire in the woods' (CM 292); just so Paul's loving embrace of Letty banishes the face, if not the fact of death.

Perhaps the true thorn in the flesh of our relation to the natural world is not nature's terrifying otherness to what Frye would say we cherish as most human in ourselves – our desire to transform our environment according to a divinely inspired vision of perfection – but the mere fact that where nature *is* we merely perceive; the fact that sentience, in which Buckler locates our true bliss, is something which can be directly experienced by individuals, but communicated only by analogy, which inevitably reduces the fire of sensation to ash. Yet though there may have been no need for words in Eden, simile and metaphor can place us back in at least a temporal garden. Through figurative language, Buckler seems to say, we can touch 'the way it was' in our lost childhood when we were at one with the world around and inside us. It is significant that the novel closes not with the vision of grace embodied in the fleeing deer, nor with the hell of fire, but with a consummate union of opposites – the intellectual Paul putting out the 'long stretching plumbing eye of longing' in 'the warm lake of [Letty's] simple flesh stretched out beside him' (CM 296).

For Paul it is immanence, not innocence, which nature now possesses: as long as he can enter into relation with the light and air and trees at Endlaw, as long as he can 'love' them, 'his eyes touch[ing] them like hands,' they will 'let down ... a rain of cleanness and eternity upon him' (CM 274). Like a milder, chaster Rupert Birkin, Paul finds in the natural world the possibility of vital relationships with things outside and beyond himself; in articulating that possibility through the unifying language of sentience Buckler allows us entrance into a world in which man, woman, and nature are finally one.

\*\*\*

Man, looking upon external nature, projects himself into her workings. His own wrath he apprehends in the violence of the storm; his own joy in the light waves running in the sun; his own gloom in the heaviness of the rain and wind. In all nature he finds but phenomena of himself.
(SPCP 279)

This chapter has attempted to show that the natural phenomena with which Maritime writers engage are projections of more than terror or submission before an engulfing, intractably inhuman environment. Yet surely there is a powerful and damning exception to this rule – the wilderness fiction of Charles G.D. Roberts, in which at least one Maritime writer and critic finds 'the inexorable process of the cycles of the forest, the uncaring vastness of nature which is intrinsic to so much Canadian writing.'[36] Even W.J. Keith, although he acknowledges that Robert's poetry makes much of the 'divine control' of nature, argues that this view is irreconcilable with that of 'Nature's never ceasing war of opposites' set forth in Robert's animal fiction.[37] In the remainder of this chapter I hope to show that Robert's presentation of nature is neither as single-mindedly 'Canadian' as Kent Thompson assumes, nor as savagely contradictory as Keith suggests; in other words, that Robert's wilderness is recognizably Maritime in conception.

In his introduction to Poems of Wildlife, Roberts makes some illuminating disclosures about attitudes towards the 'primitive' in his own society. Describing New World nature poetry as 'that characteristic modern verse which is kindled where the outposts of an elaborate and highly self-conscious civilization come in contact with crude humanity and primitive nature' (SPCP 265), Roberts sets up an antithesis between what we might call the backwoods and the drawing room. To the backwoods belongs a rejuvenating and rough-romantic concept of nature through which the essentials of existence are laid bare. To the drawing room belongs a 'restraining' or at worst 'decadent' ideal of artifice (Roberts's introduction to Poems of Wildlife and Wilde's 'The Decay of Lying' are almost exactly contemporaneous), in which the behaviour of a highly civilized society revolves around life's mere accessories. What is most interesting about Roberts's essay is that in it he plants his feet firmly in the drawing room. For while he concedes that our delight in wildlife springs from the escape it affords us from 'the artificial to the natural' (SPCP 265), he insists that the poet must continually reveal his consciousness of the difference between 'wild existence and untrammelled action' and the thoroughly civilized state of himself and his readers. Only when this self-consciousness is manifest, Roberts continues, can 'the most remote phases of human existence, the most unfamiliar aspects of the natural world [be] drawn easily within the range of our sympathies' (SPCP 265). With considerable astuteness, Roberts points out that though wildlife writings deal with the 'reality of the universal and original impulses,' they are 'apt to be regarded with distaste' if not altogether repudiated by the 'struggling civilizations' which produce them. The latter, he observes, are only too anxious to affirm their links with the thoroughly artificial and fashionable forms of long-established civilizations. 'It is to the voice from the drawing room ... that the wilderness hearkens, so the better to keep itself reminded of the ideal toward which it works' (SPCP 266).

That wilderness which hearkens to the drawing room is not only human – the backwoods settlements – but also natural, in which one species devours another in a kind of vicious spiral. For though Roberts's fiction gives abundant evidence of nature as scarlet woman rather than universal mother; though time and time again one species' young becomes the pabulum of another's; though nature's best and brightest, from butterfly to salmon, are destined to the same bloody fate as her lumpen proletariat, Roberts maintains a social and moral hierarchy in his wilderness. Just as lordly eagle and kingly moose are presented as nature's aristocrats and set over the middling beavers and porcupines, so the dutiful performance of familial responsibilities by porcupines and the unremitting industry of beavers are deemed superior to the gratuitous depredations of mole-shrew, or weasel.[38]

That some members of the animal kingdom seem to have conducted their own 'upward march of being,'[39] that there is some leaven of goodness in Roberts's creatural wilderness is, of course, perfectly congruent with his overall embrace of Darwinism in both its strictly biological and perniciously social forms. To get an adequate idea of the firmness of this embrace and the way in which it complicates his wilderness writing, we must turn to one of Roberts's lesser-known or at least lesser-celebrated works, *In the Morning of Time* – a work which alternately convulses and repulses the reader. While from a literary standpoint it is impossible to treat *Morning* as much more than a sensational yarn padded with descriptions of 'strange scenery and monstrous fauna,'[40] acquaintance with this novel is essential for any critic of Roberts's oeuvre wishing to uncover the implications of that 'intense subjectivity' which Roberts believed to characterize our perceptions of nature (SPCP 279).

*In the Morning of Time* is a form of 'backworld' *Odyssey* in which a chosen tribe – the People of the Hills, who later become Children of the Shining One – seeks out some safe spot in which to increase and multiply and further civilize itself. Through ingenuity and necessity the novel's three protagonists – the tribal chief and Master of *real-politik*, Bawr; the more contemplative and unwordly hero Grôm; and A-ya, a pre-Raphaelite prehistoric damozel with hairy legs as well as brow – discover a number of indispensable elements for the ascent of man. (Fire, strategic warfare, cookery and navigation, slavery and romantic love, maternal passion and altruism are among the list of acquired skills – racism and patriarchy, on the other hand, are presented as aboriginal traits.) It will be interesting to look more closely at the mindset of this novel if only to show that though Roberts's fiction may indeed use 'the materials of the Canadian wilderness for the purpose of expressing a coherent view of the world man inhabits,'[41] this view reflects the prejudices of the turn-of-the-century, imperialist mind.

Thus, much of *Morning* is concerned with the Hill People's eventual victory over, and near extermination of the 'foul and shaggy hordes' of the 'Bow-legs' tribe. These, with their yellow skin and stringy, inky black hair form so loathsome a contrast to the tall, white-skinned, blue-eyed Hillmen with their 'abundant locks ... of ... brown or ruddy hue' that the Hillmen prefer to spear their own women rather than have them seized by 'these filthy and bestial males who threatened to father their children.'[42] As for the red-skinned woman whom Grôm rescues from the attack of the giant dragonflies, though she is neither as 'hairy' nor as 'ape-like' as the Bow Legs, she is still 'sufficiently hideous ... and of some race plainly inferior' to the Hill People (MT 204). The black-skinned Ape people, 'plainly men, in a way, but still more plainly beasts,' are so much nearer to the primordial 'pregnant ooze' than the Hill people that they receive scant attention (MT 41).

Robert's portrayal of women in his novel is similarly more indebted to the *données* of Edwardian England than to any experience of backwoods New Brunswick, where chivalry must surely have been at a premium. Though Roberts treats it as wonderfully strange that Grôm should have an aversion to polygamy and wife-beating, he clearly considers it 'natural' for A-ya, despite her fleetness of foot and impressive musculature, to swoon and need to be carried in Grôm's arms at the climactic moment of a chase; natural, too, that she should look 'with eyes of dog-like devotion under the matted splendour of her hair [at] the man she loved, her mate and lover, yet ... also ... a sort of demi-god' (MT 75) who has mastered the secret of fire – a secret A-ya has been too timid to explore for herself.

If we look at the very structure of the novel, we will find an expression of some of the concepts expressed in Roberts's introduction to *Poems of Wild Life*. Chapter 1 acts as a prologue to the novel's true theme: 'that spirit of unquenchable expectation which has led the race of man upwards through all obstacles – the urge to find out ever what lies beyond' (MT 99). That civilizing spirit which alone permits us to sympathize with 'the most unfamiliar aspects of the natural world' is wholly absent in the first chapter of *Morning* – 'The World Without Men.' Although the action of this chapter is similar to that of Roberts's animal stories – the efforts of one creature to fend off the predatory attacks of another in a world of 'bloody turmoil' and 'violent surprises' (MT 4, 10) – and although the diplodocus protagonist possesses some rudiments of animal psychology, the essence of the animal stories – that element of 'romance' which emancipates us from ourselves, reintroducing us to 'the old kinship of earth' (KW 29) – is conspicuously absent. Roberts's depictions of the 'titanic combats' of nature's 'failures' (MT 20) are as lumbering as the dinosaurs themselves: 'A moment more, and the dreadful chase, with a noise of raucous groans and pantings, burst forth into the open ... With a horrid leap and a hoot of triumph, the pursuer sprang upon [the fugitive's] neck and bore it to the ground, where it lay bellowing hoarsely ... The victor tore madly at its throat with tooth and claw, and presently its bellowing subsided to a hideous, sobbing gurgle' (MT 78).

The failure of this passage is due not only to the stymied rhetoric which here replaces that fluency and incisive detail characteristic of Roberts's best descriptive prose, but also, to an utter lack of empathy. Unlike even tyrannical mole-shrews and vicious weasels, dinosaurs can by no possible stretch of the imagination be treated as our 'wild kindred.' An account of an afternoon in the life and death of a diplodocus cannot successfully perform the function of an animal story – 'to return us to nature, without requiring that we at the same time return to barbarism' (KW 29). Thus it is only when man and the other mammals enter *In the Morning of Time*, and when man, 'by taking thought,' is able to 'overcome the ferocity and foil the malice' of the gigantic beasts which prey upon him (MT 40) that Roberts starts to warm to his task and the reader enters a fictive world similar to that of Roberts's animal stories.

The nameless human whose victory over the last remaining dinosaurs concludes the second chapter of *Morning* is resurrected in Chapter 3 as Grôm, whose discovery and mastery of the element of fire result in his loss not only of fear regarding predatory beasts, but also of 'the beast within' – any common or base brutality of rage' (MT 78). With Grôm, his brain forever seething with new ideas for exploiting his environment, Roberts defines the essence of the human as opposed to the animal – not merely the descent from the trees and the upright walk, but also the dawning intelligence which persuades the ex-apes to 'challenge the supremacy of the hunting beasts' and to 'assert their lordship over all the other dwellers on the earth's surface' (MT 152). By the time Grôm leads his people to 'that sweetly wooded and rivulet-watered hill' (which, for all we know, might have been intended as the future site of Fredericton itself) the survival of the race of Hill Men / Shining Ones is assured.

In Grôm's personal history – his falling in love with A-ya, who had earlier saved his life in battle, and his rescue of her from a hated rival who has gone over to the yellow-skinned enemy – we have adventures akin to those in Roberts's historical romances of Old Acadie. But what significant connection can *In the Morning of Time* have with that prose form on which Roberts's own survival as a writer is considered to depend[43] – the animal or wilderness story? According to W.J. Keith, Roberts's fictions in this genre concern 'the attempts of men to survive, to come to terms with, a [natural] world which is hostile and in which they are themselves regarded as enemies.'[44] Supposedly, the key to survival is reversion to the instincts we share with the animals. Roberts's backwoodsmen are, accordingly, 'no more and no less individualized than the bears and foxes and squirrels with which they are in close contact.'[45] They come to form an integral 'connection with, and reliance upon, the world of nature,' one which allows 'no room for either sentiment or compassion' as far as both animals and humans are concerned.[46]

A reader who turns to a volume such as *The Backwoodsmen* will, then, be considerably taken aback to find fictions in which a backwoods Dr Doolittle creates a peaceable kingdom in which the woodchuck lies down with the fox, and a pig suns himself secure in the knowledge that he will never 'deteriorate into pork' ('MacPhairsson's Happy Family'); in which 'Popsie' single-handedly rescues his golden-haired little 'girlie' from a pack of ravenous wolves ('In the Deep of the Snow'), or in which a savage lumberjack is 'gentled' by the 'baby-love' of a 'tiny flaxen-haired' five-year-old by the name of Rosy-Lilly ('The Gentling of Red McWha'). It may be argued that *The Backwoodsmen* shows Roberts nodding, and that stories in which humans play such a prominent role represent an aberration from Roberts's true forte, the animal story. Yet in 'The Vagrants of the Barrens,' the first story of this collection, we surely have vintage Roberts, and a telescoped form of that vision of man and nature Roberts would set out some dozen years later in *Morning*.

'The Vagrants of the Barrens' turns upon the classic trope of CanLit, Man and Snowstorm. A fire which destroys Pete Noël's cabin pits him without warning against 'the desolation and the savage cold of the wilderness.'[47] But Pete, being 'a woodsman, and alert in every sense like the creatures of the wild themselves' (B 9), is able to rely on instincts swifter than thought to preserve himself. The drop in his fortunes seems to cause a parallel drop in his evolutionary status: 'Pete fell to his breakfast with about as much ceremony as might have sufficed a hungry wolf, the deprivation of a roof-tree having already taken him back appreciably nearer to the elemental brute' (B 14). Yet there is something stubbornly human about the way in which Pete sets off through deep snow, provided only with his clothes and the barest necessities to walk to the nearest lumber camp some fifty miles away. Floundering without snowshoes, increasingly cold and hungry, Pete would seem to be forced to 'come to terms' with the hostility of nature: 'Hitherto he had always managed to work, more or less, *with* nature, and so had come to regard the elemental forces as friendly. Now they had turned upon him altogether ...' (B 17). Yet before we can say 'wolf in the snow' we find our 'elemental brute' dictating terms to nature, offering 'challenge and defiance' to 'the savage and implacable sternness of the wild ... Against whatever odds, he declared to himself, he was master' (B 17–18).

Using his woodcraft to 'force the forest to render him something in the way of food' (B 28), relying on sheer will and patience, Noël marches on, until a blinding snowstorm cuts him off from the trail he needs to follow and the caribou he has been desperately tracking. 'Sullen, but not discouraged,' Noël, now an 'elemental creature, battling with the elements for his life' (B 23, 31), indulges in some Grôm-like reflections: 'there was no one but man who could confront such a storm undaunted ... With an obstinate pride in his superiority to the other creatures of the wilderness, he scowled defiantly at the storm' (B 25).

Nowhere does the attempt to portray Roberts as possessing a modern-

ist, quasi-existential sensibility ring falser than in the face of such a
passage. Where Conrad's Kurtz penetrates the African wilderness, ruthlessly exerting his will over its inhabitants and discovering in the
process the horror of his own human nature, Roberts's appropriately
named Noël, though he drinks caribou blood as a 'restorative' when
he finally does catch up with the herd, displays a shining nobility of
spirit in forbearing to slaughter any other caribou to make up for his
losses with pelts and meat that can be profitably sold at the settlement.
'The Vagrants of the Barren' suggests a certain solidarity between
man and beast, but strikes the chord of man's innate superiority, his
'assured ... ability to master all ... obstacles that might seek to withstand him' (B 32). Though many of Roberts's other stories portray wilderness scenes idyllic in their fresh and gentle beauty, this fiction insists
instead on depicting 'external nature' in its most savage form to render
all the more impressive the protagonist's eventual triumph over it, and
all the more human that welcoming wisp of smoke from the lumber
camp chimney with which the story ends.

Into the workings of nature at its most bleak and barren Roberts has
managed to project a kind of human courage, endurance, and dogged
mastery which have in them something both of the primeval and the
civilized, of desperate struggle and lordly assurance. *Pace* Margaret
Atwood and survivalists all, it is not only the bleats and whimpers of
dying animals that sound from the pages of Roberts's wilderness fictions, but also the shouts of invincible backwoodsmen. And as for Sir
Charles himself, penning his fictions of wild beasts and rough men for
the drawing rooms of New York and London, we could do worse than
remember that, as the White Man's Burden thesis of *In the Morning of
Time* reveals, he and his devoted public had in them something not only
of the tiger and ape, but of the Yahoo as well.

# 4

# Fictive Histories

Roger was watching when Winslow read the order to the men of
Grand Pré in their church overlooking the meadows ... What would
posterity say of all of this? Poets and romancers would have a theme
for the next five hundred years. He wondered how many would make
an honest search into its causes and stab their pens where the guilt
lay most.

THOMAS RADDALL, *Roger Sudden*[1]

la différence entre le menteur et le menteux, dans mon pays, est la même
qu'entre l'historien et le conteur: le premier vous raconte ce qu'il
veut; l'autre, ce que vous voulez. Mais au bout d'un siècle, tout cela
devient de la bonne pâte a vérité.

ANTONINE MAILLET, *Cent Ans dans les bois*[2]

(Where I come from, the difference between a liar and a teller of tales is
the same as that between a historian and a story-teller: the one tells
what he wants to say, the other, what you want to hear. But by the end
of a century, all that's become just good old truth pie.)

Our memories are killed in the flickering images of the media, and the
seeming intensity of events. There is weakened in us the simplest
form of that activity of re-collection which Plato knew to be the chief
means to wisdom.

GEORGE GRANT, *Lament for a Nation*[3]

Novelists are fictive historians; their characters possess histories, or so writers as diverse as Henry James and Margaret Laurence have argued.[4] Laurence argues that all fiction presupposes and enacts a continuum, 'the perceptions, interpretations and choices of material of particular writers giv[ing] form to our past and relat[ing] it to our present and our future.'[5] Surely, then, we might expect from historical fiction, with its deliberate focus on a collective past outside the writer's or reader's personal memory, a powerful manifestation of this continuum, radically restoring or freeing our notions of what really was, so that we can begin to see what is truly around us, and what might be actively brought into being.

To make such claims in the context of Maritime fiction may, however, appear as either perverse or deluded, given the kind of historical fiction the region has produced, and the area's very history. One historian of the Maritimes concludes that, 'for geographic reasons alone, the region was destined to be passed by or passed through' by explorers, settlers, and adventurers on their way to the productive soil and vast resources of the interior.[6] The Maritime provinces' physical proximity to Europe has led their inhabitants to cling to a submissive colonial mentality, or so a novel like *Barometer Rising* implies. Outclassed by the port cities of America's Atlantic seaboard, by-passed by the intensive railway-building that took place in the continent's interior, the Maritimes enjoyed only a brief and freakish economic boom after the decline of the region's strategic military importance during the conflicts between France, England, and America for control of the continent between the beginning of the Seven Years' War and the conclusion of the Napoleonic Wars. As William MacNutt dourly observes of the Maritimes' economic heyday,

this unprecedented prosperity of the age of wood, wind and water was something like the falling of crumbs from other tables, the consequence of the abounding expansiveness of the world economy of the 1850s ... Scores of noteworthy commercial failures had taught that prosperity could not last, that capital, when it could be accumulated, should be conserved and not risked. Behind this conservatism was a realization that in comparison with the new lands opening to the westward, the Atlantic provinces possessed no resources that promised great riches, that they could never be more than a good man's poor country.[7]

If Canadian history begins, humbly enough, in the fog-bound and cod-torn seas of the east coast, it comes of age and interest, according to the Laurentian school, in the perennial conflicts of the French and English nations, as represented by Quebec and Ontario. Though in terms of European presence the Maritimes are the oldest and historically richest part of our country, anyone raised in the centralist tradition will search for those key images and events which help to create a national story, on the Plains of Abraham rather than in the demolition of Louisbourg; in the Battle of Lundy's Lane rather than the Aroostook War; in the fur trade rather than the fisheries. The national absence of interest in the Maritimes is reflected in the fact that there is still no comprehensive study of the region's post-Confederation history. As Silver Donald Cameron lamented in 1978, though histories of Canada's other maritime province, British Columbia, abound, 'Nova Scotia's longer, richer history is still not captured in a good one-volume work.'[8]

The one event of Maritime history poignant enough to influence the national mythos – the expulsion of the Acadians – was, in fact, usurped by an American, with predictably debilitating results, as Edward McCourt observed:

it would seem only fitting that the New England bard be adopted as the patron saint of Nova Scotia, since he has created for that province a legend which has enabled the Land of Evangeline to compete on at least equal terms with Mount Vernon and the Alamo. But it is less generally recognized that Longfellow's influence on the Canadian historical novel has been equally profound. The Land of Evangeline as he conceived it ... has become a type setting for Canadian novels dealing not only with the expulsion of the Acadians, but with almost every phase of the Ancient Regime.[9]

What McCourt calls the 'mellow blight of Evangeline'[10] – an obsession with presenting the past as unconditionally, elegant, idyllic, beatific – can be designated the congenital defect of the Maritimes' premier historical novelist, Charles G.D. Roberts. His mortician's touch to the body of the past seems perfectly to fit the context in which he wrote – the Maritimes' economic and political decay following Confederation and the implementation of Macdonald's National Policy. Longfellow's and Roberts's examples would seem to have helped give the region the reputation of being a historical backwater in which can be discerned no trace of that 'type' which Georg Lukács considered the 'central category and criterion of realist,' and by extension, historical fiction, that 'type' in which 'all the humanly and socially essential determinants are present on their highest level of development, in the ultimate unfolding of the possibilities latent in them, in extreme presentation of their extremes, rendering concrete the peaks and limits of men and epochs.'[11]

And if there were a historical type native to the Maritimes, surely it would be that of the pawn or born loser – or so a roll call of the region's original population seems to argue: deracinated Micmacs and Milicetes, deported Acadians, defeated Scots Highlanders, distressed Loyalists, and that famished Irishry who so irritated Haliburton. Any historical novelist whose intention was to elevate and ennoble the past rather than merely to powder, patch, and paint it would be hard put to deal with, for example, the endemic impotence of the garrisons at Port Royal / Fort Anne, that 'ephemeral community of transients,'[12] or with Louisbourg, that collaborative disaster of 'bad construction, inadequate armament, mutinous men and inefficient officers.'[13] Fort Anne and Louisbourg stand as monuments to the criminal neglect and concerted ill will of the imperial powers towards that 'ill-thriven, hard-visaged brat' of a child, Acadie / Nova Scotia – a neglect and ill will manifested just as acutely after 1867 by Ottawa, according to the more radical school of Maritime historians. All in all, the conventional image of the Maritimes as 'everyone's half-forgotten past and no-one's future'[14] would seem to have an unimpeachable historical base.

Perhaps to compensate for the sheer dolefulness of its history the Maritimes have favoured the development of the historical romance over the historical novel. Yet the two can be seen as Siamese twins forming a single genre between them – that genre to which Scott's *Waverley* gave birth. In the best of Scott's fiction the romantic, in the form of the 'marvellous and uncommon' (with the most revolutionary or subversive of implications), is dramatically juxtaposed with the novelistic, in the form of the conventional and ordinary (with every implication of the conservatively safe and stable).[15] The case is lamentably different with the best-known Maritime equivalents, however. In Roberts's Acadian romances, the novelistic everyday is entirely absent, and in Thomas Raddall's fiction it is vitiated by an element on which both these writers depend – a flighty shadow of that Romance defined and deployed by Scott. Roberts's and, to a lesser extent Raddall's, is a Romance limited to an affair of hero and heroine, originally sworn to opposing sides, who do not so much overcome as abandon all obstacles to union by surrendering unconditionally to True Love.

This chapter makes no claims for the intrinsic excellence of most historical fiction written in the Maritimes, but it does intend to make a case for the interest and importance of some of that fiction in terms of the ideological contexts which shaped it, and of the ways in which certain texts manipulate or challenge their readers' concepts of their collective past. The texts with which this chapter will deal – Huyghue's *Argimou*, Roberts's *A Sister to Evangeline*, Raddall's *Roger Sudden*, and Maillet's *Pélagie* – recollect for us not 'the' past, but intriguingly divergent versions of it. Though all of these texts deal in varying degrees with the expulsion of the Acadians, this chapter is not an analysis of literary treatments of that historical event,[16] but rather an exploration of the inherent possibilities of the genre of historical fiction. Between Raddall's conviction that fiction can be made to search out truths about the past, stabbing at the falsehoods sentiment and ignorance foster, and Maillet's pitting of the recorded facts of history against the vision articulated and preserved by story, possibilities emerge for snuffing the 'flickering images of the media,' or at least of judging them in the light of those liberating truths and saving wisdom that fiction's histories hold out to us.

\*\*\*

They do not know it, they do it without the least provocation, even with great innocence, but it is the English that sell 'Evangeline' ... in the region made celebrated by the Expulsion of the Acadians. And this strikes your heart curiously. I should not be any happier to be offered Evangeline by the descendants of the deported.

Eugène Cloutier[17]

Charles G.D. Roberts's historical romances have received notoriously bad press. One critic has termed them 'bread-and-margarine affairs,'[18] largely inspired by a desire to milk the vogue for historical fiction – at its North American peak between 1886 and 1904 – for all the lucre it was worth. Given that the revised title for *A Sister to Evangeline* was *Lovers in Acadie*, it is perhaps unfair to expect anything remotely like *Waverley* from a writer who felt that the 'story of the French in Nova Scotia ... reads less like history than romance,' and who set out to give the expulsion of the Acadians 'the full poetic treatment' (SPCP 262).

Such an intention seems oddly redundant, given the wild success of Longfellow's poeticising of the events of 1755. It is true, however, that *Evangeline* has inspired a small but insistent chorus of dissent from readers critical of the poem's verisimilitude and its ideological intent.[19] Archibald MacMechan, in chastising the New England bard for the ignorance which made murmuring pines and hemlocks usurp the place that, had it been given to 'the desolation of the level, wind-swept marshland,' would have produced 'greater truth and deeper pathos,'[20]

seems to be directing us to the efforts made by the author of 'The Tantramar Revisited' to succeed where Longfellow failed. Yet MacMechan
is on record as declaring Roberts's novels to be 'feeble performances'
spoiled by the 'mawkish strain which affects some of his verse un-
pleasantly.'[21] The question remains, then – what other than an appropriate touch of local colour *did* Roberts achieve in his historical romances
of Old Acadie?

*The Forge in the Forest* and its sequel, *A Sister to Evangeline*, certainly
show a better grasp of Acadie's historical and geographical particulars
than Longfellow ever troubled to secure: descriptions abound not only
of apple blossom but of the freezing mud through which the deportees had to wade on their way to the ships. Details such as the alliance
between French and Micmacs against the English, and the compromising presence of the 'Black Abbé' (whom Roberts modelled after the historical missionary and *agent provocateur*, Le Loutre) give to the New
Brunswick writer's version of the Acadian 'troubles,' if not greater truth,
then at least less inaccuracy. Yet more important than Roberts's allusions to a historical context for the expulsion – a context Longfellow
almost entirely omits – are the ideological manoeuvres he manages to
carry out on the American's fictive territory, manoeuvres which have the
result of 'Canadianizing' the issues and their repercussions.

William Owen has summarized the ideological objectives of Roberts's
historical romances as the development and promotion of a harmonious reconciliation between English and Acadians in the Maritimes, and
the conflicting desire to 'revise and improve the image of the English,
specifically that of the British military, during the eighteenth century.'[22]
To achieve the impossible, Roberts relies heavily on the marriage-of-
opposing-sides device; thus a French noblewoman elopes with a gentlemanly Yankee adventurer in *The Prisoner of Mademoiselle*, or a Puritan
lily-maid and her sister are wed to an Acadian seigneur and his son in
*The Forge in the Forest*. And in *A Sister to Evangeline* a rather more
subtle reconciliation of opposites is achieved in the ultimate union of the
Acadian hero Paul Grande – already convinced that God is on the side
of the redcoats in the matter of the ownership of North America – and
Yvonne, daughter of a disaffected French nobleman resident in Acadie,
who has sworn the entire oath of allegiance to King George and be-
trothed his daughter to a handsome but dim New England Quaker.
In having Paul win Yvonne away from her Anglophile fiancé and in
allowing his Acadian lovers first to seize the ship on which they are
being deported and then to make their way to Québec and the French
cause, Roberts accords to the Francophiles a notable *coup* which al-

most distracts our attention from the fact that, in the book's last chapter, New France has fallen to the English and Paul, having sworn allegiance to King George, is living quietly and comfortably with his bride on an estate significantly located 'beside the Ottawa.'[23]

Owen implies that in *Sister*, Roberts is creating a counter to the Evangeline mythos. By making his heroine wilfully reject the traditional daughterly virtues of submission, obedience, and docility to parental or priestly decree, in order to fulfil the requirements of passionate, lofty love for the man of her choice; by making his hero not a farmer turned coureur de bois, sullenly and restlessly pursuing oblivion, but a soldier-poet who takes his destiny in his own hands by out-gallanting his farmer rival and comandeering the vehicle of his own expulsion, Roberts manages to strike a blow against the hegemony of Longfellow's history. One of the side-effects, Owen suggests, is a dexterously managed upgrading of the British position vis-à-vis the Acadian – if the latter are seen as independent agents rather than as passive victims of history, then the British can take on the role of adversaries rather than executioners in what becomes the ultimate gentleman's game – war. It is a subtler and shrewder move than Roberts's other ploy: extolling the gentlemanly restraint and tenderness of each and every deporter towards the pitiful – but also exasperating – deportees.[24]

Yet Roberts's ideological projects in works like *Forge* and *Sister* are more complex and questionable than Owen allows, as a look at what we might call the erotics and patriotics of both texts will reveal. These romances, for all their costume drama twaddle, contain significant traces of Roberts's conceptions of the Maritimes and Canada that more 'realistic' novels such as *The Heart that Knows*, or his blatantly nationalistic poems omit or obscure.

Roberts's famed restlessness finds curious expression in his Acadian romances. It is as if, harassed by the intolerable complexities of his relations with wife and family, Roberts attempted for his fictional characters in Old Acadie a simplification and resolution of duty and passion. His Jean de Mers and Paul Grandes, in quest of absolute beauty and perfect love, become pale loiterers around the dainty feet and devastatingly deep-set eyes of the unfortunately named Mizpah and the more appropriately titled Yvonne de Lamourie – ladies who, for one reason or another, are compelled to delay sexual surrender until hero and reader have been thoroughly titillated. Roberts consciously conflates the rhetoric and topoi of the religion of love and the *guerre d'amour* in order to validate the egotism *à deux* of romantic passion. (It is significant that after ten years of marriage Paul and Yvonne, prettily ensconced in post-

Conquest Québec, appear to be blissfully childless.) The 'love to which life and death must serve as lackeys' (SE 84) comes to subsume the claims of military war and power politics.

Accordingly, in *A Sister to Evangeline* rather more time is given over to Paul's *guerre d'amour* against his Quaker rival for Yvonne's affections and his actual winning of Yvonne's heart (by such strategies as feverishly kissing her little feet as she reclines in a hammock, or drinking in the empurpled bronze of her hair) than to the account of the embarkation of the Acadians onto the British ships[25] and the burning of Grand Pré. When Paul is shut up in the chapel at Grand Pré the initiative passes to Yvonne; she, however, has scarcely a moment to spare for the distress of her less fortunate neighbours, so busy is she wrestling down her sense of duty to parents and legally affianced husband, and watering the rose of romantic love that, once a-bloom, will lead her away from the safety and prosperity of her father's house into a wretched exile with the man she adores.

It is at this point in Roberts's narrative that war itself is conquered by the *guerre d'amour*. Once on board ship and officially a deportee, Yvonne conquers more effectively than her soldier lover ever will: the British 'enemy' fall over their own feet trying to provide her with luxurious accommodation and the courtesy due her rank; with general adoration and with assistance to the point of treason. When Paul and his band of fellow deportees seize the ship from its British masters, Yvonne strides forward to literally disarm all with her beauty and grace. The only Englishman who offers her even token resistance finds himself compelled to surrender his sword to the 'Queen' of the ship; so pacified and passive have the original crew become under the pressure of Yvonne's charm that when the Acadians disembark at Jemseg, en route for Québec, no one pursues or even threatens them. The fate of the French in the New World, the expulsion of the Acadians, the burning of Grand Pré – all become a subplot to the *guerre d'amour* which Roberts sustains for the full thirty-eight chapters of *A Sister to Evangeline*.

If Roberts, insistent on a happy ending for his exemplary pair of lovers, does not 'sell' Evangeline, as Cloutier puts it, does he instead sell out the French, as Owen suggests? For answer we may turn to Roberts's creation in *The Forge in the Forest* of a fiction complementary to that of the tenderhearted English he presents in *A Sister to Evangeline* – the preliminary fiction of Coulon de Villier's raid on the New Englanders stationed in Grand Pré in 1747.

Apologists for Governors Lawrence and Shirley are quick to point to Coulon's attack as justification for the decision to deport the Acadians. Thomas Raddall, no partisan of Evangeline, describes the raid in these terms: 'Coulon's war party, guided from billet to billet by the Acadians themselves, had dragged the New Englanders from their beds and tomahawked them, bayoneted them, shot them down in their shirts' (RS 230). Bona Arsenault, author of a *History of the Acadians*, which sets out to establish the reality of Acadian neutrality, gives an essentially similar account of 'this murderous battle.' Though he insists that the villagers of Grand Pré had tried to warn the overconfident Noble of the danger that awaited his men, Arsenault goes on to recount how two hundred and forty French soldiers, sixty Indians, and some twenty 'outlaw Acadians' broke with axes into the houses in which the enemy was quartered, and attacked the English, who were still half-asleep.[26]

In incorporating the French attack on Grand Pré into *The Forge in the Forest*, Roberts deliberately interrupts the run of his romance – Jean de Mer's winning the heart of a widowed Englishwoman whose only child has been kidnapped by the Micmacs under the orders of the Black Abbé – to rewrite history in his own ideological interests. Thus the novel's two penultimate chapters – 'The Fight at Grand Pré' and 'The Black Abbé Strikes in the Dark' – work to preserve the fiction that the war between French and English in North America was a chivalrous rather than vicious affair, something that led to the formation of new bonds rather than wounds between races. 'War,' Roberts has a character remark, 'becomes a gross and hideous thing whensoever it is suffered to slip out of the control of gentlemen, who alone know how to maintain its courtesies' (SE 30). Roberts's task in *Forge* is to put hostilities back in the hands of gentlemen and thus achieve parity between the races; this he accomplishes by exculpating the French, just as he would later excuse the British at Grand Pré.[27]

Contrary to Raddall, Roberts blames not Coulon de Villier's men for taking the offensive, but Noble's New Englanders for not maintaining an adequate defence. Jean de Mer is made to confess his dislike for night fighting and guerilla tactics – 'for I love a fair defiance and an open field'[28] – but also to extoll the courage and hardihood required for the manoeuvre (an epic trek across deep snow between Chignecto and Grand Pré). A practised soldier, he also acknowledges the military advantage to be gained by a surprise attack. Against the skill and courage of Coulon, Jean de Mer, and their company, Roberts pits Noble ('a man of excellent courage, but small discretion, and with a foolish contempt for his enemies' [FF 266]) and Noble's men – 'bitter fighters, drinkers of strong rum, quaintly sanctimonious in their cups' (FF 266). What follows is a combat between equals on roughly equal ground. For if Coulon's men have the advantage of surprise and Noble's men the pathos of ignorance, Roberts is careful to control our sympathies for the underdog by contrasting the luxurious comfort in which Noble's men recline indoors with the distress of the French, shivering in the wind and snow outside their doors. Roberts contrives to split up the French force so that the contingent commanded by Jean de Mer is actually outnumbered by its New England assailants; thus the actions of the French in shooting down an enemy horde rushing out of the doomed houses seem valorous rather than gratuitous. Coulon, who has had the task of actually dispatching the New Englanders in their nightshirts, goes out of his way to stress his displeasure with that regrettable strategy of 'killing in the dark' which 'the times, and the straits of New France required' (FF 288). Ever the gentleman, Coulon is made to offer honourable terms to the survivors among the enemy. And finally, the one victim on whom the narrative dwells in all this scene of 'blood-smeared thresholds and dripping window sills' (FF 292) is an Acadian, de Mer's faithful retainer Tamin. Slain by an enemy sword, he lies in a pool of his own blood under snowladen apple trees, obligingly fulfilling a prophecy darkly uttered near the text's beginning. Thus victory, honour, and pathos are accorded to the French side; courage – and incompetence – to the English. The scene will be inverted and the score balanced with the events at Grand Pré in 1755, events which Roberts uses to facilitate an ultimate reconciliation between what he perceived as Canada's opposing – and identifying – forces.

It is not out of any regional interest, but rather with nationalistic motives that Roberts rewrites literary history in *A Sister to Evangeline*. What he seeks to redress in Longfellow's *Evangeline* is not any failure of verisimilitude but rather, Longfellow's incorporation of the deportation and diaspora of the Acadians into the American mythos. For all that Roberts makes the expulsion play second fiddle to Yvonne-loves-Paul, the chapters he does devote to the Acadians' deportation in *A Sister to Evangeline* constitute the most convincing prose of his text;[29] their relative realism and honesty reveal the perfunctoriness of the mere six lines Longfellow allocates to the physical removal of the Acadians from their homeland. For the dominant concern of *Evangeline* is to illustrate that painful submission to temporal or divine authority is ultimately rewarded elsewhere by either material prosperity or spiritual ascendancy on a scale undreamed of on one's former home ground.

To appreciate the success of Roberts's revision of Longfellow, a glance at the subtext of *Evangeline* will be necessary. One of this poem's key scenes occur in the chapel at Grand Pré, immediately after Gabriel's father, the virile, choleric Basil Lajeunesse, has uttered the only words of defiance to be found in *Evangeline*: 'Flushed was his face and distorted with passion; and wildly he shouted – / Down with the tyrants of England! We have never sworn them allegiance! / Death to these foreign soldiers, who seize on our homes and our harvests! / More he fain would have said, but the merciless hand of a soldier / Smote him upon the mouth, and dragged him down to the pavement.'[30]

They who live by the sword will perish by the sword, the passage implies – thereby floating over the fact that the able-bodied Acadian men at Grand Pré so outnumbered the soldiers sent to expel them that the authorities feared for the success of the expulsion. For good measure, Longfellow has Father Felician answer Basil's challenge by gesturing to the crucified Christ on the chapel wall. To protest against deportation with anything more than violent sobs of contrition, to interpret the expulsion as an act of aggression rather than as the will of God, is to profane the house of 'the Prince of Peace' (which presumably is not profaned by being used as a prison). Needless to say, Father Felician carries the day, his parishioners praying aloud for 'strength and submission and patience' (E 30) as they go down to the ships.

The poem's 'deeper pathos' is, of course, reserved for Evangeline's self-immolation on the pyre of 'patience and abnegation of self, and devotion to others' (E 52). For her compatriots, however, a happier fate has been reserved – entry into a golden world, the 'Eden of Louisiana' (E 40), whose praises are sung by, of all people, Basil Lajeunesse. The 'ci-devant blacksmith' has quickly achieved the American Dream, effortlessly acquiring 'domains ... herds and ... patriarchal demeanour' (E 43). Gone is the staunch patriot of Grand Pré, the advocate of offensive action; in his place, an enthusiastic stirrer of the melting pot, who welcomes a party of Acadian deportees with an encomium on Louisiana: 'Welcome ... to a home, that is better perchance than the old one! / Here no hungry winter congeals our blood like the rivers: / Here no stony ground provokes the wrath of the farmer ... / All the year round the orange groves are in blossom; and grass grows / More in a single night than a whole Canadian summer' (E 45–6).

Longfellow's blithe ignorance of particulars – the almost profligate fertility of the dykelands along the Minas Basin, the length of the growing season immediately north of the u.s. border – signifies not some regrettable lapse from verisimilitude but instead, the 'sub-myth' of his poem – the discovery of a new, better (ie, American) Eden which offsets the pathos of Evangeline's and Gabriel's thwarted romance, and, more importantly, which justifies the deportation of the Acadians from

their native land. All's well that ends well – after settling the deportees on their boundless Louisiana farms, and after reuniting a rather
seedy Gabriel with his super-selfless Evangeline, the poem concludes
with a reference to Old Acadie and its forest primeval, in whose shade
the English race and language now flourish. As for the few stubborn
Acadian peasants strung out along 'the mournful and misty Atlantic,'
they will soon die out, or so Longfellow's closing lines imply.[31]

In *A Sister to Evangeline*, however, the French are made to refuse any
golden exile in America. Instead, they willingly sacrifice an exceedingly nominal 'Maritime' identity (though Paul Grande and his cousin Marc
de Mer are Acadians by birth, they are educated and pass the formative years of their adolescence in Quebec) to become Anglophile Canad-
iens. In his romances, Roberts is entirely indifferent to the fate of
Acadians seeking to retain their language and culture in their Maritime
homeland; instead, he pledges allegiance to *the* Canadian paradigm:
Canada = Quebec + Ontario. *The Forge in the Forest* makes it clear that it
is Acadie's incontrovertible 'doom' to be destroyed beyond all hope of
'renaissance,' and while Roberts may not have held that the Acadians
who *did* make it back to the Maritimes from exile in America were a
spent and assimilated force, his commitment to a vision of Canada as 'a
nation of two races' ennobled and enriched by a 'literature in two
languages' with 'no overwhelming disparity between them'[32] made inevitable his airy simplification of the French presence in Canada by
displacing Acadie by Quebec, the Acadiens by Québécois. At any rate,
his Paul Grande and Marc de Mer, having escaped from Grand Pré to
Québec, having 'fought and bled for France in all the last battles and lain
for months in an English hospital,' philosophically exchange 'the corrupt and shameless clique of plunderers who ... represented the power
of France and Quebec' (SE viii)[33] for the just and honourable English –
'the new masters of our country' and reap the requisite rewards – 'our
little estates beside the Ottawa' (SE 285).

In terms of Roberts's contribution to a national literature, the significant feature of his historical romances must be that his characters do
possess a country to which they may commit themselves – not merely an
imperial power or a colony, but a country. For Roberts in *A Sister to
Evangeline* at least, the 'great good place' is not Acadie or the flesh pots
of Louisiana, but 'Canada.' This and his dexterous manipulations to
preserve the ideological balance between French and English deserve
our notice, even if they do not redeem a prose which, by and large, is
more margarine than bread. Due credit should be given to Roberts's
historical romances for having at least provided a conceptual base

which later, better writers would exploit – or explode – according to their own visions of history, politics, and nationhood.

\*\*\*

And his is the most remembering of all bloods. The tincture of heritage from that of his forbears is always constitutively in him ...[34]

Though Ernest Buckler is here extolling the historical consciousness of the native Nova Scotian, his tribute can most appropriately be directed to the province's adopted son, Thomas H. Raddall. Though Raddall has not limited his oeuvre to historical fiction, it is the genre for which he is best known both in and out of the Maritimes. Critics have been infinitely kinder to Raddall than to his forerunner, Roberts, considering Raddall to have transcended the limitations of the historical romance rather than as having merely flogged its powdered hide: 'Rooted in a community where tradition is long by North American standards, and the urban tangles of Montreal and Toronto remote, he has absorbed the history, landscape, manners, and accent of his region with a completeness that amounts to possession. In addition, he has an unusual ability to recreate moments of dramatic action, and a vigorous, fluent, highly sensory style.'[35]

Raddall himself has few kind words for Roberts, whose fluffier efforts at historical romance – *The Prisoner of Mademoiselle*, for example – he would no doubt compare to those of the 'prostitutes of the historical novel, the writers of costume pieces' such as *Forever Amber* or *Angélique in Love*.[36] Raddall's memoir *In My Time* reveals a succinct contempt for Roberts the man, living off the largesse of susceptible wealthy women, and exploiting his status in Canadian letters to lure fledgling female authors onto the literary-critical equivalent of the casting couch.[37]

Raddall's distaste for Roberts's work can be deduced from the former's conviction that the writer of legitimate historical fiction must do more than entertain: 'Whether you write fiction or whether you write history, if you're writing honestly you have to have a constant regard for the truth.'[38] What would distress Raddall most about *The Forge in the Forest* or *A Sister to Evangeline* would be a dishonesty which it might be kinder to call historical naïveté, a conception of history as 'dealing only with matters remote and romantic' so that for Roberts, Maritime history would appear to come to an end 'with the Peace of Paris in 1763.'[39]

Raddall's best historical fiction, on the other hand, articulates the dramatic complexity of historical events in which past and present, private and public, the momentous and seemingly trivial interweave into a knot which it is the future's prime business to untangle. Though he does make questionable use of the 'marriage of opposing sides' device, Raddall, unlike Roberts, integrates his heroes' worship and wooing of fair women with the principal historical events of the novels. This gives to his fictions – which he himself calls historical romances – a credibility that has led some critics to make Lukácsian claims for him, finding in his best fiction the essential features of an entire epoch crowded into the biography of some individual type.[40] Yet while or perhaps because works such as *His Majesty's Yankees* and *Roger Sudden* belong to the 'crowded canvas' school, their heroes possess such rudimentary psyches that they fail of that 'three-dimensionality' or 'inner life of man, its essential traits and essential conflicts' which, 'portrayed ... in organic connection with social and historical factors,' creates for Lukács the possibility of great historical or realistic fiction.[41]

What Raddall's characters do share with those of Lukács's *non pareil*, Balzac, is an awareness of the 'existence of another and better truth ... poetically opposed to the squalid reality' in which they find themselves lodged.[42] In distinctly lesser works like *Pride's Fancy* this truth is found to reside in that 'abode of clean femininity,' the hero's true love,[43] and even in the novel most critics cite as Raddall's best, *His Majesty's Yankees*, David Strang is made to find in his fiancée compensatory solace for the complete collapse of his hopes that the American Revolution would spread to Britain's Maritime colonies. To replace his original commitment to the abstract ideal of liberty, David is given the new, practical goal of responsible government – foreshadowed in this novel by the presence of such figures as Richard Uniacke and Michael Francklin, with his plea for the good of the 'true country ... this queer, raw wilderness that men call Nova Scotia.'[44] With admirable dexterity, Raddall manages to replace the potentially subversive revolutionary ethos first espoused by the disaffected David with a saving vision of 'law and order' (HMY 395) serving the ultimate 'other and better truth' – a (distinctly Anglophile) vision of Canada-to-be: 'The loyalist exiles from the thirteen colonies have swelled our towns and villages and carved the new province of New Brunswick out of Nova Scotia's sprawling bulk and ... their children have married ours and turned their faces west where in the old days we looked south. Someday we shall make a nation in this northern wilderness where is now only a scatter of poor British colonies' (HMY 406).

It is Raddall's privilege as a writer of historical fiction to claim and exploit the boon of hindsight: knowing what *did* happen allows him freely to imagine what might have happened to bring particular events about, and this complex interweaving of fact and possibility becomes the index to that truth his fiction sets out to locate. For Raddall, truth and fiction are distinct categories which the novelist can bring together without adulterating their essential properties. 'Objective truth' would appear to be, for him, an unproblematic concept; indeed, it informs his activity as a revisionist – to look back over the past and correct mistaken or muddled interpretations of history in order that informed decisions may be made about the future. Certain facts or issues – the expulsion of the Acadians, for example – may be difficult for the squeamish or sentimental to confront, but the questions they raise can be definitively resolved. Thus where Roberts's romances labour to balance the stories of English and French in Acadie, and to incorporate both in his vision of Canada, in a work like *Roger Sudden* Raddall sets out to show that, whether we like to admit it or not, there is not only 'one story only,' but also one true side to that story.

Published two years after *His Majesty's Yankees* and one year before the end of World War II (in which, to his great regret, Raddall was unable to take part), *Sudden* sets out as resolutely as *Sister* to exculpate the actions of the British in the eighteenth-century Maritimes. Unlike Roberts's romance, and consistent with the tenets of *Yankees*, *Roger Sudden* conceives in its final pages a vision of Canada which makes no room for the French and which insists upon the validity and virtue of the English cause in our country's history. The novel attributes England's ultimate success not to the superiority of its military machine, but rather, to the courage and endurance of the English colonies – a fact which makes *Roger Sudden* as much a novel of the Battle of Britain as it is of the Seven Years' War.

Indeed, much of *Roger Sudden* is explicable in terms of the anxious, heightened state of the English-born Raddall's patriotic sentiments during the time of this novel's genesis. Appropriately enough, *Sudden* portrays the metamorphosis of a cynical and opportunistic survivor of the Jacobite cause into an English patriot who lays down his life for his native land. Like most of Raddall's heroes, Roger Sudden is drawn from the upper ranks of the rebellious and alienated, and is reintegrated into a social structure that is not so much reformed by conflict and struggle as redeemed by the rising winds of Destiny. Unlike these other heroes, however, Roger doesn't get the girl, or at least very much of her; more importantly, he dies to preserve the honourable identity he has at last achieved for himself. Despite pressure from his editor to

give *Roger Sudden* a happy ending, Raddall persevered in viewing his
hero's story as tragic; the result is a much sharper, finer, riskier work
than *His Majesty's Yankees*. With a minimum of 'love interest,' and disbur-
dened of the first person narrator device that dogs *Yankees, Roger
Sudden* comes close to being the right 'real thing' in Raddall's oeuvre: the
reasons for its failure are, accordingly, worth examination.

Roger Sudden, involved both economically and erotically with the
fervent and lovely young Jacobite, Mary Foy (who spies for the
French out of hatred for the English), intends for most of the novel to
run off with his lady love and the fortune he has gouged out of the
Nova Scotia wilderness. Once back in Kent, he will restore the fallen
fortunes of the aristocratic House of Sudden. Instead, he ends up in
Louisbourg during the fortress's last days, obstensibly to meet Mary, but
really to confront the conflicting loyalties his private dreams and public role as an Englishman have created. While neutrally observing the
skirmishes between French and English, Roger becomes aware that the
latter are about to fall into a murderous trap. He alerts his countrymen to
their danger and then spreads panic through the French reinforce-
ments down the line. Instead of seeking refuge on an English ship from
which he could safely watch the rest of the siege, Sudden returns to
Louisbourg to explain his actions to Mary. Arrested for high treason by
the French, he is executed by a firing squad just as the town major
formally surrenders the fortress to the English. The tone of the novel's
last pages is, however, exultant rather than tragic or even ironic; it is
as if Conrad's *Lord Jim*, instead of dying out in Marlow's uncertainty
about the truth of Jim's self-sacrifice, ended in a blaze of angels singing *Rule Britannia* at the fallen hero's feet.

Before he is dispatched, Sudden has an immoderately long time to
ponder the 'secret of French failure in America' : 'The French built
better ships, trained better soldiers; they understood the art of fortifica-
tion as no other nation did. The continent was theirs ... while the
English had no unity and no strong arm anywhere. Yet what was Louisbourg now, and what would Quebec be when another season passed?'
(RS 355–6). The answer is unrepentantly assertive:

The French in America had surrounded themselves with walls and shut up their
bodies and their minds. Only a handful of *coureurs de bois* and priests had ever
penetrated the continent – and the *coureurs* had mated with savage women, and
the priests were wedded to God. They had not left a mark ...

Walls! That was it! ... the restless English who would have no walls about
them, who demanded ... to march across a horizon that was always some-

where toward the west. The English who were not content to mate with savages but who took their women with them everywhere, resolved not merely to penetrate the wilderness but to people it ... The wilderness had purged [the common people of England] swiftly and terribly. The weak had died, the shiftless fled. In Halifax there remained only the unconquerable. (RS 357-8).

The novel's last words are, in fact, *Invicta*, the ancestral motto of the Suddens, and a fitting tribute to the common people of England who, at the time Raddall was writing this novel, were proving themselves unconquerable back on the other side of the Atlantic.

If Raddall's and Roger's upsurge of patriotism ruins the tragic project of the novel, allowing Roger to redeem his losses in the greater glory of his race, it is a débâcle prepared for by the very structure of the narrative. The text portrays Roger's transition from disillusioned chevalier to money-grubbing adventurer, to self-sacrificing patriot in three stages. First, England, on Roger's brother's ruined estate and in the slums of London where Roger hides out after turning highwayman; next, Nova Scotia's wilderness, where Sudden spends five years as captive of a repellent Micmac tribe; finally (after a brief, slavish sojourn in Louisbourg) civilization: Halifax in its boom days as 'gilded chamberpot'[45] and Louisbourg in its final glory and ashes. On these stages of his life's way, Roger first loses and then regains his soul – through the love not so much of a good woman, but of a great country. What needs to be analyzed here is the politics involved in this progress, the ideological subtext which reveals Raddall's role not as history's truth-teller but as what Maillet would term 'menteur' – telling what he wants us to hear of two groups – Micmac and Acadian – about whom the other writers this chapter treats will have a great deal to say.

Raddall's portrayal of the 'noble savage' and the Acadian *paysan* is as uncompromising as the treatment he deals out to the transported Cockney 'rabble' who are Halifax's original colonists. Yet while a saving remnant of the Cockneys prove worthy of the city they are sent to found, Raddall presents Micmac and Acadian as unregenerate, and as gaining infinitely more than they lose by their subordination to the British.

For the most part, Raddall refers to the Indians as 'savages': evil-smelling, hopelessly primitive in their subsistence off nature, and deviously cruel in warfare. The novel's one 'good' Indian, Wapke, wife of a warrior whom Sudden has had to kill in self-defence, rescues Roger from a standard form of tortune – being flayed alive by a group of giggling squaws. As is her tribal right, she takes him for her husband,

but for most of the ensuing (unconsummated) marriage she wears a repulsive mask of mud and ashes over a shapeless caribou-hide smock.
Her mourning rites over, she reveals herself to Roger as a 'bronze pixie
... young and slender ... with rounded hips and plump thighs and a
pair of breasts .. pink-nippled and erect' (RS 164). He recoils from her in
fascinated disgust. To 'mate' with this 'splendid animal at his feet' and
produce 'hybrid things, half beast and half himself' would be to 'plunge
into darkness from which there was no return' (RS 166).

Roger evades Wapke's seductions and escapes to civilization only to
be rescued by her just after he has betrayed the French at Louisbourg.
Wapke, a mere four years later, looks twenty years older, so violently as
her brutish husband, Koap, treated her. Koap, the greatest warrior
and ackowledged leader of the tribe, challenges the badly wounded
Roger to the Micmac's murderous equivalent of wrestling. Calling on
his acquaintance with sophisticated European wrestling techniques,
Sudden manages to break Koap's neck, winning both the game and
the good opinion of the tribe. He is thus in a position to team up with the
exemplary priest, Père Maillard, who persuades the Micmacs to re-
nege on their alliance with the French and to return to their old haunts
in peace, never more to harass English soldiers or settlers. As if to
clinch the argument, Wapke murders the defeated Koap, the one Micmac
whose devotion to the war against the English would have thwarted
Maillard's and Sudden's peacemaking. Almost the last word on the Micmacs is uttered by Père Maillard, and it has a dangerously proleptic
ring: 'I have long cherished a notion to prepare an account of these
people, so the world may know something of them' (RS 318) – before
they vanish, we are tempted to add.

'Cajuns ... are varmints same as Injuns,' remarks one of the minor but
respected characters of *Roger Sudden*; 'they've got to be rooted out
same as Injuns afore there can ever be peace and plenty for the English
in Nova Scotia' (RS 110). Raddall portrays both races as doomed and
has Sudden, ever the hard-headed man of business, exploit them in his
pursuit of wealth beyond measure or censure. Using the knowledge
of the Micmac tongue and customs he had been forced to amass during
his captivity, Sudden sets up trading posts in the Nova Scotia interior,
exchanging the usual cheap trinkets for valuable goods supplied by the
Indians. Similarly, having foreknowledge of the imminent fate of the
'avaricious' Acadians (RS 192) he manages to round up their cattle, abandoned during the expulsion, and – an irony he relishes – to sell the
meat at extortionate prices to English authorities desperate to feed their
troops.

As if to deliberately demolish Longfellow's Acadie-Eden, Raddall has Roger visit an Acadian farm on the eve of the Deportation, with a view to warning its inhabitants of the impending disaster: 'It was a typical Acadian farm ... a few staked fields in the wild meadows, a miserable cabin of logs (overflowing with children, dogs, fowls, and lean pigs), a crazy barn, and one or two outhouses. The people were small and lean and sharp of feature, living in a sort of dour content with themselves and at odds with the rest of the world. The women were shapeless in homespun, none too clean ... and the men ... were satisfied to till a small part of the tide meadows ... [being] in general too indolent to clear the rich soil of the upland' (RS 223).

Too lazy to embrace the hardy British style of pioneering, too greedy to preserve their neutrality by refusing the immense profits to be made off trade with Québec and Louisbourg, the 'poor stupid Acadians' (RS 246) are victims of the 'half-savage outlook' which intimate relations (sexual and otherwise) with the Indians have given them (RS 223–4). Roger's premonitory talk with Martin Muise touches on Acadian complicity with the French – the perennial harbouring of French expeditions against Annapolis, the supplying of provisions and guides to the ill-fated D'Anville in 1747, the defending of Fort Beauséjour against the English, the scalping of English settlers in the immediate vicinity of Halifax – and provides the rationale for the deportation scenes soon to follow. As does Roberts in *A Sister to Evangeline,* so Raddall in *Roger Sudden* dwells on the humane instincts and soldierly discipline of Colonel Winslow, 'on whom the greatest burden fell' (RS 227). He inverts the conventional expulsion pathos by detailing the suffering Winslow undergoes, all for the sake of 'stupid and stubborn' peasants who, 'if the shoe were on the other foot, [would] shoot [the British] down like dogs – or rather get the Indians to do it' (RS 228). Instead of compassion for the wailing deportees, Roger experiences a *frisson* at the 'uncanny quality' of the events – uncanny in that all has come to pass as he, Sudden, has foreseen it would.

The entire episode reads like the acting out of an imperative – to make an 'honest search' into the causes of the expulsion and to stab the authorial pen 'where the guilt lay most' (RS 229). Yet Raddall's last reference to the Acadians reads like a Freudian slip. One of the decorations in Sudden's Halifax mansion is a 'painted plaster figure of St Joseph from the ravished Acadian chapel at Grand Pré' (RS 251) – a poignant quotation from one of history's less estimable chapters. Raddall does not seem unduly embarrassed by the fact that New Englanders quickly took over the 'vacated' Acadian lands, nor that some of the deportees were made to perform what was virtually slave labour for these new landowners. For all that he is incomparably more ambitious, scholarly, and sophisticated a historical romancer than was Charles G.D. Roberts, Raddall possesses a naïveté Roberts never bothered to display in his narratives – the faith that in diaries, archives, textbooks, the Truth of History, inviolate against any ideological intent, lies waiting to be wed, word for word, to the honest fictions of the novelist.

\*\*\*

I love the Indian. Ere the white-man came
And taught him vice, and infamy, and shame,
His soul was noble. In the sun he saw
His God, and worshipped him with trembling awe; –
Though rude his life, his bosom never beat
With polished vices, or with dark deceit[46]

Douglas S. Huyghue's *Argimou: A Legend of the Micmac* (1847) is a self-defensively schizophrenic text: in the heyday of British imperialism it dared to declare a moral and aesthetic parity between the Micmac and English races, and to accuse the latter of virtual genocide against native peoples. Thus on the one hand, *Argimou* is the romantic account of a young English officer, Edward Molesworth, who, accompanied by his Irish servant Dennis, goes off into the New Brunswick wilderness to rescue his fiancée, Clarence. She has been kidnapped by a band of marauding 'Milicete' Indians as a prize for their thoroughly vicious chief. On another, much more compelling hand, *Argimou* is the story of the friendship which develops between Edward and Argimou, a Micmac chief whose own love, Waswetchcul, has also been carried off by the Milicetes for an equally horrid purpose. And in the interstices of these joined plots of love and friendship, another text is woven – that of the Micmac ethos as presented through legend, song, and poetry, and of its destruction by the combined ignorance and ill will of the English.

As Gwendolyn Davies points out in her introduction to *Argimou*, Huyghue's narrative is revolutionary in a number of ways. The first-hand knowledge Huyghue acquired of Indian life inspired him to sympathize with rather than recoil from or trivialize the Micmac cause: 'While other "Maritime" novelists ... work Indians into their narratives as exotic set-pieces, Huyghue makes his fiction a vehicle for prodding the New Brunswick conscience about the fate of the Micmac and the Malecite. He feels strongly that the European quest for "progress" has left a broken, deracinated people in its wake' (A iv). Moreover, Huyghue inverts the conventions of the captivity tale – in which a kidnapped white tells the brutal story of savage life – to make it a 'defence of the Indian instead of a denunciation of him' (A vi). What emerges is a relativistic analysis of two equal but opposite cultures, European and Indian – a venture staggeringly ahead of its time, as the wholly conventional 'captivity tale' embedded in *Roger Sudden* reveals.

As historical fiction, *Argimou* employs a much more complicated time scheme than either *A Sister to Evangeline* or *Roger Sudden*. The narrator addresses his gentle reader in a very mid-Victorian present, but though his Clarence and Edward may be prisoners of the pantalette and frock coat period, Argimou and Waswetchcul hark back to an earlier romantic era more consistent with the wild sublimity of the landscape and the cult of the noble savage that the text sets forth.[47] Huyghue's narrative unfolds within a carefully constructed historical frame, incorporating events such as the French / Indian raid on Beauséjour, the expulsion of the Acadians, and the final peace treaty signed between the English and the historical Argimault. Huyghue uses historical fact – the ultimate victory of the English over the French in North America – both to provide a happy ending to Clarence's and Edward's trials, and to seal the tragic end of that harmonious co-existence between European and Indian in what had been 'Acadie.' The narrative is 'infiltrated' by yet another temporal mode, the legendary as opposed to the historical, evoked through the presence of such characters as Toneas, the dying Sachem of the Micmacs, and Pansaway, Argimou's admirable father. This legendary past underscores Huyghue's claims for the Micmac as an ancient, noble race to whose present degradation our immediate attention must be paid.

The temporal complexity of *Argimou* is matched by equally complex verbal structures. The text boasts an ear-boggling excess of stilted speech on the 'Verily, it were well I go not distracted with delight' (A 166) variety, beside which Roberts's use of archaic diction seems positively clipped and spare. It is tempting to speculate that the turgid rhetoric employed by and about Huyghue's 'pure-minded' hero and his 'angel face' fiancée (whose beauty bespeaks 'a clime where bright and fadeless forms are gliding in an atmosphere of love and happiness' (A 31–2) might be self-parodic, a deliberate foil for the vigorous speech and actions of the Indian lovers. Certainly the narrative sags or bloats whenever any scene is given over to exclusively European points of view – with the exception of the comic relief afforded by Dennis who, in his stage-Irishisms, appears much more akin to the savage Milicetes than to his civilized master.[48] By contrast, Huyghue allows his Micmac characters a poetic idiom, self-consciously elevated and picturesque to be sure, but given a measure of authenticity by the considerable number of Micmac words Huyghue includes. Where Roberts sprinkles his narratives with the occasional 'tiens' or 'vraiment' to remind us that his characters are, after all, Francophone, Huyghue uses Micmac dialect to insist on the distinctiveness and integrity of the Micmac vision of the world. And the poetry of Pansaway's or Waswetchcul's speech – a function, Huyghue reminds us, of the Micmac skill at oratory and predilection for metaphor (A 94) – is complemented by that silent 'language of nature' which, for the Indian, is imprinted in 'the moss on the trees, the peculiar inclination of certain plants' – and which guides them on their journeys just as 'star and compass ... [do] the voyager on the pathless ocean ... ' (A 59).

If *Argimou* is surprisingly pluralist in its temporal and rhetorical structures, it is resolutely subversive in what it does to the genre of historical fiction. For opposed to the romance it details between Clarence and Edward, Argimou and Waswetchcul, and to the history it relates of French, English, and Indian relations in the mid-eighteenth-century Maritimes, is what à la Maillet, we might term the simple 'story' of a people for whom not written texts but the exercise and preservation of collective memory is the key to survival as a distinctive race. This 'story' spirals through the other narratives of *Argimou* so that a sense of Micmac culture and destiny vividly emerges. Thus Huyghue manipulates his narratives so that occasion may be found for Pansaway to tell Argimou the history of relations between the various Indian tribes of North America from the time when the 'great Mambertou ... bashaba of the Micmacs' made friends with the Wennocch (French), to the disruptive coming of the Anglasheou (English). This narrative is reinforced by one which, when related to Edward Molesworth, greatly disturbs the Englishman – it is the story of the rise and fall of both the ancient Ouagundy Indians *and* their white conquerors, presumably Vikings – who are destroyed by the forces of marauding 'civilization' and of omnipotent nature, respectively. Huyghue stresses the importance of both stories and 'traditions handed down by [the Indians'] fathers, from the earliest times' and which have been 'perpetuated with wonderful fidelity, by oral transmission alone' (A 94). In this context the mournful song Waswetchcul chants about the Indian maiden who loses both her lover and her memory becomes especially resonant. And finally, encoded in the narrative of *Argimou* are laments and prophecies which the reader, too, must remember in order to fully read one of the novel's subtexts – for example, the last words of the dying Toneas to Argimou:

'The red man must depart ... there are foot-prints on the graves of our fathers. Children of the Micmac, break the bow, bury the hatchet, for I tell you that you have *no* country! *The White Gull has flown over all*' (A 72). The prophecy is, in fact, fulfilled in the book's final chapters, as Argimou, in the name of all the Micmacs, buries the hatchet with the British and then collapses on the graves of his wife and infant son, victims of the pestilential disease which has been one of the gifts brought by the White Gull-English. By the end of Huyghue's novel the Indians have been driven from their ancestral territories by the English advance which Raddall was to celebrate some hundred years later in *Roger Sudden*.

Pervasive and significant as is the memorial, elegiac tone in *Argimou*, it is offset by the fiction's use of the present tense to develop another, more subversive subtext – that of the relativity of cultural values and norms. Here again language plays a key role, with Huyghue going to great lengths to prevent at least the English language from assuming complete hegemony. Once Edward and Argimou leave Fort Beauséjour, where Argimou has been held prisoner, and once they are well and truly embarked on their quest for Clarence and Waswetchcul, Huyghue has 'rude forest child' and 'polished ... stranger' converse in a tongue native to neither – Acadian French (A 82). What is more, by the journey's end Edward has 'unconsciously adopt [ed] the style of the natives' in speaking patois with Pansaway, just as he has adopted the Micmac way of dress (A 144). As if this linguistic surrender were not enough, Huyghue bends over backwards to show Edward at a disadvantage in the forest primeval – he cannot keep up with the vigorous pace the Indians set and, worst of all, he falls prey to fits of lachrymose despair which the stoical Micmacs regard with a mixture of amazed aversion and pity. Most telling of all, when the kidnapped maidens are finally rescued and reunited with their lovers, all Edward can do is to paternally fold the weeping, prayerful Clarence to his chest, while Waswetchcul and Argimou make unabashed, if metaphorical love.[49]

Huyghue's exposé of English justice, fair play, and general superiority is carried out in a variety of ways. He fulminates against the 'cruelty and injustice' of the English, who are the 'sole and only cause of [the Micmacs'] overwhelming misery, their gradual extinction' (A 173, 2). Later, he has the Micmacs innocently repeat the French priests' interpretation of England's imperial ambitions – the Anglasheou, having crucified Christ, are compelled to wander forever to the ends of the earth. And near the novel's close he resorts to broad humour, as Micmacs and English board an English frigate – 'the most beautiful creation of man' (A 166). Asked by Dickson, a pompous, condescending army surgeon, what he thinks of 'the surprising products of art and science that surround him' (A 168), Pansaway replies that one of those products – the cannon – is a much better doctor than his interrogator could ever be. Pressed to explain his comments, Pansaway states that while Dickson's medicines might easily fail his patients, anyone who received a cannon ball will 'never be sick no time anymore' (A 169).

Finally, Huyghue's *Argimou* shows itself capable of exploiting and confounding one of the principal conventions of historical romance – the harmonious integration of opposing sides by means of marriage or at least sexual union between representative 'enemies.' In *Argimou*, Edward sticks to his Clarence and Argimou to his Waswetchcul, though both men are appreciative of each woman's kind of beauty. By extension, the Micmac couple is made to refuse Edward's offer of a home for them in England, on the Molesworth estate. Significantly, the alternative possibility of Edward and Clarence casting off the 'starched petrifications' of civilized society (A 140) for the pleasant virtues of the 'green forest shade' (A 173) is not even mentioned, not because the English couple fears, like Roger Sudden, the regressive darkness of 'savage' life, but rather because they have shown themselves to be entirely inept for any kind of life-in-nature. And the dichotomy revealed in the farewells and ultimate parting of ways between English and Micmac couples is structurally reinforced by the fiction's double ending – mutedly happy for Clarence and Edward, unreservedly tragic for their Micmac counterparts. Like an earlier Fowles, Huyghue draws attention to the bifurcation of his narrative, distinguishing in Chapter 21 between those readers 'impelled by the spirit of old romance,' who would like to stop the text at the happy ending, and those 'more prone to reflect upon the dark struggle of man, for all he holds most sacred upon the earth – the want and woe which result from human oppression ...' (A 174).

In the last chapters of *Argimou*, the claims of 'old romance' are overridden by the pressure of 'an irregular narrative of vicissitude and suffering' (A 174). In flagrant contrast to the opening chapter, in which Argimou is triumphantly chosen Grand Sachem of the Micmacs at a festive gathering of the Indian nations, the work's penultimate chapter has Argimou sadly, solemnly pledge allegiance to the British. And while the Indian keeps his word to the letter of the law, Huyghue shows how deliberately the English break theirs, corrupting the Micmacs with drink, killing them with disease, seizing and polluting their forest lands, and driving away the game on which their survival depends. *Argimou's* last chapter has its hero, now an aged and dejected man, deliver an elegy on the lost patrimony of the Indians before he expires on his wife's grave. The last words of the text are a completion of the verse with which the narrative began:

Peace to the red men that are gone!
Their children are the pale strangers' scoff;
The heritage of their Fathers is a mournful thought
The memory of their glory – a broken song!

***

Chez nous l'histoire fut d'abord et est encore en grande partie l'affaire des autres ... L'effarante ruine des cultures amérindiennes a moins frappé l'imagination et produit de culpabilité rétrospective que la déroute de ce petit peuple de race blanche qui symbolise depuis toujours l'irréducibilité instinctive et fondamentale à toute forme de simplification ... L'Acadie se présentait donc en archetype, version européenne, des peuples victimes de la colonisation conquérante, dont le redressement et la renaissance justifiaient après le coup les cruelles nécessités.

Michel Roy[50]

(For us history began as, and in a large part remains, other people's business ... The alarming ruin of the Amerindian cultures has less shocked the imagination and has produced less retrospective guilt than the rout of this small people of white race who have symbolized ever since an instinctive and fundamental irreducibility to all manner of simplification ... Thus Acadie has appeared as an archetype à l'Européenne of the victimized people of conquering colonialism, a people whose recovery and renaissance have, after the fact, come to justify cruel necessity.)

If *Argimou*'s depiction of the utter ruin of the Micmac culture provides a small exception to Michel Roy's rule, then it also supports his thesis as to the irresistible attraction of the 'Acadian archetype' for Anglophone writers. Huyghue writes with special sympathy of the Acadians because of the 'singular ease and tact' with which they 'assimilated themselves in feeling and custom to the powerful nations that held a right ... to the wilderness regions' (A 21). The peaceful co-existence – even integration – of Acadians and Indians which, as we have seen, so repulsed the Anglophile Roger Sudden, becomes for Huyghue a singular achievement of fraternity between two wildly different races. He scripts an apology of sorts for the failure of Acadian neutrality in the eighteenth century, speculating that secret, hostile acts were perpetrated by the Acadians against the English because of the latter's 'narrow policy pursued towards a subjugated people' (A 20). And when the *coup* comes, Huyghue shows the solidarity which persists between Indian and Acadian by having Argimou delay the rescue of Waswetchcul and Clarence in order to reassure the 'few scattered remnants of the proscribed Acadians' who have sought 'asylum in [the] almost impervious solitudes of the New Brunswick woods' (A 21). The Micmacs, he promises the Acadians, will 'assist in erecting huts for their shelter and bring them game for food' (A 76). There is a special pathos in the encouragement Argimou gives, for as Huyghue makes clear, Acadians and Indians alike are 'two very distinct but equally doomed races' (A 21).

It is a conclusion which Antonine Maillet buoyantly rejects in *Pélagie*, which can perhaps best be described as an anti-historical novel, an attempt to turn 'History' – the property of a *parti pris* of statisticians bent on preserving the status quo – into 'her story' – the infinitely malleable dough of visionaries, story-tellers, and defiantly matriarchal epic heroes. The displaced survivors of the expulsion of 1755 whom she rescues from the exile of silence are a people without a country or a history of their own: what *Pélagie* sets out to do is to make up both losses. For the old Acadie, the golden world irretrievably gone, a new Acadie inspired by the memory of the old is substituted; as for the history which the illiterate deportees are incapable of writing or reading, an 'oral patrimony'[51] takes its place, stories of ancestors both literal and literary passed from 'mouth to ear,' parent to child, down generations sprung 'from a people of storytellers and chroniclers who had produced Gargantua and his noble son Pantagruel ...' (P 140). The woman whom Maillet chooses as instrument for this mission is both archetypal Acadienne, an anti-Evangeline, and also a representative Nova Scotian, if we may call Ernest Buckler's definition of his people into play – those who 'bend to life's prime hardships as they come, but bow to nothing ... Not to plans turned to ash. Not to the death of family or friends. Not to their own death itself.'[52]

In the most basic sense, *Pélagie* is what it defines itself to be – a 'dialectic between life and death' (P 110) which involves the destinies of unique individuals, of an entire group of homeward-trudging deportees, and of the race itself, which will need to practise the revenge of the cradle just to keep itself from dying out once it returns from exile. But the novel is also a dialectic between history and story – or what we can most comprehensively term romance in its most compendious sense –

that country of the marvelous and uncommon which in *Pélagie* includes myth, white magic, the supernatural, and, of course, a pair of lovers who are both agents and adversaries of destiny itself. What emerges from the synthesis Maillet achieves is a concept of the future and of a country shaped by imagination and volition, acknowledging brutal fact and the potential of human beings to transform, subvert, exploit, or subjugate fact. If the hero of Raddall's *Roger Sudden* is a man in quest of his soul, who, in the process of finding it, helps to fulfil his race's destiny – the conquest and possession of the North American continent – then the hero of *Pélagie* is a woman who sets for herself the task of giving back to 'bruised and amputated' Acadie 'its soul' (P 39, 42); of seizing 'an absurd and tottering future in her own two hands' (P 59) to create out of a raggle-taggle band of victims and survivors a people who will flourish and multiply in the very midst – and teeth – of those English whose authorities first deported them.

In the prologue to *Pélagie* the narrator begins her argument not only with 'that Bitch,' history (P 3), but also with those of history's interpreters who are revisionist and restrictive in spirit – for example, Pélagie-the-Grouch, a granddaughter of the first, historic Pélagie and who thus has a vested interest in tailoring history to the measure of her *amour-propre*. By taking the side of Pélagie-the-Grouch's antagonist, Louis-à-Bélonie, descended from that race of 'story-tellers and root-delvers' without whom 'History would have rolled over and died at the end of every century' (P 3), the narrator situates herself between history and story; she intervenes throughout the novel to keep the historical record straight or to point out its hopeless muddlement; to release the balloons of fantasy or to put their strings back firmly in the readers' hands. She also jumps back and forth between two temporal poles: that of the narrative proper, the ten years (1770–80) in which Pélagie's odyssey actually took place, and that of the 'hundred years in the woods' (1770-1880) at the end of which Pélagie-the-Grouch and old Louis-à-Bélonie are shown squabbling round the hearth, poised to break through silence into public speech and recorded history. The narrator's present tense interpolations – an altogether more radical affair than Roberts's or Raddall's mere flashes back or forwards – undo the convention of linear chronology on which the historical novel traditionally depends. They also gesture to the centrality of memory, without which both history and oral story-telling would be impossible.

Throughout *Pélagie*, memory acts as both tenor and vehicle: it is the memory of her dead at Grand Pré that keeps Pélagie's emotional compass pointed north, despite the suasions of Acadie-in-the-south, that

Eden of Louisiana to which some of Pélagie's people defect. At the novel's end it is the memory of Grand Pré as once it was, a golden world of freedom, peace, and plenty, as well as the reality of what it has become – 'an ancient cemetery ... an abandoned cradle' – which, Pélagie cautions her people, 'must be kept green in your hearts and blood' (P 241–2). The very ease and colloquial fluency of Maillet's complexly structured text make the narrative come across to the reader more as conversation than as print, more a product of expansive memory than of restrictive art, the words themselves, 'like the salmon remembering their spawning ground ... remount[ing] the current' of collective memory (P 77). And through the persona of the narrator, who is as much the reader's as she is both Pélagie's contemporary, Maillet is able to enact the maxim which could serve as motto for the historical novel as a genre: 'the place for the dead is in the memory of the living' (P 37).

As a historical novel, just what does *Pélagie* do to the established concept and content of that dubious archetype, the Expulsion of the Acadians? It aims to turn it inside out in a manner analogous to the Acadian march out of America – 'coming ... home through the arse end of a whale' (P 55). For most devotés of Longfellow, the Acadians' history begins and ends with the Deportation from Grand Pré in 1775. With *Pélagie* that event and date lose centrality, as Maillet insists that history be pried apart to accommodate not only the continuing survival of the Acadians as a distinctive people and of Acadie as a tangible entity post- and pre- 1755, but also the alternatives to mute and meek surrender with which non-Evangelinized Acadians responded to English aggression: hiding in the woods, seizing the very schooners carrying them off into exile and, most basic of all, verbal resistance. 'And shit to his English Majesty / Who declared his war on you and me!' (P 184) – this refrain sounds throughout the novel with all the violence of a shattered taboo. These fourteen words, more than any other, have the power to break the stranglehold of Longfellow's myth; it is as if the ghost of resistance (which, in the person of Basil Lajeunesse, Longfellow had clubbed into submission) were reanimated by electric shock. What Maillet does in *Pélagie* is to give Acadians – and all Canadians – their history back from the hands of those who, as Michel Roy implies, abused it for dubious purposes. By recording the brutality with which the Acadians were deported, their sufferings and losses on the long, hard haul back, Maillet makes it impossible for Anglophiles glibly to point to the miraculous survival and 'renaissance' of the Acadian people as justification *après coup* of the acts that made such a miracle necessary in the first place.

If Maillet delights in turning history arsey-versy, she exploits those conventions of romance which stick out their tongues at history's supposed sobriety and objective truthfulness. Pélagie's epic journey from Georgia to Grand Pré may be prompted by a visionary sense of duty and an exemplary fidelity to the past, but it is invigorated and in a large part made possible by the feats of the giant, P'tite Goule, and the sorceries of Pierre à Pitre, the fool. And her greatest inspiration, as an individual, not as a public hero, is the love of Beausoleil Broussard, the sea captain who is presented as a mix of the Flying Dutchman and Robin Hood. 'Together they would ... reverse the tide of History' (P 83) – or so the captain in his more romantic moments feels. Aided by old Bélonie, the nonagenarian story-teller who alone perceives the Wagon of Death at the heels of Pélagie's living cart, Beausoleil wrestles with destiny, keeping that cart and the hopes it comprehends from sinking without a trace in the Salem marshes. It is Beausoleil who, in the schooner he has schemed out of the hands of the English and magically transformed into a twenty-four-master, ferries Acadian deportees to the Gaspésie and to Louisiana.

Romance not only leavens the black bread of exile and wandering, but it also challenges the very authority of history. Where the historian vows to stick to the facts (in telling, as Maillet insists, what *he* wants to hear), the romancer juggles with those facts, producing countless variants and alternative versions of any one story, improvising, expanding, and accommodating myriad possibilities within her narrative in order to tell her listeners what *they* want to hear. Yet through all there is a regard for truth, not mere accuracy: the truth which is a product of remembered associations and processes, of a mythic core which stabilizes the story-teller's repertoire. In *Pélagie* this truth resides in the 'mythology of families and relationships' (P 80) which is the heritage of each deportee: the 'tree' of life and lineage (which come to mean the same thing for the Acadians) that has had its very roots torn up by the Expulsion (P 71).

Perhaps because of this all-important truth of the indestructible links between generations, of the claims the dead make on the living, Maillet carefully controls the romantic kicks and leaps of her narrative. Thus she has no truck with the conventional heroics so dear to a Charles G.D. Roberts: 'Everyone knows that Acadie was never equal to defending herself in equal combat since she was never on an equal footing with anyone. She managed just the same, like Pierre à Pitre, by brushing up on the gift of the gab and by learning that the way out of an impasse is sometimes by way of a cul-de-sac' (P 140).

As importantly, she forbids the final union of her two heroes, Pélagie and Beausoleil, allowing them, it would seem, a brief consummation of their passion on the night of Pélagie's daughter's wedding, but killing off Pélagie the day before she is to rendezvous with Beausoleil under the apple blossoms of Grand Pré. Thus Maillet prevents her 'stiff-necked, proud-browed widow' from becoming an Yvonne de Lamourie or worse still, an Evangeline twenty-years-on-from-Grand-Pré. Moreover, she knows that any long-term union between Pélagie and Beausoleil would not ring true, since both inhabit a country in which 'love songs are sung in a minor key and practically always in a whisper' (P 174).[53] Marriage in this novel is reserved for Pélagie's children – the fantastic union between Jean and his Iroquois princess, and the much more prosaic wedding between Pélagie's Madeleine and Charles-Auguste Landry.

In conceiving such a heroine as Pélagie, Maillet turns from the fairy-tale soil out of which she fashioned Beausoleil Broussard[54] to the Old Testament. For Pélagie LeBlanc is a latter-day Moses, who will 'wear her heart in splints' if need be, but will never stop marching north under the yoke of her chosen destiny (P 93). Again and again Pélagie puts the public good, the collective future ahead of private fulfilment – even that of actually living for a while in Acadie, new or old. For she is killed off on a marshland equivalent of Pisgah; it is her fate to lead her people and to suffer, but not to enjoy her labour's fruit.

Yet if she is a Moses, Pélagie is a defiantly feminist one, and this attitude does much to explode the conventions of 'vulgar' romance. Pélagie becomes the leader of more than thirty families heading back to old Acadie, not because of her golden hair and 'fairy fingers,' but because she has 'got the image of home in the gut' (P 80, 178). On her death it is not her son or son-in-law but her daughter who takes up the reins, leading the Acadians from the ruins of Grand Pré and into the woods to hide. For one of the repercussions of the splitting up of families during the deportation was, the narrator claims, that the 'batons of authority received in the Garden of Eden' perished in the woods or sea with the men who clutched them. 'As a result, the women had to face the enemy and adversity alone and wield the sceptre of the head of the family' (P 169). And so, Pélagie refuses to surrender her authority or role as leader to go aboard her lover's ship; similarly, Jeanne Aucoin acts as the 'moral chief of her clan' (P 177), while Célina, the club-footed midwife and healer, and Catoune, the 'wild child' whom Pélagie adopts, combine with the other women to take over the novel, making room only for the largely absent Beausoleil and the tottery Bélonie beside them.

Fittingly, the country which Pélagie almost single-handedly brings into being is formed in what has become her image – the ox cart she drives back to Acadie. The Grand Pré which has acted as her beacon – untouched by time, its houses aired, its barns stocked and granaries full to bursting – has been a necessary illusion, the goad which keeps the Acadians on so desperate a road home. Pélagie's guiding vision of an earthly paradise where a 'self-governing people' could live amid 'apple trees so loaded the branches are cracking at the joints' (P 76) is displaced, at the novel's end, by a new myth of a country 'patient, stubborn, wilful, vindictive against destiny, will set against history, ... advanc[ing] at an ox pace' (P 149–50). And as the novel's epilogue makes clear, the country which comes into being in the century after Pélagie's death fulfils even her visionary expectations: 'Like the wheel of a cart, like the helm of a ship, the new Acadie had spread the spokes of its compass points to the four corners of the country, without knowing it. Playing blindman's buff with Destiny, Acadie had, in the long run, reopened all its fields and replanted roots everywhere' (P 250).

Thus it would appear that Maillet's *Pélagie*, more than any other work discussed in this chapter, most closely resembles such fictions as Rudy Wiebe's *Temptations of Big Bear* or Robert Kroetsch's *The Studhorse Man* which, according to George Woodcock, may be helping to create 'a genuine Canadian twentieth-century romanticism, which must use fantasy and dream as paths to reality, which must accept myth as the structure that subsumes history ...' and, in the process, 'break time down into the non-linear patterns of authentic memory ...'[55] Yet as I have attempted to show, Maillet's text does not simply subsume history under myth, but also creates a dialectic between history and story / romance, between fact and dream, which refuses to grant victory to either side and indeed, develops a critique of both approaches to reality. The synthesis which Maillet's novel achieves is remarkable both for its complexity and its integrity. Unlike Warren Tallman, who opposed history to life and asserted that not to 'care' about history is finally to begin fully to live,[56] Maillet uses *Pélagie* to show us the necessity of remembering our past, including its horrors and terrors. Not to care about history is not to care about, for example, the gratuitously vicious manner in which the Acadians of Cape Sable were deported in 1756 (P 108) or how, in the emptied settlements of old Acadie, 'just for fun, the English soldiers had left open the cellars of families in flight to let their stores freeze or rot; how furniture, tools, even family books had been confiscated to prevent the Acadians' descendants from tracing and recognizing each other; how Acadians had been used for target practice during military exercises by new recruits from the American Loyalists' (P 233).

Whether or not one chooses to treat such accounts as 'story' or 'history,' one must recognize the irreducibly unromantic fact that, as *Pélagie* insists, English hostility to the Acadians persisted during the hundred years after the deportation and, as current language disputes in New Brunswick show, continues well into our own century. To allow history to be subsumed by myth, as Woodcock so blithely advises, is to run the risk of simplifying, folklorizing, or forgetting integral aspects of identity.[57] As Michel Roy warns of the project of neo-romanticism vis-à-vis Acadian history:

Déjà la création ... d'une mythologie parallèlle accroît le mirage et réduit infiniment le degré de notre emprise sur le réel. L'effort de mise en train d'une mythologie est sans doute nécessaire. Mais en ce domaine rien n'est moins pardonnable que la complaisance et la facilité.[58]

(Already the creation of a parallel mythology increases the mirage and infinitely reduces the degree of our hold on the real. No doubt it is necessary to create mythologies. But in this context nothing is less pardonable than complacency and facileness.)

\*\*\*

Perhaps it is a definitively Maritime trait to be preoccupied with the past, to feel, as Alden Nowlan did, a sense of 'enigmatical yet indisputable' connection with the heroes of the region's Golden Age,[59] whether those heroes have to do with the cause of the doomed French and Micmac or that of the victorious English; with ships and the sea, or with ox carts bearing a stiff-necked people back from exile. In their roles as writers of historical fiction, Roberts, Maillet, Raddall, and Huyghue have been engaged in restoring to us a part of our national memory, whatever our home region may be. In their practice as fiction writers they have actively reinterpreted, displaced, or challenged our concepts of the past, thus altering our sense of the present and shaping our perspectives on the future. Yet, as George Grant insists, 'a nation does not remain a nation only because it has roots in the past. Memory is never enough to guarantee that a nation can articulate itself in the present. There must be a thrust of intention into the future.'[60] To discover something of that 'thrust of intention' we must now turn our attention from historical to political fiction.

# 5

# Politics and Fictions

The tradition of Maritime conservatism is ... formidable to challenge. Contemporaries from outside the region have frequently attested to its existence. Scholars whose own memories date back to the 1930s affirm it unequivocally. Until recent years students of such progressive trends as the social gospel or radical politics, apparently unable to conceive of such phenomena in the 'conservative' Maritimes, have virtually omitted that region from their studies. The term conservative implies a comparison, but few scholars applying the term to the Maritimes have actually compared this region with others in any direct or explicit fashion.

ERNEST FORBES[1]

the Maritimes have a great heritage of history, more than three centuries of romantic and utilitarian endeavour as inspiring as it is interesting. The value of this heritage has too long been diminished by a tendency to concentrate upon romantic episodes to the neglect of the great social, economic and political experiments that have been made in these provinces.

D.C. HARVEY[2]

Both Ernest Forbes and D.C. Harvey point to a process of misrepresentation of what we might call political sensibility in the Maritimes – consciousness of the nature and workings of power and powerlessness; of the conflicts that form and transform a society. The 'prevailing stereotype of all-pervasive Maritime conservatism'[3] has led to a conceptual deformation, not only of the region's history, but also of its literature. Thus, radical departures from the literary norm – James De Mille's *A Strange Manuscript Found in a Copper Cylinder* or such a tour de farce as Ray Smith's 'Cape Breton Is the Thought Control Centre of Canada' – are often perceived as aberrations of the literary cottage industry that has produced such sweet-and-light Maritime works as L.M. Montgomery's *Anne of Green Gables*, Charles G.D. Roberts's *The Heart of the Ancient Wood*, and Ernest Buckler's *Whirligig*. Even the emergence of such a writer as David Adams Richards may be seen as *vieux jeu* – a regionalized throwback to nineteenth-century French naturalism. This chapter will attempt to test the validity of the conservative stereotype by looking briefly at the historical hinterland from which literary expressions of political sensibility emerge, and by examining that sensibility at work in fiction by three significant Maritime writers: James De Mille, Hugh MacLennan, and Silver Donald Cameron.

\*\*\*

The case for Maritime conservatism may well seem an incontrovertible one. The Burkean political philosophy of T.C. Haliburton is as integral a part of *The Clockmaker* as are the solecisms of Sam Slick. Haliburton's cleaving to an anachronistic, eighteeenth-century school of Toryism in the Age of Progress is as well-known a fact as Joseph Howe's buoyantly liberal and reformist politics. Yet according to Howe scholars, the Voice of Nova Scotia was raised for moderate rather than radical reform since, throughout his career, the conservatism he inherited from his Loyalist father tended to constrict his political views.[4] Moreover, Howe has generally come to be associated with a back-to-the-womb anti-Confederationism, and with a fawning colonial mentality utterly opposed to the progressive nationalism that supposedly inspired the concept of Canada.[5] And if the Loyalist backgrounds of Howe and Haliburton are of unquestionable importance in the fostering of their conservative tendencies, then this should be equally the case with a writer like Charles G.D. Roberts, who spent a great deal of his formative years in Fredericton, that bastion of ingrown conservatism and recessive gentility, founded by Loyalists aiming to create 'a well-appointed, graded society of gentry whose eminence [would be] based on the ownership of land, supported by a disciplined yeomanry.'[6] A.G. Bailey has argued that whereas the works of Haliburton and Howe are often direct responses to political challenges in Nova Scotia, the writings of Carman and Roberts express 'a crisis of the spirit after the political battle was lost, and something of the world along with it.'[7] The result was a turning away of both writers from the social to the natural worlds, from cityscape to landscape just as Canada was inexorably on its way to becoming a nation of city-dwellers. Having mentioned *Barometer Rising*, it seems apposite to remark that MacLennan is Roberts's true heir, both as the Maritimer-Who-Made-Good-Away and as a father figure for Canadian letters. With such writers as Haliburton, Roberts, and MacLennan as the Grand Old Men of Maritime literature it is perhaps inevitable that conservatism rather than radicalism, or even liberalism, should come to be regarded as the indelible dye of the Maritime ethos.

What may be the most common preconception about the Maritimes – that it is a has-been region which never quite died the decent death it deserved after Confederation came its way – is enshrined in *Barometer Rising*. MacLennan's 1941 depiction of a moribund 'rum and molasses' aristocracy, as represented by Colonel Wain and his siblings, can be related to the élite (whether family compact or mercantile oligarchy) described in D.C. Harvey's 1934 essay 'The Heritage of the Maritimes.' 'Organized society as transmitted to Maritimers of today dates from the eighteenth century, and in its origins naturally embodied the class distinctions of that period.'[8] In its origins *and* its latest manifestations, Silver Donald Cameron would argue. He points to the east coast provinces as having become, over the generations, 'the most class-structured part of English Canada,' and describes the 'control of Nova Scotia represented by the élite of the Halifax Club and the Royal Nova Scotia Yacht Squadron' as 'scarcely credible.'[9]

Economically, the Maritimes is best known as a producer of staples: nothing could be further from the microchip and Canadarm than the fish, timber and coal, the apples and potatoes the region exports. If the Maritimes' wealthy are fairly discreet, as Cameron suggests, then its poor are visibly plentiful and, according to Bruce Hutchison, docile: 'proud poverty,' he remarks, 'is accepted [here] not as a hardship but as the normal way of life.'[10] Andrew Macphail somewhat complacently described late nineteenth-century Prince Edward Island as 'the last refuge of the feudal system' (TMW 156); there are no longer any serfs in the Maritimes (though there were pauper slaves up until 1898),[11] but the working class populations of Halifax-Dartmouth and Saint John, and workers in isolated pulp, steel, and coal towns are not known for their militancy: MacLennan's *Each Man's Son* (1951) shows the miners as more preoccupied with Calvinism than Communism. And as for attitudes to class struggle, the words Charles G.D. Roberts puts into the mouth of a stalwart Tantramar boy who witnesses a dockers' strike in Barcelona may seem paradigmatic: 'Strikes were unneeded and unknown in Westcock, and Jim could not see what they were good for under any circumstances.'[12]

Finally, there is the Maritimes' presumed nostalgia for its colonial past, and that small-minded disgruntlement with Confederation which has led the region to be compared to 'a housewife who, having married for money which failed to materialize, neglected her housework, "went down to the seashore ... watched the ships go by and pouted".'[13] As Ernest Forbes and David Alexander, among others, have shown, Maritime hostility to the consequences of Confederation has been matched by the resentment of richer regions at having continually to bail out the foundering ship of the Maritime economy. Accordingly, Maritime conservatism has become conflated with notions of patriotic backsliding, with economic ineptitude and inertia.[14]

These, then, are a few of the factors instrumental in sustaining the stereotype of calcified Maritimes conservatism. And yet, there are a host of elements – cultural, social, economic, political – which complicate or even explode the stereotype. If one looks behind the ranks of frock-coated, tweed-jacketed Old Men of Maritime Literature, one finds traces of a lively subculture to which the canon – those Maritime books still in print – does little justice. For as Harvey's seminal essay on the 'great awakening' of Maritime colonial society makes clear, culture was seen as an affair not of the capitals and their élite but of the literate populace – hence the profusion of journals and newspapers disseminating throughout the colony the literature not only of Britain and America but of the Maritimes as well.[15] Folk poetry, engendered by the desire to 'caricature, satirize and ridicule' flourished in this kind of society.[16] Laurence Doyle was moved to do more than ridicule – his 'Prince Edward Isle Adieu' excoriates 'the knaves who made us slaves / And sold Prince Edward Isle.' Labourer-poets such as John McPherson (1817–45) or the self-educated radical Moses Hardy Nickerson (1846–1943) produced mortal verse indeed – but so did most of their social 'betters.' The New Brunswick lumber camps harboured balladeers such as Michael Whelan, Larry Gorman, and Hedley Parker, maintaining a thriving oral tradition in a 'free, adventurous, irreverent spirit.'[17] This subculture produced a 'literature of protest' in the sense that it expressed the experience of have-nots or have-littles, and points of view neglected by and often subversive of 'official' and 'established' writers.

Yet even texts produced by the Grand Old Men – *The Old Judge*, *The Stepsure Letters*, the *Western and Eastern Rambles* – take social, economic, and political issues as their proper narrative meat. When Robert McDougall lamented the 'abnormal absence [in Canadian literature] of feeling for class, and of concern for what the class structure can do in a developing society to make or mar the life of the individual,'[18] he failed to do justice to colonial Maritime literature. Thomas McCulloch, for example, shows a lively awareness of the claims of the rude cottage hearth as opposed to those of the polite drawing room; Haliburton and Howe at least distinguished between a leisure and a working class, between the gentry, the mercantile middle class, and the industrious, homespun farmer. Many chapters of *The Old Judge* are positive schools for class-consciousness, teaching the necessity of respecting and remaining within the class into which one was born.

Turning from literature to history, one can make a case that ferment rather than docility marked the political mood of the colonial Maritimes. Stanley Ryerson suggests that, though after 1807 the governments of the region enacted strongly repressive measures against reform movements, popular discontent still found ways to manifest itself, with citizens 'harboring fugitives from the naval press gang or from the army, and indulging with more than customary gusto in smuggling activities'[19] – acts of 'civil disobedience' which figure prominently in Thomas Raddall's short fiction. The discontented tenantry of Prince Edward Island were represented by an Escheat partly pledged to the expropriation of absentee landlords – and doomed to failure by the intransigence of the British government on the matter. There is, Milton Acorn insists in *The Island Means Minago*, a nearly invisible, unmentionable history of grassroots radicalism in the supposedly placid Garden of the Gulf. Thus incidents such as those which took place in 1843, when the Scottish tenants of Lot 45 'forcefully reinstated a dispossessed tenant on his farm and destroyed by fire the home of the landlord's agent,' necessitating calling in troops from Charlottetown to restore 'order,' can be perceived if not as regular, then as unexceptional occurrences.[20] Prince Edward Island, with its hidden history of tenant agitation and the strength of its co-operative movement, provides good evidence of the vitality of those 'great social, economic, and political experiments' Harvey saw as integral to the heritage of the Maritimes.

Where Nova Scotia had a Joseph Howe pressing for Mechanics' Institutes and Agricultural Societies, and a Moses Coady establishing the Co-operative Movement; where Prince Edward Island had a James Palmer to represent the interests of its tenant farmers in the legislature and an Edward Whelan, a protégé of Howe, to publicize comparatively radical viewpoints in his newspaper, New Brunswick had a James Glenie as an early champion of settlers' rights. He advocated, for example, the provision of parish schools for settlers' children before the establishment of any college for the sons of New Brunswick's ruling élite. Moreover, the development of a boisterous timber trade and the brief upsurge of manufacturing in that colony made for the development of 'lower orders' worlds away from the forelock-tugging 'yeomanry' desired by the Loyalists and their descendants. Of this fact Charles G.D. Roberts must have been well aware, given his depiction of human 'forest folk' – the sturdily independent, if often sentimentalized, backwoods men and women who are themselves the ancestors of the dispossessed and disillusioned characters to be found in Nowlan's and Richard's fiction.

Finally, accusations that anti-Confederation sentiment in the Maritimes is nothing more than a maundering on about how much better things were in the Golden Age of Wooden Ships and Iron Men have been admirably exploded by a number of recent studies, notably David Alexander's essays on Atlantic Canada and Confederation. Alexander adopts an aggressive rather than defensive stance, arguing that it is the policies of the federal government that are anachronistic and spineless, and not the people of the Maritimes. He further observes that in comparison with the Prairies, British Columbia, Quebec, and Ontario, Atlantic Canada has been the 'Cinderella' of Confederation and Macdonald's National Policy:

[Atlantic Canada] is the only region which secured no economic benefits (in the economist's sense) from Confederation. The nature of its economic base – ocean resources and derived maritime activities – required the energies and services of a national state with a genuinely international orientation. This is precisely what Upper Canada is not and never has been ... With an overseas trade amounting to less than 6 per cent of the GNP and in fabricated products less than 3 per cent, it is safe to say that Canada is no international trader to turn hair grey in Hamburg or Tokyo. For eastern Canada, where land resources and location discouraged replication of the Ontario / Quebec pattern, and where ocean resources required a national government with a real international focus, Confederation amounted to a disaster.[21]

Ernest Forbes, in his account of the Maritime Rights Movement, presents a portrait of Maritimers forcefully articulating and demanding their rights within Confederation. Though he shows how this 'once ... optimistic movement for progressive reform terminated in a mood of cynicism and apathy' (largely due to Mackenzie King's having opportunistically turned 'a program for Maritime economic rehabilitation ... into a

program for political pacification')[22] Forbes does manage to banish the
Bluenose bogey begot by Haliburton's portrayal of Nova Scotians as
lacking spirit, enterprise, and patriotism – sitting as stupidly as a bear in
winter 'everlastingly a suckin' of [his] paws to keep 'em warm.'[23]
Forbes shows how Maritimers fought back throughout the 1920s against
representations of them in the media as backward-looking boobies
who, rather than helping themselves, preferred 'to sit on the country
store steps and chew apples and talk politics.'[24] With his careful analysis of the region's complex economic problems, his illumination of the
federal government's vagaries concerning tariffs and freight rates and
Maritime representation in the Cabinet and Commons, and with his
exhaustive detailing of the persistent efforts of farmers, labourers,
local politicians, and those gifted native sons whose quest for education
and economic betterment did not make exiles of them, Forbes creates
a composite portrait of active, forward-thinking Maritimers who demanded to return to the roots of Confederation to redress imbalances
and grievances afflicting their region.

The chequered nature of Maritime political sensibility, with its interweaving of radical (or at least progressive) and conservative philosophies has led to the development of a literary tradition in which one
finds radical conservatives like Haliburton cheek by jowl with moderate liberals like Howe, and such idiosyncratically opposed world views
as those maintained by Milton Acorn and Alden Nowlan.[25] The fiction
the Maritimes has produced reflects this chequering in the mixed genres
it favours; thus we have works like Rockbound, whose grindingly realistic portrayal of the fisherman's lot is interwoven with fairy-tale motifs,
or The Mountain and the Valley, in which an idyllic presentation of rural
life is continually thwarted not only by the tragic imperatives of 'the
human condition,' but also by the destruction wrought by rapid technological change. Indeed, the best Maritime fiction, whether predominantly 'realist' or 'idyllic,' is marked by a dual awareness of possibilities for productive change, enriching growth, and of the perception that,
as Alex Colville has remarked, change and progress often mean loss,
that 'a lot of things actually happen for the worse.'[26]

James De Mille's A Strange Manuscript Found in a Copper Cylinder, Hugh
MacLennan's Barometer Rising and Each Man's Son, and Silver Donald
Cameron's The Education of Everett Richardson, the four works on which
this chapter will focus, are as varied and problematic a set of texts as
one could wish to find; though certainly not representative of the mass
of Maritime fiction, they do illustrate certain key aspects of the sensibility that has formed and deformed that fiction. To play these texts off

one another in this context – De Mille's fantasy, MacLennan's mythopoeic novels, Cameron's 'new journalism,' with its links to the topical,
'engaged' narratives of Howe and Haliburton – will be to follow the
theoretical initiatives of critics who argue for the interdependence, not
the separation, of culture and politics.[27] It will also help counter that
cliché of ossified conservatism by which Maritime literature as well as
politics, has long been plagued.

\*\*\*

On the high and distant rock rose one of Turner's mysterious cities, dwellings
and walls and white airy towers soaring out of unnameable gloom. I looked
and looked and could not believe my eyes, for there I knew were only squalid
hovels of the very poor, a hospital and a jail. Distance, the magic air of spring
... combined in one more miracle.

Archibald MacMechan[28]

The 'miracle' of which MacMechan speaks can be compared to that imaginative reordering of social reality undertaken by utopian writers for
whom the 'unnameable gloom' of human misery brought about by poverty and injustice can be metamorphosed into ideal 'white airy towers.'
What De Mille's most interesting fiction does, however, is to show that
the squalid hovels and airy towers are ultimately interchangeable; that
the most idealistic political philosophies, the most spiritual of values can,
if pushed to their limits, beget a gloom far more abominable than that
brought about by simple poverty and vice.

A Strange Manuscript Found in a Copper Cylinder is strange indeed: a
reactionary but radical Victorian text which is bizarrely post-
modernist in technique and conception (its characters' own reading and
critical analysis of a mysterious manuscript constituting an extended
mise en abîme). It is a novel about a narrative which has essentially written itself, since the narrator-hero-author is effectively non-existent,
his narrator's role having been usurped by his first readers, one of whom
is a literary critic who constantly calls into question the premises and
methods of the narrative itself, and another of whom refuses to finish
reading the manuscript, effectively extinguishing it and its original
author. Accordingly, A Strange Manuscript is deconstructed as it tells
itself / is read (or not read) to us / we read the characters' reading of
it. But before we travel any further into such fraught fictive territory, a
synopsis of De Mille's novel will be helpful.

A group of English gentlemen, becalmed in the South Seas on the

languid Lord Featherstone's yacht, discover inside a fortuitously re-
trieved cylinder a document recounting the exotic adventures of one
Adam More, an English sailor who has stumbled upon a South Pole
society which appears to have inverted all the norms and values cherished by the civilized Western world. In this land of the 'Kosekin,'
darkness and death are worshipped; wealth and honours are stigmas;
abject poverty is the highest mark of social and moral status. Adam
More, whose name is Kosekined to Atam-or, Child of Light, writes on
his papyrus manuscript of how he was stranded in this terrifying country, of how he came to fall in love with the beautiful Almah, who, like
him, loves light and life, and of how he was doomed to be 'blessed' by
the highest privilege the Kosekin can bestow – ritual death and cannibal-
ization. More also tells how he is all but raped by Layelah, an aberrant
Kosekin maid who discovers she quite likes the wealth and power to
which her low social status has condemned her, and who intrepidly
plans to rescue Atam-or and run away with him into a land of light
where her talents will receive the rewards and recognition they deserve. Finally, More reveals how Almah seizes the initiative to save both
him and herself from the gruesome death awaiting them: she cleverly
manipulates Kosekin psychology to have herself and Atam-or made supreme rulers of the land. (Their first act, of course, is to cancel all
plans for their killing and cooking.) The manuscript ends abruptly, not
because More has run out of papyrus or ideas – the last we hear of him
he is still plotting ways of escape back to his own world – but because
the fictive readers of the manuscript have become peckish and decide
to break for tea.

In a perverse way, *Strange Manuscript* reads like an anticipatory paro-
dy of *Heart of Darkness*, with its framing device (the group of yachts-
men leisurely listening to a horrific tale unfold), its description of a journey down a dangerous, dark river into a land of death, and its exposure of its European protagonists to the worst excesses civilized man can
imagine and commit. This said, it must straightway be admitted that De
Mille's fantasy is no masterwork – it can be tediously repetitious; there
are altogether too many saurian stage props; it presupposes a surpass-
ing pedagogical inertness in its readers, and it is frequently hilarious
in ways that De Mille could not have intended. Nevertheless, it is at
times a hauntingly suggestive text which successfully conveys its protagonist's descent into regions of psychic gloom and devastation, and
which so contorts the act of reading that we are made to share Adam
More's radical unease, desolation, and confusion.

Kenneth J. Hughes has categorized *Strange Manuscript* as 'a positive

Utopia which satirizes an aristocratic class that serves no useful purpose' and which illuminates an ideal of 'the maximum of human freedom and knowledge that can be attained given the material and intellectual limits of an epoch.' George Woodcock, recognizing the ambivalence of De Mille's text, prefers to call the work 'a satire on our own world, not a proposal for an ideal commonwealth or a warning of its opposite.' He interprets De Mille's portrayal of 'a mad and masochistic world' as an exposure of 'self-destructive elements in his own society' – Victorian 'anti-vitalism,' morbid romanticism, and fatalistic Calvinism.[29] Yet De Mille's narrative might best be described as an 'untopia' which conflates the utopia and dystopia to sabotage the very possibility of envisioning social systems radically worse or better than our own. Satiric it certainly – and heavyhandedly – is, but the most interesting and enduring feature of *Strange Manuscript* is not so much the ideas it throws out as the responses De Mille's fictive treatment of those ideas creates in the reader.

Let us begin with the Land of the Kosekin – not so much a region of contrasts as an objectified oxymoron. Here tropical seas are locked in by glacial mountains, prosperity and fertility fuel a nihilistic philosophy. Eros is Thanatos, and what could be paradise proves itself infernal. Although the Kosekin themselves cannot really be compared with Bluenoses, it may not be altogether fanciful to discern a likeness between the paradoxical regions each people inhabits. The lush valleys and green plains of Kosekin Land are ringed by islands whose jagged coast and shattered rocks recall William Cobbett's disparaging description of Nova Scotia's shores; the one trace of life and food these rocks offer Atam-or and Almah are shellfish – chief among them lobsters. Beyond these superficial similarities, however, is a conceptual bond: the Maritime mythos with its crazy quilt of golden worlds and iron ages, of Happy Valleys and Nova Scarcities, of communal bliss and mass emigration. The equation of Acadia with Arcadia is a *donnée* of Maritime writing: Maillet's prelapsarian Grand Pré, Howe's, Haliburton's, and McCulloch's agrarian ideal of trim farmers tending their own fertile fields, MacMechan's presentation of early twentiety-century Halifax (*pace Barometer Rising*) as the last refuge of gilded, gracious leisure, and of the Annapolis Valley as a land of apple juice and honey,[30] Buckler's and Montgomery's Edenizing of rural childhood all combine to persuade us that the Maritimes can be the very best of all possible worlds. Yet the Maritimes' climate and economy are also *données*: this is a land of mellow autumn, yes, but also of long winters, non-existent springs, and brief, breezy summers. More importantly, the brute facts of widespread poverty and

underdevelopment have given birth to a 'culture of patched high-
ways, reliable bootleggers .. bad dental care ... ignorance and fear'
which has permitted a Maritime province, Nova Scotia, to lead the
country 'in the rates of alcoholism and illegitimate births.'[31] Utopia and
Dystopia, mythos and actuality, not opposed but intertangled, so that
the tourist-traveller mistakes brute for 'proud' poverty, despair for docility – such is the wildly ambivalent, utterly problematic context which,
*mutatis mutandis*, must have helped shape De Mille's vision, and within
which his novel may continue to be read.

Let us briefly examine the elements of the untopia De Mille sets up and
which have important implications for what we have termed the political sensibility of the region and its art. At first glance Kosekin land seems
to represent a simple inversion of our own norms. Not only are the
Kosekin at home in darkness and incapacitated by light, not only do they
shun wealth, honour, high position, health, and long life, but they
make of unrequited love one of their greatest goods: no greater personal
catastrophe can be imagined than the marriage of lovers. There are
also, however, new rather than merely inverted features in Kosekin
society: men and women enjoy (or rather endure) not superiority but
equality of role and status. Women, in fact, commonly take the initiative
in both love- and policy-making, though since to rule and to possess
the trappings of wealth and state is to be lamentably low on the Kosekin
social scale, political power is not such a boon as might be imagined.

In some respects, the Kosekins' lust for asceticism, altruism, self-
abnegation – those virtues which, if energetically practised, lead most
surely and swiftly to the Kosekin goals of poverty and self-destruction –
can be construed as a pro-Nietzschean critique of traditional Christian, or, as one of More's readers insists, of all spiritual values. Thus De
Mille would seem to be showing up the inherent monstrousness of the
doctrine that 'human life is not a blessing; that the evil predominates
over the good; and that our best hope is to gain a spirit of acquies-
cence with its inevitable ills.'[32] Yet when the revolutionaries among the
Kosekin, heartened by Atam-or's revulsion at their society's values,
his recoiling before 'this infliction of appalling woes [poverty, physical
pain, death, cannibalism] under the miserable name of blessings' (SM
230), elect him as their political teacher and spiritural leader, not reversion but perversion of values results: 'I told [the "philosophic radical," the Kohen Gadol] that in my country self was the chief consideration, self-preservation the law of nature; death the King of Terrors;
wealth the object of universal search, poverty the worst of evils; unrequited love nothing worse than anguish and despair; to command

others the highest glory; victory, honor; defeat, intolerable shame ...'
(SM 166–7).

Layelah, the Kohen's daughter, is then made to exclaim: 'He is right ...
the rich shall be esteemed, the poor shall be down-trodden; to rule
over others shall be glorious, to serve shall be base ... selfishness, self-
seeking luxury and indulgence shall be virtues; poverty, want and
squalor shall be things of abhorrence and contempt' (SM 167).

This is not exactly the idea of a Christian or even a gentlemanly society
(though it may be the natural consequence of laissez-faire or trickle-
down economic practice). Layelah's response effectively erases the
norms Adam More so confidently expounds. Moreover, as Adam is
uncomfortably aware, many of the qualities which the Kosekin cultivate
in their repulsive quest for death and squalor are eminently desirable:
gentleness, compassion, generosity, courage. It becomes clear that by
creating the Kosekins, De Mille is not trying to attack his own society's hypocrisy or injustice, or trouncing the Kosekins' transvalued society so as to establish the superiority of his own. Rather, he is pointing
to how all societies are relative and fictive in their recognition of what is
'normal' and 'natural.' Accordingly, he sets up Adam More and an
exemplary Kosekin as double mirrors reflecting one another's incredulity
and horror at what each considers good or necessary:

'It cannot be possible that you fear death.'

'Fear death!' I exclaimed, 'I do ... Do you not understand that death is abhorrent
to humanity?'

'Abhorrent!' said the Kohen; 'that is impossible. Is it not the highest blessing?
Who is there that does not long for death?'

'... Do you love death?' I asked at length, in amazement.

'Love death? What a question! Of course I love death – all men do; who does
not? Is it not human nature? ... Who does not feel within him this intense
longing after death as the strongest passion of his heart?'

'I don't know – I don't know,' said I. 'You are of a different race; I do not
understand what you say.'

(SM 129)

One of the readers of More's manuscript, however, undercuts this professed failure to understand. A scholar and linguist by profession,
this reader conclusively proves that the Kosekin language is derived
from the Hebrew, and forwards the proposition that these strange
beings are descendants of the ten lost tribes – Shem's children. Thus
though More and the Kosekin may be of different races, they have at

least a portion of the Judaeo-Christian culture in common. And even if the Kosekin people are meant to represent the Hebraic, and Atam-or the Hellenic side of the Arnoldian dichotomy, then the Kohen's position is much closer to Adam More's than the latter would like to admit, simply by the law of attraction of opposites.[33]

At any rate, what comes to paralyze More, to throw him into an extraordinary lethargy, is the recognition that it is as 'natural' to try to end as to preserve life; as 'human' to honour a man by eating him as by preparing a banquet for him. Reason, which should clarify these issues and reveal the perversity of their ethos to the Kosekin, is of course, inadmissible to these people who find it so painful to open their eyes in the light of day. But even to Adam More reason becomes as undependable as is his only source of light during the six months' darkness into which Kosekin land is plunged each year – that aurora light 'which constantly brightens and lessens in this strange world' (SM 213).

What neither Woodcock nor Hughes remarks upon in their analyses of *Strange Manuscript* is the almost psychotically depressive mood De Mille is able to create as Adam More becomes Atam-or, increasingly enmeshed in the systematic madness of Kosekin life. He descends from active revulsion at the 'appalling desolation' (SM 198) of the world encircling him to fatalistic submission – 'I had fallen upon a world and among people which were all alien and unintelligible to me; and to live on would only open the way to new and worse calamities' (SM 210). Atam-or's psychic state is matched by a physical 'abomination of desolation' (SM 193) – the island on which, after his abortive escape attempt, he and Almah are stranded: 'It was a land of horror ... a vast expanse of impassable rocks – a scene of ruin and savage wilderness ... in ... the season of darkness and of awful gloom – [W]e stood in this land of woe; and not one single sign appeared of life save the life that we had brought with us' (SM 194).

'Life seemed over; death seemed inevitable ... we floated on the waters and waited for our doom' (SM 209). This drear, passive spirit – if spirit it can be called – weighs down the whole of Adam More's text, and it becomes distinctly uncomfortable for the reader to be pushed back and forth between Adam More's psychic desert and the bantering, pedantic chatter of the gentlemen toying with his manuscript. One of the most uncomfortable things for De Mille's reader is the way in which Adam More is stranded at the end of the fiction by the impassible closure of his situation, and by the indolence of his readers. This discomfort feeds into the cumulative effect generated by De Mille's untopia –

a vehement distaste for anything smacking of radicalism, revolution, or any alteration of established social norms and orders. So tainted and confused have the ideals of self-denial, generosity, and asceticism become that rampant self-interest, self-indulgence, and materialism come to seem laudable – much to the gratification of the langorous Lord Featherstone and his travelling companions, no doubt. It is almost as if De Mille aims to put his readers through an ideological detoxification program, wherein a desired object comes to be indelibly associated with sensations of painful confusion, disgust, and ridicule.

Radicalism, for example, gets a thorough going-over. The chivalrous Kosekin to whose keeping Adam More is given speaks with disgust of capitalism, status, wealth, and power. He seems entirely devoted to the well-being of his charge – and yet the ends to which this Kosekin are devoted are those of death and desecration. A philanthropist is defined as someone eager to give the blessing of death to all (SM 233); the Kohen Gadol, a potential revolutionary, wishes to subvert the state so that the riches and offices his inferior status have conferred upon him will earn him recognition rather than revilement. Though a crypto-capitalist, he is presented as an intensely unpleasant person precisely because he is a 'philosophical radical' (SM 165). He and his erotically aggressive daughter Layelah are described as showing 'immense strength of mind and firmness of soul' in daring 'unflinchingly the extremest rigors of the national law, and all that the Kosekin could inflict in the way of wealth, luxury, supreme command, palatial abodes, vast retinues of slaves' (SM 167). De Mille's satire does not have the terrible focus or ravening intensity of A Modest Proposal, but his technique can be compared to Swift's. The readers of A Modest Proposal should not be able to hear of the starving and indigent Irish without thinking either of actively helping them in their distress or else of eating their children, which is what their contempt or indifference would amount to. And because in this context the notion of an either / or becomes abominable, they will be moved to relieve, rather than feed on, such misery. The reader of Strange Manuscript will be conditioned in a different way – may emerge as unable to confront ideas of radical social or economic change 'animated by the desire of effecting the good of others' (SM 141) without recalling either the greed and depravity of De Mille's 'philosophic radicals,' or else the drift towards death, the passivity and powerlessness Adam More falls into during his stay with the Kosekin. Even the notion of sexual equality might be rendered noxious by the ends to which Kosekin women are shown to put their freedom and authority, and by the emasculating effect the vigorous, intelligent, unscrupulous Layelah is made to have on Adam More even before she sweeps him off his feet onto the back of an outward-bound pterodactyl.

The 'critics' who are made to discover and decode Adam More's text remain divided in their judgments – some argue for the manuscript's authenticity and scientific veracity, others deplore it as sensational, or praise it as satirical romance. One finds a 'perpetual undercurrent of meaning and innuendo ... in every line'; another sees only 'haste, gross carelessness, universal feebleness' (SM 216–17). What De Mille indisputably achieves in his strange fiction is a demolition of our generic and aesthetic expectations, and a deconstruction of those possibilities for imagining radical or alternative mindsets and models which the narrative first seems to create. De Mille's narrative frame so teases the text it infolds, Adam More's response to the Kosekin so confuses and destabilizes the reader of *his* readers, that perhaps no other conclusion is possible for writer, reader, or critic than the novel's next-to-last words, given to the lisping Lord Featherstone: 'That's enough ... I'm tired and can't read anymore.' Fortunately for Maritime readers, however, their region's writers have gone on to give more emphatic and dynamic expression to their political vision that De Mille's deconstructions permit.

\*\*\*

The skills of the writer and historian are middle-class skills, the context in which such people grow and learn is a middle-class context, and the view of the world they develop will almost certainly be bourgeois. Our intellectual life is filled with people who respect the system – which has indeed served them well – and it comes naturally to them to concentrate on the lives and works of high officials rather than on the struggles of masses of nameless workers.

Silver Donald Cameron (EER 234)

'The system' respects and has amply rewarded Hugh MacLennan; yet what exactly is this system, and what has MacLennan done for it? The author of *Barometer Rising* and *Two Solitudes* has been, in Gramscian terms, an 'organic' intellectual working from within a post-(British) colonial stratum in Canadian society to give that society 'homogeneity and an awareness of its own political function not only in the economic but also in the social and political fields.'[34] The organic intellectual attempts both to win over 'traditional' intellectuals to a new vision of society, and also to 'fuse together in a single national crucible with a unitary culture the different forms of culture imported by immigrants of differing national origins.'[35] MacLennan accomplishes the formidable task of squeezing a multicultural nation into a bicultural mould, and then compresses the latter until it achieves singular expression – we remember that the symbolic marriage between Paul Tallard and Heather Methuen in *Two Solitudes* presupposes English as being the language in which Paul makes love and writes his novels. In the course of MacLennan's oeuvre Canada, that geographical obstacle course *a mare usque ad marem* becomes conceptualized as a conflict between two founding races; this conflict becomes subsumed in a cult of the individual (*The Watch that Ends the Night*) which, in its turn, surrenders to the cult of the land (*The Rivers of Canada*; the final pages of *Return of the Sphinx*). What we might call MacLennanism necessitates an eclipse of the political and a corresponding vitiation of the social and cultural, by a mystique which involves, among other things, the bonding of exceptional individuals to their home and native land through cross-country travel by rail or car, or through the possession of summer homes in the Laurentians.

MacLennan has, indeed, done the state some service, but at some cost to his native region.[36] For in order to make his contribution to the centralist mythos, to further develop Roberts's paradigm of Canada as Quebec + Ontario, MacLennan has had to abandon any real commitment to the Maritimes. To do justice to the grievances Quebec holds against the Canadian Confederation, he has had to dismiss the plaints of the Maritimes as peripheral, or puerile. Thus he has a respectable Cape Bretoner manifest anti-Confederation sentiments – 'Since Confederation, the central provinces in this country have treated us very badly' – only to trivialize them – 'So – speaking philosophically, mind you – it is no sin for us Nova Scotians to drink smuggled liquor.'[37] Interconnected with this slighting of Maritime Rights is MacLennan's funking or sabotaging in his 'Maritime' novels, *Barometer Rising* and *Each Man's Son*, an essential socio-political issue – the existence and insistence of class conflict, or at least difference. The result is an unfortunate skewing and disempowering of MacLennan's fiction which no amount of archetypes or mythic structures can set right.

The subtitle of *Barometer Rising* could well be 'Birth of a Nation,' given that MacLennan's re-enactment of the Halifax Explosion comes to comprehend the apocalypse of a colonialist society and mentality, and the birth of a vision of Canada as a 'central arch' linking the old British Empire with the new American one. When the *Mont Blanc* blows much of Halifax sky-high it performs a paradoxical service to the city by liberating it from 'bondage' to England[38] and forcing its surviving citizens to turn their faces instead of their backs to the centre of the continent.

To do so, however, Maritimers would have to turn their backs on their native region as well as on Britain. As *Barometer Rising* opens, Halifax and the region for which it stands are a historical graveyard; as the novel closes, it has become a literal one. The future, we are told, lies elsewhere, for the Maritimes can no longer provide a significant stage or symbol for the enactment of a national role or identity. Neil Macrae, the novel's chief protagonist, admits to feeling 'rooted and at home' in Nova Scotia, yet it is 'in Montreal that all the good things had happened' (BR 73). Just as, in Neil's hymn to pan-Canadianism, the sun rolls on 'beyond Nova Scotia into the West' and the railway rises out of 'the darkness of Nova Scotia' to arrive at last 'in the flush of a British Columbia noon' (BR 32), so the theatre of the Canadian mythos is to be removed from the arch-colonial East to the symbolic centre of the land, a centre possessing political and cultural hegemony. The novel's temporarily star-crossed lovers, Neil and Penny, thus rehearse the act Paul and Janet will perform in *Two Solitudes* – helping Canada achieve her destiny by making her understand 'what her job in this world really is' (BR 357).

The Maritimes' loss, one might argue, is Canada's gain – instead of a narrowly regional writer, we have a national novelist who has provided us with the symbols and fictive structures by which we can come to know and project ourselves as a distinctive people. Yet there is a great deal in *Barometer Rising* to suggest that in becoming a national mythmaker, MacLennan sacrificed skills he possessed as a novelist – principally, a gift for social analysis, for understanding the class structures and divisions of a given human world. Given that MacLennan has come to seem 'the epitome of the conservative mind, almost a throwback to the tweedy English novelists of Georgian days in his preoccupation with his country house and his ... roses and his tennis'[39] it is refreshing to recognize in *Barometer Rising* traces of something resembling 'Literature of Protest' – a genre which, as F.W. Watt has pointed out, was in short supply in Canada even in the 1930s.[40]

Neil Macrae is introduced to us as a disaffected and dispossessed hero who spends most of his time, prior to the explosion, tramping sleazy streets in shabby clothes, and seeking help and shelter from a Halifax labourer and his family. Of course Macrae is a prince in tramp's clothing, his disinheritance the result of familial rather than class conflict, yet his 'down-and-out' disguise has allowed him both in England and Halifax to engage in some early-Orwellian social analysis, and to emerge with 'socialist' leanings (BR 160).

Neil's personal enemy is his uncle, Geoffrey Wain, pilloried for his 'low opinion of humanity' and his fervent desire that World War I, 'the greatest power bonanza in the history of mankind' should go on indefinitely (BR 101). Yet Wain, an arch-colonial and hereditary member of Halifax's élite, is also shown to be the public enemy of traditional Maritime society. His mistress is a girl from a fishing village who, in coming to Halifax to better or at least enliven her lot, has lost her 'standing in the community' to become little more than a 'domestic servant' (BR 115). Wain himself concedes that his family business is directly responsible for pushing Maritimers from the dignified poverty of the village to the disabling poverty of the city: 'Few fishermen in Nova Scotia made any money because they could not easily market their catches, and prices paid by wholesalers like himself were infinitesimal. It was steadily becoming more difficult to persuade members of the younger generation in the fishing towns to stay there' (BR 115).

Not individual ambition or desire but market forces have brought about this profound, and to MacLennan, destructive change in the very 'layout' of Maritime society. And as MacLennan goes on to insist, capitalists like Wain have not only sold out the birthright of Nova Scotia's fishermen, they have sat on the entire nation's opportunities as well. Yet before he jumps 'from colony to nation' with the observation that Canada was 'virtually owned by ... old men who were content to let it continue second rate indefinitely, looting its wealth while they talked about its infinite opportunities' (BR 357), MacLennan makes another, more trenchant and distinctively 'local' criticism. He emphasizes the link Neil Macrae's disastrous experience of an exceptionally disastrous war has led him to make between the criminal incompetence of the High Command and the criminal business sense of High Society. The Halifax élite, he realizes, have created the wretched North End slums and quite happily exploit the people 'dull and docile enough to inhabit them': 'He wondered what complacent individual in the South End owned this house [dark grey with the impressed dirt of fifty years.] He remembered someone having once said that if a man wants a profit from property he must own something in the slums, because the poor make their own repairs, and twelve renters paying twenty dollars a month are worth more than five paying fifty' (BR 146–7).

A considerable portion of the pre-explosion narrative of *Barometer Rising* is given over to the evocation of the squalid reality of Halifax – the mean streets on which ill-dressed children brawl with 'dirty faces and blank eyes' (BR 147) – and the 'rigid, automatic' nature of life among upper-class Haligonians (BR 315). Yet the explosion which one of the characters describes as a 'revolution in the nature of things' (BR 271) does not turn the world upside down for anyone. The unsightly slums and many of their inhabitants are exploded: the shabby-genteel South End is largely untouched. The figurehead oppressor, Colonel Wain, is conveniently killed and his nephew freed to pick up the pieces of his personal happiness. Fortuitous calamity obviates the need for anyone to act on the observations that have been made regarding 'what class structure can do in a developing society to make or mar the life of the individual.' Indeed, just before the explosion, Neil's argument that Nova Scotian fishermen have been ruined by the big companies – a fact corroborated by the Company Man himself – is stopped cold by the 'good' working-class character, Big Alec MacKenzie: 'Now, Mr Macrae, you're not a fisherman yourself and you don't have to worry about the prices. And I do not think it pays to have ideas like that, moreover. It makes it harder. I do not understand very much, but I have always known what it is I have to do next, and if I lose the job at Wain's there will be another one somewhere else. We are told that the Lord will provide ...' (BR 227).

Big Alec effectively defuses Neil's radicalism; in his having voluntarily left his Cape Breton home to provide his children with better educational opportunities, the fisherman redeems what has earlier been presented as a destructive process of change. We are now onto MacLennan's ideological home ground, with individual ambition, endurance, and skill, not social class or economic conditions counting for everything within and outside the world of the novel. Earlier, MacLennan has Angus Murray, the novel's Nestor, proclaim, 'all hatred is self-hatred' – a dictum that effectively annuls the idea of passionate combat against social and economic injustice. In having Big Alec help out Neil, his former commanding officer, at the risk of losing his job and plunging his family even further down the slum drain, MacLennan undercuts any suggestion of class solidarity or consciousness by a lavish show of brotherly love.

George Woodcock speaks with satisfaction of the way in which the Halifax explosion heralds 'the beginning of a new consciousness' symbolizing the 'social revolution that brings an end to the rule of the Wains.'[41] He treats the catastrophe as a species of mass cleanser, clearing the slums (and, we might add, incinerating their inhabitants). Yet it is surely doubtful that, simply by the death of Geoffrey Wain, society has been conclusively reordered. Presumably those who survived the devastation of the slums will soon be herded into other, equally profitable tenements constructed and owned by those wealthy Haligonians whose homes the *Mont Blanc* has considerately spared. Alec MacKenzie, his wife, and Geoffrey Wain's Cape Breton mistress die as well, and with them Neil's 'socialistic' speculations and concerns. Halifax, that synecdoche for the Maritimes, is of little further use to MacLennan, and when he does return to the Maritimes to 'place' a novel he choses a period, a society, and a territory more primitive and isolated by far – Cape Breton with its Homeric landscape and Calvinist soul.

\*\*\*

Many critics have argued that *Barometer Rising* can most satisfyingly be read as an allegory of Canadian nationhood; *Each Man's Son*, on the other hand, surely demands to be read as a text for and about MacLennan's 'home' people and region. Certainly it has been praised for an impassioned authenticity and authoritative rightness of tone and texture which spring from MacLennan's intimate knowledge of his subject-matter.

The novel begins with a poetic prelude celebrating Cape Breton as a Homeric land, its inhabitants – descendants of dispersed Highlanders – a Homeric people whose native courage and poetry have been dammed up and then forced tortuously back on them by the heavy hand of Calvinism. MacLennan would seem to have us believe that each Cape Breton man, woman, and child was convinced of his or her own worthlessness and damnation, and obsessed with guilt at the thought of personal happiness and pleasure. It is a little daunting to see how eager most critics have been to second the author in finding the scarlet P of Puritanism stitched on the minds of North Americans; thus, MacLennan's insistence on the predominance of Calvinist over Celt in the psyche of his Cape Breton Highlanders has been almost slavishly accepted. We are ready to admit MacLennan's gaffes vis-à-vis the French Canadians – Jacques Brazeau, among others, has pointed out just how unrepresentative is MacLennan's portrait of the rural Québécois in the first half of *Two Solitudes*, for example.[42] We defer, however, to MacLennan's delineation of the Nova Scotian 'Scotch': here the writer is on his own home ground – who better to understand the mentality of the oatmeal savage than a native son of Glace Bay? Yet a comparison of the Highlanders of *Each Man's Son* – the sin-and-guilt-obsessed Dan Ainslie, the defeated and brawling miners who perceive the misery of their lives as a manifestation of their inherent sinfulness, and their inescapable doom – with those presented by Charles Dunn in his *Highland*

*Settler: A Portrait of the Scottish Gael in Nova Scotia* – will give us considerable pause.

Though MacLennan shows himself perceptive and sensitive in recording certain aspects of the Nova Scotian Highland character and experience – the quest for education and careers in the professions, the undeniable incidence of drunkenness and brawling, the abandonment of homesteads and productive farms for the attractions of urban life – he would seem to have dramatically exaggerated the role of religion and to have underemphasized the inherited cultural forms and practices of the New World Highlanders. Thus while Dunn acknowledges that religion could 'spoil' a Highlander, turning him into a rebel or a fanatic, he argues that these extremes were not normal products of churchgoing in Cape Breton. Dunn stresses the gaiety as well as the melancholy of the Highlander, the gift for vituperative satire as well as for musical sadness, and the 'happy-go-lucky philosophy' of people for whom life was not a mere matter of toil but also of 'laughter and story and song and music.'[43] Dunn's composite portrait of the Cape Breton Gael, stressing as it does traditional Celtic rather than neurotically Calvinist elements, has much more in common with Alistair MacLeod's than with Hugh MacLennan's portrayal of Nova Scotia Highlanders.

This is not to say that MacLennan's own childhood experience was not permeated by Calvinist doctrine and puritan restraint, but to suggest that for MacLennan to attribute an equal despair and paralysis to the souls of miners as he does to a doctor for whom Homer does more than homebrew can; to portray the brutality, privation, and sheer ugliness of the miners' lives as stemming more from race and religion than economics is to practise a dubious sleight of hand by which critics appear to have been largely taken in. With dogged docility they repeat rather than resist, or even test, MacLennan's thesis:

On the symbolic level, the mine seems to be allied with the town's prevailing Calvinism and stands for man's depraved nature.

The individual miners become comments upon the narrowness and futility of the Calvinist community; their daily descent into the bowels of the earth is linked, perhaps, with the Calvinist conception of man's depraved nature.

These Highlanders, doomed to wear their vitality away in the dreary Cape Breton mines, rebel like the profound children they are by recourse to the only political action of which they are capable, their endless evening brawls.[44]

This last statement is particularly astonishing, given that, though orthodox literary historians may assert that in Canada 'the disruptive opposition of capital and labour never came to a head until after the First Wold War,'[45] a long line of violent strikes in 1882, 1904, and 1909–10, as well as in 1922, 1925, and 1930 shows the strength and persistence of a militant labour movement in Cape Breton. Nova Scotia miners, argues Ernest Forbes, were the 'hard core' of the Maritime workers' movement, developing a 'greater militancy than the international organizations with which they were affiliated.' By 1919, Forbes reveals – six years after the 'events' created in *Each Man's Son* – Nova Scotia United Mine Workers' District No. 26 'reported a membership of 13,365, the largest cohesive body of organized labour in the country.'[46]

'In few areas of Canada have strikes been as frequent and as bloody as in Cape Breton Island. Steel mills and coal pits were controlled by absentee capitalists with close links to the provincial government. The Dominion Steel and Coal Companies were in a continual state of financial crisis, and managers were told to squeeze out the last cent of wages rather than cut dividends.'[47] Even cursory reading about Cape Breton labour troubles reveals that the miners of Glace Bay were both educated and militant enough to strike on the issue of what kind of union they would be permitted to obtain – a docile 'company' one, or a radical, independent one. The political action of which Cape Breton miners were capable was thus rather more considerable than a critic like Warren Tallman would allow. We may excuse literary specialists their ignorance of Canadian labour history, but what do we make of MacLennan's own misrepresentation of the milieu from which he has created a fictive world? Do we allow the novelist freedom to write of a mining town more along the lines of the *Odyssey* than of *Sons and Lovers*, and to impose a Homeric-Calvinist schema upon the troublesome reality with which his fiction engages – or do we demand a stringent (and problematic) kind of verisimilitude? In the interests of this question, let us take a closer look at the miners and the mines which MacLennan uses as chorus and backdrop for the tragic action his novel sets up.

The prologue of *Each Man's Son* introduces the idea of a community of suffering: 'they were ... a fighting race with poetry in their hearts and a curse upon their souls. Each man's son was driven by the daemon of his own hope and imagination – by his energy or by his fear – to unknown destinations. For those who stayed behind, the beast continued to growl behind the unlocked door' (EMS xi). Yet the end of the prologue and the first chapter of the novel create a division between the exceptional individuals within this community – Dr Ainslie, Mollie, Alan, and Archie MacNeil – and the mass of miners and their wives.

Mollie and Alan clearly do not belong with the latter. MacLennan wastes no time in showing us how Alan does not build an 'ordinary child's castle' on the beach but, as his mother proudly notes, something vastly more ambitious, like 'the picture of the castle he had seen in the book she was reading to him' (EMS 4). A miner's son with a thirst for book-learning; a miner's wife who has the time and inclination to find and read improving books to her son, and who teaches him the desire to 'live in a fine house and be different' from their neighbours (EMS 6). A miner marked out not only by his physical strength and grace but also by a hatred for the mines so all-consuming that he is willing to part himself from wife and child, and to suffer mutilation and humiliation in the ring, to avoid the fate of a life in the pits. The fact that he is a prize fighter, however, lessens his stature in his wife's eyes – Mollie, we learn, yearns to be able to tell Alan that his father 'was a man with a profession like a doctor or lawyer' (EMS 118).

A Maritime version of Lawrence's Morels? Since there is no conflictual relation between the smothering ambitions of a déclassé mother for her son, and the sensual energy and physical power of a father all too present to that son, the answer must be no. Moreover, MacLennan has little interest in showing this exemplary family's complex relations with and withdrawals from the mining community. The MacNeils are hermetically sealed off from their neighbours: Alan would appear to have no friends his own age, Mollie no confidantes – and when she does take a lover it is the obnoxious outsider, Louis Camire, whose education, background, and financial prospects (his father owns a business in the south of France) distinguish him in her eyes as a likely ticket out of Broughton. As for her husband, Archie, he is presented as a loner / outsider par excellence.

In a sense, *Each Man's Son* is a critique of patriarchal authority and ambition, as Dan Ainslie, for whom 'the future of a first-class human being [had been] worth more than all the rules in the world' (EMS 135) learns the rule that, 'in comparison with a loving human being, everything else is worthless' (EMS 243). This critique, however, is consonant with a belief in the supreme rights and significance of the individual as against those of the group. MacLennan sets Dan Ainslie apart from the miners by his education, profession, and social status, and from his fellow physicians by his diagnostic skills and surgical genius, as well as by his punishing passion for Homer. He then has him proclaim that 'nothing of the slightest value has been accomplished by a crowd of people. Individual men, following ideas of their own, have given the world everything we value' (EMS 198). It is an utter disavowal of, for instance, that principle of solidarity which Conrad's Marlow comes to value over the merits of that extraordinary individual Kurtz; of the solidarity which permitted the striking coal miners of Cape Breton to 'stand the gaff' when their employers were doing their best to starve them into submission,[48] and which allowed them to show 'a fine community spirit and very efficient organization of relief forces and methods' during the appalling conditions brought about by the 1924–5 strike in Glace Bay.[49]

The only reference to labour unrest in *Each Man's Son* comes when Mollie is made to speak up against the 'radicalism' of Louis Camire. His function in the novel and the nature of his politics will be discussed later; for the present, let us simply state those of his accusations to which Mollie objects: (1) that there is no future in being an underdog; (2) that the miners are underdogs because they fight one another rather than their real enemy, the company that owns the mines. Mollie insists that 'nobody here is an underdog,' that 'nobody wants another strike' like the terrible one of 1909, and that 'the men like fighting. It makes them feel better to show each other what they can do' (EMS 21). No doubt there were many miners and miners' wives who would have shared Mollie's sentiments, but the fact that MacLennan allows the contentions of his token radical to be quashed by someone no more representative of the Cape Breton miners than Louis Camire is representative of the French socialists among whose members were such brilliant figures as Jean Jaurès is extraordinary, to say the least. When we look at MacLennan's treatment of the miners and the mines in *Each Man's Son*, however, we see that MacLennan has created a context in which Mollie's and Louis's exchange appears unexceptionable.

For MacLennan not 'underdog' but 'hangdog' best describes the miners of Broughton. Ainslie is, among other things, a colliery doctor, but it is suggested that the bulk of his time is spent on treating miners injured not at work but in drunken fights after hours. When he does treat a mining casualty, the novice Bill Blackett, it turns out that the man's own cocky stupidity around dangerous machinery is responsible for his having had most of his fingers chopped off. As for the general poverty of the miners, it would seem to stem from the fact that they drink up all their wages, and not that they are underpaid, or so the ugly scene between Angus the Barraman and his wife implies (EMS 17). In the paragraphs MacLennan does devote to distinguishing between the different types of miners – defiantly aggressive beginners, subdued, middle-aged hands, and the dignified old who manage to survive the chronic accidents of life in the pits – he sensitively communicates the horror of being broken by a life of desperate, dangerous toil, but his distress is reserved for the fact that the mines are there at all, not for the fact that those who risk their lives in them are hardly paid a living wage.

Presumably MacLennan, who has Dan Ainslie yearn back to a time when 'the past had still been honourable, unblighted by the mines' (EMS 40), wishes for the mines to be razed and the mining families to be sent back to the land they were foolish enough to leave in the first place. The lyrical description of the Margaree Valley of Ainslie's boyhood is drawn as an emphatic contrast to the needless ugliness of towns like Broughton, bulging 'black and monstrous' against the sky, the colliery bankheads 'loom[ing] like monuments in a gigantic cemetery' (EMS 44). In this novel the sordid commonness of the miners' row housing is somehow made to seem more the fault of the occupants than the owners: 'Ainslie felt he could almost smell their dusty, dark interiors, the rooms where they lived crowded together, the kitchens steamy from dishwater and the perpetually boiling kettle, the diapers of the babies and the sweaty underwear of the men, the high odor given off by heavy muscles' (EMS 87).

Whereas Lawrence allows his miners engaging qualities of camaraderie and sexual vitality, MacLennan presents the Broughton workers as zombies – Alan shudders at the sight of them walking home from work with 'black faces and staring white eyes' (EMS 179) – or as mere animals – in his encounter with the drunken Red Willie MacIsaac, Ainslie dismisses the former as a 'swine'; not a man but a mere 'living thing' (EMS 184). The one trace of vitality he concedes to them lies in their speech, invigorated and made musical by 'the Gaelic.' Of course it is the melancholic and not the satiric propensities of the Gaelic tongue that MacLennan stresses, as when he has Archie meet a fellow Cape Bretoner in a Trenton bar, or when Angus the Barraman, after a violent domestic scene, sits 'croon[ing] a Gaelic song ... soft and plaintive as the cry of a sea bird lost in the fog' (EMS 18). Failure and fatalism are the miners' native element: when Archie loses the big fight at Trenton the Broughton men are said to feel at one with him 'because they knew that luck was certainly working against themselves' (EMS 148). MacLennan strongly implies that it is as much the Celtic spirit as the killing purposelessness of 'being a miner in a pit, boring into the black till the seam runs out' (EMS 188) which dooms the Highlanders: 'They were all lost here in the mines. They were inextricably lost in their own sea-deep feelings and crazy dreams' (EMS 40).

Thus far it may be objected that MacLennan is entitled to interpret and symbolize the life of the mines in any way he chooses, as long as the result is a rhetorically convincing, aesthetically satisfying text. *Each Man's Son* may be inadequate in mimetic terms, since MacLennan distorts the historical, social, and political context of his subject-matter. Yet as many critics have shown, MacLennan creates powerful mythic types and structures in this novel – surely one should base one's judgment of the novel's success or failure on mythic rather than mimetic grounds. The mythos of *Each Man's Son*, however, is vitiated by an ideological animus which ruptures the Calvinist schema underpinning MacLennan's mythic structures. To recognize the substantial flaw in the fabirc of *Each Man's Son* – a flaw influencing MacLennan's representation of Broughton and its people – we must examine the role MacLennan assigns in this novel to Louis Camire.

As Robert Cockburn has pointed out, 'somehow one cannot reconcile oneself to the presence of such a bizarre type [as Louis Camire] in Broughton. Why not a man from Ontario (or even New Brunswick) instead of a left-wing fanatic from France?'[50] Why indeed? To be sure, MacLennan needs an agent who will not so much create as facilitate the catastrophe – Archie's murdering of Mollie to permit the adoption by the Ainslies of Alan. Yet why voluntarily introduce a representative from the world MacLennan has striven to exclude from his novel – the world of radical politics and militant labour? George Woodcock describes Camire as 'a perverted product of the doctrines of class struggle that in the early twentieth century were agitating the masses of Europe, and thus he contrasts with the Cape Breton Highlanders, who think of themselves not in class terms, but rather as a homogeneous society in which degree exists, but no antagonism bred of it.'[51]

But Camire does more than show up the utterly apolitical nature of MacLennan's Cape Breton Highlanders – he is also made to play the role of rival to Archie (by becoming Mollie's lover) and to Ainslie as well (by forcing himself on Alan as prospective stepfather). Camire, however, is such a repulsive character that Alan rejects him almost immediately: how then, can Mollie, however desperate she is to get out of Broughton, finally allow this 'perverted product' of a foreign tradition into her bed and, presumably, her heart? Would it not have been more plausible – and interesting – for MacLennan to have provided Mollie with an attractive rather than a villainous seducer?

Physically and temperamentally, Camire cannot hold a candle to Archie. 'Even with his padded shoulders [Camire] looked frail' (EMS 18). He has a vicious temper, too; as his final battle with Archie reveals, he is the kind of cowardly bully who fights not with his fists, but with broken bottles. (He is in Broughton, it is rumoured, to evade military service in France; his own explanation is that he is paving the way in Cape Breton for a great social revolution. Neither explanation endears him to the Broughton miners.) And intellectually, Camire is hardly a match for Ainslie. Yet Camire's socialist doctrines, which boil down to 'Nobody does something for anybody without they want something back' (EMS 196) are, though rather crude for a man of his supposed background and education, entirely correct in the context of this novel. Dr Ainslie, after all, provides Alan with a train ride to Louisbourg, books and well-balanced meals, a private hospital bed and free treatment when the boy is stricken with appendicitis, not out of the goodness of his heart, but in order to seduce the child from Mollie.

Camire, it is quickly established, has little luck as an organizer or *agent provocateur*. For a time he had tried to advance himself in the local of the union, but he got nowhere with the men, 'who ... dismissed him as a foreigner who talked too much' (EMS 14). Despairing at the miners' lack of sympathy for his views, Camire nevertheless stays on, presumably because of the attractions of the stubbornly virtuous Mollie. For Ainslie he has an implacable hatred, simply, it would seem, because the doctor has a voluptuous wife, a magnificent home, and a thriving practice. Perhaps the nastiest thing MacLennan has the Frenchman do is to hint to Bill Blackett that Ainslie has purposely amputated the miner's fingers. With his Napoleon worship, his lustful designs on Mollie, his 'dirty' way of fighting, and perhaps most reprehensible of all to the reader, 'is veree Franch way of talkeen', '*Name of God!*' – Camire emerges as an altogether detestable creature whose attack on the status quo does not even convince an eight-year-old boy: 'Mr Camire said that the wealth of the world was like a pie. There was plenty of pie but only a few people were cutting it and of course they cut all the big pieces for themselves, but when the rulers were hanging from the lampposts there would be plenty of pie for everyone. Alan wondered if this was true, and he ... hoped that nobody would be hanged in Broughton. He fell asleep remembering Angus the Barraman's warning that it was not safe to believe everything a foreigner said' (EMS 165–6).

When it comes to the crunch, Archie is easily able to overcome Camire, who 'dart[s] back and forth across the room, trying to find a place to hide as he [gives] mouselike squeaks of terror' (EMS 233). All in all, Camire is so inept a radical and so despicable a man he can't help but fail in the tasks MacLennan has set him. Why then did MacLennan choose to include him in his novel when it would have been dramatically simpler and infinitely more convincing to have made Mollie's lover

a white-collar worker from the colliery, or even Ainslie himself, for
whom Mollie's Celtic eyes are supposed to have such a haunting appeal?
If a suitor was required to round out the Homeric parallels, why did
not MacLennan choose a character as imposing as Antinous instead of
the ratlike Camire?[52] However successfully MacLennan may be in control of one of the ideological axes of this novel – the disastrous influence
of virulent Calvinism and its patriarchal God – he flounders with the
other: the absurdity and alienness of political explanations for and solu-
tions to the Cape Breton 'troubles.' Consequently, 'politics' sabotages
'mythos' with the result that the all-important ending of *Each Man's Son*
becomes overdetermined, and ambivalent to the point of confusion.
Penelope is killed off with her suitor *and* her husband, while Ainslie,
who has been Alan's and indirectly Mollie's suitor, is allowed his
heart's desire – a son, and experience as well as knowledge of the redeeming power of love. If patriarchy is meant to be rejected, and
loving mothers substituted for savage fathers, why is Mollie, that paragon of maternal devotion, so conveniently killed off? And why the
privileging of Ainslie, whose inability to love has blighted his wife's
existence and whose surgical skills have, however inadvertently,
made her barren? If Ainslie is meant to be a tragic hero, then why does
not MacLennan have him strike Archie or Mollie down – as Ainslie
has been trying to do in a less physical sense throughout the novel? Why
is it only that exceptional individual, Daniel Ainslie, who is allowed to
have his cake and eat it too? In part, to show up the meaninglessness
and futility of that policy of collective action which his rival, Louis
Camire, has supposedly stood for.

In *Each Man's Son* there is a thematic confusion aggravated by ideological cross-purposes that, for this reader at least, prevents the novel
from being the rhetorically convincing, aesthetically satisfying work
many critics claim it to be. In its own terms, the novel ends in a curiously anti-climactic sort of draw. Though its protagonist wins the tug-
of-war for possession of young Alan MacNeil, he does admit failure
in a more public domain: at the last possible moment before the outbreak
of World War I, Daniel Ainslie, his wife, and adopted son set sail for
England, never more, apparently, to set foot in Cape Breton. Daniel
seems finally to have acted on kind, wise old Dr MacKenzie's advice:
'I'm convinced that God himself can never lick the mines. It's a kind of
blasphemy, I know – fighting clans going into the blackness of the
earth to dig coal. But *you* can't solve the problem. At least not here'
(EMS 67).

The violent strikes of the 1920s didn't solve the problem either. Yet the 'fighting clans' did at last come out of the blackness of the earth onto the streets of Glace Bay. By organizing themselves and 'standing the gaff' they proved themselves as 'wonderful and gallant [as] the Highlanders of legend' (EMS 30); as heroic as Daniel Ainslie could wish, though not in ways that he or his author would ever recognize or represent. It is this kind of collective heroism which Silver Donald Cameron attempts to portray in *The Education of Everett Richardson*.

\*\*\*

In the end this is not a story of the fishermen alone, or even of the labour movement. It is a story about privilege and poverty and injustice in this country, and about the social and political arrangements which cheat and oppress most Canadians, which stunt our humanity and distort our environment ... [I]n the end, I hope, it is a story about democracy, and the way Canadians might hope to achieve it. (EER 18)

Silver Donald Cameron's account of the 1970–1 Nova Scotia Fishermen's Strike is a multiple birth, generically speaking: part new journalism, pointing out the inevitably fictive nature of our efforts to record fact, part *Bildungsroman* as the title, *The Education of Everett Richardson*, would suggest, part satire, and part encomium on a certain kind of rural community. It manages, despite such diversity, to provide an intelligible overview of an immensely complicated event in Canadian labour history. In its lively engagement with social and political issues it revives the tradition in which a writer like Haliburton flourished; in its focus on conflictual class relationships it works as a kind of photographic negative to such a text as *Each Man's Son*, and finally, like Day's *Rockbound* it demystifies and deromanticizes the common conception of who and how fishermen are. The book's title is thus deceptive or at least incomplete, for the education Cameron records is undergone not only by the fishermen of Canso but also by Cameron himself and his readers, most of whom are not likely to jig cod for a living.

Describing himself as 'a chronicler with a tape recorder' (EER 19), Cameron explores the world of the Canso Strait in a manner not wholly dissimilar to (though with results dramatically different from) De Mille's untopian discovery of the land of the Kosekin. Reminding us that fishing, especially as carried out under modern methods, is 'the hardest life by which men still earn their daily bread' (EER 29) Cameron soon dashes the stereotypes of sou'westers and schooners with which the Tourist Board has made us overfamiliar: 'If fishing tells Nova Scotians what they are, part of what it tells them is not pretty. It tells them that they live in an essentially feudal society' (EER 26). It is a society in which 'diabetes is frighteningly common, the rates of maternal and infant mortality are similar to those of Kenya, and dental care is virtually unobtainable ...' (EER 25–6).

Cameron effectively portrays the strangeness of this kind of world by asking his urban, middle-class reader to consider 'what it is like to take a break from *The Mary Tyler Moore Show* by going out to the back-house for a crap when the temperature is 20 below zero and a gale from Greenland is slashing between the cracks in the wall. You *know* you work hard and live thriftily and yet somehow you can't be permitted a flush toilet' (EER 25). But where Adam More is faced with an abominable confusion of normal and abnormal human practices and values, Cameron discovers among the striking fishermen and their families a courage, dignity, and low-key heroism that reaffirms his faith in human society and its ability to withstand the erosion of values caused by big business, government, and North American consumer culture.

As Cameron explains, the industrialization of fishing after World War II, the introduction of prohibitively expensive steel stern draggers which are able to stay out in all kinds of weather, allowing workers to dress fish non-stop sixteen hours a day, has turned fishermen – who were once self-employed – into blue-collar workers in a capital intensive industry. Thus where fishermen used to be 'co-adventurers' with the men who owned the boats and equipment used in offshore fishing, sharing the risks and profits of each voyage, they are now employees on floating fish factories, receiving a ludicrously small cash return for their labour. Yet as Cameron explains, the fiction of fisherman as co-adventurer persisted, allowing the courts to refuse certification to fishermen's unions that otherwise would act as bargaining agents in disputes with management.

The multinational corporations with which the Canso fishermen were involved in 1970–1 agreed to give voluntary recognition to a union of the company's own choosing – a union compliant to the wishes of management, rather than responsive to the needs of the fishermen themselves. Striking on the issue of their right both to the union of their choice and to a contract, the fishermen were dealt a court injunction ordering them back to work while the issue was studied by legal experts. Ignoring the injunction, the fishermen continued to picket, even though some received jail sentences for their actions, with the result that the plant remained closed. Ultimately, the judge concerned handed down his decision: 'A properly-certified union can and will remove many of the deep-seated problems and bring mutual benefits to all concerned' (EER 141). The workers, having obtained a less than satisfying contract, agreed to go back to work, and were outmanoeuvred by the company into joining a 'symbiotic' rather than independent union. Symbolic protests were made; one of the companies involved went bankrupt;[53] the other pulled up stakes and moved to Newfoundland.

Because of mercury pollution and general overfishing the fishermen's situation had become disastrous by the time Cameron wrote his epilogue, although Canso, he found, had managed somehow to pull through. Summarizing the achievement of the strikers, Cameron sounds an unabashedly heroic strain:

In the end the fishermen were collective heroes and martyrs who lost the battle for themselves but won it for their brothers. They smashed the archaic prohibition on fishermen's unions and left unionism firmly established on the draggers. They changed the law, changed conditions on the boats, and left the see-saw of power balanced a little more evenly.

... They showed us what the labour movement was really all about ... Thousands of Nova Scotians who had dismissed the labour movement ... suddenly saw anew its fundamental glory, its insistence on respect for human labour and its resistance to the moral squalor of exploitation. If the strike was a failure, let us pray for more failures like it.
(EER 236)

It is clear that what fires Cameron's imagination and pervades his narrative is the larger symbolic value of the strike, its power to 'educate' us into a sense of our fundamental human rights and responsibilities, regardless of class background or social position. Yet *The Education of Everett Richardson* is, as its dedication discloses, written *for* the fishermen: Cameron sets himself the task of creating a text which will not only interpret and convey the significance of the strike for his largely middle-class readers, but which will also communicate that information to the fishermen and their families, an essentially non-literate audience making use of other means of entertainment and instruction than reading and writing. It is in his attempt to bring together these two audiences that the main literary interest of Cameron's text resides.

Cameron organizes his narrative into chapters whose headings – 'Grade School,' 'Junior College,' 'Graduate Study,' and so on – both mock and reassert the value of education in contemporary Canadian society. Satirizing the reprehensible ignorance of the educational system's *fines fleurs* – judges, lawyers, law officers, Church executives, and corporate businessmen – celebrating the kind of experiential education which involves the crossing of boundaries and rerouting of minds, Cameron shows how one heterogeneous group of people – fishermen and their families, an Anglican clergyman, a number of radical middle-class students and, of course, the author himself – learned together a lesson about the uses and abuses of power, and the ways in which a system created to maintain the privileges of an élite can be subverted to sustain the rights of the mass.

The text opens with a prologue which serves a purpose similar to that of *Each Man's Son*: creating a historical backdrop for the story into which the reader is to be launched. Thus in some three pages Cameron introduces us to his representative fisherman, Everett Richardson, and to the interrelationship of Europe, Canso, and the fisheries – a factor of some importance, as one of the companies picketed by the fishermen is owned by a British corporation. Where MacLennan moves from the general (the geography of Cape Breton and the temperament of the Highlanders) to the specific (the predicament of one Daniel Ainslie). Cameron reverses this order, opening with the circumstances in which Everett Richardson signs his first union card, and then moving into a synopsis of Canso's original historical and economic importance, to finish with the fact of the strike and its significance to those who participated in or read about it. Since one of Cameron's aims is to reveal the dignity and importance of the fishermen, he needs a prologue to create appropriate expectations: who of his readers born and bred west of the New Brunswick-Québec border will know anything about a 'backwater' like Canso, or care about people named Eddie Dort or Edison Lumsden?

In the prologue, too, Cameron identifies himself as narrator, indicating where his sympathies lie. By mid-text his 'I' has become 'we' as he identifies himself with the fishermen and their cause, and attempts to reassure his readers as to his narrative integrity: 'I *am* biased, but I hope I'm not unfair. In general I'm sympathetic to the workers, not to the multinational corporations, and I think their account of the strike and its causes is a load of horse-shit. But I've given it to you as completely and fairly as I can. You can judge it for yourselves' (EER 119). Remembering MacLennan's presentation of Louis Camire, it must be admitted that Cameron, despite his rhetoric, has indeed been fair to both sides, letting representatives of each tell their story. The first of his three 'Interludes' is a case in point; here Cameron introduces us to two principal figures of the fishermen's strike in Canso. In the context of MacLennan's penchant for classicizing local history, the Interlude's opening sen-

tence is especially felicitous: 'The two symbolic figures, grappling together like some downeast Hector and Achilles, are Donnie Cadegan
and Homer Stevens' (EER 42).

Essentially, Cameron lets Cadegan, the manager of Acadia Fisheries,
speak for himself and his company; then, Cameron lets others speak
about Stevens, organizer for the United Fishermen and Allied Workers,
and a member of the Canadian Communist Party. What fascinates
Cameron is not the differences between the two men but rather their
similarities – and, of course, the intensely dramatic situation into
which both men's political choices have led them: 'Sons of fish merchants
in Glace Bay and Port Guichon, peddling fish from door to door. Poor
boys, full of intelligence and energy. Boys with a mark to make. Eyeball
to eyeball in the Strait of Canso in the spring of 1970' (EER 54).

The economy and clarity of Cameron's comparison of this Hector and
Achilles are masterly, as is his manipulation of that primal element of
conflict which makes any strike, properly explored, consummate dramatic material. Yet Cameron refuses in the remainder of his narrative to
stage a piscine Trojan War – having isolated Cadegan and Stevens for
our consideration in this Interlude, he promptly sets them down again
into that 'crowd' of scabs and strikers whose collective story he has set
out to tell. Dramatic situations continue to crop up throughout his
narrative, but no one individual claims centre stage. Though Cameron
needs a character through whom to thread his narrative line, in choosing the unexceptional Everett Richardson for this purpose he manages to
maintain and to further delineate his focus on the group and on that
collective heroism his narrative celebrates.

If Cameron satisfactorily handles the problems of his own narrative
role and alignment, and of his text's commitment to the collective as
opposed to individuals, how then does he deal with the dilemma posed
by the two different kinds of people for whom his book is written –
the fishermen, whose largely oral tradition he emphasizes by using traditional folk songs and shanties as epigraphs to some of his chapters –
and the 'book-learned' reader? Let us look first at Cameron's second
'Interlude,' which is a species of apology, placating the reader whose
expectations that Cameron's account of the strike will read like a novel
are being utterly frustrated:

Cherished reader, if you are bored by now I don't blame you. The summer went
on like the dull pain of a toothache: meetings and statements, resolutions and
pamphlets, as though the sharp and urgent cry of the fishermen for justice had
somehow been absorbed by bureaucrats. We are waiting, waiting, waiting for

something decisive to happen. It doesn't … If this were a novel I could wave a hand and abolish the tedium. But it's not a novel and these are real people, real events … In a way it's *important* that you and I endure together the irritations, the frustrations, and the ennui of that long, inconclusive summer. We're following a strike, and strikes have periods like that. (EER 118–19)

Inviting the reader to identify with him – 'We're following a strike' – Cameron returns to his embrace of the fishermen's experience: 'The days grind by, like sandpaper. We're low on food, the phone is cut off, the power commission is sending dunning letters … [I]f we express our frustration, the press will thunder at us for violence and irresponsibility. If we take it out on one another, our unity will dissolve and we'll drift back to the boats, one at a time … You're bored, cherished reader, and so am I. And so were the fishermen for whom there was no mid-term break, no relief, no clarity' (EER 119–20).

Here Cameron turns the disadvantages of his chosen 'chronicle' form into an argument for that form's epistemological validity: you can't *know* how the fishermen felt unless you *experience* a bit of what they felt – if not the penury then at least the boredom and frustration. In the process, Cameron argues, the reader will learn the reality and value of those skills of 'self-discipline, will, and forebearance' which successful strikers must develop (EER 120). This second Interlude succeeds, as does the first, in engaging the reader and schooling her or his expectations without compromising Cameron's primary narratological commitment to the fishermen.

When we consider the final Interlude, however, we find Cameron attempting, not to involve his readers in the fishermen's strike, but rather, to involve the fishermen in his narrative. Entitled 'Country Cunning and Unofficial Life' and prefaced by a Nova Scotia folk song in which grog, rum, tobacco, and gin-drinking lassies feature prominently, the chapter is couched in the form of a letter to Everett from Don, a piece of private correspondence set out for the public good. In it Cameron celebrates the people of Canso precisely because they are not middle-class, middle-income, middle-brow. 'Warm-hearted, raucous, vital and vulgar' with 'a sound set of values' which only insiders can recognize for what they are: such are the people of whom Cameron has come to think himself part (EER 166). Much of the Interlude is given up to describing the ways in which country people get round the values imposed on them by the 'polite, dutiful and mealy-mouthed,' and the regulations set up by a 'liberal-capitalist' system (EER 166–7). What the system terms unreliable and irresponsible Cameron finds full of *élan vital*: wildcatting so that 'the boys' can go hunting or swimming once in a while; couples deserting the production line to make love in the woods; bootleggers leading Mounties on wild goose chases; workers pinching tools from the worksite.

Manoeuvres like these Cameron classifies as 'country cunning'; by 'unofficial life' he means the life that no one in the centre or the city knows or cares to find out about. It is 'peasant' life, by which, Cameron reassures Everett, he means praise and not insult. The peasant, he argues, is someone living outside the cash economy, someone who can shift for himself in a countryside he knows intimately and expertly. The kind of life Cameron's fishermen-peasants lead is one centred on local, community affairs; it ignores the metropolis just as the metropolis ignores it. But unofficial life is endangered as 'peasants' become a rusticated industrialized proletariat; as corporate capitalism brings about the 'gradual reduction of rounded human beings into workers and consumers' (EER 173) — the major reason that a strongly independent union is essential for the fishermen of Canso.

The trouble with Cameron's third Interlude lies in its premise that the narrator can become one with his subjects and interpret them to themselves. The only possible way for Cameron to write a book *for* the fishermen, to let them, as much as possible, author the text is to let the fishermen speak for and among themselves — which they do with verve, dignity, and acerbic intelligence through most of the narrative. This Interlude, which Cameron intends as a hymn to the rural Maritimer, is, however, really aimed at ignorant urban readers who need to be taken down a peg in their probable condescension regarding the fishermen and their plight. And just as MacLennan fails in his ultra-negative portrayal of the socialist Louis Camire, so Cameron fails in his glorification of the Canso 'peasants.' Under a critique of urban values he slips in a sentimental portrait of country people that reads all too much like a cross between *Anne's House of Dreams* and *The Rowdyman*. What Cameron manages to achieve in his first chapter — a convincing tribute to the unpretentious courage and vitality of the fishermen — eludes him in this Interlude, often because his tone falters or becomes fatuous: 'Most lives include too much boredom and too few outdoor orgasms' (EER 167). When he tells Everett that he and his fellows 'have become for Nova Scotians what Mahatma Gandhi and Martin Luther King had been in their communities' (EER 174) the result is bathos — not because the fishermen have not indeed endured and in some ways triumphed over colossal odds, but because Cameron's sympathy with the fishermen has turned to kitsch.

Milan Kundera's novel *The Unbearable Lightness of Being* defines kitsch as 'excluding everything from its purview which is essentially unacceptable in human existence.'[54] What Cameron excludes from his account of 'unofficial life' are the elements of that life unacceptable, not just to consumer-cultured, but also to the kind of people who will read and sympathize with Cameron's book. In his opening pages Cameron touches on the 'dark side' of life in the fishing village: 'if you are interested in books or music or science, in the world of ideas, you will not find your growth in the village' (EER 224). The limitations to which Cameron here alludes are precisely those against which a Daniel Ainslie butts his head.

Kitsch, declares Kundera, is a special sort of feeling; to transpose Cameron's text onto the example Kundera uses, we might say that kitsch is not simply the statement, 'How good it is to find people who are still freely, freshly vital and vulgar'; it is more the reflection, 'How good to feel good that people who are freely, freshly vulgar still exist.' Kundera's conclusion that 'The brotherhood of man on earth will be possible only on a base of kitsch'[55] becomes especially apt when we encounter our narrator in the epilogue of his text, seating himself in the bait shed 'to read to my brothers the final pages of the book I had written for them' (EER 236–7). Again, it is not the reading itself which makes one wince – one of the most poignant parts of *The Education of Everett Richardson* occurs when Cameron, asking Everett his opinion of the book is told that the man for whom he has written this book has never finished it. 'Everett doesn't read very fast,' his wife explains. 'So I was reading it out in the evenings to the whole family ... But then it got to be summer ... and visitors and what not, and we put it aside and just never got back to it' (EER 233).

Cameron then tells how, at Everett's suggestion, he read aloud the end of his text to a group of fishermen gathered in the bait shed: their responses and his analysis of what the strike achieved bring *The Education of Everett Richardson* to a close. Cameron is almost able to let the fishermen have the last word, in their own words, but the call of kitsch is too strong. He ends his narrative with a chorus from *Solidarity Forever*: 'We can bring to birth a new world from the ashes of the old / For the union makes us strong.' However heartfelt, this sentiment betrays the very strength of Cameron's book, its rootedness, not in the *Internationale*, not in working-class or bourgeois kitsch, but in a unique and saving, *local* 'history, geography, language, tradition' (EER 174).

***

This chapter has attempted to reveal a cross-section of Maritime political sensibility as reflected in the region's fiction: the weirdly concerted inertia of De Mille's conservatism, MacLennan's dedication to the rights of the exceptional individual and his animosity towards collective action and achievement, and finally the radical 'conservatism' of Cameron, born-again Maritimer, defending like another former west coaster, David Alexander, 'the integrity and validity of the small society and culture in the great economic blocks and political federations of the modern world.'[56] Elements of all three kinds of sensibility feature, as we shall next see, in the development of a significant Maritime mode – realism.

# 6

# Reading the Real:
# Maritime Strategies

Nowlan's stories ... reveal his preoccupation with class; most of them are about the working class, the mill workers and loggers without much education, and their wives and lives of quiet desperation.

WILLIAM FRENCH[1]

It would be fun to write about the curious habits of the bourgeoisie as observed by a spy from the lumpenproletariat. There's an old joke to the effect that God segregates the Baptists in Heaven because He can't bring Himself to dispel them of the illusion that they're the only people there. The middle classes suffer from much the same delusion.

ALDEN NOWLAN[2]

As these epigraphs testify, our understanding of our common world and of those literary texts which attempt to explore and reveal it is often skewed by schematic misreading, by expecting every text to reproduce the perspectives and conventions belonging to our own social class and context. As Nowlan might have argued, we can imagine a Miramichi reader finding Timothy Findley's fiction as preoccupied with class – upper-middle rather than working – as French finds Nowlan's. What is revealing about his response to Nowlan's work is not only French's own unacknowledged class preoccupations but also his critical discomfort with a mode of Maritime fiction which eschews the lyrical vision and style of a writer like Ernest Buckler. In an initial review of David Adams Richards's latest novel, *Road to the Stilt House*, French ex-

pressed the fear that Richards's 'desolate and depressing' subject matter
will alienate readers – 'Who wants deliberately to court melancholia
when so many pleasant diversions are within easy reach?' In urging him
to quit the dreary precincts of the proles and 'expand his horizons,'
French would seem to have been counselling Richards to produce not
'antidote[s] to middle-class smugness' but rather anatomies of it.[3] Re-
viewing an earlier Richards novel, Douglas Barbour makes the assumption that readers can't be expected to care for 'crude' characters or to
enjoy reading about dark, bleak lives (which would presumably put *King
Lear* or *Waiting for Godot* beyond the pale); Fraser Sutherland, for his
part, seems barely able to tolerate such a work as Alden Nowlan's *Various Persons Named Kevin O'Brien*, given its lack of 'life-affirming'
qualities.[4]

   If the business of realism is mimesis, the text's faithful re-presenting of
a 'given' reality, then perhaps these critics' real quarrel lies not with
these texts but with the region which authors them. In the Maritimes,
isolation and impoverishment have nearly always been the normal
conditions of life for a hefty number of people. This is a fact we prefer to
leave 'outside the canon' of what we recognize as real, and there
would seem to be something profoundly shocking, even subversive in
writers like Maillet and MacLeod suggesting that the lives of dirt-poor
charwomen, fishermen, and coal-miners are as significant – as 'real' – as
those of the educated and urbane, for whom poverty is exclusively an
existential, even a metaphysical affair.[5] What this chapter will attempt to
show is that in the work of recent Maritime writers new strategies
have emerged to help us read the lives of the inarticulate and impoverished; to comprehend and indeed, value them. Once proficient in this
kind of reading, we may also come to understand how, as at least one
critic has argued, the 'pervasiveness of human degradation' in the
work of a writer like David Adams Richards is not a mere shock tactic to
jolt 'the reader secure in his garrison of Vancouver or Toronto, who
knows the Maritimes only from the songs of Anne Murray or an auto trip
along the Cabot Trail.' It stems, rather, from a vision of life 'closer to
the Canadian reality than either the traditional True North self-
glorification or the more recent self-pitying Victim / Survival syndrome
...'[6]

   If the reality that Maritime fiction explores is intensely regional and yet
national as well, the realism of which writers as diverse as Alistair
MacLeod and David Adams Richards make use is an equally complex
matter. Realism, as traditionally defined, explores the lives of individual characters within the social, economic, and broadly political contexts

which shape those lives. It does not, as George Woodcock would have it, preclude the creation of an 'alternate world of the imagination.'[7] Rather, as Georg Lukács has shown, it pits the privately imagined and desired against a brutal public world which resists all attempts to reform or remake it. In exposing these contradictions between public and private worlds, realism becomes, for Lukács, 'a search for that deeper essence of reality that is hidden under the surface.'[8]

Finally, realism may be described not only as a literary mode but as a language as well, a way of speaking the world. Nowlan and Mac-Leod, Antonine Maillet and David Adams Richards all use this language in widely different ways to create fictive worlds which themselves articulate, accentuate, and rephrase significant aspects of the writers' and readers' 'given' world. In the process they contest 'canonical' reality – that which is complacently and agreeably life-affirming – and take their place within a long-standing literary tradition in the Maritimes, a tradition in which the facts of poverty and the experience of impoverishment engage both author and text. From Thomas McCulloch, describing how the poor stuff broken windows with rags to keep out winter winds in The Stepsure Letters, to Ernest Buckler noting that Nova Scotia is 'more locust for the heart than lotus,'[9] Maritime writers have acknowledged an inescapable home truth. Kent Thompson has pointed out that in the stories of Alden Nowlan 'poverty is not even the point, but simply an assumption, a fact of life.'[10] It is, however, an assumption that Nowlan explores as well as exploits in his fiction: 'the distance between the rich and the poor,' he notes in Various Persons Named Kevin O'Brien, 'is less than the distance between the poor and the poverty-stricken. The problem of the poor is that they lack money, while to the poverty-stricken the lack of money is almost irrelevant, in the sense that the cause of his disease is almost irrelevant to the victim of cancer.'[11]

Those who fault the prose of Nowlan or Richards for its joylessness might well recall that life in the Maritimes, particularly New Brunswick, has not always been the idyll that we associate with the writings of Charles G.D. Roberts and Bliss Carman. As Nowlan pointed out, New Brunswick, up to the 1950s was 'still in the era of the Parish Overseer of the Poor.'[12] And until 1928 traces could be found of the 'contract system' whereby 'farmers, shopkeepers and others could arrange to house, feed and clothe paupers for a certain yearly sum to be paid to them by the parish ... [I]t was in the contractor's interest to poorly treat his charge in order to get as much work out of his paupers [as possible] at least expense to himself.'[13]

The fact of poverty and the experience of impoverishment in contemporary Canadian society have been overlooked or minimized by many prominent critics. One of George Woodcock's reasons for undervaluing realism as a literary mode is that, since 'we all live in the supermarket, hire-purchase, high-living standard environment that extends from El Paso to Yellowknife,'[14] realism has nothing to tell us any more about ourselves or others. Bruce Hutchison acknowledges the omnipresence of poverty in the Maritimes only to transvalue it beyond recognition. His decently, unashamedly poor Maritimes in which everyone's clothes are neatly patched and shoes shined; in which 'every face glistens with soap and water,'[15] has nothing to do with Nowlan's or even Richards's 'world of Maritimers, who, when they tire of dancing, go down the road to drink white lightening, wearing their spiked logging boots and home-made brass knuckles, a world where one finds "men ... who have never heard of Canada".'[16]

To make fiction out of this kind of impoverishment one needs, to quote Nowlan's Kevin O'Brien, a mind which doesn't discriminate between the 'flesh and blood and bone' of experience and the 'urine and excrement'; between 'what ought to be assimilated and what ought to be evacuated' (VP 117). Ever since 'Censor' rapped Thomas McCulloch over the knuckles for mentioning flatulence and chamberpots in front of the gentle reader, Maritime writers have trespassed against the oughts and ought-nots. This is not to deny that the region has produced its share of unregenerate idylls, but to point out that there have always been writers able to comprehend within their fictive worlds both the beauty of landscape and the brutal conditions of much Maritime life. Silver Donald Cameron argues the east of Québec lies 'the most realistic, concrete, anecdotal region of Canada,' a region which has produced writers formed for the most part, not by universities and artistic coteries, but 'by the truths taught by a kind of life few artists ever see at all' – the truths of 'ironstone and brine.'[17]

That Cameron's words are not merely a convert's whistling in the dark may be determined by a brief look at the tradition of Maritime realism – a state of mind as well as pen – from Haliburton's time on. Blurb-fabricators praising The Clockmaker for its 'fresh and funny' observations on human nature make no comment on chapters equally fresh if less amusing – not only the celebrated 'The White Nigger,' but such chapters as 'Setting Up for Governor,' in which the following vignette appears: 'to look round and see the poverty – the half-naked children, the old pine stumps for chairs; a small bin of poor watery yaller potatoes in the corner; daylight through the sides and roof of the house ... all black where the smoke got out; no utensils for cookin' or eatin', and starvation wrote as plain as a handbill on their holler cheeks, skinny fingers and sunk eyes – went right straight to the heart.'[18]

Even Charles G.D. Roberts when he wrote of lovers not in Acadie but in the Tantramar veered towards realism. Fred Cogswell – in 1967, before the arrival of David Adams Richards on his province's literary scene – described *The Heart that Knows* as 'the best realistic novel of New Brunswick yet written,' praising its 'attack on the "respectable" morality of the province.'[19] (Unfortunately, Roberts was unable to resist cooking up a cream-puff ending for his tale of a 'fallen woman' who refuses to see herself as others see her; otherwise his novel would have been remarkable indeed.) And Frank Parker Day's *Rockbound*, for all that its final chapters collapse into fairy-tale, does for Maritime fishermen and their families something of what Frederick Philip Grove did for the homesteaders of the West.

Thomas Raddall, in spite of the fact that his considerable descriptive skills have been channelled into historical romance – or romance pure and simple – has also contributed to the development of realism in Maritime literature. In *Tidefall* and *The Wings of Night* Raddall manages to create powerful evocations of economic realities. The first novel opens with a convincing account of a depression-era Nova Scotia seaport, its straggling, unpainted houses, decrepit wharf, and crumbling warehouses: 'A reek of fish and decayed lobster shells hung about the waterfront and crept about the houses on the cold breeze from the sea. The whole history of Port Baron was one of exposure and hard living and it was written on its face.'[20]

Before this fiction succumbs, à la *Rockbound*, to romance, Raddall manages to set up a near-Balzacian conflict between the ethos of those nineteenth-century adventurers who, after amassing fortunes, attempted to become moral and economic benefactors of their societies, and that of the modern capitalist who, by grossly immoral and illegal means, makes his bundle without a thought either for the well-being of his fellows or for the state of his own soul. And in *The Wings of Night*, Raddall throws away what could have been a superb account of the moral, social, and economic effects of political corruption in a small Nova Scotia lumber town. Yet before love takes its toll Raddall manages powerfully to evoke the decay of the old lumber aristocracy, with its disintegrating wooden mansions and emotionally paralyzed children.

Raddall, however, is ultimately a realist *manqué*: absent from even his non-historical fiction is that awareness of a 'language of reality' which makes of novels like *The Mountain and the Valley* and *The Channel Shore*

landmark texts in the revitalization of Maritime realism. While both
Buckler and Bruce deal with communities to whom Hutchison's diagno-
sis of 'proud poverty' might apply; though both emphasize beauty of
place and richness of experience, they do engage with a fundamental
problem that has preoccupied their successors, particularly David Adams Richards. In a rather grudging review of *Blood Ties*, Douglas Barbour
yet manages to put his finger on the nature of Richards's achievement:
'Richards is trying something pretty tricky here, the articulation in his
fiction of the feelings and half-thoughts of basically inarticulate people [who] ... cannot clearly speak their own feelings of despair or fear,
not even to themselves.'[21]

Buckler's approach to this problem was, as Barbour notes, to create
the 'highly articulate, psychologically acute' David, a character of and
among the inarticulate villagers but who has been given the gift of
tongues – a language and vision to perceive and communicate the significant reality of his people's ordinary lives. Yet one of the most disconcert-
ing features of *Mountain* is the enormous discrepancy one finds between the farming life and natural world whose directness and simplicity
Buckler values so highly, and the philosophically burdened prose in
which he evokes this life and world. To compensate for the cultural
impoverishment of his chosen rural scene, the 'hi-yup-fuhllas' nature
of popular speech, Buckler steeps the reader in aesthetically heightened,
often torturous prose, a language of educated consciousness to which
none of his characters save David has access. It is as though Buckler
cannot trust his reader, cannot let his people speak for themselves –
he must 'tell' them for us in order to reveal not just their crude surfaces
but more importantly, that essence which the narrator can express
only in super-literary language. At times, indeed, it is as if Proust's
Marcel had woken up, not in a strange Parisian hotel room, but in an
even stranger farmhouse in the Annapolis Valley.

Charles Bruce, on the other hand, avoids major transitional shocks
between the dialects native to farmers and fishermen, and to university graduates, by adopting one language in which all characters including
the narrator speak and think. It is a low-key 'correct' as opposed to
rough-and-folksy speech, lacking the lyricism and grandiloquence of
Buckler's chosen mode, but it acquires an incremental power and
dignity through Bruce's manipulation of recurring rhythms and speech
patterns. Yet this very homogeneity of speech, this merging of narrative voice and the native speech of his characters can be seen as a blur-
ring or misrepresentation of the distinctive reality Bruce is striving to
convey.

It is with Nowlan, Richards, Antonine Maillet, and Alistair MacLeod that Maritime realism truly comes of age as a literary mode and as a language which accommodates both illiterate character and educated reader, linking the worlds of the poverty-stricken and the aimlessly affluent. To representative works by each of these four writers we will now turn.

\*\*\*

'Help me,' she writes. 'I need coat, I need shoes. I need medicine, I am old. Help me.' *Help* is one of the words that convey a special meaning, not to be found in any dictionary, in the dialect of that part of Nova Scotia where I was born and grew up ... *Help* ... meant not comfort or advice but goods or money that, at least in the opinion of the recipient, were not so much given as shared.

Alden Nowlan (VP 98)

*The Mountain and the Valley* is a significant work of Canadian literature, and it is certain that no case can be made for the 'superiority' of a text like *Various Persons Named Kevin O'Brien* over Buckler's acknowledged masterpiece. Yet Nowlan's novel is of immense value precisely because it is so defiantly *not* a lyrical, life-affirming evocation of rural life – because it is 'hard,' not 'soft' realism, with all the sharp discomfort that hardness entails.

In his fiction Nowlan is able to convey, as did Haliburton and McCulloch, dirt poverty and its attendant ills – the brutalizing of human relationships, the extinction of hope for anything brighter or better than brute subsistence. In *Miracle at Indian River* and *Will Ye Let the Mummers In?* the narrative voice is discerning and dispassionate in recording the squalor in which the rural poor eke out their lives. Yet if the narrator insists that such conditions are abominable and intolerable he is just as insistent that the people trapped in them are not. And in his finest stories – 'The Glass Roses,' 'At the Edge of the Woods,' 'Nightmare' – we find a sensitive and open consciousness pitted against the crude, closed mentality of place. Often the 'open' character is a child – no David Canaan, gifted with extraordinary imaginative and linguistic skills, but just an ordinary child with the child's birthright of wonder, terror, and delight not yet extinguished by the stupidity and bleakness of the adult world. Through such fictive but not literary children, the educated, sensitive, middle-class reader is given an emotional entrée into a world that otherwise would remain repugnant and impenetrable – for Nowlan, though he occasionally totters into sentimentality, can be ruthless about presenting the warts-and-all of his backwoods people, as the right-wing rednecks in a story like 'Prisoners of War' reveal.

One of the essential features of 'hard' realism as it has developed in the Maritimes is a consciousness of how language is implicated in the process of impoverishment, victimizing those who cannot aspire to correct or educated speech, and liberating those who can. In *Kevin O'Brien* Nowlan uses language to create an anatomy of poverty, making us see and know 'his' people, and as importantly, interrogating his own relation to literacy, that power which has both rescued and alienated him from 'his own.' This 'fictional memoir' is the story of a returned prodigy, not prodigal; it is a self-conscious narrative in a much different sense than is *The Mountain and the Valley*. Buckler's narrative consciousness is supersaturated with the sense of his role as priest of the Annapolis Valley imagination, its aesthetic smithy. Nowlan's O'Brien, on the other hand, is obsessed both with his own sense of dislocation – 'it's as though I were dreaming and knew I was dreaming but couldn't remember who I was or where I lived when I was awake' (VP 1) – and with the problematic nature of truth wherever memory and human relations are involved. He is out to present Lockhartville as he finds it and not, like Buckler, to 'make the light shine kindly' on its people.[22] Whereas David Canaan is in thrall to a past so beneficient and idyllic that it prevents him from living the present, Kevin O'Brien is 'the prisoner of a past that he is unable either to accept or reject' (VP 5) because of its continuing ugliness, desolation, and pain.

Much of what Kevin O'Brien remembers once back on his inhospitable native soil can be found anywhere: the inventive cruelty of children towards one another, the first ecstatic and first disillusioning experiences of sex. Other flashbacks – to the atrocious lives of his parents or the disintegration of his Aunt Kathleen, for example – need to be mediated by a narrator who can make real for the outside reader a world of absolute misery and closure. One way to accomplish such mediation is through that staple of realism, the creation of a convincing fictive world, in this case the appropriately named village of Lockhartville.

Lockhartville is outside the world – the introduction of television, we are told, has only widened an already immense gap, 'since little or nothing that appears on the screen has the remotest connection with what can be seen from the window' (VP 13). Even the sounds of the radio, we are told, are like 'the images seen by the inhabitants of Plato's cave' (VP 39). It is this abyss between Kevin's village and the larger world which is his salvation and damnation; since there *is* another world, he can escape into it; because he escapes, he betrays all those who couldn't, all those who weren't able even to imagine anything other than their poverty.

What Kevin escapes he makes damningly clear: 'poverty unlike that which afflicted the urban middle classes during the Depression. That kind of poverty compares with ours as a hit-and-run accident, in which the victim escapes death or serious injury, compares with a cogenital and incurable disease' (VP 79–80). In this 'almost intolerable environment' joy can be found only rarely, even miraculously – at a country dance, or on Christmas day. Nowlan's description of Christmas celebrations in Lockhartville should be read alongside Buckler's Christmas chapter in *Mountain* as an illustration both of the enormous difference between 'poor' and 'poverty-stricken,' and of the contrast between the consummate nostalgia of Buckler's fictionalized memories and the knifing clarity of Nowlan's.

Lockhartville is an infernal antidote to the paradise of Buckler's Entremont; it is composed of a different set of realities than those Buckler (whom Nowlan greatly admired) emphasized in his writing about Nova Scotia. The very landscape in which O'Brien grew up is impoverished – 'Good-for-nothing trees. Grotesquely overgrown weeds' (VP 4). Struggling up from 'thin-soil country' (VP 89), the village offers bare subsistence to its inhabitants, raised on bread, molasses, hard liquor, and violence. Recalling how he went barefoot to school, limping over stones and broken glass, O'Brien implies that his home ground was little different from the benighted European villages which immigrants forsook for a 'better life' in Canada (VP 138).

As bad as the material deprivation is the servile mentality it engenders. Thus Kevin's father admonishes him after his son has sent a sympathetic letter to a left-wing newspaper (and consequently, been visited by the Mounties). 'People like us,' he counsels, 'should keep our mouths shut and our arses down' (VP 125). This, of course, is the father who 'has worked for fifty years and never once had a permanent year-round job ... [or] a job that a machine couldn't have done better had there been a machine to do it' (VP 47).

Predictably, Kevin's relations with his father are minimal, as they are with most of his family, even the sister to whom, in his childhood, he was literally hyphenated as 'Kevin-Stephanie.' As a child he had been intensely ashamed, and, as an adult, uneasily proud of 'his grandmother, an old peasant woman, [who] had sat up all through the last night of her life, singing songs to entertain herself and Death' (VP 64). Everyone else he describes, however, lacks the passion, humour, dignity, and active cunning that characterize Antonine Maillet's Sagouine and her peers; the integrity which makes Alistair MacLeod's poverty-doomed Cape Bretoners almost terrifyingly noble. There are some kinds of poverty, Nowlan makes clear, which reduce people to 'work-beast[s]' (VP 97) whose only achievement is subsistence itself. Rarely do the inhabitants of Lockhartville revenge themselves on the world outside – once in a while they manage to sell to townspeople organic 'country' pumpkins that they have, in fact, harvested from the town dump (VP 59).

Such a life Kevin compares to protracted drowning or execution (VP 97); intolerable as it is, it breeds a worse condition – 'the reality of nightmare [forcing itself] ... into the very core of the mind' (VP 16–17) – nightmares the terror of which readers of Nowlan's poetry will know well. Yet outside the everyday horror of Lockhartville and the reality of nightmare there exists not so much another reality as the believable fiction 'that there must be more to the world than he had experienced in this village.' To have lost faith in that something more, Kevin confesses, would have been to lose 'any reason to keep in touch with reality' (VP 122). Yet once he has escaped from the village, once he feels safe enough to return temporarily, O'Brien feels compelled to get back in touch with the very reality he has abandoned, and to get in touch with it through his very means of escape – written language.

Nowlan begins the first chapter of his memoir with an authorial 'we' addressed to a readerly 'you,' but this quickly changes to a fluctuating 'I-he' as the reader is moved back from the present impressions with which each chapter begins, into shifting, formless memories. O'Brien's motives for writing his past are mixed – 'to explore and explain' (VP 23), to exorcize (VP 41), and also to make the reader – a sympathetic member of 'that great communion, the human race' (VP 51) acknowledge the existence of Lockhartville and its people within the same communion. This he does by translating forms of speech – for example, the word 'help' as understood in Lockhartville – or by translating people and their actions. Kevin's memories of the mother who abandoned him – or rather his memories of what people have told him about the 'big blonde,' 'that stinking bitch, that cow' (VP 31–2) are presented to us in such a way that the child's hurt, love, loss, and revulsion disarm us – we accept his mother, however reluctantly, as one of us. Even the savage aunt who reviles Kevin's mother to his face is made human by her very inarticulateness, so that we acknowledge even if we do not absolve her: 'In Aunt Lorna's voice a deep-throated adult sorrow gave way reluctantly to a whine almost like that of a small girl screwing down the lid on a sob ... [H]e could not distinguish sentences, only words jutting out like rocks from a river of murmurs' (VP 54).

Because Nowlan mediates the reality of Lockhartville through the persona of Kevin O'Brien, because his narrative successfully deploys two languages – that of the 'work-beasts' of Lockhartville, and that of the educated, middle-class reader – we can be moved, even as we are shocked by life at economic, cultural, and social degree zero. The fictive door through which we enter this appalling world is also the door by which we exit from it – ironically, it is because Kevin O'Brien is such a successful interpreter, because there is an appropriate intermediary in the first place, that we can ultimately dismiss Lockhartville to the periphery of our consciousness. After all, whereas the child Kevin can only believe in the existence of a larger, wider, better world, Nowlan's readers have most likely always inhabited it. In David Adams Richards's fiction, however, no intermediaries are permitted. We are plunged into the raw speech, consciousness, reality of the radically poor, a reality so insistently presented that it becomes the larger world, banishing the reader's clean, well-lit accustomed place to an invisible periphery.

\*\*\*

I was born of slaves, thinks Kevin O'Brien as he drives away from the mill. I was born of slaves and because the brand of slavery is burnt into my flesh I have been prey to dreams in which I could be omnipotent. But I am putting that behind me now; I am squeezing the slave from my ego and need no longer play at being lord of the universe. (VP 117)

David Adams Richards's characters have squeezed the slave from their ego and ceased lording the universe in their dreams – but at a price; they no longer possess any notion of freedom and if they still have dreams they are almost all the kind that one instantly forgets upon waking. Among Richards's Miramichi people we find no David Canaans or even Kevin O'Briens; their speech (most of which consists of variations on 'fuck' as noun, adjective and verb) and their consciousness alike are minimalist, and Richards's narrational style, with its repetitions and fragmentations does not relieve but rather increases the pressure of an intolerably dreary, foreclosed reality.

Richards is impressive not only for his precocity and the sheer volume of his ouevre but also for the development of his aesthetic, from the dogged naturalism of *The Coming of Winter* to the complex realism of *Lives of Short Duration*. With the latter novel Richards has outgrown the irritating mannerisms of his earlier prose while retaining the distinctive, authoritative voice that work engendered. Without sacrificing the *donnée* of *Winter* – that the Miramichi is not just some grimy corner of the world, it *is* the world – he is able to expand and deepen his fictive world by introducing historical and symbolical elements. Moreover, he is able to create a narratological overview that permits the possibility of analysis, interpretation, and judgment of this world – all within the idiom and consciousness of representative characters – the old patriarch Simon Terri, for example, or his grandson Packet.

*The Coming of Winter* details the indeterminacy and immediate meaninglessness of experience among people for whom survival has ceased to be an active issue and subsistence has become a norm. *Blood Ties* creates a comparatively pastoral vision of life-in-the-family, introducing a new element of pathos to the narrative and permitting its characters to move from mere sensation (the stock-in-trade of *Winter*) to perception, however fragmentary. *Lives of Short Duration*, however, presents the reader with a fictive world completely realized according to an artistic vision mature enough to create a convincing political, social and economic context within which the lives of individual characters can be not merely comprehended but also felt as real.

*Lives of Short Duration* adapts certain high-modernist literary techniques for its own post-modernist purpose – to bring to life a sub- or post-literary world. Thus, the errant, dissolute George Terri is pursued, rather like Leopold Bloom, by snatches of song – not 'those lovely seaside girls,' but a jingle for a supermarket chain: 'Check, Check, Check Out the Difference at Sobey's.' (This jingle acts to tie together that gross bundle of trivia which constitutes his swill of consciousness.) *Lives*, like *Under the Volcano*, is spirally structured: we are given multiple perspectives on the same series of events, and we move backwards and forwards through time, the novel ending where it began, with a party on high school graduation night in backwoods New Brunswick. Like Lowry's Mexico, Richards's Miramichi is supersaturated with symbols and portents: garbage dumps, American voodoo jets screaming overhead, Begin and Sadat on television, the continual appearance in front of one character's house of the van that will eventually run him down. And finally, there is a quasi-Faulknerian element in Richards's use of local history – his recurring allusions to the 1880s murder of an Indian woman, Emma Jane Ward, and the story of a certain Hudson Kapochus setting out in 1825 'on a journey to kill a man.'[23] Richards skilfully interweaves these elements to give a sense of density and urgency to his fictive world. *Lives of Short Duration* makes it clear that this author is no *idiot savant* of the Miramichi, bludgeoning the life around him into novel-sized chunks, but an artist distanced enough from his material to find an authentic shape for its disjointed, discontinuous nature – his characters, after all, inhabit a world in which nothing means or matters any more.

The world of *Lives* is also one in which traditional social structures have rotted away, with not a moral or cultural touchstone left in sight. Nothing more noxious could be imagined than the novel's opening scene – a party at which a bridge is set on fire for fun, while guests consume massive quantities of charred pig, ogle one another, and belt out obscene songs. The party sequence brings together the familiar figures of Richards's New Brunswick, and introduces a new element – the politicians who blatantly sell themselves to higher-ups, and who buy, then betray, their constituents. But in addition to characters who suffer from a general cultural impoverishment while remaining well above the poverty line – entrepreneurs, winners of the Atlantic Loto, bootleggers, and drug peddlers – Richards's novel includes the Masey family, living in what can only be called a leprous poverty, exploited and reviled by their neighbours, and Indians such as the Wards, their circumstances so desperate they attempt a family suicide. The Miramichi, as Old Simon Terri has come to understand, is really a Third World country: 'People with swollen bellies lay in various corners of the earth – so Anne Murray told him on television, people with their skins wracked with sores, or hungry – and he'd seen on television ... the Palestinians – and children with flies crawling over their body, as he'd seen them crawl over Daniel Ward's children in Daniel Ward's house' (L 107).

Industrialism has brought vitriolic changes to a once self-sufficient region; spray planes buzz malevolently overhead, sulphuric acid dumped into the river burns the children who swim there, the landscape is despoiled as trees are razed to 'be sold, pulped, transported to the United States, made into toilet paper and sold back to us' (L 267). The Miramichi becomes Canada itself, that land 'bought and played with by foreigners ... When the woods were gone the rivers'd be gone, but there'd be iron ore, and when that was gone there was uranium also' (L 138). Yet more than the exploitation and destruction of material resources, Richards portrays the devastation of human lives. His novel literally overflows with passages such as the following lamentation:

'fuck ya, fuck ya,' for 'I love you, I love you' or 'Help me, help me.' The passionless day in the schools where nothing was said or learned, the poor teachers with baseball caps on their heads, their university rings polished on their fingers, looking at the fifteen- and sixteen-year-old girls, and the docile, never-be-taught Indians, some pregnant, sitting at the back with their heads on the desks, some knife-scarred along their bellies in the rites of drunken manhood, as day by day the afternoon winter months played on resolute, determined ... (L 110)

If Maritime realism is indeed a language, a means of communication between the speechless illiterate and the articulate educated, then Richards is a master of this language. The opening ten pages of *Lives* show the amazing flexibility of his prose, his ability to combine minimal sentence fragments with elaborately run-on sentences, to punctuate maundering monologues by his drunken characters with terse, pointed description and commentary so as to produce a narrative capable of conveying both the crudity and density of experience in this particular world. The structure of the novel is appropriately baggy-loose and yet held together by a story of three generations: the old patriarch Simon Terri who has spent sixty consecutive winters in the bush and who manages, in the course of the novel, to escape from his hospital bed and die in the woods; his grotesquely ignorant, exploitative, and luckless son George; and finally, George's children – Little Simon, a dope-pusher and petty gangster; Lois, who has borne three children by three different men and who lives scuzzily in a trailer; and Packet, who has somehow broken his family chains, given up drink and drugs, and who lives on the edge of the community with a great-great-granddaughter of the murdered Emma Jane Ward. The interstices of this backwoods *Buddenbrooks* are filled with violent, randomly related incidents – the botched killing of a moose calf, the bathing of an Indian child in scalding water, an abortion, a rape cum seduction, a father pushing his children's heads into a toilet bowl and flushing, the biting off of a man's ear in a fight. Richards relates the decay of the Terri family not to 'the human condition' but to economic exploitation and general social breakdown in the region; most of his characters show signs of this decay in their very speech: nasty, poor, brutish, and short, it is epitomized by the declaration 'I don't give a fuck fer nothin – never did, never will' (L 60).

Richards does, however, allow certain of his characters a species of interrogative consciousness. Packet, surveying his native place and people after a prolonged absence, asks himself: 'And didn't he grow up and fight in the school and fight on the way home from school and drown the cottagers' kittens if they paid him a quarter, by putting them in a feed-sack and standing on them ... And didn't he corner Billie

Masey one afternoon with his sister Susie? And while they crouched down in the corner of Alewood's store holding hands and huddling against each other, crying, did he or did he not threaten them with a burning cattail, the smell of black oil. Susie Masey's white dirty underwear' (L 238).

He ends his self-interrogation with 'all this ... *means?'* (L 254). This posing and half-answering of questions, after the near-complete passivity of speech and consciousness in the previous novels gives *Lives* a necessary anger and energy. The narrative shifts from dispassionate direct statement – 'They bootlegged and sold marijuana, they had bottles all over the kitchen. They had fights over hockey games' (L 59) – to orchestrated overview:

children staring from metal cribs into the long dark empty corridors with the sparse winter light coming through the grey venetian blinds – in a house that had not only no drink but not a book either, with vases and imitation fruit on their dusted furniture ... and the sad cardboard light-shades in the living rooms which no one entered until the priest / minister was invited for Sunday dinner ... Until the one thought in a child's mind was how fortunate you were to live here in a nice community without drink or books either, except the encyclopedia – until out of that, out of it all it would take an imbecile or a lunatic not to become a drunk before he was twenty. A thousand such hallways and rooms and lampshades on one of the most violent rivers in the country. (L 113–14)

This kind of generalization and judgment – alien to a work like *The Coming of Winter* – becomes the narrative equivalent of a wide-angle lens. It affords a degree of relief from Richards's focus on the minutiae of impoverishment without, however, diminishing the intolerable pressure of reality. Richards does not pacify or placate the reader by condemning the brutishness of the Miramichi. His judgments further tighten the screws on our perception of the viciousness of our common world, as, for example, when he has one of the novel's true villains, the 'uneducated, ignorant and stupid' Bennie show to his mistress's children 'a picture of a woman in such an obscene position that not only was it beneath eroticism it was beneath common lust' (L 199). Moreover, Richards combines discourse of this kind with responses true to the experience and consciousness of his characters. Thus old Simon Terri, who has lived through the virtual annihilation of his way of life as a backwoodsman and guide, moves through stages of awareness to anomie regarding the 'grey clouds of sulphur' from the nearby paper mills: 'For a long time he'd not minded the mills and then he saw a rinse in the water – and parr floating belly-up (like they did when someone blew a pool with dynamite) – and then he minded it. And then, now, he didn't mind it anymore' (L 99).

Richards's empathy with his characters, the very eloquence of his awareness of their desolation and despair, makes it necessary for us to understand rather than summarily reject the inescapable vileness that such poverty and impoverishment breed. More importantly, he forces us to acknowledge it as part of our own reality. We witness the aggressive loathing shown by Richards's New Brunswickers towards Vietnamese and Pakistani refugees and towards native Indians – 'squaw meant nothing more than cunt, and buck nothing other than cock' (L 224). We see how the very Acadians are perceived by their Anglophone neighbours as 'malfunctioning creatures who for some unknown reason preferred a mud bank beside a ditch to the river, a mosquito swamp to the bay' (L 153). These are sentiments we prefer not to hear; they do not belong to the Canada of our patriotic imaginings, a cheerfully tolerant multicultural haven. Richards presents prejudice and racism in their unadulterated, vigorous, damning forms, but prevents us from simply 'reading off' the region in which they flourish. These responses are too vicious for us to ignore or wish away; moreover, they are contrasted in the novel with a set of values encoded in the narrative – values which were barely latent in *Winter*, erratically present in *Blood Ties*, but which inform the whole of *Lives*. The river for all its violence, the woods, the old way of life-in-nature (as represented by an ancient photograph of two backwoodsmen, now gathering dust in a provincial archive) – these all make up that menaced 'beauty of the earth' surrounding the 'steel rod of pain' at the centre of life (L 237). As *Lives* reveals, the degradation of human life and the despoiling of the natural world are not mere *faits accomplis* – alternatives exist, however shakily. For the reader to merely shrug them off is to become complicit in the very degradation and despoliation this fiction represents.

The complex nature of Richards's own relation to the reality his novels confront may be seen in his treatment of Old Simon's slatternly granddaughter Lois. One of the most powerful moments in the novel occurs in the telling of Lois's loss of innocence – her virtual rape by a much older man who had been led on by the foul language and provocative manner the girl has ignorantly copied from the mother who has totally neglected her. Lois gives birth to children who grow up just as deprived: she makes her five-year-old roll tokes for her; before he is ten he is nearly picked up for trafficking by the RCMP. Yet against what seem

insurmountable odds, Richards succeeds in making us include Lois
within Nowlan's 'great communion, the human race.' His unsentimen-
tal, sensitive portrayal of her is one of the finest achievements of this
novel. Lois's paradoxical 'motif' – a rose tattoo which 'signified something pure and life-giving about her, exuded from her a quality of love,
though she said she'd gotten the rose tattoo on a $20 bet with a man, she
said, who couldn't hold his own piss' (L 123) – seems emblematic of
Richards's own conception of the Miramichi.

'He'd known men who would beat men senseless for no reason – and
women with narrow souls who would laugh and ridicule the beaten
men. These youngsters were no different. Their women would be no
different' (L 123). Such is the 'hard' realism of *Lives of Short Duration*, a
work which succeeds in communicating the full 'terror of brutish life'
(L 53). Ambitious, complex, the novel is certainly not without flaws and
overreachings, yet Richards's accomplishment is staggering. By the
sheer, passionate integrity of his vision, and the quality of his novelist's gifts he is able to relocate the 'canon of reality' from the civilized
'centre' to the backwoods 'region.' So insistently detailed and so per-
suasively evoked is the world of his rednecks and yahoos and blind,
damned souls that we end by recognizing the Miramichi as 'ours' and
not 'theirs.' No outer, other world exists to which a character like Packet
can escape or in which the reader can take refuge: Richards's is truly
a global village with its Boat People, its New York executives who
fly down in private planes for a weekend's shooting, its television
screens showing the whole world's brutality and suffering. If, as one of
Richards's characters suggests, Canada is a country 'where a person's
gloating ignorance of his fellow countrymen was considered the height
of achievement' (L 258), then Richards has jarringly turned the tables
on those who would have him quit his seedy provincial corner and move
on to brighter, better territory at the centre. As James Doyle has
remarked:

Richards's Miramichi, on first encounter, seems unique in the pervasiveness of
human degradation; but the drunkenness, the violence, the marital and family
conflict gradually emerge as concentrated reflections of modern North American
society. This society destroys nature and aboriginal peoples, ruthlessly sets
individuals against each other in economic, social, and sexual competition, then
salves its conscience with meaningless gestures of institutionalized benevolence ... In the mood of self-pity, Canadians are fond of complaining that their
country, and the world as a whole, is being Americanized; Richards suggests,
on the contrary, that the world is being Canadianized, a process which, even

more than Americanization, is terrifyingly redolent of universal decay and death.[24]

\*\*\*

Nous autres, j'avons jamais vu une graine d'allitérature de notre vie. Je parlons avec les mots que j'avons dans la bouche et j'allons pas les charcher ben loin. Je les tenons de nos péres qui les aviont reçus de leur aïeux. De goule en oreille, coume qui dirait.

Antonine Maillet

(Us guys, we never seen a drop of alliterature in our life. We speaks with words we got right in our mouths, and we ain't got far ta go ta find 'em. We gets 'em from our fathers who got 'em from their fathers before 'em. From trap ta ear, ya might say.)[25]

Like Richards, Maillet has focused in her writing on the uneducated and economically deprived; unlike Richards's, however, her people, though poverty-stricken, are not impoverished – such is their heritage of courage, imagination, and humour that they at least question their fate rather than passively live it out. Maillet's vision is ultimately comic and romantic: there are strong elements of the fabulous in such texts as *Don l'Orignal* and *Pélagie*, elements which permit the development of a dialectic of hope whereby the possibility of change for the better becomes as real as the grim, grudging reality of the present. Perhaps what has enabled Maillet to keep her lightness of vision is her faith in the language of her people – the grammatically anachronistic, increasingly Anglicized but still vital Acadien which, in the mouth of a character like the Sagouine, manages to be richly expressive and yet representative of the condition of the poor French of New Brunswick. Where Nowlan's destitute characters are largely silent and Richards's manage to communicate with a vocabulary limited to 'fuck,' 'Oh ya,' and 'asshole,' Maillet's characters emerge as powerfully articulate, their very solecisms and malapropisms rendering their speech subversive, as, for example, when the Sagouine speaks of the Rusurrection in her speech on religion.

Maillet's most obvious influence is, of course, Rabelais, and in terms of Canadian literature she would seem to have much more in common with a writer like Jack Hodgins than Alden Nowlan or David Adams Richards, since much of her work can be described as fabulation. Yet there is an overwhelming sense of particular time and local place in her writing, an impassioned commitment to 'mon pays' as a social and political entity, and a need to make that country comprehensible to itself and recognized by outsiders. To this end she employs conventions of epic and romance which suit the non-industrialized, extraliterary character of traditional Acadie.[26] Yet she also depends on an Auerbachian sense of realism to communicate the harsh, immovable realities that cannot be talked around or beyond, realities that stem from the brutal treatment the Acadians have received from history, and that have been aggravated by class divisions and institutions that can be found in Montreal as well as in Buctouche or Caraquet. (Since Maillet has been criticized by her Acadian peers for folklorizing and thus trivializing the realities of Acadian experience,[27] analysis of the realist grounding of Maillet's work will lead to no critical disservice.)

A work like *Mariaàgélas*, for example, can be described as a species of 'epic realism'; a hybrid of legend, tall tale, and novel, it grounds the exploits of its smuggler protagonist (who possesses the kind of courage, intelligence, and sheer audacity of such fairy-tale heroines as Mollie Whuppie) securely within the day-to-day life of a 1930s fishing village. The difficulty of earning a living is made tolerable by the richness of community life, with all its religious and social rituals, and the endless intrigues that closely-knit communities breed. Fascinated as Maillet may be by the mock-heroic battle of wits and fists between the young Maria and her arch-enemy, a shrewish old widow; revel as she may in the elaborate techniques of the story-teller's art, she nevertheless manages to create a mimetically convincing world in La Baie, the poor and isolated settlements she also calls 'mon pays.' Her people, by turns forgotten and exploited by Ottawa, Toronto, and Montréal, are driven not just by the brute need to get food and clothes enough to keep body and soul together, but more importantly, by the desire to remain within the community, to resist the economic necessity that drives so many Maritimers to 'the Boston States.'

Maillet's chosen characters are, like Nowlan's and Richards's, the non-respectable of society – bootleggers, smugglers, scrubwomen, hard-luck fishermen – all those whose poverty extends as far back as their genealogies and who possess only one form of wealth, their native tongue. Not only does Maillet faithfully record Acadian speech, taking special pleasure in its saltier, earthier locutions, she also legitimizes it by making dialect words and indigenous grammatical forms the very stuff of her narrative. Indeed, the fabulistic and folkloric aspects of Maillet's writing reflect not only her vision of the Acadians as the true heirs of Rabelais and his epoch, but also her need to show the Acadians of La Baie not as boors or rednecks or pathetic victims but as the magnificently indomitable people they really are, *pace* Longfellow, Raddall, et al.

Nothing could be further from the sordid depression of Richards's Miramichi than the vigorous survival of Maillet's Acadie; the very *élan vital* Maillet's prose exudes may even make her suspect in the eyes of Acadian writers who, like Michel Roy, find more to lament than to celebrate in the present state of Acadian affairs. Yet while the romance conventions in *Pélagie* and *Cent Ans* may certainly cloy or gall – too much marrying off of pretty heroines and hardy heroes – Maillet's eschewal of a happy ending for her early novel *Mariaàgélas* both requites and frustrates the reader's expectations. The work ends on a tragic note, for though the valiant, cunning Maria ultimately routs her vituperative enemy, it is a pyrrhic victory which brings about the maiming of the widow, the murder of an Acadian customs officer, and the orphaning of his children. Maria is left profoundly disillusioned; after struggling against colossal odds to avoid a life of servitude in the shops or factories of New England, after trouncing those who would have gladly sabotaged her operations, she discovers that the world of La Baie is too small and sheltered for her. The person of extraordinary vision and abilities, be she writer or *contrabandier*, seems fated to exile from the very source of her identity and worth. This problematic fate of self-exile permeates the pages of *Mariaàgélas*, a novel whose narrator seems always to be shifting self-consciously between telling stories and writing literature, between recounting the conditions of life in Acadie and valorizing them, translating them into terms outsiders can understand and appreciate. The novel's subtext could be described as the narrator's own search for a tenable position among her people, of whom she is one by birthright but from whom she is estranged by her knowledge of the world outside the confines of La Baie, and by her very articulateness.

It is significant that the epilogue to *Mariaàgélas* deals only vaguely with the ultimate fate of Maria, who, the narrator hints, has been drowned off the Îles de la Madeleine. Its real purpose is self-reflexive, to legitimize the novel *Mariaàgélas* by having one of its characters, a fortune-teller named La Bidoche, predict that the narrator will realize her heart's desire – 'to write one day the marvellous adventures of one Mariaàgélas who so joyously battled against the sea, customs officers, fishermen, priests, the village gossips, and life itself during the most glorious and the most tragic epoch in the history of my country.'[28] In *La Sagouine* (a dramatic monologue which I am here taking the liberty of considering as narrative, and thus fiction), such problems of narrative identity, of the relation between the narrator and the people whose lives she tells, do not arise. The narrator is the text's sole character; her discourse, in comically heightened dialect, the narrative – no intermediary is necessary. In this way *La Sagouine* embodies the fusion of realism as a language as well as a literary mode.

In an essay on 'The Language of *La Sagouine*,' André Belleau argues that the speech of Maillet's charwoman – whose name means 'filthy slob' or 'pig' – is inseparable from her condition, a condition not vaguely 'human' but concretely economic and social. What the text reveals, he argues, is 'the disdain of the rich towards the poor, of those who dress themselves from the best shops towards those who frequent Eaton's bargain basement' (s 37). The central paradox of Maillet's work, he suggests, is that the power and beauty of the Sagouine's speech – her very diction and syntax – strive to express that which works to negate them – misery, injustice, and the stupidity of the present age (s 38). Nevertheless, what emerges from that verbal powerhouse, the Sagouine, is a disarming denunciation of the hypocrisy of her 'betters,' the deliberate saying of that which most of us agree remains best, or safest, unsaid. Reality, in effect, becomes redefined as that which we do not tell, whether it is the meanness of giving cast-off or broken toys as 'charitable' Christmas presents to the children of the poor, or class barriers at work in the church, so that 'the best seats in the house' are reserved for those who can pay for them, while the penniless take standing room at the back, where their smell will not offend the pious rich.

The Sagouine's husband, Gapi, whose blasphemies and grumblings she is careful to repeat word for word before reproving, speaks for those 'poor people, those low-down' (s 88), whose only possible response to injustice is to 'bad-mouth' the tyrants. The Sagouine herself, however, goes beyond cursing – she translates the world into her own words, and if she cannot right wrongs she can at least reveal them, in so ingenuous a manner that she never sounds like a dog in the manger. When she tells how 'good times' are always bad times for the poor (since you need war, flood, and economic chaos to prick society's conscience and remind it there are people around with nothing to eat or wear [s 135]) or when she expresses a wish that she and her kind could be regarded as heathen by the church so that they could receive the social and economic benefits that accompany missionary work, her restraint and ironic naïveté make possible a critique of society, politics, and organized religion that works on the principle of the double-take, and is all the more effective for it. By recounting without rancour or self-pity her sufferings – bruising work, losing nine out of her twelve children to cold and hunger – by questioning rather than roundly accusing everything from the misogyny of priests to creation itself (s 181); by telling how it is in such a way as to ask, 'need it be like this?', Maillet makes her spokeswoman do more than represent the poverty-stricken – she empowers her, as all interrogators are empowered.

The conventions of the monologue necessitate the Sagouine having, not just the last word, but all the words. By giving her a language whose roots go back to Rabelais and beyond, a language both literary and extraliterary, since it survived virtually without benefit of writers or readers for some three hundred years, Maillet allows her scrubwoman heroine to speak with an authority that neither literary critic nor common reader can contest. Maillet's is a 'telling' realism, and if her work lacks the devastating, relentless pressure of Richards's, the degree zero of Nowlan's, she, better than any other Maritime realist, is able to refute implications that fiction which has to do with the working-class, the crude and the illiterate need be too desolate or dreary for words.

\*\*\*

It is as if all of the worst things one imagines happening suddenly have ... I realize ... with a sort of shock that in spite of Scott's refusal to go on the truck nothing has really changed ... that all of the facts remain awfully and simply the same: that Scott is old and that we are poor and that my father must soon go away and that he must leave us either with Scott or without him. And that it is somehow like my mother's shielding her children from 'swearing' for so many years, only to find one day that it too is there in its awful reality in spite of everything that she had wished and wanted.[29]

With Alistair MacLeod's *The Lost Salt Gift of Blood* we arrive at a species of realism which, though lyrical, is as constrained by the harsh conditions of everyday life as is Nowlan's or Richard's, and which is as dependent on history and cultural tradition as is Maillet's Most of the stories in this collection are narrated through intermediaries, either supersensitive children or the adults they have become, natives and exiles of Cape Breton, a country as independent and isolated as Maillet's Acadie. These narrators evoke, reminisce, question and, most often, lament. For while Maillet's 'epic' realism derives from her belief in the spirited endurance of the Acadians, their will to survive on their own terms as a people, the work of MacLeod is overcast by a sense of loss and ending; the culture which authenticates and dignifies his povertywed Cape Bretoners is being steadily eroded by the kind of North Americanism which Richards excoriates in *Lives of Short Duration*.

Like *The Mountain and the Valley*, *The Lost Salt Gift of Blood* derives its poignancy from a sense of unequal conflict between old and new, past and present; between that which is desired, and that which cannot be avoided. Unlike Buckler, however, MacLeod is not preoccupied with the nature of time and memory, the suasions of solipsism, or the phenomenology of perception. He is closer to Nowlan in his engagement with the inevitable, intolerable real: the poverty which defines his people. This poverty MacLeod realizes for us by means factual (the fact, for example, that the cod which is bought from fishermen at 12 cents a pound sells in Ontario cities for $1.65 a pound) and experiential: the process whereby, under the relentless pressure of poverty, all the forms of love – of place, of wife or husband, of parent or child – become entrapment by regret, betrayal, or sheer necessity.

If Antonine Maillet adapts the epic and the romance for the purposes of realism, MacLeod appropriates traditional Gaelic music, as the sonorous modulations and phrasing of his prose reveal. Often he seems to sing rather than tell his stories. Occasionally, he slides into sentimentality; most often, he achieves that haunting and powerful resonance characteristic of the Gaelic music which is his characters' best means to self-expression and communication. Yet there is a knife-edge to MacLeod's most mellifluous prose: his superb characters – the grandparents in 'The Vastness of the Dark' or 'The Return' – share their world with creatures like the foul-mouthed MacRae, with his 'odour of manure and sweat and fear' (LSG 20). Similarly, MacLeod's evocations of Cape Breton, the vastness of the sea, the wild beauty of the land, do not block out the views with which his characters are most familiar – views of 'slate-grey slag heaps and ruined skeletal mine tipples' (LSG 45). The poorness of the soil, the violence of the sea, the exhaustion of the mines prevent his people from earning more than a bare living and drive, perhaps not the strongest, but certainly the most ambitious into exile. Those who go are crippled by a sense of shame and loss; those who stay, like the mother in 'The Boat,' become almost dehumanized by loyalty to a place which seems reduced to primal elements – wind, water, rock.

Where Maillet's characters possess a marvellous resilience and vitality, MacLeod's protagonists are given such pride and independence that their struggle with perpetual poverty achieves tragic dimensions.

'Ashamed yet proud, young yet old, and saved, yet forever lost' (LSG 140) they are a 'people it is impossible to ever know or fully understand' (LSG 162). Because so much of their culture lies beyond language, or at least the English language; because the very work they perform – coal-mining or fishing, subsistence farming, the raising of large families – lies outside the experience of most of his readers, MacLeod acts as much as translator as teller of their lives. The sonority and biblical cadences of his prose ('And there came into my heart a very great love for my father' [LSG 147]; 'And the fish had eaten his testicles and the gulls had pecked out his eyes and the white-green stubble of his whiskers had continued to grow in death, like the grass on graves ...' [LSG 151]) convey something of the timeless assurance and presence of his people. By making frequent use of the first person and the present tense with such opening sentences as 'I am speaking now of a July in the early 1970's' (LSG 155), MacLeod's fiction, like James Agee's A Death in the Family demands from the reader an immediate emotional involvement. To read MacLeod, one must take on the narrator's own charged feelings and claim his people for one's own; one must jump into their sea and cling to the raft of his prose. For MacLeod there seems to be no problem of the overeducated and articulate narrative voice jarring with the speech and experience of his characters; rather, his difficulty lies in finding a prose rich enough to translate with any adequacy their characteristic modes of expression: gesture, music, silence.

Here, then, is one great difference between MacLeod's characters and those of Nowlan and Richards – their symbolic stature and function. If sex for Kevin O'Brien is an exercise in random ecstasy and sudden disillusionment; if for David Adams Richards's characters it is an affair of casual violence; then for MacLeod's people it becomes and confers a kind of death, passionate and inevitable, bringing 'grim release' more often than joy (LSG 39). Like Nowlan's characters, MacLeod's are workbeasts, yet vastly more – they possess a 'second sight' of which the ignorant mill-workers of Lockhartville are incapable: even when 'the darkness of their labour ha[s] become that of their lives' (LSG 39), MacLeod's Cape Bretoners possess a tragic knowledge of self and world that is all the more profound for the fact that they cannot speak it. In a way, the narrator's very eloquence plays second fiddle to the all the more conspicuous silence of such protagonists as the man and wife whose wordless embrace at the end of 'In the Fall' becomes elemental, like the wind and snow whirling round them.

Accordingly, the fundamental point of difference between the other writers discussed in this chapter and MacLeod can be found in the close connection between the material and the metaphysical on which his realism insists. Nowlan and Richards are concerned primarily with life in a surface hell, the lower depths raised to open view. Maillet, though she has the Sagouine speculate on the existence of a paradise in which the angels would come round with plates of chicken stew and coconut cream pie, with God himself calling the dance on Saturday nights, is more involved with the basics of survival, spirit intact, in a world which does its best to quash her and her like. But MacLeod, careful as he is to make real for us the material conditions which pressure his characters, is also concerned to show us how their entrapment has a significance which transcends particulars of period and place by the universals of time and death.

The first and last stories collected in *The Lost Salt Gift of Blood* show this connection between the 'material' and 'metaphysical' in MacLeod's fiction. 'In the Fall,' a finely controlled account of a child's perception of the powerlessness and pain of his parents' lives lays bare the iron laws of poverty. The boy's father, we learn, must take on a variety of jobs which paradoxically take him away from his wife and six children in order that he may 'support' them. So great is the need for cash that his wife begrudges him the rare returns he makes to the farm from the Halifax shipyard where he spends his winters. She also insists that whatever cannot pay its way, whatever is there merely for love and not for food or shelter – in this case, Scott, a beloved horse too old to be worth the expense of feeding him – must be got rid of. As in most of MacLeod's fiction, it is the women who must be ruthless in their labour to make ends meet and keep the family together; it is women, too, who are most locked into silence. The narrator tells us how, whenever his mother does speak, 'she does something with her hands. It is as if the private voice in her can only be liberated by some kind of physical action' (LSG 14).

Though the husband and wife of 'In the Fall' possess heroic qualities of endurance, their 'congenital' poverty paralyses them so that they can neither speak nor move freely: the most they can attempt is 'to hold their place' in 'fear and pain and almost a mute wonder ... trapped by what seemed all too familiar' (LSG 30, 20). Poverty is the trap, poverty, and life itself under such conditions where love yields not pleasure but children, and children, further entrapment in unceasing labour and conflict between man and wife, child and parents, freedom from and loyalty to the place which has become oneself.

The protagonist of the last story in the collection, 'The Road to Rankin's Point,' discovers the absolute of entrapment – not the epic poverty his grandmother knew, widowed at twenty-six, with seven children to support, but the certain knowledge of his impending death. The story unfolds in a context of idyllic summer beauty – wildflowers rampant, bees swarming – which makes all the more stark such presentiments of death and ending as the impossibly overgrown road to the Point, the car crashed at the base of the cliffs, the grandmother's frailty and the decay of her farm. Leaving Toronto to come home to die, twenty-six-year-old Calum falls back into the past, remembering the absurd yet appropriate way his grandfather met his end – bleeding to death one winter's night after shattering a bottle of rum in a fall on the way home – and recalling the practical stoicism, courage, and self-sufficiency with which his grandmother met this castastrophe. They are qualities he feels his own generation has betrayed, just as he must betray his grandmother's hope that, by taking over the farm at Rankin's Point, he will save her from finishing her days in a nursing home. Knowing that Calum cannot help her, she wills her own death – he finds her still-warm body on the path by the cliffs. The story ends with Calum reaching out to death, envisioned as the perfect meeting of 'internal and ... external darkness' (LSG 187).

It is more than personal and private death that this story comprehends: it suggests the ending of a world and time and code of values destroyed by urban affluence, junk yards, strip joints, and supermarkets. Calum's grandmother dies and at Rankin's Point 'for the first time in the centuries since the Scottish emigrations there is no human life at the end of this dark road' (LSG 189). Calum comes back to confront 'the darkest truth' that words cannot reach – death itself (LSG 179). In so doing he discovers the place his dying has in the natural order and the history of things – he is like 'the diseased and polluted salmon, [returning] to swim for a brief time in the clear waters of [his] earlier stream' (LSG 174). Like his grandfather he is doomed to die young, at the very moment when the culture which gave his grandparents' lives dignity and meaning is itself dying. At the finish of this story, Calum does indeed discover 'the ending that we have' (LSG 187) but this revelation is coupled with, made intelligible by, a 'material' truth he has learned from his grandmother, a truth which could serve as epigraph to that literary mode and language to which this chapter has been devoted:

It does not matter that some things are difficult. No one has ever said that life is to be easy. Only that it is to be lived. (LSG 181)

# 7

# Pigs in the Pinewoods: Self-Destructing Regional Idylls

'Don't be led away by these howls about realism. Remember *pine woods* are as real as *pigsties*, and a darn sight pleasanter to be in.'

LUCY MAUD MONTGOMERY, *Emily's Quest*[1]

If the idyll may accurately be described as a 'prose composition which deals charmingly with rustic life; ordinarily ... describ[ing] a picturesque rural scene of gentle beauty and innocent tranquillity and narrat[ing] a story of some simple sort of happiness'; if it creates 'a picture of life as the human spirit wishes it to be, a presentation of the chosen moments of earthly content,'[2] then it must be admitted that the idyll is one of the favoured modes of Maritime fiction. Admitted with trepidation, for once idyll is prefaced by the adjective 'regional' the whole takes on a pejorative cast, as far as most critics of Canadian literature are concerned. It has been argued that, Maritime culture being intrinsically nostalgic, the region's writers have been compelled to produce 'almost nothing except historical romances and regional idylls.'[3]

In defence of the idyll, however, it should be pointed out that for Maritime writers this literary mode may represent an inevitable rather than merely escapist response to the natural world that surrounds them. Northrop Frye, though he considers as truly Canadian the myth of a hostile or indifferent, morally silent environment does acknowledge, almost as a triumph of imagination, this myth's polar opposite – that 'sentimental pastoral myth' which produces the idyll. Frye's implication would seem to be that the greatest literary works comprehend both the notion of life-in-nature as harmonious and spiritually restorative,

and the idea of nature's 'sinister and terrible elements,' connected
with the death wish in man.[4] Ernest Buckler's *The Mountain and the Valley*
would seem to provide a classic illustration of this thesis. Yet in most
Maritime writing it would seem that the 'pastoral,' sentimental or not,
predominates over the terrifying 'existential' – an inevitable consequence in a region characterized not by extremes but by an evenness of
climate and geography. Thus we should not dismiss but rather concede to Maritime writers the idyll – a term synonomous with Frye's
'sentimental pastoral' – in order that we may better appreciate what
the more original and reflective among them do with this literary
mode.

Though there is nothing inherently wrong in writing lovingly and
knowingly of one's native place, there is certainly something rebarbative about fiction in which 'trials and hardships are not completely
ignored, but ... are overcome or circumvented, and we are asked to
believe that the world is essentially a good place in which such qualities
as thrift, industry, and integrity will always, in the long run, triumph.'[5]
With the Pollyannish idylls of minor Maritime authors this chapter does
not concern itself, and yet a word must be said about the common
tendency of more important writers to wax idyllic in their fictions.
Thomas Raddall's heroes and heroines, for example, habitually flee a
problematic society for some Edenic retreat – the Annapolis Valley
(*The Nymph and the Lamp*), a backwoods farm (*The Wings of Night*), or a
near-deserted island (*Tidefall*). In the backs of her characters' minds
Antonine Maillet plants the lost Arcadia of Grand Pré, still blossoming in
post-Expulsion Acadie in the true love of properly romantic heroes
and heroines. Even David Adams Richards in his fleetingly pastoral
fiction, *Blood Ties*, evokes Eve, Adam, and the Garden (albeit bog-
tree'd and mosquito-infested) to portray the loving relationship between
a husband and wife.

Thus the idyll can be seen not so much as a literary mode as a frame
of mind for many Maritime writers; that the frame is often warped or
cracked only the rare realists like Alden Nowlan would seem to show. In
the short story 'Will Ye Let the Mummers In?' he topples the idyll a
self-exiled American university professor and his wife have put together
like a child's block tower. Having abandoned the criminal violence
and *anomie* of the big city, the couple buy a beautiful old wooden house
in bucolic New Brunswick and painstakingly refit themselves for country
pleasures. In so doing, however, they sabotage their project: overeager
to see only innocence, beauty, and bovinity about them, they shatter
local taboos and, more importantly, refuse to acknowledge and make
provision for the inevitable serpents lurking in the most blissful of

bowers – prejudice, jealousy, lust, and fear. To wish to live an idyll, Nowlan implies, is eminently human; to actually believe you can do so is naïve if not downright cretinous.

Nowlan, however, is not alone in his subversive treatment of the idyll. In some of the work of Charles G.D. Roberts and Lucy Maud Montgomery, and in certain fictions by Ernest Buckler and Donna Smyth we find idylls presented as self-consciously fictive worlds, temporarily self-delighting but never self-sustaining. Death, the bloody laws of nature, the tyranny of adults, violence – all poison the sweetness of these writers' Arcadia. And yet the idyllic vision is also undercut by what we might call meta-idylls, realized through the forces of magic, fantasy, mass-cultural cliché, and language itself. Together, 'menace' and 'meta-idyll' produce subversive subtexts to each idyll. This chapter sets out to explore the relations between text and subtext in four representative idylls: Roberts's *The Heart of the Ancient Wood*, Montgomery's *Anne of Green Gables*, Buckler's *Oxbells and Fireflies*, and Smyth's *Quilt*.

\*\*\*

That Lucy Maud Montgomery deserves to be taken as seriously as is Charles G.D. Roberts as a Canadian culture hero should be accepted as a truth self-evident. None of Roberts's work – neither his animal stories nor 'The Tantramar Revisited' – will ever attain the national or international fame of that flawed but authentic children's classic, *Anne of Green Gables*.[6] Yet while many critics grudgingly admit Roberts's historical if not literary importance, and others extoll his originality and achievements as a poet or nature writer, most would probably share George Woodcock's assessment of Montgomery as a devotee of 'the pseudorealistic North American local-color movement, with its aim of giving authenticity, through a vivid and detailed depiction of the setting and the characteristic local way of life, to a sentimental plot and a group of conventionally typed characters.'[7] Perhaps the various putdowns of Montgomery's work – from Archibald MacMechan's contention that *Anne of Green Gables*, while capable of captivating 'the unreflecting general reader' fails in that 'truth of representation' which convinces the critic, to E.K. Brown's pronouncement that Montgomery was 'aggressively unliterary' and more concerned with 'making an abundant living by [her] pen' than with striving for artistic excellence[8] – may have been aggravated by a sexist bias: is not Montgomery simply one more dreary bead on that interminable string of lady writers which has so choked and cluttered the bosom of Canadian letters? We rarely hear mention of the mother of Canadian literature, yet surely Montgomery, even more so than her contemporary Sara Jeannette Duncan, did as much to put Canada on the literary map as did Charles G.D. Roberts. And since recent literary theory has encouraged a new catholicism in our cultural awareness and interests, the fact that *Anne of Green Gables* falls into the category of children's literature or regional idyll should not preclude an analysis of it as literary text and conceptual structure.

Let us, then, go so far as to accept works like Roberts's *Heart of the Ancient Wood* and Montgomery's *Anne* as textual equals, whatever their deficiencies as works of literary art. In fact these books are similar enough to force the critic to the conclusion that Roberts and Montgomery, especially in their rapturous response to natural beauty – trees, lakes, sunsets, moonlight – are, in Anne's terms, 'kindred spirits.'

Like the orphaned Anne Shirley, Roberts's Miranda Craig is thrust by circumstance into a strange new world which she proceeds to master and transform. Where Anne calls upon extraordinary (and comic) powers of language and imagination to turn prosaic Avonlea into an enchanted world, Miranda develops quasi-occult powers of communication with the animals in that ancient wood to which she and her mother have exiled themselves. In the solitude of the backwoods, Miranda and her mother, Kirstie, hope to escape the vicious tongues of the 'Settlement' gossips – Kirstie's husband has deserted her, giving rise to speculation that the couple were never properly married at all and that Miranda is thus a bastard.

Both Anne and Miranda enjoy unwonted liberty and power in their new-found worlds. Miranda goes to no school but that of a gentle and permissive Mother Nature: she is allowed to wander at will through the woods, accompanied only by the adoring she-bear, Kroof. 'Queen of the Forest,' she achieves 'sovereignty' over the animals: lynx and panther are made to lie down defenceless at her feet; birds, caribou, and deer to take food from her hands.[9] Anne Shirley is permitted to break almost all the burdensome taboos of life in a fearsomely strict and dull Presbyterian community, openly accusing her elders of hypocrisy and convicting them of physical ugliness, dyeing her hair, intoxicating a teetotaller's daughter, and successfully refusing to attend school. Despite the drawbacks of low social and aesthetic status (orphanhood, violently red hair, and freckles) Anne becomes undisputed leader among the pallid little girls of Avonlea. Finally, Anne and Miranda are made to experience the transformation from child to adult, girl to woman – a transformation, their creators hint, fatal to what is best and brightest in them.

Let us look in greater detail at the idyll which Roberts creates in *The Heart of the Ancient Wood*. The clearing in which Miranda and her mother settle is, as Roberts takes pains to emphasize, paradisal after the 'stupidly inhospitable' Settlement (HW 27). Although the clearing is first perceived as 'cut ... off from all the world of men' (HW 20) and viewed in terms of 'immeasurable desolation' and 'unspeakable loneliness' (HW 18, 28), it soon comes to be associated with 'wide wonder' and 'peace' (HW 124, 33). Before long the deserted cabin in which Kirstie and Miranda settle becomes homelike: flowers blossom round it, fertile meadows are fenced in, and the clearing comes to resemble 'a little beautiful lost world' (HW 146). Far from having a 'shut-in valley loneliness, without horizons and without hope,' the Craig's cabin enjoys a 'high, austere, clear loneliness' (HW 216–17). Altogether, the clearing comes to seem truly idyllic, as close as one could safely come to regaining Eden in a fallen world.

So peaceable is the kingdom Miranda establishes that neither guns nor meat are permitted within its precincts. What this pacifistic rule confirms, of course, is the complete independence of Kirstie and Miranda from a world, not only of gossiping women, but of men as well. (The exceptions to this rule are the Tituses, Old and Young Dave, who prepare the cabin for Kirstie's arrival and play an important, but minor role in the narrative.) When wolves attack the women's caribou Kirstie routs them with an axe; when two 'surly and mutinous' lumberjacks blunder into the clearing and begin to harass them, Kirstie and Miranda quickly and contemptuously send them packing. What Roberts sets up, in fact, is a kind of backwoods Cranford where women are able to exist happily, harmoniously, prosperously, and safely without the guidance or support of men.

Yet for all the remarkable beauty and productivity of life in the clearing, there is something lacking, or at least limited, in this idyll, as Roberts demonstrates by creating an idyll-within-an-idyll through the aptly named Miranda. 'Elvish,' 'fairylike' (HW 39, 36), Miranda grows impatient not with the clearing itself but with her mother's acceptance of it as the sum total of their chosen world. Miranda, it soon becomes clear, attains to 'semi-occult' experience of the woods and their inhabitants: her eyes 'had the keener vision, the subtler knowledge ...' – they are 'eyes that see everything and cannot be deceived' (HW 224, 31). And this is no mere matter of optics – neither Miranda's strong, spirited but sombre mother, nor the lively trapper, Young Dave, manages to perceive what Miranda does in the forest that engulfs the clearing. The mysterious stillness and confusing light of these woods 'distur[b] the accustomed perspective, and hin[t] of some elvish deception in familiar and apparent things' (HW 2). An 'enchantment' seems to have brought about 'the confusion of near and far, the unreality of the familiar' (HW 197–8). In spite or perhaps because of this, Miranda is able to discern even the most insistently camouflaged of creatures: it is she who first sets eyes on and is later 'adopted' by Kroof; with the bear, and indeed with all the wildlife around her she establishes a 'mysterious communion' and 'kinship' (HW 39–40) so that she is 'initiated ... into the full fellowship of the folk of the ancient wood' (HW 72). Gossip in the Settlement has it that Kirstie is a witch and her cabin protected by 'familiars' in the shape of panther, bear, or wolf; while Roberts clearly ridicules this speculation he insists that there is white magic at work in Miranda, who grows into 'a faun woman or a wood goddess' (HW 157) as if 'a soul not at all human dwelt in her human shape' (HW 124).

Roberts, however, sabotages the magical powers of his Miranda. The girl who can tame a rutting bull moose by the mesmeric power of her eyes is undone by the 'riotous cravings in her astonished appetite' (HW 188), cravings stirred not by the sight of the young man who disturbs the Edenic serenity of her world, but by the smell of the meat he fries for his supper.[10] Yet before the narrative becomes a 'last battle' fought between herbivores and carnivores and between the mother-substitute bear and her rival for Miranda's heart and allegiance, Young Dave, Roberts does manage to create a convincing 'meta-idyll' in the mysterious and masterfully evoked 'ancient wood' which is Miranda's preferred home, and before which the tame delights of a cabin wound round with scarlet runner beans in a bee-loud glade soon pall.

The most interesting aspect of *The Heart of the Ancient Wood*, however, is that Roberts should feel compelled to bring both idyll and meta-idyll toppling down upon his characters. From the very beginning we are told that the woods can be not magical, but merely 'lonely, menacing, terrible' (HW 67) and Roberts stresses that, at least when Miranda is a young child, the forest remains a 'forbidden realm' (HW 103) whenever her protector, Kroof, is absent. Moreover, the 'elvish' child has irrevocably human instincts and commitments: though she chooses to dress in homespun rather than pink gingham in order to better blend in with her surroundings, Miranda insists on wearing around her throat a scarlet ribbon that sets her off as a creature mysteriously superior to the 'woodfolk,' and which links her to the experience and sensibility of her mother. Miranda's love of laughter, her compassion, her horror of bloodshed mark her as ultimately alien from the wilderness and its creatures. At her first encounter with a sick child she is made to exhibit a 'mothering hunger' (HW 217) which alerts the reader to the fact that Young Dave will have no insurmountable task in humanizing his 'wood goddess.'

Two-thirds of the way through *The Heart of the Ancient Wood* Roberts broaches the question of whether any 'understanding between the world of men and the world of the ancient wood is possible' (HW 161) – whether, in other words, Miranda can have both Kroof and Young Dave, peaceable affection and, presumably, the sexual experience and satisfaction the meat-eating Dave proffers. The answer is simple and final. The moment Miranda discovers the 'beautiful' young trapper, rifle propped up against a tree as he sleeps 'the luxurious sleep of an idle summer afternoon' (HW 128) her very 'system of life' is threatened (HW 134). The wholly female idyll enjoyed by Miranda, Kroof, and Kirstie is exploded by the man who causes Kroof's death, encourages Kirstie in her desire to eat meat and return to the humanly social world, and who succeeds in 'mould[ing] Miranda to his 'will' (HW 134–5). The novel ends with a double destruction – that of Miranda's magical communion with the world of the ancient wood, and of Kirstie's self-sufficient, solitary but ennobling life in the clearing. Having shot Kroof in order to save Dave's life, Miranda, who had previously scorned her lover's attempts to either protect or solace her, hides her face in his breast, murmurs 'take mother and me away from this place; I don't want to live at the clearing anymore. You've killed the old life I loved,' and then breaks into a 'storm of tears' (HW 233). The hero she has saved, but to whom she feels compelled to surrender, announces that he'll give up his hunting and trapping, sell the clearing, and take Miranda and Kirstie down to the Miramichi, where he can find work as a lumber surveyor. Presumably they will live happily and heartily – on a non-vegetarian diet – forever after.

Halfway through *The Heart of the Ancient Wood* Roberts states the ostensible reason for the destruction of the idylls he has sketched: 'Miranda had regarded the folk of the ancient wood as gentle people, living for the most part in a voiceless amity. Her seeing eyes quite failed to see the unceasing tragedy of the stillness. She did not guess that the furtive folk, whom she watched about their business, went always with fear at their side and death lying in wait at every turn. She little dreamed that, for most of them, the very price of life itself was the ceaseless extinguishing of life' (HW 105–6).

This, of course, is orthodox Roberts – Nature red in tooth and claw. Yet it was precisely this bloody natural law that Miranda was able to countermand or at least suspend in the first half of the novel. Miranda can hardly be accused of moral blindness if, with few exceptions, she has so charmed the beasts that no killing goes on in her presence, and that accordingly, all appears to her peace and beauty in the world of the ancient wood. Nor does the fact that she 'cheats' in her vegetarianism by expertly catching, killing, and eating fish console the reader for the fact that she will be 'giving up her freedom and her personality to a man – a strong man, who would ... absor[b] her' (HW 223). True, Dave does 'submit' to Miranda by giving up his career as a killer of animals – but he does take her away from the clearing which, as Roberts has clearly shown, is a workable idyll and backwoods Eden. Given Roberts's equation of meat-eating with sexual experience, of rifle with phallus; given Dave's thesis that, until Miranda overcomes her aversion to 'flesh food' she will not 'become sufficiently human to understand human love or any truly human emotions' (HW 174), it would appear that in dismantling the female idyll in the clearing – Kirstie and Miranda flourishing without the aid of men as hunters or lovers – Roberts is funking issues which have less to do with nature's laws than with sexual politics. Nowhere is this clearer than in the ludicrously framed 'crisis' of the novel – Kirstie's galloping anemia, cured by the provision of venison steaks and her sudden discovery of a need for social intercourse after all these years alone in the clearing.

It may well be that hidden personal reasons underlie Roberts's ambivalence towards this female idyll – after all, what drives Kirstie Craig to seek out a solitary clearing in the wilderness is her husband's abandonment of her and their child. 'Frank Craig, dilettante and man of the world,' painter, poet, musician when the mood takes him, lacks the 'steadiness of purpose, the decision of will, the long-enduring patience' (HW 35) which would make of him not only a successful artist but also a faithful husband and father. After a few happy years of marriage he simply falls prey to restlessness and disappears from the Settlement, never to be heard of again. Perhaps the 'strange conflict between honesty and inconstancy' (HW 35) that goes on in the depths of Frank Craig's beautiful eyes was similar to that which afflicted Roberts himself in his own married life. To his credit, Roberts does not have the abandoner return to the domestic fold at the novel's end, as he does in *The Heart that Knows*; nevertheless, in his need both to envision a world in which women and children can happily and successfully manage without husbands and fathers, and to undermine and eventually cancel that self-sufficient world, a curious double standard is at work. If there were no mystique of the ancient woods, if Miranda, instead of breaking the laws and controlling the forces of nature, merely grew up in wilderness solitude, there would be no need for her to abandon the clearing in order to become 'completely' human, and for her sadly to submit to the man who has been anything but a knight errant and princely rescuer to her. In this sense, Roberts's creation of a meta-idyllic magical forest may be a subterfuge allowing him to have his cake and eat it too, to salve his conscience by proving that a man's desertion of his family need not have doleful consequences, and to reassert machismo by showing that, given a proper chance, even the most independent of women will choose dependence on male strength and presence over reliance on female support and company.

If an outsider is made to destroy the idylls created in Charles G.D. Roberts's novel, then it is Montgomery's own heroine who subverts the nominal idyllic world in *Anne of Green Gables*. Though in such works as *Jane of Lantern Hill*, *The Story Girl*, and *The Golden Road* Montgomery presents the 'Garden of the Gulf' as a little paradise in comparison with the grim grey world of Toronto, in other texts, notably *Emily of New Moon* she shows how even the lushest landscapes could be peopled by cruelly narrow-minded and manically authoritarian figures. *Anne of Green Gables*, it is true, boasts descriptions of beautiful haunts and seasonal set-pieces, many of which bear comparison with Ernest Buckler's depictions of idyllic rural scenes. The very name Avonlea conjures up the English pastoral tradition, and the novel's first pages, replete with orchards in 'a bridal flush of pinky-white bloom, hummed over by a myriad of bees,'[11] set up expectations of an earthly paradise – expectations which seem clinched by the book's closing line: 'God's in his heaven, all's right with the world.' Throughout, the cohesiveness and rootedness of community life are stressed, with not only the people but also the very lakes and trees of Avonlea becoming an extended family for the alien, orphaned Anne. Yet one of the surprises of Montgomery's narrative is the fact that Anne, plucked from 'a life of drudgery and poverty and neglect' (GG 54) and set down on the rich red earth and rolling hills of Avonlea, continues that habit of fantasizing alternative worlds she first formed in her harsh foster homes, and that she perfected in the desolation of an orphanage. It is not enough to find herself among unimaginably lovely surroundings; like Roberts's Miranda, the 'witchlike' Anne must have an enchanted element to exist in. This is not due merely to an extravagant love of beauty or an extreme proclivity for romance, though these are indeed dominant characteristics of Montgomery's heroine. As importantly, Anne's creation of a fantasy world points to non-idyllic, even ugly and malicious aspects of life in Avonlea.

As Muriel Whitaker has described it, Montgomery's Island Eden is blighted by smallness and closure:

It is a highly ritualised society, supported on the twin pillars of church and work. Labour in the rural community is determined by the cycle of the seasons, social intercourse, by the round of Sunday church, midweek prayer meeting, Ladies Aid, and school. Propriety and conformity, a regard for 'decency and decorum,' prevail. Explanations must be found for uncharacteristic behaviour, a necessity that leads to the prying and gossiping that characterise any closely knit society ... The odd and the out of place are immediately suspect ... Almost as suspect as the odd is the beautiful, utility being preferred when it comes to making value judgements ... [T]he rigorous criteria regarding clothes extend also to reading material (novels are 'wicked books and have ruined many souls'), to bangs, to whistling; in fact, a 'great many jolly things' are, if not wicked, at least unladylike.[12]

As her biographers have demonstrated, Montgomery suffered all her life from the repressions and restrictions attendant on her role first as granddaughter to strict Calvinists, then as schoolteacher, later as companion to her ailing and cantankerous grandmother, and finally, as wife of a Presbyterian minister suffering from acute melancholia – the Reverend Macdonald, it appears, frequently collapsed under the conviction that he was predestined to an eternity of hellfire – a condition his wife had to hide from the congregation, lest the minister's family lose its daily bread. In her *Emily* series Montgomery portrays something of how hellish a writer's life in a resolutely Philistine community can be, and in her memoir, *The Alpine Path*, she focuses equally on the beauty of nature and the cruelty of adults in the passages she devotes to her childhood. The humiliations, injustice, and concerted teasing children suffer at the hands of their elders, the threats that 'did not make us good, [but] only made us miserable,' and profound experiences of bereavement and loss[13] would seem to have driven Montgomery to use imagination as 'a passport to the geography of Fairyland,'[14] a realm which for her was more 'real,' because desirable, than a world structured according to what a biographer has termed 'the forbidding Calvinism of Presbyterian dogma.'[15]

Calvin's skeleton does not exactly rage in the closets of Green Gables farmhouse, yet one cannot read far in the first two-thirds of *Anne* without encountering what might be called the corrective subtext of the Avonlea idyll – the pigs befouling the pine woods. The first character to whom the text introduces us is the sharp-tongued, ferret-minded Rachel Lynde who, on hearing that the Cuthberts are about to adopt an orphan, warns that asylum children are prone to burn houses and put strychnine down wells. Later the same Mrs Lynde takes it upon herself to point out to Anne her obvious physical deficiencies. Anne's response is all we need to convince us of Montgomery's skill in depicting 'the plight of sensitive children under the authority of uncompromising adults'[16]: 'I hate you – I hate you – I hate you ... How dare you call me skinny and ugly? How dare you say I'm freckled and redheaded? You are a rude, impolite, unfeeling woman! ... How would you like to have such things said about you? How would you like to be told that you are fat and clumsy and probably hadn't a spark of imagination in you?' (GG 83–4).

The scenes which follow, wherein Anne is imprisoned in her room until she agrees to apologize for her intolerable truth-telling, and then proceeds to glory in a rhetorical extravaganza of an apology are not merely humorous highlights. They introduce the battle waged between truth and propriety, life and mere behaviour, beauty and decency, love and obedience all through Anne's early adolescence. Although the novel's 'authority figure,' Marilla, is made to mellow in the course of Anne's growing up, there remains enough of the moral terrorist about her to push Anne through reality's exit doors into fantasy. Unable to express or respond to emotion, distrustful of the 'dancing and irresponsible' things of life (GG 5), spurred by an iron sense of duty to drill Anne into 'a tranquil uniformity of disposition as impossible and alien to her as to a dancing sunbeam in one of the brook shallows' (GG 228), Marilla is only one of the adults who attempt to deform and control Anne. Mr Phillips, the incompetent and hypocritical schoolmaster who unjustly punishes and humiliates her; Mrs Barry, who, again unjustly, accuses her of being a 'thoroughly bad, wicked little girl' unfit to play with her daughter; Marilla, again, wrongly accusing Anne of stealing and forcing her into a lie in order to be forgiven, embody those negative elements against which Anne fights through language and fantasy.[17]

The primary theme of Montgomery's work, one critic has suggested, is 'the encroachment of the real world on the child, and the need to leave childhood behind.'[18] Not only children but also adults, Montgomery shows, create compensatory worlds if they are starved of love or experience: thus the twenty-nine-year-old heroine of The Blue Castle continues to seek refuge in a fantasy world where she possesses all the love, beauty, and happiness her family denies her; so too the fortyish Miss Lavendar of Anne of Avonlea sustains a dream world in which she can pretend to have everything reality denies her. The fact that at the end of both books Montgomery lavishes 'real' Prince Charmings and idyllic homes on these characters only compounds the pathos, the texts themselves sealing their heroines into a land of dreams-come-true they should have long ago outgrown. And yet, though Anne Shirley's realization of the necessity and desirability of quitting her fantasy world speaks well for her psychological health, in terms of the authenticity and simple pleasure of Montgomery's text, Anne's abandonment of fairyland is decidedly destructive.

Let us look for a moment at the meta-idyll which Anne begins to create almost the moment we meet her. One of its defining characteristics is not merely beauty, but a sympathetic magic released by the naming of things. Driving along 'the Avenue' – 'one long canopy of snowy fragrant bloom' through which 'a glimpse of painted sky shone like a great rose window at the end of a cathedral aisle' (GG 23) – Anne becomes ecstatic. To Matthew's comment, 'It is a kind of pretty place,' she responds: 'Pretty? Oh, *pretty* doesn't seem the right word to use. Nor beautiful, either. They don't go far enough. Oh, it was wonderful ... But they shouldn't call that lovely place the Avenue. There is no meaning in a name like that ... When I don't like the name of a place or a person I always imagine a new one ... Other people may call that place the Avenue but I shall always call it the White Way of Delight' (GG 25).

'Like Adam, Anne Shirley's first important act after coming to Avonlea is to rename the external world she finds ... She takes the commonplace and makes it beautiful.'[19] Hence Barry's Pond becomes The Lake of Shining Waters; an apple tree outside her bedroom window, Snow Queen; the woods, Lovers' Lane or Willowmere or Violet Vale; a creek, the Dryad's Bubble. To give romantic names, however hackneyed to an adult's taste, to objects in nature is to recreate the world. Anne's remarkable powers of language[20] have other equally important uses: she literally talks Matthew and Marilla into keeping her at Green Gables – the barrage of words she aims at them destroys Marilla's firm resolution to send Anne back to the asylum. Whether addressing God or Mrs Lynde, Anne is equally loquacious and self-assured – her melodramatic contributions to the 'Story Club' secure her the admiration of her peers, as do her considerable abilities as an elocutionist. Indeed, it is Anne's pyrotechnics with language which enable her to hold her own in Avonlea, to be adopted by the Cuthberts, accepted by her schoolmates, and encouraged by her teacher to get the education which will take her beyond the bounds of Avonlea.[21] They also help her to overcome what would otherwise be the unbearable placidity of pastoral life. To be capable of self-dramatization, of uttering, when forbidden to play with one's best friend, 'I must cry. My heart is broken. The stars in their courses fight against me' (GG 165) is to prevent one's being swallowed up by the uniformity and sheer utility of adult existence. Anne's childhood 'effusions' are her only effective defence against the constant moralizing and carping most of her elders aim her way.

Like her fictional *semblable* Emily Byrd, Anne lies 'between the world of fact and the world of words.'[22] She learns, as did Montgomery herself, that fantasy and fact clash 'hopelessly and irreconcilably.' Yet where Montgomery 'learned to keep them apart so that the former might remain for [her] unspoiled,'[23] Anne merely abandons fantasy slowly but surely. Her life in Avonlea becomes a series of improving incidents whereby she is 'cured' of all those flaws and faults which made her a breaker of taboos, a defier of conventional wisdom, and a creator rather than mere lover of beauty. Her outstanding vice, according to the sages of Avonlea, is her linguistic extravagance: by the time she turns sixteen and confesses to Marilla, apropos a bitchy schoolmate, 'I've made what I would once have called a heroic effort to like her' (GG 384), we know Anne has been cured of this besetting sin. Indeed, what formerly were spirited and humorous rhetorical overreachings become, in the older Anne, maudlin moralizing or sententious exhortations to be good, pure, and noble. As her disfiguring freckles and carrot-red hair give way to creamy skin and Titian tresses, Anne's 'magical' and subversive powers of speech, along with the fantasy world they bring into being, wither away. The matronly Anne, of course, cannot hold a candle to the child: as Gillian Thomas observes, the older Anne becomes 'a willing victim of social convention ... a woman intent on observing the social proprieties and for whom "imagination" has come to mean something which very closely resembles sentimentality' – hardly, as Thomas adds, a 'kindred spirit' to 'the young Anne Shirley, with her sharp eye for social hypocrisy.'[24] And since the matronly Anne has lost all of the subversive spirit that made her such an attractive child, she is finally at home on the Island which, in the rest of the Anne books, is, with few exceptions, complacently idyllic.

'She writes often like a woman thrust out of Eden,' a biographer observed, noting that though Montgomery often reproved the sentimental excesses of Anne's or Emily's language, she was incapable of correcting her own.[25] Yet for all her limitations, Montgomery was able to communicate in a work like *Anne of Green Gables* not an unadulterated idyll of childhood, or a harmonious pastoral symphony, but rather, the inescapable injustices, malice, and authoritarianism to which children are heir even in the pleasantest of physical surroundings. The very will to create idylls or to shore them up with unbridled imagination and splendiferous language is, after all, testimony to the fact that the idyll is a consciously and consummately fictive construct: that popular enthusiasm for the genre can be attributed in great part to the idyll's very impossibility outside the pages of fiction. We are all thrust out of Eden, adult and child alike – the most we can do is, through imagination and language, to write and talk ourselves 'back,' as do Lucy Maud Montgomery and her creation, Anne.

***

Happy the man, says Ronsard, *qu'une même maison a vu jeune et viellard*. It is of that house and place, in which I was born, in which I still live, and of those who dwelt therein, that I propose to write, with such skill in the use of words as I first began to learn it, and have ever since striven to perfect. The remembrance of any life, rich and fresh, should not be lost to the world.

Sir Andrew Macphail (TMW 1)

If Robert's magical 'ancient wood' proves irremediably alien to humankind, so that the backwoods idyll created by his three heroines cannot be sustained; if Montgomery's Avonlea is less than Edenic and Anne's heightened fantasy world doomed to be outgrown and effectively discarded, then surely the world of country pleasures Ernest Buckler celebrates in his writings is Arcadian rather than naïvely idyllic, and thus invulnerable to the deconstructive force of meta-idylls. In all his fiction Buckler creates a dialectic between beauty, growth, love, and the 'destructive element': *The Mountain and the Valley* is ultimately a tragic novel, the utterly desirable natural world of *The Cruelest Month* is ravaged by fire, and in the 'fictionalized memoir' *Oxbells and Fireflies*, 'the great sabled presence' of Death enters on the opening page.[26] Alan R. Young, in his introduction to Buckler's memoir, argues that *Oxbells* is not an idyll answering to wish-fulfilment, to simplistic desires as to what human life might be, but rather, a form of pastoral, evoking 'that universal human desire to return to some lost paradise world ... against which the spiritual poverty of our present existence may be evaluated' (OF xii). Yet I would argue that this discrimination between literary categories blurs the issue: Buckler does create an idyll in the fictional world of Norstead, a 'land of lost content' which can be regained not only through memory but, more importantly, through language. In so doing Buckler goes a step further than Montgomery's Anne, who recreated the given world through words, translating the mutely pretty into the magically expressive and eloquently beautiful. Buckler, author, narrator, and character of *Oxbells and Fireflies*, takes remembered experience and transforms it through and into language, creating Eden in the eternal present tense of a narrative that celebrates a vanished way of life. Paradoxically, his treatment of language both realizes and subverts the idyll of Norstead, as we shall soon see.

First, however, let us look at the idyllic elements which define Norstead. That it is meant as new Eden we may assume from, among other things, the names of its principal inhabitants – Joe and Mary. Not only chosen individuals but the entire community is part of a 'family compact': 'neighbours were ... like brothers' (OF 109), blessed with 'extraordinary good humour and grace' (OF 150), compassion, and the ability to communicate their understanding of and love for one another. Buckler makes a habit of contrasting the average Norsteader with the typically alienated, 'invisible' city-dweller, insisting that an exemplary fellowship and the best of blood ties make Norstead, paradigmatically, a community.[27] That Norstead is idyllic in this human sense is emphasized by the inclusion within the narrative of a counterworld or anti-idyll, the village of Claymore and its inhabitants:

Their senses were deaf as adders to the voice of the eternal around them ... their hearts ... pocked with pettiness ... cramped with caution.

To look at them and their like was to see better what Norsteaders and *their* like were not ... Their houses were of two kinds. One as narrow-eyed as themselves ... the other ... slovenly as the hair in the gravy, or the urine-scalded legs of the children with the neglected diapers. (OF 265–7)

This is as close as Buckler ever comes to the kind of 'hard' realism practised by a Nowlan or Richards. And while Buckler admits that his Norsteaders could be odd or even cruel, he neutralizes the criticism by insisting that 'even the ore they were flawed with was as purely itself as a member of the Table of Elements' (OF 265).

The inhabitants of Norstead occupy an existential paradise in which 'your presence exactly filled the space that your eyes encompassed, with nothing stern or unrelated in any object it came up against or in any of your senses' (OF 94); 'light and air were themselves at table with you, like fellow workers' (OF 98). Even the sign of our banishment from the Garden, labour, becomes emblematic of harmonious integration:

Wheels went round in the field and sled runners ran straight in their tracks, bearing the loads of food and heat that would go back into the breath and blood and muscle that had gone into the raising of them, while the broad day smiled. Water obeyed its quenchless memory always to boil at a certain heat, the particles of things clung together in the shape their physics said they must, rock was immutably rock, green grew exactly as its seed said – but they did this not as if they were sullen in their implacable yoke (as the steel of cities is) but as willingly as if they had made their own laws. (OF 301–2)

To be sure, Buckler provides ample evidence that this kind of 'work to be rejoiced in and rested after' (OF 198) is attended by back-breaking fatigue, yet such exhaustion is perceived not so much as a consequence of as an enemy to labour. The farmers and farmwives of Norstead are not the 'work-beasts' of Nowlan's Lockhartville; rather, they are just a little below the angels in their ability to carry out with immense dignity and skill their 'earth-sourced tasks' (OF 86) and thus enter into a kind of communion with nature and each other. Their work does not prevent them from knowing themselves or their world, as labour in city factories would. 'Work for the hands' provides 'wealth for the senses' (OF 88); 'muscles ... had the knack of what they were doing built into them like a recitation' (OF 90).

Such 'recitation' is carefully defined by Buckler and distinguished from other forms and uses of language. Just as the narrator must re-present and thus validate the farmer's age-old tasks and implements – peavy and scythe, sowing and haying – so he must authenticate and valorize the speech native to these exemplary villagers. '"That hay's made good," he kept exclaiming again and again. It was like a benediction' (OF 99). Simple words, fundamental perceptions, universal truths. Often Buckler's narrative falls into an entranced naming of things: 'Kraut knives and brace bits. Earwigs and compasses. Linchpins and patchwork holders' (OF 215). At frequent intervals he points out the superiority of 'folk' to 'educated' speech: 'What medical term is as dead-on as "that 'gone' feelin"? What better picture of a woman plagued with neuralgia than "she looks like a hen with an egg broke in her"? How better describe a man after a bout of quinsy than "He looks as if he'd been pulled through a knothole and beat with a sutt bag"?' (OF 129).

And a whole chapter, 'As the Saying Went, or Slugs and Gluts,' is a kind of *apologia pro lingua sua*, for the 'ticktock of empty rote' that is Norstead's daily speech. 'People whose senses graze always in the same pasture have a wordless intercourse circling among them without stop' (OF 160) – therefore their words will be 'tools as blunt and honest as the work tools of the field' (OF 161). Although Buckler gives abundant examples of earthy or piquant local dialect, he insists that his people's 'talk was no measure of them. Laughable or weedy as it might be, it did not spatter *them* with its weediness' (OF 167). He praises the Norsteaders' 'art of instant translation. From sense to sense. From self to self. So that half a dozen words from one man was all that was needed to set up a whole mirror of response in the other' (OF 167). Opposing the true if sometimes halting speech of his 'rustics,' and the 'little air-bubbling of the learned that, for all its ease and slickness ranks them with people who can fart at will' (OF 277); discriminating between substance and sound, words and 'a man's word,' Buckler undercuts talk itself, extolling a wordless language of feeling, gesture, perception: 'when the child looked at his brother's foot bleeding from the spike, as if it was his fault not to have defended enough this flesh that was all at once closer than his own. Or when he saw his father's broad hands bend down on the blustery day to fasten the scarf snugger around his throat before he'd known himself (until he felt suddenly warmer) that he'd been cold …' (OF 178).

Buckler epiphanizes moments when one touches 'the very meaning of the thing itself that the word for it had always stood in front of' (OF 124). And he spends considerable time declaring the redundancy or spuriousness of books in such a community as Norstead:

When everyone had read with his nerve ends the only great writers – earth, sky, rock and tree (not *these* the petticoated little penmen mooning about doubt and heartburn) – and been strengthened by them. When familiar faces held all the texts that mattered … When there were whole libraries in the eyes … which had themselves read … the only records that are printed without falsity (on field and kitchen), messages that make words the mere chips and whittlings of feeling entire … Who needed books, when he had memory? (OF 193–5)

Here, of course, is the paradox. *Oxbells and Fireflies*, we presume, must be written for all those with no experience and no memories of these essential moments and relationships; written by a member of a community for whom literacy, language, books themselves possess little value and less significance. In writing *Oxbells and Fireflies* Buckler is celebrating an idyllic world and at the same time lamenting its erosion and disappearance. The world he loves is dead; only in 'literary' language can he call it back into being and communicate its essence to those who never knew it. And in using such language – by turns laboured and playful, metaphysically charged and down-to-earth, transparent and opaque – Buckler is defining himself against the world of simple farmers and farmwives whose limited but honest, heartfelt speech he takes pains to reproduce in his text. Alan R. Young describes the chief feature of Buckler's style as 'its daring and innovative search for metaphors and verbal effects that will express the complexity of ideas and feelings that he wishes to communicate' (OF xvi). Yet surely this aesthetic imperative feeds on psychological and philosophical pressures stemming from Buckler's radical unease in the rural paradise he creates with his pen.

Norstead, I have argued, is a supra- and non-verbal world: its values and worth do not appear in, though they can be communicated through, its indigenous speech. And yet Buckler, like some linguist's King Midas, cannot help turning everything he touches into words. When he describes a man fishing on a summer's day he must translate the pleasure and gratification of trout-catching into both words and Platonic ideas: 'suddenly the surge of a trout would stretch your line taut and all at once ... you would know exactly what trout*ness* was. And *brook*ness. And *leaf*ness. And, yes, *world*ness and *life*ness itself' (OF 52).

Ordinary household objects become transfigured by simile and metaphor – 'Appetite shimmers. The meat and the bread and the tea are like the host of some affable religion whose only creed is the denial of sternness ... The plainest of mysteries, facelight, knits its shield above the table and around us' (OF 35). The narrator, remembering his childhood, speaks of the alphabet blocks carved by his father, and of his own games with them, the building of houses and the making of words which become not only animate but human: 'I make "thing." I change the *g* to a *k* and I have "think." I change the *i* to an *a* and I have "thank." I see that vowels are the eyes of words. I see how they change the word's expression' (OF 38).

The very implements of labour become an alphabet, 'the Z-shaped iron dogs, sawed into O-faced blocks by the W-shaped teeth of the cross-cut' (OF 101). And Buckler carries his verbalizing of the world into grammar itself, vivifying even those intractably dead parts of speech, articles definite and indefinite: '"The" points to something particular. "And" connects two things that are different. In the city, so much is alike that only a few "the's" are found, no more than a handful of "and's" needed to couple them. Here the "the's" were numberless, the "and's" infinite' (OF 212).

Beatific moments of experience become 'sentences ... in the book of your life' (OF 103); the days 'a train of quotes from the letter writing between sense and object' (OF 115). Time itself become a species of 'ink that dried on the air' (OF 186). And, if all aspects of existence can be translated, the flesh made word, then words themselves can be spoken in flesh: '[A man] climbs the hill. He has never been sick a day in his life. Then, between one step and the next ... comes the faceless smoke of mortality. A traitor cell unlocks itself and death is inside him. "Death" that has "the" in it. All the "the's." And "had." And "eat" in the middle' (OF 220).

The 'realism' – in the Platonic sense – of Buckler's concept of language, his finding deliberate and essential correspondences between words and things, his turning words into homunculi and microcosms, each with its own centre and beating heart, is fundamental to his idyllic vision of Norstead, that harmoniously integrated, blessed, and blissful world. Yet there are moments when the pressure of language threatens to break down or deform his narrative and the world it brings into being. It is not that his prose, at times superbly charged, often tumbles into mere preciousness, or that he develops certain tiresome verbal twitches – for example, 'triplets' such as 'A joy of brooks. A sigh of hemlocks. A grief of stones ...' or 'Mixing bowls, cheerful as stars. Barrel hoops as secure as a month. Roosters, regal as noon' (OF 201, 203). It is more the tortuous quality of much of his prose – a quality that the relaxed tone for which the narrative strives with such conversational ploys as 'And who could ever forget ...' (OF 63) or 'There was one young man ...' (OF 172) does not so much camouflage as openly battle against.

Buckler's true narrative voice is, of course, not artless and folksy, but contrived, convoluted. Such a passage as the following clearly reveals how difficult it was for Buckler to integrate 'literary' language and idiomatic speech, his chosen roles as writer and farmer: 'We used to laugh at Howie's crazy rhymes. How would he rhyme us now? ... We try to escape. We talk fast, we smoke, we drink. But time's rhymes have turned against us too. To smoke is to choke a little, to drink is to stink a little. To screw is to rue. Pain stains our brains. Words are now curds. The fair air is now bare. Worries, with their little moles' teeth, nibble the casings off our nerves. The cold scolds. The sun is done' (OF 299).

There are, in fact, three different voices in *Oxbells and Fireflies*: the 'down-home' which repeats and imitates the actual sayings of the villagers of Norstead; the 'impersonal literary' which translates the

sights and sounds of the village into imperishable moments of significant beauty, and a third voice which Buckler often cages within parentheses – the disembodied voice of loss, regret, loneliness: the voice of
Adam, unEdened while still in paradise: 'Sometimes, happy in a group,
in the middle of a laugh, the self of yourself that has gone its own way
with yourself alone (so long that their two faces, turned so jealously
toward each other, turn the other faces away) stands suddenly on a
vast twilight shore that the others' gaze falls just short of' (OF 300).

It is not Death which squats in Buckler's heartland, threatening the
idyllic vision his language so insistently creates. The 'Sable Presence'
is a mystery which ultimately sanctifies and revitalizes living. Lovingly,
Buckler evokes the ritual that surrounds the death of a family member
or a neighbour, the ways in which the dead are remembered and the
manner in which their presence allows unabashed tenderness, compassion, love to surface within the community. Thus it is not death but
another, more destructive force that is the interloper and outsider in
this idyll.

'The heart, born solitary' (OF 84) searches for its like, for objects or
persons to which to attach itself, Buckler insists. Aboriginal isolation
is the 'third Narrator's' great fear and affliction – not only the isolation /
alienation which for Buckler is an inescapable condition of city life,
but more significantly, the sense of being self-exiled on one's own
home ground, islanded in strangeness:

Silence tortures. It is the loudness of yourself alone. Speech tortures. It is the
husk of speech forever falling short of the wall that the voice crying beneath it
knows it can never penetrate or reach over. Music tortures. It holds out to you
the leap beyond yourself to where it promises to fuse all things, but lands you
there to find nothing but its orchestration of your singleness. Living tortures. It
will give you no clear space in its mirror where you can see both yourself
defined for everyone and yourself reflected out into all things. And because it
will not stop. (OF 84)

'This these people knew nothing of,' Buckler insists of his Norsteaders. Yet the narrator himself intrudes this alien knowledge within his
'story of some simple sort of happiness.' Humorous anecdotes, lush
descriptive passages, reverent evocations of the rightness, the beauty, the overwhelming meaning of Norstead life are 'interrupted' by
gain-saying parentheses:

I see the hardwood hills blazing (though not yet haunted) with remembrance ...

The air is as still as the Bible; pure and clear as the brook in a psalm. The velvet afternoon light sprawls in this once and total gift of itself, bemusing the senses. I glory in its dreamy ambience.
(Not yet the ravage of the perfect moment by the need to grasp it entire, knowing that all you ever find in grasp's palm when its fingers open up again is echo.) (OF 33)

Unquellable anxiety invades the text in passages like these, an anxiety rooted in our general human lot of loss and grief, but compounded by that creeping solipsism which is Buckler's bad angel as well as his daemon. In the last chapter of *Oxbells and Fireflies* he takes his narratorial alter-ego, the 'boy' of Chapter 1, into the memory of a perfect summer's day. For almost everything the wonderstruck child perceives comes the refrain. 'I have created it' (OF 296–8). Perception, for Buckler, becomes creation; it is this which kindles his prose, making it evocation and not mere description, epiphany rather than simple observation. Just as with David Canaan in the final section of *The Mountain and the Valley*, so with the narrator of *Oxbells*: there is ecstasy, but even more, terror in thus taking on responsibility for the very existence of things – to fail to name and write them down is to have them perish. Not to be able to pressure language, to coin new ways of expressing 'how it was or is' is to fall down some black hole, some unfillable blankness. To talk to one's neighbours in Norstead is to make one another 'solid as places' (OF 87), yet such talk does not suffice for the narrator – one cannot talk to time, except through memory, and even then while recapturing lived time one simultaneously confirms present absence.

The verbal binges on which Buckler goes, his wildcatting with words, are not necessary risks taken in an inventive and experimental context so much as a frenzied whistling in the dark. And while much of *Oxbells and Fireflies* consists of passages superbly tempered, where emotion and language perfectly mesh, there are enough instances of what we might call verbal despair – manic punning, verbal vivisection, unstoppable listing of phenomena (as if the mere naming of things could not only preserve them, but bring them into being in the first place) that the reader is ultimately jostled and jerked, not led, through the narrative. The idyll of Norstead self-destructs under the textual pressures Buckler brings to bear upon it. His narrative's penultimate focus on unreality, isolation, blindness, despair (OF 299–300) is followed by a catalogue of beneficent images – 'snowflakes cosy as locks and sun flakes (under the apple boughs) the image of keys' (OF 301) – that cloy in the sweetness and light squeezed out of them. The dialectic between the dark – 'the bag of day-old kittens in the pail drowned with their eyes shut ... And old men with a milky film over their pupils tapp[ing] their way querulously with their canes to the outhouse they had once swapped the roaring jokes about with the neighbor who was helping them build it, their thin streams now missing the hole' – and the light – 'rabbits r[unning] in the calm clear moonlight while the children dreamed of brooks and spring ... and the fir trees prayed with the cows on Christmas Eve' (OF 302) – comes to an unconvincing synthesis in the 'fireflies and freedom' of the text's last words. This is the same sort of solution which blurs the ending of Buckler's fine short story 'Man and Snowman,' in which a dying farmer's disillusionment with the health, home, and happiness he had once taken for granted is conveniently transcended by the 'peace' which death brings.

Oxbells and Fireflies does, as the blurb of the New Canadian Library edition insists, magnify 'the rural Nova Scotia of decades ago into a magnificent macrocosm of humanity.' As importantly, however, it deconstructs that idyllic macrocosm through a subtext of creative anxiety and personal isolation – 'the unshielded consciousness of one who does a thing alone' (OF 109). The result is problematic, affecting in the way a merely nostalgic celebration of and lament for a vanished way of life could never be. In Buckler's hands the 'regional idyll' takes on a radically new interest and significance; in subverting this genre, as, in their different ways did Roberts and Montgomery, he carries on a tradition that has found more recent expression in the work of Donna Smyth, whose Arcadia is post-Bucklerian, almost post-rural altogether.

\*\*\*

A woman, a dog and a walnut tree,
The more you lick them the better they be.[28]

In Quilt the 'anxiety of exile' that so pervades Oxbells and Fireflies is absent – or at least quiescent. The inhabitants of the idyllic-sounding 'Dayspring' are presented without verbal embellishment or apology: they pickle vegetables, piece quilts, go down to the old swimming hole or to their jobs at the power house without the narrator's making any special claims for the inherent dignity of their labour or nobility of their relationships. Neither language nor loneliness is the serpent in Dayspring; rather, it is sexually rooted violence – that of a jealous tomcat biting off the heads of newborn kittens, that of a luckless man who savagely beats his equally luckless wife. Death, the traditional trespasser in Arcadia, poses less of a threat than such violence – thus the protagonist's husband, dying by inches of arteriosclerosis, at last convinces his wife to give him an overdose of the medication which has only prolonged a death-in-life. For him death is a release, an inevitable ending. Aggression, on the other hand, is irredeemable. Myrt, the young wife who is repeatedly beaten, becomes helplessly inert, ready, in her confusion and boredom, to leave the shelter a social worker has found her and to go back to Ralph, who cannot help abusing her. One of the subtleties of Smyth's novel is its compassionate delineation of Ralph, who ends by shooting himself out of his rage and pain and puzzlement at not being able to get his wife back, and its equally understanding portrayal of the wronged wife whose sullen indecision and idleness are contrasted to the spirited dignity and power of the novel's heroine, old Sam Sanford.

*Quilt* is an altogether less complex and bedevilled work than *Oxbells and Fireflies* – more a novella than a novel, with a limited number of characters and conflicts. Generically, it is a regional idyll or rather, a cracked mirror of that genre. The narrative shifts from passages of unvarnished dialogue or exposition to pools of consciousness reflecting the redeeming stillness and rootedness of the natural world and its markers – clouds, rocks, trees, the river: 'And the elms rustled and moved overhead full of elm life after a hundred years, crammed from the inner bark to the secret core, pith and heart of tree where sap-life flowed between the earth and sky in the shape of a tree. And the elm leaves muttered and sighed, shadow and sun, leafy interfringe woven. Green.'[29] Without such markers pointing to 'something ... not beyond [the things themselves] ... but through them' (Q 119) there is no significance to rural life, however prettily pastoral it may appear.

Smyth shows how the human and natural worlds intersect in Dayspring for better or worse. On Sam and Walt Sanford the sunlight falls 'so strong and clear it was like part of them and how they lived that part of their lives in the light' (Q 107). The infernal summer heat, on the other hand, burns and bakes the earth 'where it was open to attack' (Q 60) and helps push Ralph to suicide. Despite this interconnection between women and men and the earth itself, the idyll which Smyth's text creates is less heightened, smacks less of special pleading than Buckler's. Where his sensuous, intricate narrative is juxtaposed against the limited speech of the Norsteaders, Smyth makes verbal awkwardness and limitation the authentic stuff of her text: 'Hazel grabbed the dishes to clear the table and she cleared it like a whizz, she was some mad that she cleared it like a whizz and he went on at her while she was clearing, went on and on about the beans, the blessed beans, and the raspberries rotting' (Q 33).

While sharing Buckler's reverence for the beauty of the rural world, Smyth resists aestheticizing it – unlike the photographer who moves to Dayspring and attempts to '"clean up" the swimming hole – as if the kids were garbage' so as to create an 'environmental studio' in which he can take photographs of engaged couples from Halifax (Q 22). Like Nowlan or Richards, Smyth relishes the real – if she describes how, at the swimming hole, 'dapple light ... came down like a blessing on the hot day' she also mentions the beer and blankets that have become as integral a part of the place as the light and water. A passage distilling the quasi-mystical, jewel-like beauty of preserves gleaming on dark pantry shelves (Q 10) is put into the context of the labour which produced them, the 'prickles of heat ... in the armpits and .. crotch' of the cook (Q 9). And in showing the 'good neighbourliness' of the women who assemble to make the quilt and to unlock the stories latent in the bits of cloth with which they work, Smyth breaks with the Bucklerian tradition of depicting rural women as silent in their sexuality: 'They'd talked a lot and laughed a lot. Laughed at silly things like Sam's friend, Dot, giving her a water pistol shaped like a man's thing for a joke. And Sam had squirted it at them and made all kinds of jokes like she used to. She was a devil that way but they always knew she was joking' (Q 48).

Smyth's Dayspring is a Norstead on which the foreign forces of Welfare, the Shopping Mall and Television have encroached. The 'destructive element' is duly acknowledged in, for example, the persistent references to flies, glistening like 'living jewels' but battening on death and decay (Q 90), or in the 'stretch of beach littered with garbage from ... the filthy sea' (Q 111). Even violence when it is accidental – Ralph's father cutting off his hand with a chain saw – is part of the natural order and law. What truly destroys the possibility of some simple sort of happiness in Dayspring is the development of false idylls threatening the rural world's identity and integrity. Chain stores where you can buy 'sweet sticky lemon pie' and 'Love's Own Red' lipstick, country and western songs advising girls to stand by their man no matter whether he's out to 'screw or beat [them] up' (Q 104), the television 'stories' with characters named Naomi and Bruce carrying on their adulterous affairs against a background of super-suburban affluence, the mystique of marriage, with brides in white carrying 'baby pink roses' and hungover grooms 'who knew about love ... knew all about it' (Q 80) – these form the antithesis of Buckler's world in which 'common decency' prevails and everyone knows the difference between sex and love, misunderstanding and aggressive hatred, the salt of the earth and city flummery.

Most dangerous, however, is the meta-idyll constructed by the victim of violence – that 'holy stillness the other side of pain'; that 'blessed silence' and perfect safety 'where only [Myrt] was allowed and nobody, not God, not nobody could touch her' (Q 102, 16) and which she begins to crave like some lost Eden. This paradise Myrt reaches only after having been beaten into unconsciousness shows the inevitability of the rural world's contagion by general social problems and disorders; the false idylls Smyth recounts call into question Ernest Buckler's conviction that young Maritimers, even if they don't go back to the plough, will turn their backs on the nefarious influence of the urban, industrial, and generally modern, and take a stand against 'annihilation by the juggernaut which levels all things to sameness.'[30] Though by the end of *Quilt* Sam Sanford's face regains its strength, becoming 'a rock, part of the earth that you wanted to touch and hang onto' (Q 121), the idyllic possibilities of Dayspring have been 'broken up, crumbled and creased' so that they resemble not a rock any more 'but a face in pieces, a face in tears' (Q 88).

The work of Buckler and Smyth, Roberts and Montgomery would seem to show that for the idyll to survive as an authentic and valid genre it must deconstruct itself, work against its traditional premises and strategies. Thus texts like *Quilt, Oxbells and Fireflies, Anne of Green Gables*, and *The Heart of the Ancient Wood* become not exercises in sentimentality and nostalgia but rather, intriguingly problematic manifestations of desire for that which we can never have, and knowledge of that which we cannot help but desire.

# 8

# Going or Staying:
# Maritime Paradigms

'The seasons in this colony,' said the Judge, 'are not only accompanied
by the ordinary mutations of weather observed in other countries,
but present a constant and rapid succession of incidents and people.
From the opening of the ports to the close of navigation, everything
and everybody is in motion, or in *transitu*. The whole province is a sort
of railroad station, where crowds are perpetually arriving and departing. It receives an emigrant population, and either hurries it on-
ward, or furnishes another of its own in exchange. It is the land of
'comers and goers' ... [R]icher lands, warmer climates, and better times,
those meteor terms that seduce them hither, still precede them, and
light the way to Canada or the far west, to ruin or the grave.'

THOMAS CHANDLER HALIBURTON[1]

The Maritimes, as writers from Haliburton to D.C. Harvey have pointed
out, are exporters not only of fish and timber but, more importantly, of
people: so exigent and incessant have been the pressures of making and
keeping a living for most Maritimers that throughout its history this
region has been one 'you had to choose not to leave.'[2] As a work like *The
Master's Wife* reveals, 'escape' has been for ambitious young Maritimers
what 'success' was for Richler's Duddy Kravitz – escape not merely
from the drudgery of the family farm or fishing boat, but also, from the
inevitable constrictions of Maritime society. Three avenues of escape
have traditionally been open: running away to sea; finding work in
New England factories or western cities; or getting an education and
going not on, but out to university.

In 'the Boston states' and the great cities of central Canada; on the prairies and the 'other' coast, exiled Maritimers abound. Contrary to Haliburton's pessimistic forecast, many of these *dépaysé* have thriven, pursuing the goals and realizing the ambitions which continued residence in their native region would have denied them. Yet for the writers among them the fact of successful escape is complicated by the condition of exile it necessitates. The successful labourer or would-be entrepreneur, the 'educational and professional' people whom Harvey resignedly described as 'men who have been educated here for eminent positions elsewhere,'[3] can hope to make enough money to retire or at least occasionally visit the region. But Maritime writers resettled in Toronto or Montreal, Vancouver, or Calgary will, in Ernest Buckler's words, have 'excommunicated' themselves from their imaginative homeground – should they continue to write about their native region, they risk becoming permanent tourists and nostalgia-mongers. As W.H. New has observed, the sense of exile from a time or place or stable moral order is a recurrent motif in Maritime writing;[4] as Fraser Sutherland has pointed out, it may well be an endemic one: 'How can such a rare species as the artist survive in the Maritimes save by becoming a hermit or, at the other extreme, pretending to be one of the boys in such traditional pursuits as collecting unemployment insurance and swilling Moosehead ale in the corner tavern?'[5]

'Is one's birthplace Canaan, or the land that God gave Cain? Every writer born in the Maritimes must answer that question; how he answers it will determine whether he remains home to work, or goes away.'[6] Almost from the beginning of literary culture in the Maritimes, writers have faced this conundrum. Against the Joe Howes and Thomas McCullochs, Ernest Bucklers and David Adams Richards who have elected to stay are all those who have conspicuously gone away – Haliburton, Charles G.D. Roberts, Hugh MacLennan, Antonine Maillet. One critic has argued that had MacLennan, for example, remained in the Maritimes, he would have been nothing more than a professor of dead languages at Dalhousie;[7] others have suggested that if Richards were to quit his preoccupation with the Miramichi and move on to more life-enhancing material he would find a wider, more appreciative audience. The implication seems to be that there is something intrinsically barbarous, philistine, passé – at all accounts inimical to the creation of literature – in the characteristic life of the Maritimes; that whatever a MacLennan might have been able to write as a Maritimer rather than a Montrealer would never have had the remotest interest or cultural significance for Canadian readers.[8]

This chapter will examine the major paradigms established by Maritime fiction regarding the vexed question of going or staying, a question which many writers have shown to comprehend more than mere geography and economics. The writers with whom I will be concerned, Hugh MacLennan, Ernest Buckler, Charles Bruce, and Alistair MacLeod, have all produced different answers to that question which, according to Sutherland, it is the definitive task of the Maritime writer to pose. Because MacLennan and Buckler are widely regarded as *the* major Maritime writers, and because their lives and oeuvres represent such dramatic contrasts, the bulk of this chapter will be devoted to them. Yet the paradigms established by Bruce and MacLeod, writers who have avoided the absolutes elected by MacLennan – who left for good – and Buckler – who defiantly and defensively stayed – will also be examined as important alternatives to the traditional literary models according to which Maritimers have perceived their own possibilities and those of their region.

\*\*\*

[In the mid-nineteenth century] the Maritimes began to build up the tradition of being an exporter of educational men to the United States and Western Canada ... [Maritimers] are reconciled to their loss if these sons can build up their own careers in helping to build up Canada as a whole.

D.C. Harvey[9]

Hugh MacLennan is perhaps the perfect representative of Harvey's Maritime man. Born in Cape Breton, bred in Halifax, MacLennan found himself exiled to Montreal after his studies at Oxford and Princeton by the simple fact that he couldn't find work in Nova Scotia. It was, MacLennan has stated, a most fortunate irony that the post at Dalhousie he had been educated in England to fill went to an Englishman instead of himself, since in leaving the Maritimes and encountering central Canada for the first time he entered at last into his true birthright and vocation – that of being a twentieth-century Canadian, interpreting his country to its own citizens and to the world.[10]

The question of MacLennan's status and stature in the field of Canadian letters should long have ceased to be a burning one – like Charles G.D. Roberts, MacLennan has become a fait accompli – the necessary cultural product and producer of his time. The presence of novelists of the calibre of Margaret Laurence and Robertson Davies, Timothy Findley and Margaret Atwood on the Canadian literary scene permits us the luxury of recognizing MacLennan for what he is – not *the* Canadian

novelist (and hence one whose literary virtues *must* be shown to out-
weigh his vices), but as a kind of *homme signe* on the Canadian literary
map. MacLennan's vision of Canada, elaborated in *Two Solitudes* and
*The Return of the Sphinx* has become part of our general cultural history.
As for the role MacLennan has consistently assumed, let us take it as
he wishes it to be perceived. *Pace* Woodcock, MacLennan is not Canada's Balzac, but rather, its self-styled Galsworthy, his essays and
novels revealing the mindset of a Middlebrow *Agonistes* and serving as
moral and ideological touchstones for a generation of educated Sunday
readers.[11]

It is when we come to consider MacLennan's credentials as a Maritime
writer that awkward problems arise. For it seems to be a regional tic to
claim this eminent Canadian as Forever Bluenose, to protest – too much
– that '[a]lthough MacLennan has lived in Montreal for many years,
he remains a staunch son of Atlantic Canada. He is by far our most
distinguished man of letters.'[12] Yet MacLennan has always seemed
baffled, even evasive, when interviewers attempt to pin him down on
the question of regional identity and loyalty. Thus although the Win-
throp Pickard Bell lectures MacLennan delivered as Professor of Maritime Studies (1982–3) at Mount Allison University bear the title 'On
being a Maritime Writer,' they have almost nothing to do with that topic.
MacLennan begins by considering what it means to be and how he
became a Canadian, and suggests that all writers need to leave their
native regions for one of the nation's cosmopolitan cities, since in
them real power lies. Declaring that 'Maritime Writer' is an 'inaccurate
title' to apply to anyone writing in so diverse a region as the Maritimes, implying that there are no common characteristics that define a
distinctively Maritime corpus of literature, MacLennan stresses that
Maritime writing should not consider itself to be 'regional' at all, but
rather, an unapologetic part of world literature. Finally, he concedes
that the Maritimes did form his sensibilities and values, but leaves us in
no doubt that whatever importance his work possesses stems from his
identity and role as a Canadian, not a Maritime writer; that the value of
his work lies in its having helped Canadian literature out of those
cages of colonialism and provincialism into which its critics, at home and
abroad, had tried to lock it.[13]

MacLennan's reluctance to call himself a Maritime writer, coupled
with his insistence that Canadians must transcend regional loyalties
in order to unite in discovering a national sense of self should put paid
to the notion of this writer as an east coast Odysseus, bound, after
much dalliance with the Calypso of Montreal, home to the patient

Penelope of Halifax. Certainly the course of his oeuvre after *Barometer Rising*, in which he explodes that colonial mentality which has traditionally been seen as the Maritime's ne plus ultra, represents a steady west-to-centre movement. Having found Canada in Quebec, or more precisely, Montreal, that microcosmic example of 'two nations warring in the bosom of a single state,' MacLennan set out to write his first truly Canadian novel. The rest is *Two Solitudes* – or so it would seem. Yet MacLennan's oeuvre does not follow a straight line towards a fictional realization of his concept of Canada, but rather, a curious zigzag, his westerly course being regularly deflected back to the sensibility and values he connects with his Maritime birth, chief among them a terroristic Calvinism and a strict submission to paternal authority.[14] To get a rudimentary idea of the pattern which results let us take a brief tour round MacLennan's fictive estate. So brief will this tour be that MacLennan's oeuvre will appear reduced to a series of theses or themes – since he is, however, largely a thesis-novelist this reduction will not be altogether unjust to his texts.[15]

After examining the psychological roots of the French-English question in *Two Solitudes*, MacLennan launched on a companion study of the WASPish North American psyche in *The Precipice*. Both novels attempted to answer the question MacLennan would later rephrase from Crèvecoeur – 'Who then is this new man, this Canadian?'[16] – by literally marrying different national types, respectively, Canadien and Quebecker, Scotch-Canadian and All-American. While the first novel laments and lambastes the stock prejudices and resulting blindness that made French-English relations in Canada a dialogue of the deaf, MacLennan turned in the latter work to another obstacle in the way of Canada's attaining to the kind of national identity 'that grows spontaneously in small peoples and in individuals out of the instinct of self-preservation.'[17] This obstacle is that 'dourness in English-speaking Canada that came from the raw Calvinism of the Scotch and the diluted Calvinism of the United Empire Loyalists and that infected even the French Canadians. The Irish only brought the cholera with them, but so far no antibiotic has been able to eradicate from the national bloodstream what the Scotch brought. It makes us allergic to great expectations.'[18]

Accordingly, MacLennan in his next novel got back to origins – not only his own but also those of Scotch dourness, by which his personal life had long been dampened.[19] As a result *Each Man's Son* is as much an exposition of the spiritual roots of that destructive Puritanism which in *The Precipice* MacLennan had portrayed as afflicting Americans and

Canadians alike, as an account of life in a Cape Breton mining town. The Broughton of this novel could not breed even petty, never mind great expectations: it is a ghost town in which that spiritual terrorist, Jean Calvin, continues to Rule O.K. When Daniel Ainslie and the miner's son Alan MacNeil make their escape from it at the novel's close, it is as though they are quitting the ruins of a town as dead as Troy after the Greeks had done with it. In *Each Man's Son* MacLennan had supposedly wrestled down that slavish respect for paternal authority his Calvin-fearing father had drummed into him as a child.[20] In *The Watch that Ends the Night* MacLennan felt free enough from Calvin's clutches to set out what can be called his gospel of humanistic individualism, in which graciousness in social relations and spiritual grace are presented as the greatest goods with which human beings can be blessed, and as utterly transcending socio-political realities. Yet George Stewart's search for a father and a faith in the figure of Jerome Martell would seem to show that the ancestral ghosts MacLennan had tried to exorcize in *Each Man's Son* were very much alive and kicking him still.

Despite, or perhaps because of his renunciation of politics and society in *Watch*, MacLennan was hit particularly hard by the radical mood and events of North America in the 1960s. The political consequences of Québec's Révolution Tranquille must have seemed to him a particularly monstrous attack upon his previously worked out concept of 'the essence of Canadian nationhood' – the fact that our country is 'a political fusion of the two elements in North American history which refused to belong to the United States.'[21] Not only was one of those founding elements attempting to rupture its ties with the other and to seek closer economic links with the Americans; it was also repudiating what MacLennan came to define as Canada's sole hope for sovereignty – the manifestation of 'a single constructive idea that [would make] her national survival of value to the rest of mankind.'[22] This idea was not the exceedingly naïve one expressed in *Barometer Rising* of Canada as a central arch uniting England and America, but rather the notion found first in *Two Solitudes* of Canada as a haven of racial tolerance and co-operation – or, as MacLennan expressed it in his essay 'Scotland's Fate: Canada's Lesson,' the vision of a society north of the 49th parallel resistant to 'Romanization,' that is, being turned into a racial and cultural melting pot *à l'américaine*.

It is not mere coincidence that in *The Return of the Sphinx* MacLennan resurrected the boy-hero of *Each Man's Son*, Alan MacNeil-Ainslie, for in this novel one of the most important components of MacLennan's obsession with puritanism – the absolute authority of the father, be he divine or biological – comes to the fore. Daniel Ainslie had attempted to evict from his soul a tyrannically patriarchal God, making room for a gentler, maternal, loving-and-forgiving divinity. It would seem that his adopted son Alan hankers after the old-time religion, or at least for a patriarchal God to whom His creatures would owe filial respect and obedience. Elspeth Cameron has commented on MacLennan's embrace of G. Rattray Taylor's *Sex in History* with its theory of history moving in recurring cycles of 'patrism' – restrictive and authoritarian – and 'matrism' – permissive, sexually and politically liberating.[23] In *Sphinx* Alan Ainslie – a Modern by virtue of his appalling experiences in World War II, a Victorian by virtue of his commitment to civilized (patriarchal) values – has his political career and very nearly his sanity destroyed by his confused and rebellious son, who not only falls into bed with his girlfriend's mother – what else could be expected of someone who has come of age in a 'matrist' epoch? – but who also nearly succeeds in blowing up a building to show solidarity with the terrorist / liberationist cause.

If the Daniel Ainslie of *Each Man's Son* was a fictional portrait of MacLennan's own father, then the Alan Ainslie of *Sphinx* would seem to be MacLennan's desired self-portrait – the respected, responsible man his father had educated him to become, freed of that father's sexual guilt but yearning for the authority and respect his father possessed and commanded. In this context MacLennan's latest novel, *Voices in Time*, represents a wish-fulfilment: whereas Alan Ainslie is nearly destroyed by his son, the elderly John Wellfleet is rescued from ignominy and oblivion by the young André Gervais, who sits at his feet, receives his (transcribed) word, and comes both to revere and to love him as a dutiful son. The new generation which MacLennan imagines as surviving the 'clean' nuclear destruction of civilization is one which respects traditional forms of morality and authority: Gervais addresses Wellfleet as 'Sir,' is repelled by the accounts of drug-taking and promiscuity among the young that the Timothy Wellfleet Papers reveal as having been prevalent before 'the Destruction,' and is shown to be an affectionate father and loyal husband – in other words, a perfect petit bourgeois in a world where, although individual nations no longer exist, conditions are ripe for a muted kind of Renaissance.

One of the MacLennan's most recent critics has argued that his 'portrayal of the individual's relationship to the external world is frequently modelled on the relationship of a child to an arbitrary and powerful parent': 'He habitually sees national, or collective psychology as extensions of individual psychology, and he often understands national

and international politics as family dynamics writ large ... Therefore
the social and religious dimensions of MacLennan's fiction are often
simply enlarged versions of his recurrent subject, the patriarchal
family.'[24]

It is this habit of vision which MacLennan owes to or perhaps conflates with his Maritime heritage. His oeuvre, as we have seen, shows
his 'Maritime sensibility' to be partly objective – a historian's awareness
that the political, economic, and cultural importance of the Maritimes
is very much a thing of the past – and partly intensely personal – a son's
combined fear and love, anger and submission towards the religion
and authority of his father. It is this sensibility and not his concern with
*the* Canadian identity that remains a constant throughout his fiction,
for with *Voices in Time* MacLennan's preoccupation with Canada's survival is subsumed by his concern for human survival. What persists is
an obsession with the destructive or disabling force of Puritanism, for all
that it is displaced into a kind of old man's yearning for the deference
and reverential affection that in previous societies the young were accustomed to show their elders. But though the shaping forces this writer
connects with his native region are still at work in his latest fiction,
MacLennan has eliminated all references to the Maritimes in *Voices in
Time*. The only place that survives is MacLennan's true Penelope –
Montreal and that Laurentian countryside to which the useless John
Wellfleet has been rusticated by the governors of his section of the
World State. Ultimately, then, MacLennan can be described as a re-
gionalist – on the understanding that his chosen region is not the Mari-
times, but that curious country, an Anglophone's Quebec.[25]

If it has been MacLennan's example, not his practice as a writer that
has been of most significance for the emergence and survival of an
indigenous literary culture in this country, then what of that example in
the context of Maritime literature? It would appear that none of Mac-
Lennan's regional 'heirs' have concerned themselves with the humanly
oppressive force of Calvinism or with the chimera of Canadian national identity – perhaps because MacLennan has himself exhausted these
concerns. Nevertheless, the roles performed by the protagonists of
MacLennan's fiction, the notion of Maritime possibilities they express
must have influenced, however subliminally, readers and writers in
the Maritimes. What MacLennan has done, of course, is to progressively
write the Maritimes out of his fictive worlds. We have seen in a previous chapter how the hero of *Barometer Rising* is made to turn his mind's
eye from the wreckage of colony to the reality of nation – a process
that will involve Neil Macrae's phsical removal from the Maritimes. (The
only hero of the novel voluntarily to remain in the Maritimes is Angus

Murray, the amiably tippling doctor who spouts Latin tags during the chaotic aftermath of the Halifax explosion, and who more or less puts himself out to pasture in his native Cape Breton once he realizes that he has no chance with the novel's heroine, Penny Wain.)

In MacLennan's next novel a Maritimer takes on an important, if peripheral role: Captain Yardley, the archetypal Nova Scotian sea captain, not only plays Nestor to Paul Tallard's Telemachus but also serves as a repository of authentic human values, as opposed to the pseudo-civilized ones of his 'High-Society' daughter, an impeccably lifeless Montreal matron. The reasons MacLennan gives for this Maritimer popping up in the little village of Saint-Marc-des-Érables are almost as farfetched as those he gives for Louis Camire's presence in Broughton, Cape Breton. Presumably MacLennan needed to introduce a character who would not only possess qualities of bluffness, compassion, intellectual curiosity, existential insight, and the earthy wisdom that allows him ultimately to affirm life and have a quasi-mystical vision at the moment of his death, but also whose very age and *métier* – he was one of the iron men in the wooden ships – show him to belong to a vanishing breed. Paul Tallard and Heather Methuen can receive Yardley's practical assistance and his blessing, but cannot model their own lives and characters after his: when Yardley dies – appropriately enough, in Halifax – an epoch dies with him.

The Maritimes, MacLennan seems to suggest, is a country for old men; in *Each Man's Son* the youthful characters – Mollie and Archie – are killed off, their son Alan is whisked to parts abroad, and the novel's hero, Daniel Ainslie, only shows signs of vitality and growth once he makes up his mind to heed everyone's advice and leave the Maritimes to study in Europe. Jerome Martell in *The Watch that Ends the Night* is portrayed as having outgrown provincial, pre-war Halifax just as he has outgrown the Boy's Own Christianity in which he was raised. Though he maintains the virility and naïveté which are his backwoods New Brunswick birthright, Martell must quit the Maritimes in order to realize his destiny: becoming a top Montreal surgeon, marrying Catherine Carey, getting trapped by his own idealism into a political involvement which leads him literally round the world, and, most importantly, realizing the error of his ways and coming into a state of grace while having a vision of Jesus in a jail cell. Significantly, Jerome Martell does not return to the Maritimes after his climactic meeting with his former wife in Montreal – rather he heads for pastures new in the northwest. The Maritimes, for MacLennan, have become nothing more than a *terminus a quo*.

Similarly Alan Ainslie, the last Maritimer we meet in MacLennan's pages, rejects any notion of going back as more than a tourist to the region of his birth. His career in ruins due to his son's trafficking in terrorism, Ainslie flees Ottawa and Montreal to drive from coast to coast in an attempt to renew his faith in Canada. He visits his birthplace, but his use of his real name, Alan MacNeil, on motel registers in the Maritimes is no more than a filial gesture. Rather like Neil Macrae with his vision of the miraculous railway spanning the continental breadth of a magnificent nation, Alan Ainslie realizes the Canadian dream by driving cross-crountry on the Trans-Canada, coming to realize that the distinctive essence of Canada is simply the land itself – 'Too vast even for fools to ruin all of it.'[26] And the part of that land to which Ainslie clings is his country place in the Laurentians – his and MacLennan's elected home.

Thus the regional heritage this 'staunch son of Atlantic Canada' has to pass on to his literary successors is a thoroughly confused one. If Cape Breton made him, Montreal certainly has him now; furthermore, the making of the man has perhaps been the undoing of the novelist. T.D. MacLulich has argued that MacLennan could never realize his full potential as a novelist because of his father's unshakeable influence upon him – and we know from Elspeth Cameron's biography that MacLennan wrote regularly to his father long after the old man's death. To be a worthy son of a father whose life was dedicated to the principles of self-denial and service to others, MacLennan felt compelled to create fiction that would serve 'an obvious social and moral purpose'[27] instead of creating fictive worlds to explore his own profoundest experiences and impulses. Certainly MacLennan's post-*Watch* thinking represents a return to the father, to a milder form of those patriarchal values and concepts he had tried to reject in *The Precipice* and *Each Man's Son*. Yet his fiction has never enacted a parallel physical return to or validation of his father's and his own native region.

Despite their affection for and pride in an eminent exiled native son, Maritimers must deal with the fact that in his novels MacLennan has effectively written off their region, portraying it as a graveyard of desires and ambitions, and creating a whole range of characters who re-enact his own story – not an odyssey back to, but an abandonment of, the Maritimes. Perhaps the literary character one should think of in connection with MacLennan and the Maritimes is not Odysseus, but rather Lord Jim, with the Maritimes being his Patna; Montreal his Patusan. At any rate, the paradigm his career and oeuvre offer to Maritime writers is both destructive and dubious, and it is surely time that MacLennan's position as this region's predominant literary figure – a position he himself lays no claim to – is put into perspective by looking at other Maritime writers and the alternative paradigms their work offers.

\*\*\*

Whether, as it sometimes seemed, he had a love of the place as binding as blood, or, as it sometimes seemed, a hatred of it so dark and stubborn as to fascinate him beyond the fascination of any possible kind of love ...

Ernest Buckler[28]

The farmer-writer from the Annapolis Valley is in almost every way a contrast to MacLennan. Both men possessed the intelligence and ambition to 'escape' from their native regions via higher education – MacLennan at Oxford and Princeton, Buckler at graduate school in Toronto – but there the resemblance ends. For Buckler found little delight and less literary stimulation during his working years in Toronto; by returning to the Maritimes to farm and to write (in that order) Buckler consciously and conspicuously chose not to leave. Where MacLennan's novels vividly depict the excitement of living in great cities like Montreal and New York, Buckler's fiction is adamant on the alienation, isolation, and ugliness endemic to urban life as opposed to the country pleasures an Entremont, Endlaw, or Norstead offer. Except for a few stories, Buckler's fiction is set firmly within the rural Maritimes, and within the same section of the Annapolis Valley to boot. He has gone out of his way to insist that this area is a microcosm, not a backwater; that it affords him both 'great sustenance' and that isolation in which, as an artist, he needs to work: isolation, he stresses, from other writers who 'are just stuffed with words, like dry-bread dressing up a Christmas Eve goose's ass.'[29]

There is no question that Buckler is a finer artist than MacLennan, though he may be a less 'successful' novelist and was certainly less prominent as a cultural figure. Perhaps the most distinguishing feature of Buckler's career was not his managing to combine the careers of farmer and writer, but rather, his profound and unshakeable ambivalence about the act of writing, an ambivalence most succinctly expressed in his essay 'My First Novel': 'if writing is hell, not writing is worse.'[30] Buckler's distrust of language, particularly literary or 'educated' language, was rooted in the two consuming concerns of his existence: First, his philosophical awareness of the solitariness of individuals, their separateness from the natural world, and the disjunction between things, and thoughts, and the words in which we try to express them. And second, his unremitting commitment to a kind of people and a way of life in which not alienation but harmonious integration between self and other, being and world was possible – largely because language (not perhaps the cause but certainly the vehicle of loneliness and apartness) becomes in this world subordinate to wordless labour, gesture, and touch.

These two concerns give to Buckler's fiction and to his conception of writing a schizophrenic cast, since he never resolved the fundamental contradictions they begat. For Buckler to have given full rein to what one critic has called his 'metaphysical'[31] preoccupations would have involved his leaving behind not so much the family farm as the intense guilt and indeed, the contempt which his farming made him feel towards those who made their living and perceived the world primarily through language and the intellect. On the other hand, for Buckler to authentically have given voice to the inarticulate rural people he loved and respected, to have truly 'spoken' the land and their attachment to it, he would have had to reject those intimations of isolation and solipsism which made his perceptions of reality so intense, and his expressions of them so tortured. As it is, Buckler's oeuvre is almost intolerably problematic, contradictory, fraught – reading the major works of this writer is like trying to drink out of a shattered glass. Time and time again, Buckler's very medium, his acutely figurative prose, sabotages the vision of life it tries to communicate – that idyllic integration of man and nature that, as we have seen, *Oxbells and Fireflies* attempts to celebrate. If, as Buckler once claimed, the writer's task is to observe people 'who just act simply, and are not introspective in the least, and draw [his] conclusions from them,'[32] then why are the more interesting of his characters introspective to a fault – David and Anna in *The Mountain and the Valley* and everyone except Letty in *The Cruelest Month*? Any why do these characters and the narrators themselves spend so much time and linguistic effort analysing, exposing, and communicating the essence of simple people? One answer must be that this writer has an impossibly complex relation to the very medium he must use to accomplish his 'simple' task.

The 'human condition,' for Buckler, was essentially a linguistic one. And since language both delights and deceives, destroys and preserves, unites and divides, it comes to be a particularly poisonous serpent in his fictive garden. If Buckler compared the writer's practice to the mowing, reaping, and bundling of what has 'blossomed' during the day, he also compared it to the less attractive bodily functions – defecation, masturbation, vomiting, and the eruption of boils.[33] And Buckler posited not only isolation, but something altogether different – abject loneliness – as 'almost the *sine qua non* of the writer's art,' insisting that it is 'the *sick* whale that produces the ambergris, it is the *irritated* oyster which produces the pearl.'[34] What I would like to suggest is that Buckler's defiant refusal to concede a higher value to writing than to farming, and his insistence on remaining physically isolated from other writers and intellectuals as the truest means of keeping faith with his 'own' people, led not to the production of literary pearls, but to writing that, however magnificent, evocative, original it may be in a great many of its parts, is irritating – even sick – as a whole. Buckler – for better and worse – was no David Adams Richards, able to convey the reality of impoverished, inarticulate people's lives from within their native idiom and set of mind. Instead, he attempted to apotheosize the Josephs and Marthas, Juds and Steves of Entremont by situating them in elaborate fields of language, and by deliberately undercutting the one word-artist in their midst, the luckless David Canaan. The result was inevitably problematic.

For Alden Nowlan, Buckler compared with D.H. Lawrence in his ability to create fresh and true similes; Buckler's weaknesses, Nowlan argued, his letting his 'similes slip out of his hands' were but 'exaggerations of his strength.'[35] Buckler's critics have been less generous, and certainly more exasperated than Nowlan. Of *The Mountain and the Valley* Stuart Keate wrote: 'Had his excesses of imagery, his infatuations with the language, been curbed by a somewhat sterner editorial pencil, this good book might have been a great one.'[36] John Orange has commented on how the tension created in Buckler's texts between 'an intuitive view of life and a distrust of words to communicate this view results in a kind of prose that is obsessed with clarification.'[37] Claude Bissell, complaining of the 'vexatious obscurity' of Buckler's prose, has pointed out how Buckler's 'pursuit of the microscopic detail has become an obsession, and often brings the flow of the narrative to a halt'[38] – though he palliates this criticism by suggesting that such obsessions are to be found among all great writers. R.G. Baldwin is less kindly and more accurate in his perceptions: for him, Buckler's is the obsession of a 'neurotic perfectionist': 'Here is a man giving everything he has. The trouble is he tries to give more – at least in his style, which is sometimes grotesquely difficult, almost self-consuming as it turns in on itself.'[39]

As John Orange elaborates,

Buckler time and again comes back to the paradox that the writer expects words to clarify, and to give unity and meaning to experience in some transcendent way, when in fact they always seem to fragment, separate, and focus our attention on individual things both inside and outside of ourselves. In fact this paradox finds its way into Buckler's own writing style which struggles (sometimes painfully) to capture every nuance of texture and feeling in relationships either among people or between people and their surroundings, while at the same time it ironically expresses the idealistic expectations of artists who try to do that very thing.[40]

It is in *The Mountain and the Valley* that the Bucklerian paradox emerges most clearly. David Canaan is the born artist who possesses, *ab ovo*, the 'secret extra senses' (MV 28) that allow him to take an extreme delight in the phenomena around him, to develop a 'negative capability' which enables him to understand how other people feel and to express their thoughts for them in the words they cannot command, and finally, to recognize the disjunction between his perceptions of things and the language in which those perceptions must be communicated: 'When he was alone with his father he didn't know what to say. The quick things in his mind sounded foolish even to himself ... [S]omehow David would be struck shy when he started to talk; and then, when he didn't speak true to his thoughts, he'd feel as if he were keeping a secret from the person he could most trust' (MV 27).

Throughout the novel David experiences moments of ecstasy and fulfilment whenever thoughts and words seem to touch, either in the books he finds to read or in the phrases he puts down in his scribbler. And time and time again, David is humiliated and betrayed by such congruence, as when, enchanted by his lines in a school play, he conflates fiction and reality, kisses the pretend princess and is mocked by Jud Spinney, or when, having become so engrossed in writing a story that he doesn't notice his sister and brother-in-law coming into his room, he throws his entire manuscript into the fire lest they read his work and laugh at him. His experience is an endless seesaw between acceptance and rejection of his artistic sensibility, between fostering his writing and lashing out at it as he does to the turnips he hacks to pieces after Toby's train has passed him by and revealed the horrible emptiness and stagnation of David's life on the farm. As D.J. Dooley has observed, painful futility is the condition which characterizes all of David's artistic endeavours – 'All his attempts at writing are torn up, or blotted out, or consigned to the flames.'[41]

David rides this agonizing seesaw, alternately exulting in and repudiating his artist's vocation, precisely because he has chosen to stay in his parents' world and to live as they have done. As long as he has his sister to talk to and share perceptions with, he manages to have the best of both worlds – a rich inner life, and a secure, beneficent environment sustained by the dignified labour and emotional strength of his parents. Once Anna goes away, however, David loses one of the main props of his balanced world; with his fellows 'he has to adopt an alien mode of discourse in a very self-conscious way,'[42] and though Anna comes back from time to time David never recaptures his previous intimacy with her. The utter lack in Entremont of a *semblable*, even a friend, however different from himself, makes it impossible for David to stand up for his truest self: as Dooley argues, 'when [the community's] perspective intrudes into his life, he has neither the confidence in himself nor the confidence in the values of literary creation which would enable him to pursue his own goals in his own way.'[43]

Yet if David 'has no system of values to oppose to that of [a] community [which] could place a value upon farming or logging, [but] not upon writing'; if he becomes a prisoner 'not just of his valley, but of his valley's moral outlook,'[44] he retains a peculiarly ironic authority throughout the novel which prevents *The Mountain and the Valley* from becoming that novel-of-the-land-and-its-people which David finally envisions writing. Buckler's text has an omniscient and supposedly objective narrator, but it is David's sensibility that predominates: the passages given over to Martha's enchantment with her household tasks, Anna's complicated feelings for the happy-go-lucky Toby, Ellen's memories, Joseph's contentment with the farm are more like narratological asides than chapters furnishing authentic alternatives to David's vision and perceptions. We are made to feel that a complete congruity exists between the narrator's way of seeing and depicting a landscape or situation for us, and what David's response to these same things would be. This feeling comes to the fore in the epilogue, where David's vision of his world and his idea for textualizing that vision suggest a proleptic kind of *déjà vu*: the novel David projects we have, in fact, already read. And whereas Buckler ironically qualifies David's mountaintop vision of himself as the greatest writer in the world,[45] he lets stand the whole intricate narrative of perception that begins with David's setting out on the road that leads to the mountaintop (MV 281), and which ends with his reaching both the very top of the mountain and the realization that he can become the things he perceives, and, in finding their 'single core of meaning' tell everything exactly as it is in itself. It is this 'narrative of perception' with which Buckler is most insistently engaged, and, whatever his intentions, it has almost nothing to do with his attempts to give 'an absolving voice' to the 'misread' lives of the ordinary, inarticulate people of Entremont.

All during his climb, David has been assaulted by the multiplicity and essential difference of things, and by a sense of perceptual regression *ad infinitum* – 'Myself amongst [things and thoughts] … *thinking* of myself amongst them … thinking of myself screaming "stop," thinking of myself thinking of myself thinking of …' (MV 297). This perceptual hysteria is nothing new for David – it has constantly animated his various responses to the world around him. Moreover, there is something disturbingly rapacious in David's excessive responses to snowy fields or autumn foliage or Christmas. If a thing is 'imperfectly known' it remains 'unpossessed' for him (MV 119) and just as David must demonstrate his machismo to Toby by casually fornicating with a passively reluctant Effie, so he must demonstrate possession of the phenomena around him, using heightened sensation and throbbing language in order to penetrate them. This 'phallogocentricity' is the hallmark of Buckler's narrative style. Writing for him was not so much expression as possession: as David is made to remark: 'There was only one way to possess anything; to *say* it exactly. Then it would be outside you, captured and conquered' (MV 195). The books which David comes to admire are those in which, through metaphor, simile, and acuteness of diction, sensation is translated into perception, meaning added to sentience, so that one not only feels but *knows* how something is, for oneself and for everyone else. In this way the almost neurasthenic David Canaan can become the voice of Everyman in Entremont.

Such consummate knowing 'how it is' presupposes a belief in the universality of events and phenomena, a conviction that we can all experience 'moments when the simplest things … [are] suddenly, sweepingly, shot with universality. As if [we have] happened on some shockingly bright phrase in the very language of meaning' (MV 195). Yet once again 'the thought breaks down like a stream forking in the sand. Then the forks fork. Then the forks' forks fork …' (MV 296). For opposed to this intimation of universality as a 'language of meaning' which all can share, illiterate and educated alike, is the rampant solipsism which afflicts David Canaan and, as we have already seen in *Oxbells and Fireflies* and *The Cruelest Month*, Buckler's writing as a whole. That six years' 'almost complete isolation' in which Buckler wrote *The Mountain and the Valley*[46] would seem to have exacerbated his habitual anxiety that, unless he not only saw but said a thing, it did not exist.

The intensity with which David feels things comes to serve as a guarantee that they *are* there to be felt, and that they are perceived by others who haven't the words to capture and possess them. Conversely, the bluntness and inertia of perception which characterizes, for example, his neighbour Steve, the last person David ever sees and speaks to, must be both reassuring and terrifying. For Steve, coming down the mountain, was assaulted by no such multitudinous perceptions as swarm to David walking up the mountain, and which cause him nearly to lose his sanity. But if David's perceptual world is unreal, as much a fiction of his own creation as is the heightened, romantic world of feeling his acting in the school play had so disastrously created, then how can he use it to validate the lives of his neighbours? The narrative suggests that David's family, at least, perceives the beauty and meaning of the rural world in the same way David does though they have no language to express it. Yet as soon as extravagantly literary language is used to communicate how Joseph or Chris or Martha feel about their world, the feelings stop being theirs and become David's, or the narrator's. And this is the point at which the futility of David's vocation becomes apparent: the ordinary people of Entremont speak best through touch or even through silence; accordingly, not verbal but visual and tactile mediums would best express their lives.

David's language and process of perception, his 'word-shaped' thought isolate him and his fiction of the world within the ordinary rural world of Entremont. Though he is fluent in the speech of the community, with its painfully limited vocabulary, tropes, and topics, whenever he is by (and therefore most) himself he speaks a private, 'literary' language. Perhaps the most poignant aspect of his life lies in the fact that there is no one to listen to him and to talk back – 'almost all his conversation involves play-acting, from his first meeting with Effie to his last encounter with a human being ... in the Epilogue.'[47] All David's best conversations go on inside his head, about the world in his head. That this may have been Buckler's own situation seems painfully likely when one turns to the novel that followed *The Mountain and the Valley*. In *The Cruelest Month* what is intended as conversation between imaginative, educated people emerges as ruminative monologues. As Robert Farlow has pointed out, in Buckler's second novel the 'talkers are ... unreal because they only talk about themselves, or more impossibly, about something that interests the author.'[48] Once again, Buckler seems unable to trust either the tale or the tellers – pages and pages of 'book-talk' are hoisted on the petard of the novel's one illiterate character, Letty, who observes that all the readin' and writin' in the world don't add up to a fart on the plains of Arabia. Yet Letty's hostility to learned language is in itself suspect, since she has fallen hopelessly in love with the book's most learned and literary character – the supersensitive Paul Creed, who, as D.O. Spettigue has suggested, 'is a David who has "gone outside," has been a city sophisticate and now has returned to the home soil (as Buckler himself did in 1936).'[49]

Deliberately, dispassionately Buckler kills off David Canaan just at the moment he has looked into his heart and is ready to write. Yet what else could he do? For it is manifest that David Canaan could never have written a book that would do justice both to his own tormented sensibility and to the robustly natural life of the villagers of Entremont. Ernest Buckler himself could not manage this in *The Mountain and the Valley* – hence his going on to author *The Cruelest Month* and *Oxbells and Fireflies*, texts which deal respectively with the tortured sensibilities of an educated, urbanized élite, and with the profoundly simple labours and pleasures of country people. It is only in his first novel that Buckler attempted to integrate the two, and ended by annulling both – not only David but Joseph and Martha are dead; Anna and Chris as-good-as-gone, by the novel's end. Perhaps more importantly, Buckler kills off the artist whom David might have become, sparing only the near-senile Ellen, whose artistic medium is not alien, treacherous words, but good solid cloth, and whose products are not books which the community will never read, but rugs they will gratefully wear under their feet.

'[I]n David — perhaps in Buckler himself – ' Spettigue has argued, 'one detects ... that sense of guilt on the part of the very articulate person that an anti-intellectual society fosters, as though too great a facility with words implied a lightness of character.'[50] Certainly Buckler portrays David as becoming enraged whenever someone in the community imputes extraordinary intelligence, sensitivity, and hence weakness, to him. His astonishing quickness and cleverness at school, his learning of foreign languages, and reading of books are things he must hide because they show him as different from his father and brother, as not really belonging to their world. As a result of having to hide or internalize what matters most to him, David develops a remarkable sensibility which he cultivates in an almost decadent way – he is forever drawing things out, delaying gratification so that he can anticipate and savour the sounds, smells, look, and feel of them. He 'works himself up' to feel even more by creating peculiar kinds of fictions – to heighten his feeling for his sister, for example, he observes how terribly frail she is, then imagines she is dead and how terrible *that* would feel, and then, how exquisite it is to know that she *isn't* dead, after all. It is a mildly masochistic practice he intensifies and elaborates in adolescence and maturity. Thus David's response to Effie's death (which Buckler allows him to believe he caused) is '[t]o stoke his frustration (as always) with bitter and bitterer self-destruction. To shock back the immediacy of the death-sadness by the very shame of defiling it' (MV 151). Later, he comes positively to caress the isolation which overtakes him on his parents' deaths, taking 'a self-biting satisfaction in deliberately making himself lonelier still' (MV 229). Even the aesthetics of perception become contaminated – at the novel's end Buckler implies that David's demand, in the face of the 'infinite divisibility' of things, for 'complete realization' of the world around him, feeds a peculiar kind of desire – the 'exquisite parching for the taste of completion' begets an equally 'exquisite guilt' and 'exquisite accusing' (MV 292), all of which shows how consummately David loves to hate himself.

In fact, Buckler's hero is often made to resemble an overgrown spoiled child.[51] Though Buckler spares no pains to *tell* us how wonderful everyone in Entremont – not only David's family, but the whole community as well – thinks David is, among the things he *shows* us are David's colossal egotism and vindictiveness. His love for Anna and Toby because in them he finds reflections of his own self; his churlish treatment of Effie, the pleasure he takes first in his own remorse, and then, in his lack of remorse for her death; his manipulation of Chris's guilt at the accident that befalls David, not because Chris has goaded him into showing off his toughness, but because David furiously resents Chris's recognition of his younger brother's hypersensitivity; his frequent exercise of 'that exquisite power which only the lonely have ... of inflicting it on [others]' (MV 145); the whole *symphonie pathétique* of David's guilty consciousness – all these deliberately make of David Canaan what Henry James called 'that queer monster, the artist, an obstinate finality, an inexhaustible sensibility.'[52] It seems entirely possible that Buckler makes his protagonist such a rebarbative character precisely because David is an artist, an embryo writer, and as such, a powerful contradiction to the very way and values of life in Entremont.

Of course one can always damn these ingrown, incestuous complications and point out that though David Canaan and his family may be killed off by the end of The Mountain and the Valley, the novel itself was born and continues to survive. As, unquestionably, it should – it may be one of the most problematic novels we have, but it is also one of the most powerful and ambitious as well. Yet what of the works which followed this remarkable début? The Cruelest Month, though some of its language is marvellously acute, and its evocation of the pastoral world is a tour de force, implodes as soon as its characters are made to open their mouths (and that is almost all they ever do). Paul Creed, the hero of this novel, is not a writer manqué as was David Canaan, but rather a man who, having written, decides that writing has absolutely nothing to do with the value or meaning of his existence. He destroys all his manuscripts and notebooks at this novel's end, and though he is given a twelve-month reprieve from death, it is not to write his book, but instead to live as much as he can with Letty, in Letty's way – wordlessly, in the flesh. From *Oxbells and Fireflies*, as we have seen, Buckler tries to banish the writer-as-character altogether, though his anguished consciousness keeps intruding into the narrative and curdling the prose. The memoir reads, in fact, like a truncated version of *The Mountain and the Valley* – we keep trying to read David Canaan into the narrator. And in Buckler's last book, *Whirligig*, he abandons his epistemological and metaphysical preoccupations to tell 'how it is' with country people. In so doing he adopts a crackerbarrel persona and a *Saturday Evening Post* sensibility that makes one yearn for the ultra-literary talk of *The Cruelest Month* and the vexatious complexities of *The Mountain and the Valley*.

Buckler's first novel, I have suggested, betrays a schizophrenic kind of creative consciousness – the text itself can be thought of as the verbal equivalent of those standardized images of ambiguity – rabbit or duck, wineglass or two profiles. Thus *The Mountain and the Valley* can be read, as D.G. Jones does, as an account of how an artist 'escapes from the isolation and unreality' caused by his 'self-conscious awareness of other possibilities, of a different mode of life from that of his parents and neighbours' into the joyful realization that 'his salvation lies not in leaving, but in accepting and articulating the very world that had seemed to threaten him.'[53] But it can equally well be read as 'an extremely moving and convincing account of the buried life ... [a] description of the mental torment of a sensitive man living in a restricted environment.'[54] The point would seem to be that Buckler may have conceived his novel as the former, but actually wrote it so that both interpretations become equally necessary to a complete understanding of his text. In the same way, an awareness of the Buckler who knew 'the stupid, static ... spying rigidity of the one who waits, before the mobile freedom of the one who comes' (MV 134); the 'excommunication' (MV 132) that derives from isolating oneself from people unashamed of their learning or writing, is as necessary to an understanding of this most complex writer as is recognition of the Buckler who posed for a cover of *Books in Canada* with a piece of hay between his teeth.

Ernest Buckler's career comes, in fact, to serve as an ironic counterpoint to Hugh MacLennan's – whereas MacLennan, had he 'stayed home' in the sense of wrestling in complex and profound ways with the faith of his father, might have written more powerful and complex novels, so Buckler, had he not felt compelled to make so absolute a division between learning and living, literature and farming, word-shaped and wordless speech, might have gone beyond the schizophrenic consciousness of *The Mountain and the Valley* to produce an oeuvre which would have represented a development and not a paralysis of his particular vision and skills. In their very different ways, Hugh MacLennan and Ernest Buckler are trapped in the same limbo; like the invalid and isolated David Canaan, '[they] could neither leave nor stay' in their imaginations' own home ground (MV 171).

\*\*\*

'Everyone comes and goes around here ... So, like the wanderer, the sun gone down, darkness be over me, my rest a stone – that's your Nova Scotian, if you've the eye to see it. Wanderers. Looking all over the continent for a future. But they always come back. That's the point to remember, they always come back to the roots ...'

Hugh MacLennan (BR 223)

If the paradigm offered by Hugh MacLennan's work is overwhelmingly negative vis-à-vis the Maritimes, and if Buckler's commitment to his native region and chosen people has resulted in a body of fiction tortured and truncated by the isolation he imposed upon himself, then Charles Bruce may stand as an example of a writer whose life and work are rooted in the region he left behind him, and the project of whose fiction can be described as 'looking back' without nostalgia or cynicism in order faithfully to represent a dynamic, not stagnant communal world.

*The Channel Shore* is a work that redefines the concepts of kinship and community by emphasizing the needs and claims of 'spirit' over those of 'blood.' Just as Grant Marshall is not compelled by necessity but chooses out of love and a larger sense of moral responsibility to take on the roles of son to the Gordons, and of father to Hazel McKee's illegitimate child, so Charles Bruce chose to become the chronicler of a particular form of Maritime experience even though he no longer lived or worked in the region. Both *The Channel Shore* and *The Township of Time* (which deals with some two hundred years in the collective existence of a shore community in Nova Scotia) are exhaustive accounts of Maritime life. It is through his first novel, however, that Bruce works out a paradigm whereby the gifted, the 'different,' the ambitious need not treat their native region as 'a place to be born in, to grow your teeth in, and to get the hell away from' (CS 205), but rather as a place in which one's most fundamentally human qualities can best be tested and realized. True, there is no would-be artist among the characters of *The Channel Shore*, but an authentic work of art *is* realized by Grant Marshall and his son – a new form of community, a living narrative of communal experience. As Grant comes to realize, 'It's easy enough to leave. Nothing new in that. But when you take the old stuff, the country that's under your feet and all around you ... when you take that, and build something they said you couldn't, and grow something they said would die: that's new, boy. That's something really new' (CS 269).

The novel opens with one of its central characters, Hazel McKee, alreading turning over ideas for getting off the Channel Shore which, since the passing of its prosperous days, has become 'a breeding-place for migrants, men and women who were born there, raised there, and who left the Shore in youth for the States and the West' (CS 12). Before the novel's close a varied assortment of characters will leave the Shore – Anse, out of 'hard scorn' for the 'commonness of life and things at Currie Head' (CS 14); the pregnant Hazel, out of shame and pride; her brother Joe, for whom the Shore is merely a place 'to raise a stake to get somewhere else' (CS 163); and finally, Bill Graham, Bruce's alter ego, who goes back to Toronto after just one summer at the Shore, and who comes back some thirty years later to discover that the place has become 'part of him, a habit in the flesh, like breathing and sleep' (CS 176).

With continued hard times, the Shore has evolved its own 'tradition': '[t]he smart ones leave ... [for] University. Summers at paying jobs, away from the Shore, and occasional visits ... back for a day or two between terms, and finally not back at all' (CS 217–18). Yet in the teeth of this tradition both Grant and Alan, the wandering Anse's son, choose to stay, treating the Shore neither as an idyllic retreat nor as a *pis aller* but as 'a living part of the larger world' (CS 261). Able to discriminate between 'joy in brief adventure, the passing urge to new experience, and the fact of exile' (CS 221), they realize that the price of leaving would be that full moral consciousness possible only in small communities in which one can trace to one's every action another's equal and opposite reaction.

It is not the physical beauty of the land, 'sensuous with the sound of seas and voices' but that land's translation into 'a country of the mind, the remembering blood' to which Bruce commits both characters and readers, as the novel's prefatory epigraph predicts. At the very end of his novel, Bruce has the regretfully departing Bill Graham encounter one of the Shore's prodigal sons, Stan Currie. Currie's ancestors settled the Shore out of an unquenchable desire for independence and a profound 'sense of venture' (cs 395). Stan, ironically, left the Shore for the same reasons, only to return years later to raise a family. As he confesses to Bill, 'I looked at what I'd got by leaving. Running water and central heat and something – oh, *cultivation* ... Well, they seemed to me to be cancelled out by the pulling and hauling, the pressure to say "Yes" when you wanted to say "No" ... *There was venture in coming back'* (cs 395).

This 'venture' he associates with living in a place to which one is bound by past and future generations, and in which one can constantly 'look back' to the courage, rebelliousness, and integrity of one's ancestors. Rooted in values and associations that have some proven and continuing worth, empowered by these very roots, the people of the Channel Shore can work to transform settled opinion and blind prejudice so that the stability of Shore life does not become stagnation. And if characters like Grant, Alan, and Stan Currie come to 'author' the collective story of community, their text is 'read' by the one character who is both within and outside the community, Bill Graham. Like Bruce himself, Graham has had to exchange 'the rough well-being' of Shore life for the 'ice of surface living' in Toronto (cs 271); yet, though 'he would never live on the Channel Shore,' 'in blood and spirit this was the country he belonged to ... [I]t was home' (cs 396).

What Bruce creates in *The Channel Shore* is a paradigm which liberates reader and writer, text, and subject. Unlike MacLennan, who points in his work to the impossibility of realizing or sustaining a full and significant life within the Maritimes; unlike Buckler, whose insistence on the artist's complete enclosure within rural Maritime life strands him in the deep-ends of solipsism and 'schizophrenia,' Bruce shows in his fiction that physical departure from a region need not entail spiritual exile from it; that informed 'looking back' is in itself a form of return, and that, even if one is condemned only to visit rather than actually live in one's native region, one can still make it the source and substance of one's fictive worlds. In the remainder of this chapter I will attempt to indicate how Bruce's paradigm is complemented and extended in the work of a fellow writer and partial exile from the Maritimes, Alistair MacLeod.

***

it seems that we can only stay forever if we stay right here. Because in the end that's all there is – just staying.

Alistair MacLeod (LSG 96)

Of the seven stories collected in *The Lost Salt Gift of Blood*, five have to do with a character's decision to guiltily abandon or else needily return to his birthplace – a Cape Breton whose terrible beauty is a product of savage poverty and of land- and seascapes which can only be called sublime. The characters driven from the coal towns and fishing villages MacLeod so powerfully evokes are never identified as writers-in-embryo, but they all possess the education and sensibility to be accomplished tellers of their own stories. MacLeod's relentless use of the first person voice and the present tense pushes his readers through the doors of his texts; narrator, author, and reader seem to become one, a disquieting proposition, given the nature of the fictive world created in *The Lost Salt Gift of Blood*.

In choosing to go or to stay, MacLeod's characters are caught in a particularly vicious trap: for the most part, their mothers strive to bind them to their birthplace and family, while their fathers, whose own escape plans have been thwarted by love or loyalty, urge them to go. Unlike David Canaan, who has the choice of a paradisal valley or a city of strangers, MacLeod's protagonists must choose between a punitive land and sea or the inchoate dark of the world outside these elements. As the story 'The Boat' makes clear, to leave is to betray a fiercely unforgiving mother; to stay is to reject the only gift it is in a father's power to give – encouragement to flee both the annihilating labour exacted by the sea and the mines, and the kind of marriage in which tenderness and joy become impossible luxuries. One is a traitor whether one goes or stays.

For the protagonist of another story, 'The Vastness of the Dark,' answering the question of whether to go or stay has become an essential part of coming of age, 'to have come almost with the first waves of sexual desire.' On his eighteenth birthday he decides to leave 'this grimy Cape Breton coal-mining town whose prisoner [he has] been for all of [his] life' (LSG 39). Yet in the very act of going away he comes to a recognition that what he is running from is not a Cape Breton coal town but the 'reality of where I am and what I think' (LSG 59):

I had somehow thought that 'going away' was but a physical thing. And that it had only to do with movement and with labels like the silly 'Vancouver' that I had glibly rolled from off my tongue; or with the crossing of bodies of water or

with the boundaries of borders. And because my father had told me I was
'free' I had foolishly felt that it was really so ... And I realize now that the older
people of my past are more complicated than perhaps I had ever thought ...
[T]hey have somehow endured and given me the only life I know for all these
eighteen years. Their lives flowing into mine and mine from out theirs. (LSG
59–60)

The paradigm which emerges from MacLeod's first book of fiction is a
tragic one. In 'The Return' an exiled Cape Bretoner and his son leave
their wealthy Montreal suburb for a brief visit back 'home' to the 'green
hills with the gashes of their coal deeply embedded in their sides'
(LSG 105). Instead of feeling joy or nostalgia, the father rediscovers how
bitterly his family grieves over his having left them; his son comes to
understand that in going back to Montreal after this brief and rich 'im-
mersion in family' he will become, like his father, 'silent and alone'
(LSG 105). And in the final story of the collection, 'The Road to Rankin's
Point,' a young man comes home only to learn how to die. His is the
consummate return, that of dust to dust, of 'inner' to 'outer' darkness. It
is as though MacLeod has taken Bruce's injunction to 'look back' and
translated it into metaphysical terms, so that questions of coming or
going, staying or leaving reach an ultimate intensity and significance.

   Having returned to his childhood home in order to confer some sort of
dignity and meaning on his dying, MacLeod's protagonist comes to
learn that all deaths, wherever they occur, are the same in the end; what
he does discover at Rankin's Point, however, is not death but 'the
intensity of life' (LSG 168) as personified by his frail but indomitable
grandmother, who stubbornly refuses to leave the farm she still manages to run for the dubious comforts of a nursing home. Just as the
young hero of 'The Vastness of the Dark' discovers that he is, in
effect, who his grandparents have been, so the narrator of this final
story finds his own life and death, and those of his grandmother are
fastened tightly together. Just before he meets his own death he 'looks
back' as Bruce's Stan Currie had: 'Sometimes when seeing the end of
our present our past looms even larger because it is all we have or think
we know ... My twenty-six years are not enough and I would want to
go farther ... back through previous generations ... through the super-
stitions and the herbal remedies and the fatalistic war cries and
the haunting violins and the cancer cures of cobwebs ... Back to
anything rather than die at the objective hands of mute, cold science'
(LSG 184–5).

   Calum's premature death will have broken this chain of generations:

his grandmother had wanted him to leave off teaching 'the over-urbanized high school students of Burlington and Don Mills' (LSG 174), to marry a Cape Breton girl and work the farm at Rankin's Point. Her grandson's response to this request destroys the matted web of loyalty and betrayal, guilt and grief which makes the question of going or staying so hopelessly fraught. In 'The Road to Rankin's Point' MacLeod relocates 'home' as death itself. If it is 'universal significance' which ultimately validates regional art, then this story, developed as it is within the context of that peculiarly Maritime dilemma, going or staying, can stand as what MacLennan desired Maritime writing to be – an unapologetic part of world literature.

The 'greater world' intersects with the regional in MacLeod's latest collection of short fiction: *As Birds Bring Forth the Sun*. In it we discover narrators who are no longer oppressed by the implications of going or staying, but who are simply at home. In its social and linguistic configurations, the imaginative world of *Birds* is the Cape Breton of *Lost Salt Gift*, but freed of any fierce sense of closure. MacLeod has found ways of opening his fiction by returning to the roots of his native culture: that Gaelic gift of second sight and belief in what we call superstition, which play a relatively minor role in 'Rankin's Point,' become the foreground of 'As Birds bring Forth the Sun' and the collection's superb final story, 'Vision.' Both of these works are radically 'fictive' in ways that the elegiac accounts of experience in *Lost Salt Gift* are not, as though MacLeod were coming closer to forms of writing favoured by surrealists or 'magic realists' precisely through his 'at-homeness' on his chosen fictive ground. The title and final story of *Birds* possess a 'meta-fictional' quality, as does the more traditional opening piece. 'The Closing Down of Summer.' It is in this story that MacLeod embeds the collection's most significant creative paradigm.

'Closing Down' is an encomium on the life of the mines. The narrator, an older man, waits with his companions for the last days of an unusually balmy August to give way to autumn gales, 'making it impossible for us to lie longer on the beach,' ignoring telephone calls and telegrams.[55] For the narrator and his friends are 'perhaps the best crew of shaft and development miners in the world and ... were due in South Africa on the seventh of July' (BBS 12). The trail they will eventually take from the beach at Cameron's Point has already taken them to Quebec, Ontario and the Yukon, Mexico and Africa: their earnings are deposited in 'the metropolitan banks of New York or Toronto or London, from which our families are issued monthly cheques' (BBS 22). These miners, then, are constantly at the moving centre, not the periphery of things. Yet wherever they go they take their Cape Breton with them, just as they take their unique skills whenever they go down the mine shafts.

With loving particularity the narrator evokes the lives and livelihood of himself and his fellow miners; though the vision of 'Closing Down' is expressed in the fifteenth-century lyric quoted on the story's last page, 'I wend to death, knight stith in stour,' MacLeod's story consists of a gentle raging against a variety of nights – the narrator's own death, the death of his profession, the silence which prevents the miners from communicating with those they love. Thinking of his sons, none of whom have followed him to the mines, the narrator remarks, 'I have always wished that my children could see ... how articulate we are in the accomplishment of what we do' (BBS 28). He proceeds to translate this accomplishment so that they, and we, 'might appreciate the perfection of our drilling and the calculation of our angles ... and that they might understand that what we know through eye and ear and touch is of a finer quality than any information garnered by the most sophisticated of mining engineers with all their elaborate equipment' (BBS 28).

With the pride and assurance of a master of his craft, the narrator articulates the 'eloquent beauty' of the miners' work (BBS 28), a beauty they are '[u]nable either to show or tell' their children (BBS 29). What the narrator does succeeds in telling the reader, at least, is the paradoxical nature of human freedom, symbolized here by labour that goes beyond the mere digging of coal: 'We are big men engaged in perhaps the most violent of occupations and we have chosen as our adversary walls and faces of massive stone. It is as if the stone of the spherical earth has challenged us to move its weight and find its treasure and we have accepted the challenge and responded with ... all our ingenuity' (BBS 30). This response is an ironic and contradictory one, as the narrator concedes: 'In the chill and damp we have given ourselves to the breaking down of walls and barriers. We have sentenced ourselves to enclosures so that we might taste the giddy joy of breaking through. Always hopeful of breaking through though we know we never will break free' (BBS 30).

The struggle of the miners is also the writer's struggle, MacLeod seems to imply. Certainly in the stories of *As Birds Bring Forth the Sun* Alistair MacLeod has discovered narrative and rhetorical strategies for 'breaking through' in his writing without 'breaking free' of his native region. It is a paradigm MacLeod's fellow writers can explore and rework for themselves, finding new ways of using the particulars of their time and place to break through the enclosures which prevent us from knowing ourselves and our world.

\*\*\*

Recent developments in Maritime letters would seem to show that what I have argued for – the dethroning of MacLennan's paradigm, the questioning of Buckler's and a recognition of the importance of the alternatives Bruce and MacLeod have offered Maritime readers and writers – has become a quiet fait accompli. For the latest generations of this region's writers are composed of artists like Nowlan and Richards, who have stayed because it has become the natural thing to do, and immigrants like Susan Kerslake and Nancy Bauer who have come and stayed on because conditions in the Maritimes have proved encouraging for their writing. Some of these conditions, of course, have to do with such manifestations of reborn cultural confidence as the emergence of regional presses and the development of writers' associations; others have to do with the very nature of the region – its distinctive history and landscape; its places and people. The Maritimes, it would seem, is no longer a country for old men or old paradigms.

# 9

# Words and Women

The Maritimes, we concluded, is no country for old men or old paradigms: moreover, as far as recent fiction is concerned, it may most hospitably be a country for women. It is an interesting and justly retributive fact that much of the best Maritime fiction of the last ten or fifteen years has been authored by the sex which this region's writers – almost exclusively male – have traditionally represented as merely gossipy, or else silent, or, worst of all, implacably hostile to the written word.

Antonine Maillet, Susan Kerslake, Nancy Bauer, and Donna Smyth among others, have upset that literary apple cart in which Lucy Maud Montgomery (who, after all wrote for *children*) would appear to be the only orange.[2] Thus it would seem fitting to bring this study to a close by looking at the specifically literary role allotted to women by traditional Maritime writers, and by briefly examining a work by the writer who, more than anyone else, allowed women to move from the sphere of literary imagination into that of literary production – Lucy Maud Montgomery. Finally, representative fictions by two of Montgomery's 'successors,' Nancy Bauer and Susan Kerslake, will be examined to show how powerfully Maritime women have moved from silence into speech.

***

And now, my fair countrywomen, at the risk of some score of frowns ... I cannot refrain from asking whether you think that nature intended ... that your lives should be passed in combing children's hair and making pies and pastry, and entertaining your visitors with a long list of your domestic handicraft. Were your minds formed for nothing better than this? ... Is there no pleasing study, no literary or scientific pursuit, that without interfering with or weaning you from your domestic duties, might elevate and enlarge your understandings? Away with the old objection that intellectual pursuits interfere with domestic duties ... [T]o the bright galaxy of peerless females who shed such radiance over the British Isles ... the duties and charities of life are matters of vital interest: but in their leisure hours – the odds and ends of existence – they ... enrich their literature and adorn their age; and why should not women on this side of the water 'go and do likewise.'

Joseph Howe (WER 69–70)

Why, not indeed? One answer immediately suggests itself. It was presumably as difficult to be a superwoman in the nineteenth-century Maritimes as it is in twentieth-century Canada. Mrs Frederick Beavan and Susanna Moodie may have somehow found 'leisure hours' enough to adorn the colonial literary scene, but if the account Andrew Macphail gives in *The Master's Wife* of unremitting domestic toil is representative of the average woman's lot in Maritime Canada, we should be surprised to learn that women *were* able to produce 'domestic handicraft,' never mind carry out 'literary or scientific pursuits.' Of course, Howe is here addressing not rural matrons but 'Society' women of the ilk of Griselda Tonge, who died at sixteen in Demerara[3] – but then, as Archibald MacMechan observed from a representative funerary monument to his 'Townswoman of the Olden Time': 'she seems to have married early, borne many children, and died before she was thirty-five. Her husband's grief is always great, and he marries again within two years.'[4]

The second reason that Maritime literature has not abounded in Fanny Burneys, Jane Austens, Emily Brontës, and George Eliots may well be the constant pressure women were under to keep silence, or at least, to use as few and as simple words as possible in their daily living. Thus to upbraid the Bluenoses for always talking when they should be working, Sam Slick lights upon the example of the Lowell factory girls who (despite the fact that 'a woman's tongue goes so slick of itself, without water power or steam, and moves so easy on its hinges, that it's no easy matter to put a spring-stop on it') keep total silence at their labour, bursting into chatter only 'at intermission and arter hours.'[5] Ernest Buckler makes an especial cult of the wordlessly contented farmwife who speaks a language of washing, dusting, baking, and placid sexual service. And even the schoolteacher heroines who crop up again and again in Maritime fiction do relatively little with the education they receive, except to inspire occasional (mostly male) students to achieve academic goals. Day's Mary Dauphiny, Buckler's Miss Merriam, Bruce's Renie Fraser decidedly do *not* write anything in their leisure time – the creator of each of these heroines envisages her highest attainment as marriage to the proper hero. Of course, that 'real life' schoolteacher, L.M. Montgomery, *did* write – not in her daily 'leisure hours,' since a country school marm of her day didn't possess such a thing, but at four or five or six o'clock of a morning, before the fires were lit, and while it was still so cold that she had to dress in her outdoor clothes to avoid freezing at her desk. And yet Montgomery's Anne, for all that she acquires a college education, does marry the local hero and goes on to produce babies, not books – or at least, instead of books, little trifles for children that she almost apologetically pens in her rare, spare time.[6]

To be sure, literary texts receive short shrift in Maritime fiction. We recall the narrator's insistence in *Pélagie* that the Acadians had to do without a written language and books of any kind during their exile and 'hundred years in the woods'; we remember the abandonment of Adam More's precious manuscript in De Mille's novel; Everett Richardson never getting round to finishing the book Cameron has written for him; the copy of *The Tempest* that David Jung decides is not much use to him after his shipwreck in *Rockbound* ('Dem poets is de bunk' [R 202]);

Andrew Macphail agreeing with his mother that Shakespeare can't hold a candle to Holy Writ; and Alden Nowlan remarking that 'I wrote (as I read) in secret. My father would as soon have seen me wear lipstick. Books belong to The Big Man, he would have said if words had not come so painfully to him, and not to poor folk like us.'[7]

Nowlan links writing with masturbation, emphasizing the secrecy and guilt traditionally associated with the act. Ernest Buckler compares writerly talk about literature to onanism[8] and, in his frequent comparisons of writing with defecation, shows an obvious need to de-idealize the production of literary texts and the process of inspiration. In *The Cruelest Month* Buckler compares Paul Creed's notebooks to a 'guano island' and compares not writing to constipation; writing itself to shitting or farting (CM 273). There, too, he plays the paradoxical postmodernist game of writing about how writing is inherently duplicitous – 'A novel had to squint, to keep its target focussed'; 'No writer ever gets it right. How can they get it true to life when life's not true or faithful to itself?' (CM 274, 284). For Buckler's hero, even the mere use of 'clever words left behind it a soiling like any other kind of drunkenness ... a subtle shame and guilt, as of a traveller returning home from some trip the others couldn't share' (CM 103).

And then, of course, there are all those book-burnings that go in Maritime fiction: Paul Creed's destruction of his 'jottings ... for the novel (maybe) he'd one day write' (CM 273), David Canaan's impulsive burning (rather than have Toby read it) of the short story he had so joyfully produced, Emily Starr's burning of her private notebooks so that her Aunt Elizabeth shan't be able to demand to read them,[9] and later, her destruction of her first novel on the advice of her fiancé, who tells her that, though it's nice to have a 'little hobby,' she will never be 'a Brontë or an Austen' and that besides, she can 'do more with those eyes – that smile – than [she] can ever do with [her] pen' (EQ 41–2).

Yet if male and female writers have had a hard time of it within the fictive worlds that Maritimers have created, it is largely women who are represented as having the biggest, most destructive grudge against literature. From Macphail's mother, who refused to read books or write letters, and who proposed that the authors of any other kind of book than grammars and spellers 'knew nothing, and even if they did know anything serious they could not teach it by writing. One learned by doing and seeing done' (TMW 66) to the narrator's mother in Alistair MacLeod's 'The Boat,' with her virulent hatred for the books which take her husband and children from the sea; from Margaret Ainslie's (justifiable) resentment of her doctor-husband's devotion to Homer in

*Each Man's Son*, to the sadistic Miss Brownell who humiliates Emily
Starr by jeeringly reading the girl's poetry in class and then attempting
to burn it (ENM 168–72), women have been presented as enemies of
the word. And with one Maritime writer, Ernest Buckler, a woman not
only objects to literature and literary talk, she would seem to replace
its role and place in the life of the novel's true writer – Paul Creed.

It is true that Buckler makes the highly educated and articulate Kate
(daughter of a Dalhousie University professor) inspire the novel's
'surface' writer, Morse, to begin writing again, after he has become bitterly disillusioned with the act and sceptical of his powers. Kate agrees
to marry Morse, talks him into writing a certain kind of honest, as
opposed to fashionably cynical novel, and foresees that the most important part she will play in his life and her own is to bear a child before
her biological clock (no relative of Marie Bashkirtseff's) runs down.
Yet Morse and Kate are not the authoritative characters of this novel:
Paul (Buckler's fictive alter ego) and his housekeeper Letty are. Paul,
it is repeatedly suggested, has fathomed the depths, and knows exactly
what his 'prattling notebooks' are worth (CM 272). He has the courage
and integrity to burn his books, to transcend the limitations of literary
language, and to join with Letty who, as we know, has contemptuously dismissed reading and writing as useless occupations. Through
the characters of Paul and Letty, Buckler sets up a battle between
words and worth, and it is Letty who wins, resoundingly.

Very early on in the novel Buckler makes it clear that where Paul and
his sophisticated friends are associated with the 'long unfamiliar
words' you lose yourself by, Letty incarnates 'the short words you live
by' – she is 'the simple monosyllable of home' (CM 8, 296). She is also
the novel's touchstone, with the various characters of the novel being
judged by whether or not they are capable of sharing or at least appre-
ciating her mode of speech. The novel's other unintellectual (though
literate) character, Rex Giorno, is perhaps closest to Letty in his chosen form of discourse – literally, feeling: 'His hands started their conversation with her body, their language expressive beyond any possible
speech, always to be relied on for the exact translation of whatever could
not be put into words' (CM 123). Bruce, a character country-born and
-bred like Letty, has acquired a university education yet still shares Letty's language – he spends most of his time in the novel, when not
remorsefully remembering his dead wife and son, working the land, his
hands 'fluent in the earth' (CM 132). And as for Paul, learning to love
Letty is a matter of learning both to read her correctly, and to speak her
language. When he realizes the profundity of her love for him, he

becomes 'mortifi[ed at] his own correct syntax, as if it were some foppish garment specious to a wonted ground of trust' (CM 295). Sex with Letty, we are told, prunes his mind and heart of 'their clusterous, strangling ivy of wilted clauses' (CM 296). The novel ends, in fact, with Paul and Letty the 'morning after' – not langorously abed but with Letty, aproned and still rather cowed by the privilege Paul has bestowed on her between the sheets, telling him that, after he has 'drank' his coffee, they will go into town to see the doctor about his ailing heart. The true test of Paul's embrace of Letty, as a woman and a mode of discourse, is shown to be his acceptance – not automatic, but then not grudging, either – of her ungrammatical usage.[10] And here, of course, is the familiar Bucklerian paradigm: integrity and honesty in life are somhow guaranteed by illiterate, or at least unliterary speech; honesty and integrity in the text are somehow guaranteed by tortuous expression and artificial language.[11]

Thus Letty, the creation of the Maritimes' most self-consciously literary writer, stands as the antithesis of the articulate, educated, reader-writer whom Joseph Howe envisioned as raising the 'intellectual and moral character of the Province' (WER 71). Where there is at least a Packet in *Lives of Short Duration* to read the Everyman edition of Marlowe's plays, and a Stewart Gordon in *The Channel Shore* to peruse *Nicholas Nickleby* while his farm quietly falls apart, is there any female character in Maritime fiction who is passionately, singlemindedly devoted not just to reading and talking about books but most importantly, to writing itself? Of course there is, and she is the creation of the often maligned and distinctly troublesome writer, L.M. Montgomery. Not Anne, and not the 'story girl,' Sara Stanley, but Emily Byrd Starr, whom Montgomery created towards the end of her literary life, and who can be seen as a mirror image of the writer Montgomery was – and was not.

\*\*\*

[W]riting, to Emily Byrd Starr, was not primarily a thing of worldy lucre or laurel crown. It was something she *had* to do. A thing – and idea – whether of beauty or ugliness, tortured her until it was 'written out.' (EQ 3)

Lucy Maud Montgomery was neither a literary light nor a hack; some of her books have become classic works of children's literature, others – *Anne* after Green Gables, volumes such as *The Blue Castle*, her poetry – cannot be read without a sigh – and not a rapturous one, either. Yet

Montgomery was a writer born, as were Virginia Woolf and Vladimir Nabokov. I choose the names not randomly, and not to suggest that Montgomery's oeuvre, or her genesis as a writer can even remotely be compared with theirs, but because all three shared vital prerequisites for writing – a compulsion, physical as much as psychological, to know and manage the world in terms of language, and unusual, almost praeternatural modes of perception. Where Nabokov speaks in his memoir of possessing 'colored hearing' – actually seeing the distinctive colours of the different letters of the alphabet – and of having been able to see, as a child, objects of which he had no prior perceptual knowledge, Montgomery-Emily[12] would seem to have possessed a related 'gift' – the ability literally to 'lift' patterns from wallpaper or prints and 'see' them suspended in air before her eyes.[13] And where, as Woolf's letters and diaries make clear, writing was for her passion, a plank across an abyss, and an indestructible weapon against those who hurt, annoyed, bored, or rivalled her, for Montgomery-Emily, writing was 'an outlet for the violence of emotion that racked her being' (ENM 109); a means of turning pain and humiliation into the 'exquisite satisfaction' of finding the right words to describe those set in authority over her, and thus to destroy their power. Had Montgomery been born, as were Woolf and Nabokov, into literary and comparatively enlightened families; had she, like her heroine in *Jane of Lantern Hill* grown up in a large city as well as in the idyllic country, and above all, had she not been born and married into familial situations where imagination – and therefore freedom – had always to be pitted against duty – and therefore submission – might she have developed into a Canadian Virginia Woolf? The question cannot and need not be decided. What *is* important is to recognize the impassioned voice Montgomery gave in *Emily of New Moon* to the process of writing, whatever the merits of her products may be.

Briefly, the *Emily* series relates the development of a young, imaginative girl into a mature writer and woman. Unfortunately, the fact that Emily becomes a woman effectively cancels her status as a writer, at least for the modern reader. For while Emily does win out over the well-educated and aesthetically accomplished fiancé who implies that her writing is 'pretty cobwebs' (EQ 41); though she writes another novel to replace the one she had burned for him, she does so by rebound, spurred by thwarted love for her childhood sweetheart, who has become a successful painter, and whom, of course, she does eventually marry. The best part of *Emily's Quest*, Montgomery's evocation of 'the loneliness of unshared thought,' the frustration of being considered mad or temperamental because one is slightly different from one's neighbours, the erotic intensity that underlies Montgomery's descriptions of that natural world which, along with writing, offers Emily a magical escape from the constricting life of Blair Water, do not quite make up for the 'Woman's Own' romance that ruins the novel. The middle book in the series, *Emily Climbs*, in which our writer sees herself becoming a 'High Priestess of beauty' and vows, 'I shall always end my stories happily. I don't care whether it's "true to life" or not. It's true to life as it *should* be, and that's a better truth than the other'[14] makes tiresome reading. But *Emily of New Moon*, in which the project of freeing oneself from the tyrannical and unjust authority of one's family (in this case, substitute parents) is enmeshed in the project of realizing one's literary voice and wresting 'recognition' and 'standing' from one's world (ENM 210, 120), is a compelling *Bildungsroman*, a classic work of children's literature, and an overt defiance of the taunt whose debilitating power Woolf's Lily Briscoe knew well: 'Women can't paint, women can't write ...'[15]

From the moment we first encounter Emily we are aware of her extraordinary nature: as sensitive as Buckler's David Canaan to the beauty of the natural world, she is much more precocious and disciplined than he in that she constantly writes down descriptions of the phenomena which physically hurt her until she has found language to express them (ENM 7). Like David's, Emily's perceptions have a metaphysical direction: 'It had always seemed to Emily, ever since she could remember, that she was very, very near to a world of wonderful beauty. Between it and herself hung only a thin curtain; she could never draw the curtain aside – but sometimes, just for a moment, a wind fluttered it and then it was as if she caught a glimpse of the enchanting realm beyond ... and heard a note of unearthly music' (ENM 7).

Enchanting, unearthly – clichés, yes, and wilted rhetoric – Montgomery utterly lacked a poetics of desire whereby she could give convincing form to her perceptions. But this sense of the gaps or absences between the life she had and the only world she wanted, this awareness of traces and signs of something absolutely other than the limitations and constrictions of her existence as a woman and a writer, is as powerfully present in her work as is the astonishing vividness of her understanding of child life, the power politics of child rearing, the humiliations, shames, injustices imposed by adults on children in the name of responsibility and perhaps even love.

Emily, orphaned by the death of the literary if dilettantish father she adored, goes to New Moon farm to live with her autocratic Aunt Elizabeth, her kind but weak Aunt Laura, and her Uncle Jimmy – who is said not to be 'all there' after having been pushed into a well when a child (he makes up eerie poetry which he recites to Emily, and thus fulfils the poet-madman equation so dear to the folk of Blair Water). It is with Aunt Elizabeth whom Emily fights her major battles – Aunt Elizabeth who forbids her to read the books in the parlour and who confiscates from Emily the books her father had left her, because of the child's 'carelessness' – that is, her having 'put a tiny pencil dot under every beautiful word' she found in them (ENM 190). Just as Emily, out of some mysterious 'irresistible surge of energy' summons the authority and the very words to forbid her aunt to cut off her hair – 'Aunt Elizabeth, *my hair is not going to be cut off*. Let me hear no more of this' (ENM 111) – so she summons the will and sheer stubbornness to refuse to obey her aunt's injunction to give up writing stories – much to the bewilderment of her kindly Aunt Laura, who 'thought Emily ought to yield in such an unimportant matter and please Aunt Elizabeth' (ENM 318). Montgomery insists on Emily's refusal to be covert about the matter; when Laura advises her to 'hoodwink' Aunt Elizabeth into thinking she has given up writing, but to continue her scribbling on the sly, Emily 'found she could not do it. *This* had to be open and above-board. She *must* write stories – and Aunt Elizabeth *must* know it. She could not be false to herself in this – she could not *pretend* to be false' (ENM 319).

Emily eventually wins a decisive battle against her aunt – again, a battle connected with her writing. Before Emily had come to New Moon, she had disgraced herself in her relations' eyes by hiding herself in the room in which they were gathered to discuss her faults and decide her future. Emily responds to the cruel things said about her by silently 'talking back' word for word to her relations; when they attack her father, however, she forgets herself and bursts into an impassioned defence of him. She is reproved for the wickedness of eavesdropping by all her relatives, most cuttingly by Aunt Elizabeth. Appropriately, it is Elizabeth who is later caught out by Emily in the same crime – or rather, a worse one, since the child hadn't known that eavesdropping is an immoral act, whereas the woman does, and goes ahead anyway. What Emily's aunt has done is to find and read the letters the miserably homesick Emily had written to her dead father, just after her arrival at New Moon. Emily discovers her aunt *in flagrante delicto* and quickly makes the woman feel shame at her actions, and then fury at having been set right by the child she is supposed to be raising. After a climactic battle of wills, Aunt Elizabeth concedes defeat, stiffly admits to Emily that she has been wrong, and, as stiffly, asks for the child's forgiveness. The momentousness of the occasion is underscored: 'Elizabeth Murray had learned an important lesson – that there was not one law of fairness for children and another for grown-ups' (ENM 326). Seemingly flat, uninspired, platitudinous, these words are embedded in a context which makes them remarkably powerful for the reader.

Emily's defeat of Aunt Elizabeth is not absolute – her aunt will later forbid her to write 'anything untrue' – that is, fiction – for a period of three years and this time she will submit. Emily's moral victory against Aunt Elizabeth vis-à-vis eavesdropping, however, signals Emily's having come into maturity, both as a human being and as a writer. Her development in the latter domain is no affair of a *Wunderkind* monotonously tossing off deathless prose, but rather, a slow apprenticeship whose stages Montgomery clearly outlines. First, there is Emily's transition from scribbling random stories, anecdotes, and descriptions into old account books, to writing letters to her dead father – letters focused and sharpened by her unhappiness at New Moon, the coldness and unfairness of Aunt Elizabeth's treatment of her, the limitations imposed on her liberty, both physical and imaginative. One of her triumphs over this inauspicious environment is to discover a horde of paper – the blank backs of 'letter-bills' left over from her grandfather's days as postmaster – that will enable her to write at length and 'empt[y] her soul ... [of] evil passions,' particularly those prompted by the schoolmistress, Miss Brownell, who has tried to shame and bully Emily out of her love for poetry (ENM 97).

One can, of course, see Emily's writing as a species of 'logotherapy,' turning the strong feelings her society has deemed inadmissible into tangible words on paper; one can also see it as a means of gaining power and autonomy in a world which denies her any expression of self. We remember the scene in which Aunt Elizabeth has accused her niece of 'staring at nothing in that queer way' (Emily has been 'seeing' the wallpaper patterns in the air):

Emily shrank into herself ... 'I – I wasn't staring at nothing.'

'Dont contradict, I say you were,' retorted Aunt Elizabeth. 'Don't do it again. It gives your face an unnatural expression.' (ENM 57)

It is in coming to New Moon that Emily does not so much discover as avow her vocation as writer, rather than scribbler. Taunted at school for her strange clothes and unconventional looks – Emily is no all-adorable Anne – having to admit that she cannot sing, dance, sew, cook, knit lace, or crochet, she protests '"I can write poetry," without in the least meaning to say it' –

But at that instant she knew she *could* write poetry. And with this queer, unreasonable conviction came – the flash! Right there, surrounded by hostility and suspicion, fighting alone for her standing, without backing or advantage, came the wonderful moment when soul seemed to cast aside the bonds of flesh and spring upward to the stars. (ENM 83)

Having professed that she can write poetry, Emily sets out to do so. Montgomery reproduces a few of her verses, and creates critics for them as well – Emily's relations, the priest, Father Cassidy, and, most important of all, the new, marvellously unorthodox and alcoholic schoolmaster, Mr Carpenter. When Emily's benign Aunt Laura objects that her niece's writing doesn't sound like poetry, since it doesn't rhyme, Emily protests that she is writing blank verse. '*Very* blank,' adds Aunt Elizabeth, after which Emily decides to write rhyming poetry ever after, 'so there will be no mistake about it' (ENM 102–3). Father Cassidy is rather more encouraging after Emily quotes him her 'Evening Dreams': 'Of course, it *was* trash. All the same, for a child like this – and rhyme and rhythm were flawless – and there was one line – just one line – 'the light of faintly golden stars' – for the sake of that line Father Cassidy suddenly said, 'Keep on, – keep on writing poetry' (ENM 210).

To some extent, Mr Carpenter shares the priest's 'one line' theory of poetic promise – a theory the reader cannot endorse, since the many 'one lines' we are given as proof of Emily's genius add up to less than zero. Yet the climax of Emily's progress towards being recognized as a writer comes when she summons the courage to show her acerbic but scrupulously fair teacher her work. In her nervousness she does not give him the 'pretty dream of hopes come true after long years' she has entitled *The Disappointed House* but, by mistake, the notebook in which she has produced 'mercilessly lucid' sketches of everyone in her community, including the vulnerable Mr Carpenter himself. He responds with: 'I wouldn't have missed this for all the poetry you've written or ever will write! By gad, it's literature – *literature* – and you're only thirteen. But you don't know ... the stony hills – the steep ascents ... the discouragements [ahead of you]. Stay in the valley if you're wise' (ENM 349).

Emily is not wise. Ironically, at the very moment she has received badly needed recognition of her talent from the only critic who matters to her, she disregards his advice, with consequences that will become fatal. Emily sets out on what she calls ' the Alpine Path' – the title Montgomery herself gave to an account of her life as a writer. It is painful for anyone who reads Montgomery's oeuvre to see the cross-purposes at which this woman always wrote; the unbreakable dichotomy created between duty and imagination in her very conception and execution of fiction; the resolute blindness with which she walks into the traps from which her critic-characters have the sense to warn their protégés away. So much of Montgomery's fiction is written after *The Disappointed House* pattern, so much of it represents ever more fanciful variations on the theme of wish-fulfilment, and so little of it exhibits the 'merciless lucidity' in which Mr Carpenter found the promise of *literature*. That lucidity surfaces at moments in *Anne of Green Gables*, and persistently in *Emily of New Moon*. It becomes smeared by the 'romance-element' and the concatenations of mystery, supernatural gifts, and fairy-tale inversions in *Emily Climbs*. And though the relationship in *Emily's Quest* between Emily and her mentor Dean Priest crystallizes all the traditional impediments in the way of a woman's ever being recognized and conceded standing as a writer – recognition and standing without which she cannot continue to produce and publish – the novel sabotages itself in having Emily's 'hopes come true after long years.' Not of course, the hope of becoming an Austen or Brontë – rather, the hope of being Mrs Teddy Kent and, as Joseph Howe would have approved, of giving 'in [her] leisure hours ... the reins to fancy [so as to] enrich [her] literature and adorn [her] age.'

Montgomery's own writing life demonstrates perfectly the 'failure of success' – she remained trapped by requests to produce more Anne books, and locked into her role as 'the minister's wife' who must hear and say everything that is expected, nothing which is interesting. Had she, after dutifully sacrificing her youth to a tyrannical grandmother, not married the unfortunate Reverend Macdonald and thus been able to express her passion and frustration in fiction that did not have to meet the approval of Presbyterian parishioners, who knows what she might have written? Perhaps her most important contribution to her country's literature will turn out to be the private journals in which she wrote out the feelings and experiences which both tortured and liberated her – perhaps, for all her publications she was, as so many Maritime women have been, a prisoner of silence.

\*\*\*

She belonged by right divine to the Ancient and Noble Order of Story-tellers. Born thousands of years earlier she would have sat in the circle around the fires of the tribe and enchanted her listeners. Born in the foremost files of time she must reach her audience through many artificial mediums. (EQ 2)

Born not in Howe's or Montgomery's, but in Margaret Laurence's, Mavis Gallant's, Margaret Atwood's, Alice Munro's era, women writers in the Maritimes may now use whatever 'mediums' they choose to reach their audience. In ending this study of Maritime fiction I would like to touch upon the work of two writers who have stressed the special importance of language to women. The very title of Nancy Bauer's novel *Flora, Write this Down* is significant in this context, as is the fact that her latest book, *Wise-Ears*, is structured around the letters and fictions a newly 'liberated' woman comes to write. And in Susan Kerslake's *Middlewatch* and *Penumbra*, we find a Maritime writer whose love of language is as intense and complex as Buckler's, but whose texts display no crippling ambivalence towards the world of words.

Nancy Bauer's first novel has a deceptively offhand title – no *Lives of Short Duration* or *Painted Ladies*, but *Flora, Write this Down*. It is as if someone had asked the novel's heroine to jot down certain events and impressions, in the way she might scribble a shopping list or casual letter to an old schoolfriend. The novel tells the story of an unremarkable woman – wife and mother – who returns with her young son to what has become the family home in the town where she grew up. The son is to have a minor, but difficult operation in a famous children's hospital nearby, but the bulk of the novel focuses on the sustenance which his mother, Flora, draws from going back to her human roots, and the patterns she is able to perceive in the ordinary, yet delicate web which connects different members of her extended family.

Bauer's writing is thoughtful and wryly sensitive, yet the concerns of her fiction would be accessible to women readers in just those isolated, ordinary places and occupations in which Maritime writers have traditionally situated their female characters. It is only when Flora returns from her pilgrimage to her home town, back to the life she has made for herself in New Brunswick, that she actually begins to write things down – to become, by a kind of ritual initiation, a writer. She deliberately separates herself from her own house, her husband and children, going out to the family cottage, and living alone there. She overcomes fears about intruders and about her own ability to write; she keeps a journal which establishes her individuality outside the octopus embrace of family life. In the end she succeeds: not only has she stayed for the full term of her 'initiation' but out of the journal she keeps emerges the 'family chronicle' we have just read. It is the chicken-and-egg phenomenon familiar to readers of *The Mountain and the Valley* – a novel in which the protagonist spends her time getting ready to write the novel we are in fact reading – but as with Montgomery's Emily, Bauer's fledgling writer does survive the first flight out of the nest – we are left with the sense of Flora's writing as a process which will continue beyond the covers of her journal or the book in our hands.

*Wise-Ears*, Bauer's next novel, is in many ways a revisioning and re-fashioning of *Flora*. The second paragraph of *Wise-Ears* has its protagonist, fifty-eight-year-old Sophie Aspinwall, also a wife and mother, listening to a church choir sing 'I Love to tell the Story,' and from that moment the project of this novel is clear – Sophie is going to experiment with different ways of telling stories, extraordinary stories which incorporate elements of her experience and consciousness that she cannot otherwise deal with or even articulate. The bulk of her experience is common-garden fare: her children have grown up and left home – she keeps a diminished house, worrying over the success of her children's marriages, and increasingly anxious at the thought that she may never have grandchildren. It is this anxiety which, more than anything else, propels Sophie's writing – her sole purpose in life has been to marry and raise children who will in their turn raise more children, so that the human chain can be sustained from one generation to the next. Yet none of her children shows any signs of wishing to secure the chain – one of her sons has a vasectomy, another, she suspects, is homosexual, and her only daughter, unmarried at twenty-six, shows no signs of settling down. Nevertheless, Sophie's experience of mothering, and even her stint as a volunteer at a local shelter for battered wives and their children, confirm the belief that family life can be our greatest good, one of our most poignant and fulfilling reasons for being. It is this knowledge she attempts to communicate to her refractory children.

At first she chooses a non-verbal means of expression: she redecorates the guest room in extravagant fashion, putting huge mirrors on the ceiling over a new bed with 'magic' massaging 'fingers' and built-in trays to hold the elaborate breakfasts-in-bed which she loves to prepare for her homecoming children. This combination of the erotic and domestic, Sophie's wish to shower affection and understanding on her children, and also to entice them into procreating, sets the tone and direction of Bauer's novel. For when, after a weekend in the newly refurbished guest room, her son and his wife announce an irreversible intention never to have children, Sophie looks for less threatening and more persuasive means of getting her message across. She decorates the crawl space under the house, originally intending it as an exotic playroom for her future grandchildren, replete with a hidden taperecorder which will tell fairy stories of her own devising, but gradually the room becomes her own – a private place in which she can accomplish the realization of her mature self, scribbling her thoughts down on the meaning and the very shape of her life, her relation to God and the world He has created. Over and over again the refrain sounds: 'I love to tell the story / Because I know it's true, / It satisfies my longings / As nothing else could do.'

Sophie tells her stories by concocting a fairy-tale about an orphan named Snowflower, by writing idiosyncratic letters to her children, and, most interestingly of all, by undertaking a series of letters to her sister, in which she deliberately creates a fantasy life, inventing herself first as a missionary midwife in China and then as Anna, the housekeeper and mistress of a mysterious Chinese. Sophie's fiction is no milk and cookies affair – the Chinese man Anna is made to keep house for is portrayed as a pederast who abuses a succession of young boys; she is persuaded by a Buddhist higher-up to bear the pederast's child, and to seduce him performs actions which, it is safe to say, Sophie Aspinwall, née Taylor, would never have practised with her devoted and genial husband Harold. She herself is shocked by the tenor her 'China' fantasy has assumed, until she realizes that her suspicions about her son's homosexuality, and the knowledge of child abuse she has gained through watching documentaries and working at the transition house, have assumed this particular configuration in her unconscious and have demanded expression in her writing. Thus the various forms of storytelling in which Sophie engages continue side-by-side: she keeps writing letters to her children, brings the stories of Snowflower and of Anna to fitting conclusions, persists with her efforts to describe God and understand death, and learns to live with her children's decisions. In the process she gains the two things she realizes she has needed most – freedom, and the ability to invent something – to bring things into being. We leave Sophie engaged in a new form of invention, experimenting with something as frivolous and fascinating as breeding tomatoes to discover all the possible variants on the colour red. Yet she is still writing – not for future grandchildren, now, but for God, the peculiarly desultory and approachable 'Wise-Ears' with whom she has open conversations. The novel ends with Sophie in the act of writing.

Sophie describes writing as a 'soothing' activity,[16] and indeed there is something low-key, laid-back, resolutely un-high-literary about *Wise-Ears* and Bauer's style in general. It is as though she has given a voice to generations of Maritime women who have been handmaidens of silence – who simply hadn't the leisure or the authority to speak and write down. Of course there were women for whom the act of writing would have seemed an absurd and unnecessary exercise – no one would doubt that the Renies and Margarets, Lettys and Marthas whom Charles Bruce and Ernest Buckler portray are convincing mimetic types. The point is, however, that they do not exhaust the possibilities, and that more and more, Maritime writers have tried to free other voices, those of women for whom verbal expression and communication have become essential. The Floras and Sophies created by Nancy Bauer come into literary language and being in a fashion which is consistent with their possibilities – I have used the term 'common-garden' in reference to the qualities and characters about which Nancy Bauer writes, and it should be clear that I use the term in no derogatory sense. For it is one of the hardest things in the world to bring off the portrayal of the everyday and ordinary, to make it worth reading about – and Nancy Bauer achieves just this. Yet there are, again, other possibilities, and I would like now to turn to a writer whose female characters are portrayed not as handmaidens to, but as prisoners of silence – women, moreover, who learn to come out of this silence into speech and into the invention of themselves through language.

Susan Kerslake's first novel, *Middlewatch*, is the story of a young girl, Sibbi, who is psychologically and physically abused by her much-older brother. At the novel's opening, we come upon the girl lying spreadeagled, naked on a bed, her wrists and ankles roped to the posts so that 'raw snakes burn[ed] below the bleached skin, down to where there [was] still blood.'[17] In a series of narratological manoeuvres artful, subtle, and complex enough to deserve a better name than 'flashbacks,' we learn that the brother Jason, having sustained a head injury while out cutting wood, has finally lost his slippery balance between inchoate inner darkness and outer strength, practicality, and sheer volition. He abandons the sheep farm he has struggled to create, after first destroying everything he can lay hands on – including his sister. But the physical damage he inflicts upon Sibbi is only a supreme violence – for the previous ten or so years of their life together he has punished her by total silence, refusing, or unable to speak to her, so that she is forced upon her inner life and an internal language of perception to keep herself alive at all. It is only in the rare days she is able to spend at the school run by the young teacher who unties her from her bed and painstakingly coaxes her back from the frozen darkness in which she has lost herself, that Sibbi learns the uses of language. Her attempts to read and write are described as 'feverish' (M 15) and though she does master both arts, she cannot practise them except by translating them into the terms of her peculiar environment. She learns to read the natural world around her – the ocean, stars, forests, and meadows surrounding the rude cabin in which she lives. Perhaps her most intense experience of happiness comes from hearing the schoolteacher, Morgan, read a poem to her – fittingly, it is Hopkins's 'Pied Beauty.' And when she finally meets someone with whom she can speak – the gypsy boy who has helped her brother after his accident – her sexual awakening is described as a welcome invasion of the silence at her core.

Unable to break through her brother's terrifying silence, Sibbi had told herself stories in order to survive. Yet as Jason's physical brutality plunges her into a perpetual winter darkness, Sibbi herself succumbs to silence. Morgan's attempts to help her are met by a 'dumb stare' and 'animal sounds' instead of language (m 11, 42). When he provides her with pen and paper she leaves the sheets utterly blank – it becomes apparent that she must complete her descent into darkness before she can find any way out again. And in evoking that darkness, and the effects it has on Morgan's own perception of himself and the world, Kerslake is breathtaking. *Middlewatch* becomes a brilliant narrative of perception, a sensuous interrelation of the physical reality of a remote coastal village and the mental landscapes of certain of its inhabitants. Just as in Bauer's novels, there is no tightly structured plot, no driving narrative thrust, but rather a free play of associations, perceptions, ideas. In Sibbi, we are made to live through what might be called 'the going of winter,' as slowly, almost inconsequentially, she is drawn out of darkness.

Typically, her emergence is signalled by speech – an expression of concern for Morgan, who is wrestling with his own inner darkness: 'What. What is it. What's the matter?' Sibbi finally asks – and Morgan, instead of rejoicing in her words, almost resents them. For with this speech, Sibbi shows herself to be subject to no one and nothing – she is active, asking questions, persisting, demanding an answer. We are told that Morgan 'wanted her secrets, her private being opened to him, but she had found his first' (m 94). Thus Morgan, whose obsession with drawing Sibbi back into life is portrayed through predominantly sexual imagery – he continually presses Sibbi to 'admit' him, let him inside (m 75–7) – is himself invaded and overpowered. Sibbi's last act is to offer him her hand: he thinks it fragile, vulnerable, but as he grasps it he realizes it is 'quite steady, offered as a solid thing, a story' (m 133). The novel ends on an indeterminate note – Sibbi has indeed broken free from winter, but Morgan isn't altogether sure that she will accept him as a reward for coming back to life. Rather as in Gide's *La symphonie pastorale* the helpless silence and blindness of the abandoned girl child and the knowledge, power, and authority of the teacher come to be both reversed and intermingled. Helping these women into the world of light and language, the rescuers discover abysses within themselves; confident that they have won the love of these victims, they discover themselves powerless before their own love of women who have grown independent of, and indeed, beyond them.

The female protagonists of Kerslake's next novel, *Penumbra*, reveal three different approaches to, or ways of being with, language. The novel is set, like *Middlewatch*, in the past – in this case, the heyday of the whaling ships. And while a great deal of the novel explores the horrific mindscape of the sailor Hebel and the compassionate consciousness of the asylum-keeper, John, an equally powerful section of the novel details the lives of the women who are stranded with Hebel and John on the island of Lune, which houses lunatics from the coastal settlements. One of these women, Mercy, is, like Hebel, an inmate on the island. Like Sibbi at the opening of *Middlewatch*, Mercy is plunged in darkness – for her, however, it is the darkness of total madness and possession. In a remarkable chapter of the novel, Kerslake is able to slip below the skin of this character and, weaving together heightened and abnormal perceptions of the real world, superstition, magic, and the supernatural, allows Mercy to turn her silence into a form of speech. For this woman, who was born with her eyes staring open, and who, for three nights after her birth, speaks out to her mother, saying that she was sad to have been born, never speaks again. 'The earth was not for her,' we are told: 'She held her hands at odd angles in the sky exploring the qualities of light.'[18] Yet she does listen to the gossip and cures of the 'herb-craft lady' and midwife who had pulled her to birth and in whose speech Mercy strains to hear the words that will make her night terrors stop, or allow her to be finally possessed by the spirits she perceives in everything round her.

The way in which Kerslake communicates the unsayable, the purely phenomenal, is startling – here, for example, is Mercy's perception of night terrors:

they would ignite the marrow in her bones until the steam seeped out from beneath her nails and eyelids. They transformed her silent tears into beads of glass that broke. The walls sunk into deep alleys that were raw and humid as if the passageways of animal bodies, of her own body had been sucked out and embedded there. She watched the flames swirl in there and felt the burn in her body. Then the sweat glistened all over her skin and put out the fire before it froze. She knew it froze and flaked off her because in the morning light when she looked out into the hall her footsteps were in the frost on the floor. As she breathed over them they melted. She felt the walls lightly in case they gave in, but the morning light was mortar and the walls were solid. The sun and the moon were in the sky together. (P 57)

This is the language of pure perception – not just heightened or intensi- fied speech, but a different kind of articulation that is at times terrify- ing in its power and very fluency – how do you learn such a language, the reader asks: how is it possible for anyone to give words to sensa- tions which are both invisible and all-consuming? In this extraordinary way, Kerslake frees the voice of madness and makes it intelligible – which is perhaps the most frightening thing of all. Yet in *Penumbra*'s other female characters she is able to portray alternatives to Mercy's kind of speech – for example, in the ordinary and quite rational fear of Sarah, the wife of the asylum keeper. Sarah wakes in the middle of the night, stifling cries and expressing herself to her husband in eloquently broken speech: 'Oh God, John, of my children, myself ...' (P 13). Like Sibbi in *Middlewatch*, she is stricken by the silence which walls in her existence.

The burden of her complaint is that she has no one to talk to. Her daughter, the unnamed heroine of *Penumbra* who is for a large part of the novel a first person narrator, reflects that while her mother has known another world than that of Lune, she, having grown up with her brother on the island, and knowing no other world than that of the lunatics, and the little fortress of ordinary living her mother has erected against them, finds Lune a world which is 'quite possible' (P 13). When she does make a trip to the mainland, she acquires a lover, another sailor, who comes to her on the island. The narrator's world is communicated to us as an amalgam of the ferocious strangeness of Mercy's and the inescapable reality of Sarah's – yet what the narrator is able to bring out is the fierce beauty and freedom of the life she lives, until it is brought to an end by her father's performing a mercy killing – itself an act of communication between the insane Hebel, who can no longer endure the torment of his memories, and the 'keeper,' John, who has promised Hebel his friendship.

When news of the killing reaches the mainland, John and Sarah are taken off the island with their children – John, we may assume, to be convicted of murder, and the pregnant Sarah to somehow survive with her children. *Penumbra* ends with the narrator lying in bed, listening to her mother tell her young brother a story, and then hearing her mother talk in her sleep, trying to piece together the reasons for what has happened, the justification for her husband's having helped Hebel to death at the price of abandoning his own family. We are left with the sense of words spoken disjointedly in darkness, of ordinary speech being used to state and understand that which is incomprehensible, unforgiveable. In this way the experience of Kerslake's female characters underscores the antithesis *Penumbra* creates between the organized and socially sanctioned lunacy of whaling, with all the terrors it involves, and the profound human decency and sanity of John's treatment of the certified lunatics on his island – a decency which ends in death and desertion.

*Penumbra* is an extraordinarily complex and difficult novel – the reader is at turns exhilarated by the power and beauty of Kerslake's metaphors and unnerved by her uncanny recreations of disordered or deranged consciousness. No two writers could be more dissimilar than Nancy Bauer and Susan Kerslake, yet both, as I've attempted to show, are compelled by the same need to give voice to those who have traditionally kept silent or been silenced, the majority of them women. And the very qualities of these women's writing, the spiralling movement of their narratives, the refusal of linearity, their sense of language as something with which one may joke, play, or which one may scrape like matches against rough, dark walls are recognizably new qualities in Maritime fiction. This freeing of the text from the yoke of linear narrative and also from the magisterial, perfected structure one gets with *The Mountain and the Valley*, for example, is, of course, part and parcel of postmodernism in fiction – and yet it is interesting to note how many of the best postmodernists are women, and to speculate on how much of their energies derive from this sudden sense of being freed from silence into speech, and of their perceived need to speak for those who were previously excluded either from the expression, or else from the recording of their identities.

\*\*\*

In writing thus briefly of the way in which the relationship between words and women in the Maritimes has traditionally been perceived, and the rather miraculous way in which women's silence has been so compellingly broken – a miracle in which, as I have tried to show, Lucy Maud Montgomery played no small part – I do not, of course, mean to suggest that the only fine writers who have emerged recently in the Maritimes have been women. Indeed, the present literary scene in the Maritimes is as varied as it is lively: to find oneself compelled nowadays to 'Go to Halifax' – or Fredericton or Charlottetown, for that matter – is not only, as MacMechan said, to be blessed against one's will. It is also to find oneself among some of the finest writers, and on the home ground of some of the richest literature to be found anywhere in that happily diverse country we call Canada.

# Notes

PREFACE

1 Archibald MacMechan, *Headwaters of Canadian Literature* (1924; rpt, Toronto: McClelland & Stewart 1974) 19
2 George Rawlyk, 'The Atlantic Provinces: History and Politics, in Robert Fulford et al., eds., *Read Canadian: A Book about Canadian Books* (Toronto: James, Lewis & Samuel 1972) 30
3 Donald Stephens, 'From the Maritimes,' *Canadian Literature* 3 (Winter 1960) 84
4 Douglas Daymond and Leslie Monkman, *Canadian Novelists and the Novel* (Ottawa: Borealis Press 1981) 253. Robert Kroetsch proves the exception to this rule of critical neglect: in 'Beyond Nationalism: A Prologue' he speaks briefly of *The Mountain and the Valley* in post-modernist terms as 'that story of the novelist looking for both the tale and the teller' (Evelyn J. Hinz, ed., *Beyond Nationalism: The Canadian Literary Scene in Global Perspective* [Winnipeg: University of Manitoba Press 1981] ix). George Woodcock, on the other hand, though he makes fleeting reference to Haliburton and McCulloch, Montgomery and Roberts, and spends considerable time on James De Mille in a discussion of Canadian fiction, omits Buckler altogether. See 'Possessing the Land: Notes on Canadian Fiction' in David Staines, ed., *The Canadian Imagination: Dimensions of a Literary Culture* (Cambridge, MA: Harvard University Press 1977).
5 'Thomas Raddall: The Past Is Always Important,' in Donald Cameron, ed., *Conversations with Canadian Novelists* (Toronto: Macmillan 1973) 107
6 'Fiction 1940–1960' in Carl F. Klinck, gen. ed., *Literary History of Canada: Canadian Literature in English* (Toronto: University of Toronto Press 1965; 2nd ed., 1976) II, 205

CHAPTER ONE: POLEMICAL INTRODUCTION

1 Archibald MacMechan, *Headwaters of Canadian Literature* (1924; rpt, Toronto: McClelland & Stewart 1974) 17

2 Despite, or perhaps because of, the influence of Charles G.D. Roberts and Bliss Carman, important poets have not thriven in the Maritimes to the extent that prose writers have – with the notable exceptions, of course, of Alden Nowlan and Milton Acorn. This is not to deny that many fine poets are currently writing in the Maritimes but rather to suggest that Maritime poetry, from its origins to its most recent developments, is a subject which demands its own extended study. On the subject of Nowlan a word needs to be said: though his fiction can hardly be considered as accomplished as his poetry, it does voice significant indigenous concerns and makes an invaluable contribution to the development of realist fiction in the Maritimes. The work of David Adams Richards, for example, owes much to the fictive ground broken by Nowlan.

3 Patrick O'Flaherty, *The Rock Observed: Studies in the Literature of Newfoundland* (Toronto: University of Toronto Press 1979) 115

4 Ibid. 186

5 Ibid. 187

6 Sandra Djwa, 'No Other Way: Sinclair Ross's Stories and Novels' in George Woodcock, ed., *The Canadian Novel in the Twentieth Century: Essays from 'Canadian Literature'* (Toronto: McClelland & Stewart 1975) 127

7 See O'Flaherty, *The Rock Observed* (p 112): 'the nineteenth century's most enduring fantasy about Newfoundland, the idea that the country was a treasure house of riches which, once unlocked, would provide boundless wealth and opportunity for a vast population' remained, O'Flaherty points out, a fantasy or else a grim joke.

8 O'Flaherty, *The Rock Observed* 100

9 *A Literary and Linguistic History of New Brunswick*, ed. Reavley Gair (Fredericton: Goose Lane 1985), is a recent, welcome attempt to bring English- and French-language writing in New Brunswick under one scholarly roof.

10 Ronald Sutherland, 'The Mainstream,' *Canadian Literature* 53 (Summer 1972) 32

11 Ernest Buckler, *Nova Scotia: Window on the Sea* (1973; rpt, Toronto: McClelland & Stewart 1978) 98

12 A.D. Nuttall, *A New Mimesis: Shakespeare and the Representation of Reality* (London: Methuen 1983) 75

13 Ibid. 82

14 Ibid. 90

15 Ibid. 95

16 Silver Donald Cameron, *Seasons in the Rain: An Expatriate's Notes on British Columbia* (Toronto: McClelland & Stewart 1978) 13

17 Alden Nowlan, 'My Canada,' *Maclean's* 84:6 (June 1971) 17

18 Archibald MacMechan, *The Book of Ultima Thule* (Toronto: McClelland & Stewart 1927) 24–5

19 Janet Giltrow, '"Painful Experience in a Distant Land": Mrs Moodie in Canada and Mrs Trollope in America' in Evelyn J. Hinz, ed., *Beyond National-*

*ism: The Canadian Literary Scene in Global Perspective* (Winnipeg: University of Manitoba Press 1981) 132

20 Joseph Howe, *Western and Eastern Rambles: Travel Sketches of Nova Scotia*, ed. M.G. Parks (Toronto: University of Toronto Press 1973) 73. All subsequent quotations from this text will be taken from this edition and incorporated into Chapter 1 using the abbreviation WER.

21 Nowlan, 'My Canada' 17

22 D.C. Harvey, 'The Heritage of the Maritimes,' *Dalhousie Review* XIV (1934) 28

23 *Ultima Thule* 251–2

24 'An Afternoon with Milton Acorn,' *New Maritimes* (May 1984) 4

25 Alden Nowlan, 'The National Whipping Boy,' *Atlantic Advocate* 67:11 (July 1977) 71

26 Margaret Laurence, 'Down East' in *Heart of a Stranger* (Toronto: McClelland & Stewart 1976) 159. Laurence refers here to both Quebec and the Maritimes.

27 William French, 'The Write Stuff,' the *Globe and Mail*, 14 June 1986, c1–c3. In the defence of the 'Toronto-based,' it must be acknowledged that critics such as Robert Weaver, with his receptiveness to all fine Canadian writing, regardless of regional origin, and Claude Bissell, with his championing of Ernest Buckler, have done much to make Maritime literature better known and appreciated. And William French, despite his initial lukewarmness to the work of David Adams Richards, has recently 'come round' – as 'The Write Stuff' reveals. Needless to say, what needs to be attacked is not 'Toronto,' but a mentality that tends to associate most things Maritime – including literature – with spruce bogs and codfish.

28 That Maritimers have no comprehensive history of their region or adequate general critical study of their region's literature may be seen as evidence of their lack of basic interest or enthusiasm in these subjects, but it may also be interpreted as a reflection of their state of demoralization. If one's home region has traditionally been seen as an 'anachronistic backwater,' to quote George Rawlyk, an exporter of the talented and harbourer of the shiftless, then there will hardly be the confidence to undertake major studies that will show one's region to be as worthy of scholarly and critical interest as more politically and economically favoured regions. For information on denigratory perceptions of the Maritimes by 'outsiders' and how these affected Maritime morale see Chapter 5's discussion of Ernest Forbes's *The Maritime Rights Movement 1919–1927: A Study in Canadian Regionalism* (Montreal: McGill-Queen's University Press 1979).

29 Nowlan, 'My Canada' 17

30 E.K. Brown, 'The Problem of a Canadian Literature' in A.J.M. Smith, ed., *Masks of Fiction: Canadian Critics on Canadian Prose* (1961; rpt, Toronto: McClelland & Stewart 1969) 52

31 Hugo McPherson, 'Fiction 1940-1960' in Carl F. Klinck, gen. ed. *Literary History of Canada: Canadian Literature in English* (Toronto: University of Toronto Press; 2nd ed., 1976), II, 219

32 Sutherland, 'The Mainstream' 38

33 Ibid. 41
34 Don Precosky, 'Seven Myths about Canadian Literature,' *Studies in Canadian Literature* 11:1 (1986) 89. The anti-regionalist bogey emerges most powerfully, of course, at times of national crisis. Recent cuts to the CBC in the interests of deficit-slashing have resulted in fears that regional programming will not so much suffer as be suppressed altogether (see Anna Cameron's interview with Terry Campbell on CBC's Stereo Morning program, 22 March 1985). And with free trade looming, and cultural sovereignty threatened, there is a strong possibility that centralist-nationalism and its corollary, anti-regionalism, will again be slouching towards Bethlehem.
35 John Metcalf, *Kicking against the Pricks* (Toronto: ECW Press 1982) 14–15
36 Northrop Frye, *The Bush Garden: Essays on the Canadian Imagination* (Toronto: Anansi 1971) ii
37 Ibid. iii
38 Terry Whalen, 'Atlantic Possibilities,' *Essays on Canadian Writing* 20 (Winter 1980–1) 53
39 David Frank, 'Regional Disparities Reviewed,' *Atlantic Provinces Book Review* 10:2 (Sept. / Oct. 1983) 2
40 Ibid.
41 See Rawlyk, *Read Canadian*. 'In terms of the historiography of the Atlantic provinces, what is most striking is the initial absence of any book-length studies specifically dealing with the post-Confederation period.' The one comprehensive study of the pre-Confederation Maritimes that is easily available, W.S. MacNutt's *The Atlantic Provinces: The Emergence of Colonial Society 1712–1857* (1965; rpt, Toronto: McClelland & Stewart 1968), suffers, Rawlyk claims, from the fact that its author was required 'to cram into one volume what should have been contained in at least three or four' (*Read Canadian* 32).
42 William Kilbourn, 'The Writing of Canadian History,' *Literary History of Canada*, 27–8
43 Ibid. 30
44 Ibid. 28
45 *The Bush Garden* 217
46 Ibid.
47 'From Nationalism to Regionalism: The Maturing of Canadian Culture. Robert Fulford Talks with Northrop Frye,' *Aurora: New Canadian Writing 1980*, ed. Morris Wolfe (Toronto: Doubleday 1980) 8
48 Northrop Frye, 'Culture as Interpenetration,' *Divisions on a Ground: Essays on Canadian Culture*, ed. James Polk (Toronto: Anansi 1982) 24
49 Frye, 'Across the River and Out of the Trees,' *Divisions* 31
50 Frye, 'Culture as Interpenetration,' *Divisions* 24
51 Frye, 'National Consciousness in Canadian Culture,' *Divisions* 49–55
52 Ibid. 52. Douglas Lochhead has also contested the applicability to the Maritimes of Frye's notion of Canada as a journey without arrival, a horrific wilderness, a vastness of space that devours us; in 'The Literary Heritage:

The Place, the Past, the Prospects,' collected in *The Atlantic Provinces Literature Colloquium Papers* (Saint John: Atlantic Canada Institute 1977) he declares, 'No nonsense about being swallowed up. The sense of place is everywhere in our writing' (p 8).

53 Northrop Frye, 'Conclusion,' *Literary History of Canada*, III, 323
54 Ibid.
55 'Hugh MacLennan: The Tennis Racket Is an Antelope Bone' in Donald Cameron, ed., *Conversations with Canadian Novelists* (Toronto: Macmillan 1973) 136
56 Ernest R. Forbes, *The Maritime Rights Movement* ix
57 See Michael Cross, 'Canadian History' in *Literary History of Canada*, III, 63–83. Cross argues that through the 1930s to the 1960s, 'metropolitanism [combined with] the Laurentian hypothesis had become a dogma reverently repeated rather than intellectually tested.' In the 1960s Laurentianism lost its ideological hold, and with it 'the dead hand of the Toronto-centred, conservative interpretations which had dominated historiography for three decades' (p 63).
58 Patricia Barclay, 'Regionalism and the Writer: A Talk with W.O. Mitchell,' *Canadian Literature* 14 (Autumn 1962) 53
59 Margaret Laurence, 'Ivory Tower or Grass Roots?: The Novelist as Socio-Political Being' in Douglas Daymond and Leslie Monkman, eds, *Canadian Novelists and the Novel* (Ottawa: Borealis 1981) 254–5
60 Might it not be possible that only in new, sprawling countries politically and economically dependent on another, overwhelming power, does the term regionalism inspire such vituperation? Certainly American writers from 'the South' or, more recently, Bobbie Ann Mason country, seem not to suffer from the Canadian dilemma of whether to be 'regional' as opposed to 'national' writers. Again, the interpenetration of culture and politics seems the key to the issue: since Canadian culture is such a fragile, vulnerable entity, under constant bombardment from the American entertainment industry, we seem desperately to seek a uniform, all-inclusive Canadian ethos to be expressed in our art – a kind of cultural Great Wall against the New Romans.
61 These stories are to be found in the collections *The Moons of Jupiter* and *The Expatriate* respectively.
62 David Staines, introduction, *The Canadian Imagination: Dimensions of a Literary Culture* (Cambridge, MA: Harvard University Press 1977) 3
63 David Alexander, 'Convocation Address,' *Atlantic Canada and Confederation: Essays on Canadian Political Economy* (Toronto: University of Toronto Press in association with Memorial University of Newfoundland 1983) 144–5
64 Alden Nowlan, 'The National Whipping Boy,' *The Atlantic Advocate* 67:11 (July 1977) 71
65 Julia Beckwith Hart possesses the entirely dubious distinction of being the first Canadian-born novelist by virtue of her adolescent opus *St Ursula's Convent*.

66 While it is true that New England transcendentalism did influence Maritime poetry (whether for the better or worse is a moot point) the best and most significant fiction produced in the Maritimes is not dependent upon New England models. Susan Kerslake's *Penumbra* is, of course, indebted to Melville, but stands on its imaginative own.

67 *Ultima Thule* 19

CHAPTER TWO: COMMUNITY

1 Thomas Chandler Haliburton, *The Old Judge: Or Life in a Colony* (1849; rpt, Ottawa: Tecumseh Press 1978) 143. All subsequent quotations will be taken from this edition and incorporated into the text of Chapter 2 using the abbreviation TOJ.

2 Sandra Djwa, 'No Other Way: Sinclair Ross's Stories and Novels' in George Woodcock, ed., *The Canadian Novel in the Twentieth Century: Essays from Canadian Literature* (Toronto: McClelland & Stewart 1975) 142

3 With few exceptions, Maritime fiction does not feature the city: Halifax is usually presented as a place to go to be miserable without attracting attention, or as a place to get out of by any possible means. Such is the experience of Anna and Margaret in *The Channel Shore*, Isabel Jardine and Matthew Carney in *The Nymph and the Lamp*, Anna in *The Mountain and the Valley*, and the narrator of *Oxbells and Fireflies*.

4 Hugh MacLennan, interviewed by Ronald Sutherland in *Canadian Literature: Special Issue on the Maritimes* 68–9 (Spring / Summer 1976) 41

5 See R.E. Watters' introduction to his edition of *The Old Judge* (Toronto: Clarke Irwin 1968).

6 D.C. Harvey, 'The Heritage of the Maritimes,' *Dalhousie Review* 14 (1934) 29

7 Thomas Vincent, 'Eighteenth-Century Poetry in Maritime Canada: Problems of Approach – A Research Report,' *Atlantic Provinces Literature Colloquium Papers* (Saint John: Atlantic Canada Institute 1977) 18

8 Leaving aside Francophone Maritime literature, the most notable exceptions to this rule are Howe's *Acadia*, Thomas Raddall's oeuvre (which, however, maintains a distinctly condescending attitude to the Maritimes' native peoples), and Huyghue's *Argimou*, which will be discussed in Chapter 4.

9 Thomas McCulloch, *The Stepsure Letters* (Toronto: McClelland & Stewart 1960) 14. All subsequent quotations will be taken from this edition and incorporated into Chapter 2 using the abbreviation SL.

10 See Jars Balan, 'The Maritimes' in *Salt and Braided Bread* (Toronto: Oxford University Press 1984) 20–1.

11 Quoted in W.H. New, *Articulating West: Essays on Purpose and Form in Modern Canadian Literature* (Toronto: New Press 1972) xvi

12 *Ninety Seasons*, ed. R. Cockburn and R. Gibbs (Toronto: McClelland & Stewart 1974) 13

13 The term is Harry Bruce's; Silver Donald Cameron develops the concept in his essay 'The Maritime Writer and the Folks Down Home' in *Canadian Literature: Special Issue on the Maritimes*.

14 Silver Donald Cameron, *Seasons in the Rain: An Expatriate's Notes on British Columbia* (Toronto: McClelland & Stewart 1978) 10

15 Alden Nowlan, 'My Canada,' *Maclean's* 84:6 (June 1971) 17

16 In the NFB film 'Margaree People,' rural Maritimers present this paradox in their own terms.

17 See Cameron, *Seasons* 13.

18 Raymond Williams, *The English Novel from Dickens to Lawrence* (London: Paladin 1974) 13

19 W.H. New, 'Maritime Cadences,' *Canadian Literature: Special Issue on the Maritimes* 5

20 'Ernest Buckler: A Conversation with an Irritated Oyster' in Silver Donald Cameron's *Conversation with Canadian Novelists* (Toronto: Macmillan 1973) 5

21 Alden Nowlan, 'Something to Write About,' *Canadian Literature: Special Issue on the Maritimes* 11–12

22 Ibid. 7

23 'Alden Nowlan's Notebook,' *The Atlantic Advocate* 72: 1 (Sept. 1981) 78

24 Millar MacLure, 'Literary Scholarship' in Carl F. Klinck, gen. ed., *Literary History of Canada: Canadian Literature in English* (Toronto: University of Toronto Press 1965; 2nd ed., 1976) II, 73

25 While it would be hypocritical to expect from a McCulloch or Haliburton or even a Macphail a sympathetic consideration of, never mind an interest in, the Indian and Black population of the Maritimes, it is unpalatable food for thought that these 'outsiders' are virtually banished from the fictive worlds of Bruce, Buckler, and MacLennan; that one must turn to the writers of historical fiction – Roberts, Raddall, Maillet – before we find Blacks or Micmacs appearing even as marginal characters in Maritime writing.

26 Susanna Moodie, *Roughing It in the Bush* (Toronto: McClelland & Stewart 1967) 159

27 It may be argued that the later careers and interests of Joseph Howe and T.C. Haliburton are linked by their shared concern that the British imperial system provide a place in the sun for its ambitious and enterprising colonial sons.

28 See Haliburton's credo as expressed in *The Old Judge*: 'A man who steps out of his proper sphere in life must inevitably provoke ridicule.' (TOJ 46)

29 A place for everyone and everyone in his place, as the cliché goes, though it must be remarked that just as Haliburton refuses to make room in his society for destitute Irish immigrants, so he refuses to accommodate Nova Scotian Blacks, whom he presses into the stereotype of 'the merry, thoughtless Negro' (TOJ 158), too lackadaisical to ask even for crumbs of the social pie (though they were allowed the pie into which a child's shoe had accidentally fallen during that same 'pickinick' at which Sally Horn so charmed her gentlemen friends.

30 Ian Ross Robertson, introduction, New Canadian Library edition of *The Master's Wife* (Toronto: McClelland & Stewart 1979) x. All subsequent quotations will be taken from this edition and incorporated into Chapter 2 using the abbreviation TMW.

31 The epic 'duel' which took place between two Island fiddlers, detailed in the chapter 'The Musicians' in *The Master's Wife*, is an episode which belongs to Macphail's adult life. When he was a child, 'musical instruments were not held in favour. One young man who performed very well on the bagpipes abandoned the practice at the time of his conversion ... The violin was unknown, except among the Irish. It was considered a dissolute instrument.' (TMW 149)

32 This is not, of course, to argue for the greater racial tolerance of Orwell – the case of the 'Esquimau wife' would prove the contrary. Yet it is interesting to compare the 'good-humoured toleration' and 'amusement' of Malpeque society towards the 'segregated class' with Macphail's depiction of his mother's attitude towards Blacks: 'The Master's wife found something unseemly in ... consternation over the negro ... With her intense human sympathy, her devotion to those who were kind, with her inability to believe anything contrary to her desire, she had two explanations of the negro [in this case, a particularly attentive porter on a train]: either he was not a negro, or he could be white if he preferred that colour' (TMW 16–17).

33 The last two chapters of *The Master's Wife* are disappointing in tone and conception, perhaps because in them Macphail deals with his post-Orwellian adult life, and a degree of self-consciousness, sentimentality, and pompousness infects the narrative.

34 It is also terrifyingly clear as to the absolute self-sacrifice such economy made upon the women who practised it – all of which should give those keen to get back to the land lengthy pause.

35 *Oxbells and Fireflies* is, of course, steeped in the mystique of community, but there is an elegiac tone in that narrative which suggests that even communities less beneficent than Norstead exist now only in memory and desire.

36 Charles Bruce, *The Channel Shore* (1954; rpt, Toronto: McClelland & Stewart 1984) 196. All subsequent quotations will be taken from this edition and incorporated into Chapter 2 using the abbreviation CS.

CHAPTER THREE: THE BOOK OF NATURE

1 Charles G.D. Roberts, 'The Poetry of Nature,' *Selected Poetry and Critical Prose*, ed. W.J. Keith (Toronto: University of Toronto Press 1974) 277–8. Subsequent quotations will be taken from this edition and incorporated into Chapter 3 using the abbreviation SPCP.

2 Hugo McPherson, 'Fiction 1940–1960,' in Carl F. Klinck, gen. ed., *Literary History of Canada: Canadian Literature in English* (Toronto: University of Toronto Press 1965; 2nd ed., 1976), II, 233

3 Northrop Frye, 'Conclusion,' *Literary History of Canada* II, 342.
4 Ibid. II, 338.
5 Warren Tallman, 'Wolf in the Snow,' in *Contexts of Canadian Criticism*, ed. Eli Mandel (Chicago: University of Chicago Press 1971) 253, 247–8
6 Malcolm Ross, 'Critical Theory: Some Trends,' in *Literary History of Canada* III, 167
7 John Moss, *Patterns of Isolation in English-Canadian Fiction* (Toronto: McClelland & Stewart 1974) 110
8 Ibid. 113
9 D.O. Spettigue, 'The Way It Was: Ernest Buckler' in George Woodcock, ed., *The Canadian Novel in the Twentieth Century: Essays from Canadian Literature*, (Toronto: McClelland & Stewart 1975) 146
10 See Sandra Djwa's essay, 'No Other Way: Sinclair Ross's Stories and Novels' in Woodcock, *The Canadian Novel in the Twentieth Century* 144n.
11 Rudy Wiebe, 'Passage by Land' in Douglas Daymond and Leslie Monkman, eds, *Canadian Novelists and the Novel* (Ottawa: Borealis 1981) 262
12 Ernest Buckler, *Nova Scotia: Window on the Sea* (1973; rpt, Toronto: McClelland & Stewart 1978) 97
13 Frye, 'Conclusion,' *Literary History of Canada* II, 355
14 Archibald MacMechan, *The Book of Ultima Thule* (Toronto: McClelland 1927) 204–5
15 Silver Donald Cameron, *Seasons in the Rain: An Expatriate's Notes on British Columbia* (Toronto: McClelland & Stewart 1978) 12
16 Oliver Goldsmith, *The Rising Village*, in Brown and Bennett, eds, *An Anthology of Canadian Literature in English* (Toronto: Oxford University Press 1982) I, 52
17 Thomas C. Keefer's *The Philosophy of Railroads* appeared in 1849. It was reprinted in 1972 (Toronto: University of Toronto Press).
18 Lucy Maud Montgomery, *Anne of Green Gables* (1942; rpt, Toronto: Ryerson 1962) 394
19 Despite Roberts's contention that his kindred of the wild play out tragedies and comedies on the stage Mother Nature sets, such stories as 'In Panoply of Spears' or 'The Homesickness of Kehonka' are scarcely tragic – the untimely end of an infant porcupine or melancholy goose may be lamentable but is hardly to be compared with the death of such a character as Dr Fennison in *The Cruelest Month* or Gershom Born in *Rockbound*.
20 Buckler, *Nova Scotia: Window on the Sea* 98
21 The massive spoliation of Maritime forests brought about by 'clearcutting' and the lack of any adequate program of reforestation is another matter – one which, to be appreciated, needs to be observed from the air.
22 D.C. Harvey, 'The Heritage of the Maritimes,' *Dalhousie Review* XIV (1934) 28–9
23 MacMechan, *The Book of Ultima Thule* 230
24 Susan Kerslake's recently published novel *Penumbra*, indebted to *Moby Dick* and set on a remote island governed by the symbolic forces of moon and

sea, could very well represent a new trend towards sea-centred fiction in Maritime writing.

25 See Thomas Raddall's foreword to *Pride's Fancy* (New York: Doubleday 1946) v: 'I live in a small Nova Scotia seaport which in colonial times had a great deal to do with the West Indies. More than one garden blooms actually in West Indian soil, brought north as ballast in the days of the Caribbean trade. Street corners are marked by half-sunken cannon, muzzle down, which once upon a time spoke sharply for their owners in the Caribbean waters. Other relics are carefully preserved, and tales of the old wild days survive in family legend as well as in letters, diaries, logbooks, and other documents of the time.'

26 Ernest Buckler is the great exception, but his metaphysics is complicated by solipsistic tendencies, and it is only his exceptional characters – a David Canaan or Paul Creed, and no equivalent of Conrad's MacWhirr or Whalley – who wrestle with it.

27 Thomas Raddall, *The Nymph and the Lamp* (Toronto: McClelland & Stewart 1968) 153. All subsequent quotations will be taken from this edition and incorporated into the text of Chapter 3 using the abbreviation NL.

28 Frank Parker Day, *Rockbound* (1928; rpt, Toronto: University of Toronto Press 1973) xxvii. All subsequent quotations will be taken from this edition and incorporated into the text of Chapter 3 using the abbreviation R.

29 An understanding to which Hugh MacLennan's Captain Yardley also comes in *Two Solitudes*, as he contemplates the senselessly beautiful and destructive swimming of sharks and barracuda round his ship.

30 Where Day differs from Conrad in his vision of human possibility and metaphysical truth is in the certainty and clarity with which he distinguishes these opposed factors – there is none of Conrad's infinitely suggestive doubt, which finds expression in Marlow's compulsive narratives and in the multiple perspectives Conrad brings to bear upon individual characters and events in his novels.

31 Raddall's Isabel Jardine, Bruce's Renie Fraser, and Buckler's Miss Merriam are other examples. The role of schoolmistress permits to heroines who are the daughters of farmers or fishermen the possibility of enhancing their status and pursuing a profession without having to marry (or to marry outside of their social group), to leave their home ground, or to betray their community's customs and values.

32 D.G. Jones, *Butterfly on Rock* (Toronto: University of Toronto Press 1970) 8

33 Raddall presents Isabel as the incarnation of Womanly Service and Self-Sacrifice; her passion is not so much for Matthew Carney as for her vocation of Mother / Helper to an increasingly blind and helpless husband. Raddall also implies on the novel's last page that it is feminine vanity as much as altruism which sends Isabel back to the near blind Carney – he will always remember her as he last sees her: a sexually attractive woman in her prime.

34 Ernest Buckler, *The Cruelest Month* (Toronto: McClelland & Stewart 1963) 116.

Subsequent quotations will be taken from this edition and incorporated into Chapter 3 using the abbreviation CM.

35 'Even in Arcadia, there am I, [Death]'
36 Kent Thompson, introduction, *Stories from Atlantic Canada* (Toronto: Macmillan 1973) xiii
37 W.J. Keith, *Charles G.D. Roberts* (Toronto: Copp Clark 1969) 22
38 For an extended discussion of the class system of Roberts's wilderness see my article '"With a Pistol in His Paw": The Anthropocentric Animal Fiction of Charles G.D. Roberts, Kenneth Grahame, and Franz Kafka,' *Revue de l'Université Sainte-Anne* (1982) 19–28.
39 'The Animal Story,' *The Kindred of the Wild* (London: Duckworth 1903) 29. Subsequent quotations will be taken from this edition and incorporated into Chapter 3 using the abbreviation KW.
40 The blurb on the original dust-jacket of *Morning* reads as follows: 'Mr Roberts gives us a story of a man in primeval times, and introduces descriptions of the strange scenery and monstrous fauna. It is likely to prove one of the most successful of the author's many popular works.' Part of that popularity may have depended on the cover illustration – a hairy hulk of a man carrying off a scantily clad, unconscious female.
41 Keith, *Charles G.D. Roberts* 96
42 Charles G.D. Roberts, *In the Morning of Time* (London: Hutchinson 1919) 48. Subsequent quotations will be taken from this edition and incorporated into Chapter 3 using the abbreviation MT.
43 Most critics would agree with Keith's thesis that Roberts's skills as a writer are shown to best and most enduring advantage in his animal fiction. See Keith's *Charles G.D. Roberts* 59.
44 Ibid. 96
45 Ibid. 100–1
46 Ibid. 102
47 Charles G.D. Roberts, *The Backwoodsmen* (London: Ward Lock 1909) 9. Subsequent quotations will be taken from this edition and incorporated into Chapter 3 using the abbreviation B.

CHAPTER FOUR: FICTIVE HISTORIES

1 Thomas Raddall, *Roger Sudden* (Toronto: McClelland & Stewart 1944) 228–9
2 Antonine Maillet, *Cent Ans dans les bois* (Québec: Leméac 1981) 13. My translation, as are the subsequent passages from Michel Roy. I would like to acknowledge the kind help of Professor René LeBlanc of Université Sainte-Anne in checking the accuracy of my translations.
3 George Grant, *Lament for a Nation: The Defeat of Canadian Nationalism* (1965; rpt, Toronto: McClelland & Stewart 1971) vii
4 See Henry James, 'The Art of Fiction' in Morris Roberts, ed. *The Art of Fiction and Other Essays* (New York: Oxford 1948) and Margaret Laurence, 'Ivory Tower or Grassroots: The Novelist as Socio-Political Being,' in Douglas

Daymond and Leslie Monkman, eds, *Canadian Novelists and the Novel* (Ottawa: Borealis 1981).

5 Laurence, ibid. 252
6 W.S. MacNutt, *The Atlantic Provinces: The Emergence of Colonial Society 1712–1857* (1965; rpt, Toronto: McClelland & Stewart 1968) 1
7 Ibid. 267–8. It can be argued, of course, that MacNutt himself is under the sway of the centralist school, which has treated the Maritimes as Canada's historical, economic, social, and cultural *Ultima Thule*. For a historian who sees the Golden Age of the Maritime economy as a result of vigorous north-south trade relations and the absence of tariffs on imported goods – all of which Confederation annulled – see David Alexander's *Atlantic Canada and Confederation: Essays in Canadian Political Economy* (Toronto: University of Toronto Press in association with Memorial University of Newfoundland 1983).
8 Silver Donald Cameron, *Seasons in the Rain: An Expatriate's Notes on British Columbia* (Toronto: McClelland & Stewart 1978) 8
9 Edward McCourt, 'The Canadian Historical Novel' in Daymond and Monkman, *Canadian Novelists and the Novel* 168
10 Ibid. 168
11 Georg Lukács, *Studies in European Realism* (New York: Grosset & Dunlap 1964) 6
12 MacNutt, *The Atlantic Provinces* 23
13 Edgar McInnis, *Canada: A Political and Social History* (1947; rpt, Toronto: Clarke Irwin 1959) 108
14 W.H. New, 'Maritime Cadences' in *Canadian Literature: Special Issue on the Maritimes* 68–9 (Spring / Summer 1976) 3
15 See Andrew Hook's introduction to *Waverley* (Harmondsworth, Eng.: Penguin 1972).
16 For such an analysis see my article 'The Ideology of Innocence: Anglophone Literature and the Expulsion of the Acadians,' *Revue de l'Université Sainte-Anne* (1984–5) 39–46.
17 Eugène Cloutier, 'In the Land of Evangeline' from *No Passport: A Discovery of Canada*, collected in *The Oxford Anthology of Canadian Literature*, ed. Robert Weaver and William Toye (Toronto: Oxford University Press 1973) 65
18 Gordon Roper et al., 'Writers of Fiction: 1880–1920' in Carl F. Klinck, gen. ed., *Literary History of Canada* (Toronto: University of Toronto Press 1965; 2nd ed., 1976) I, 336
19 See 'The Ideology of Innocence: Anglophone Literature and the Expulsion of the Acadians' 39–46.
20 Archibald MacMechan, 'The Orchards of Ultima Thule,' *The Book of Ultima Thule* (Toronto: McClelland & Stewart 1927) 289
21 Archibald MacMechan, *Headwaters of Canadian Literature* (1924; rpt, Toronto: McClelland & Stewart 1974) 125
22 William Owen, 'Vision and Revision in Roberts's Acadian Romances' in *The Sir Charles G.D. Roberts Symposium* (Ottawa: University of Ottawa Press 1984) 117

23 Charles G.D. Roberts, *A Sister to Evangeline* (London: John Lane 1900) 285. Subsequent quotations will be taken from this edition and incorporated into the text of Chapter 4 using the abbreviation SE.
24 Lower class deportees, that is. Though *A Sister to Evangeline* describes the pain and sheer messiness of the deportation – shrieking women, lost children, the struggles through mud flats to the ships – Roberts does suggest that the splitting up of families was partly due to the women losing their heads and weeping when they should have been keeping track of their kinfolk. For Roberts's gentry, deportation is an altogether different affair – Paul Grande, for example, is incarcerated by Lieutenant Waldron in Grand Pré Chapel with such exquisite tact and delicacy that the two men can become the best of friends when they meet up in post-Conquest Québec.
25 As Thomas Raddall has pointed out, it was the New England bluecoats, and not the British red coats, who carried out the Deportation. See *Halifax, Warden of the North* (Toronto: McClelland & Stewart 1971) 46.
26 Bona Arsenault, *The History of the Acadians* (Québec: Conseil de la vie française en Amérique 1966) 100
27 *A Sister to Evangeline* describes the courtesy under pressure with which the British treated Acadians during the Deportation: 'The soldiers toiled faithfully, and their leggings to the knee were a sorry sight. They were patient, these red-coats, with the women, who often seemed to lose their heads so that they knew not which boat they wanted to go in. To the children every red-coat seemed tender as a mother' (SE 203).
28 Charles G.D. Roberts, *The Forge in the Forest* (Boston: Lamson Wolffe 1896) 266. All subsequent quotations will be taken from this edition and incorporated into the text of Chapter 4 using the abbreviation FF.
29 The 'calamitous confusion' (SE 204) over which Longfellow passes so lightly is communicated by Roberts's general description of the embarkation in Chapter 28. For an idea of the chasm between his treatment of the expulsion and Maillet's, compare Roberts's vignette of the lost child, tossed from ship to ship (SE 204–5) and the account given in Maillet's *Pélagie* of the abuse of the child Catoune.
30 H.W. Longfellow, *Evangeline* (Toronto: McClelland & Stewart 1962) 26. Subsequent quotations will be taken from this edition and incorporated into the text of Chapter 4 using the abbreviation E.
31 The last three verses of the French translation by Léon Pamphile Lemay, on the other hand, give a much solider sense of continuing French presence in what was Acadie.
32 See Roberts's introduction to his translation of Phillipe Aubert de Gaspé's *The Canadians of Old* (Toronto: McClelland & Stewart 1974).
33 Charles G.D. Roberts, *Lovers in Acadie* (London: Dent 1924) viii
34 Ernest Buckler, *Nova Scotia: Window on the Sea* (1973; rpt, Toronto: McClelland & Stewart 1978) 126
35 Hugo McPherson 'Fiction: 1940–1960,' *Literary History of Canada* II, 207–8

36 Donald Cameron, 'Thomas Raddall: The Art of Historical Fiction,' *Dalhousie Review* 49:4 (Winter 1969–70) 546
37 Thomas H. Raddall, *In My Time: A Memoir* (Toronto: McClelland & Stewart 1976) 252
38 Cameron, 'Thomas Raddall: The Art of Historical Fiction' 546
39 The crime of which MacMechan accused Haliburton. See *Headwaters* 41.
40 Cameron, 'Thomas Raddall: The Art of Historical Fiction' 544, and Georg Lukács, *Studies in European Realism* 72
41 Lukács, *Studies in European Realism* 6, 8
42 Ibid. 62
43 *In My Time* 128
44 Thomas H. Raddall, *His Majesty's Yankees*, (1942; rpt, New York: Popular Library, nd) 294. Subsequent quotations will be taken from this edition and incorporated into the text of Chapter 4 using the abbreviation HMY.
45 Raddall, *Halifax, Warden of the North* 151
46 Samuel Douglas Smith Huyghue, *Argimou: A Legend of the Micmac* (Halifax, Nova Scotia Morning Courier Office 1847; rpt, Sackville, NB: R.P. Bell Library, Mount Allison University 1977) 1. All subsequent quotations will be taken from this edition and incorporated into the text of Chapter 4 using the abbreviation A.
47 Huyghue's portrayal of native peoples in *Argimou* is, however, not entirely sympathetic; the deep-dyed villains of the romance are not the English, but a rival Indian band – the vicious 'Milicetes,' for whom the author has no sympathy whatsoever.
48 Huyghue would seem to share Haliburton's scathing view of the Irish.
49 'In the deep, solemn night – dark as their eyes, voiceless as their sealed lips – the *Flower of the Wilderness* unfolded its leaves beneath the warm atmosphere of passion, whose mild dew descended, pouring a refreshing balm into its depths, enhancing its fragrance … [N]or were … its stores of unrifled sweets withheld sparingly in return' (A 140).
50 Michel Roy, *L'Acadie des origines à nos jours: Essai de synthèse historique* (Montréal: Québec / Amérique 1981) 11
51 Antonine Maillet, *Pélagie*, tr. Philip Stratford (1979; tr. Toronto: General Publishing 1983) 173. Subsequent quotations will be taken from this edition and incorporated into the text of Chapter 4 using the abbreviation P.
52 Buckler, *Nova Scotia: Window on the Sea* 109
53 The equivalents to Pélagie and Beausoleil in *Cent Ans dans les bois*, the sequel to *Pélagie*, are allowed to marry but are drowned on their wedding day on the way to their new home in Prince Edward Island.
54 The historical Beausoleil was a guerilla fighter implacably hostile to the British, or so claims Thomas Raddall in *Halifax, Warden of the North* 45.
55 George Woodcock, 'Possessing the Land: Notes on Canadian Fiction' in David Staines, ed., *The Canadian Imagination: Dimensions of a Literary Culture* (Cambridge, MA: Harvard University Press 1977) 73–4, 95

56 Warren Tallman, 'Wolf in the Snow' in Eli Mandel, ed., *Contexts of Canadian Criticism* (Chicago: University of Chicago Press 1971) 251–2

57 *Cents Ans dans les bois*, unlike *Pélagie*, fails to successfully synthesize history and myth – the 'vulgar' romantic element (in the shape of star-crossed lovers finally allowed to marry and live happily forever) predominates, while the historical element (the convention at Memramcook in which the Acadians finally achieve a public voice and re-enter the collective historical record) seems merely tacked on at the end.

58 Roy, *L'Acadie des origines à nos jours* 229

59 Alden Nowlan, 'My Canada,' *Maclean's* 84:6 (June 1971) 17

60 Grant, *Lament* 12

CHAPTER FIVE: POLITICS AND FICTIONS

1 E.R. Forbes, *The Maritime Rights Movement, 1919–1927: A Study in Canadian Regionalism* (1979; rpt, Montreal: McGill-Queen's University Press 1980), ix

2 D.C. Harvey, 'The Heritage of the Maritimes,' *Dalhousie Review* xiv (1934) 32

3 Forbes, *Maritime Rights Movement* 111

4 It was Howe who lambasted the citizens of the Canadas for resorting to armed rebellion to try to secure governmental reform; Howe, too, whose anti-democratic ideas led him to oppose extending the franchise in Nova Scotia. See J. Murray Beck's article 'Joseph Howe, a Liberal, but with Qualifications' in Wayne A. Hunt, ed., *The Proceedings of the Joseph Howe Symposium*, Mount Allison University (Halifax: Nimbus 1984).

5 For a balanced view on Howe's evolution as a 'Canadian' see J. Murray Beck's article, note 4 above, 5–26.

6 W.S. MacNutt, *The Atlantic Provinces: The Emergence of Colonial Society 1712–1857* (Toronto: McClelland & Stewart 1968) 139

7 A.G. Bailey, quoted by Malcolm Ross, 'A Strange Aesthetic Ferment' in *Canadian Literature: Special Issue on the Maritimes* 68–9 (Spring / Summer 1976) 14

8 Harvey, 'The Heritage of the Maritimes' 29

9 Silver Donald Cameron, *The Education of Everett Richardson: The Nova Scotia Fishermen's Strike 1970–71* (Toronto: McClelland & Stewart 1977) 30. Subsequent quotations will be taken from this edition and incorporated into the text of Chapter 5 using the abbreviation EER.

10 Bruce Hutchison, *The Unknown Country: Canada and Her People* (1942; rpt, Toronto: McClelland & Stewart 1965) 167. Certain fishermen have recently begun radical action to protect the very survival of their livelihood: they are, however, not the 'chronic poor' but a well-established group who have invested considerable amounts of money in their equipment.

11 See J.M. Whalen and W.A. Oppen, 'Poor for Sale!' *The Atlantic Advocate* 67:1 (Sept. 1976) 50–1.

12 Charles G.D. Roberts, *The Heart that Knows* (Toronto: Copp Clark 1906) 160

13 Forbes, *Maritime Rights Movement* 216n

14 See Forbes, Chapter 6, 'A National Appeal,' and David G. Alexander, 'New Notions of Happiness: Nationalism, Regionalism and Atlantic Canada' (Ch. 5) in *Atlantic Canada and Confederation: Essays in Canadian Political Economy* (Toronto: University of Toronto Press in association with Memorial University of Newfoundland 1983).
15 D.C. Harvey, 'The Intellectual Awakening of Nova Scotia,' collected in G.A. Rawlyk, ed., *Historical Essays on the Atlantic Provinces* (1967; rpt, Toronto: McClelland & Stewart 1971) 99–121
16 William Hamilton, *Local History in Atlantic Canada* (Toronto: Macmillan 1974) 145
17 Desmond Pacey, 'Contemporary Writing in New Brunswick' in *Arts in New Brunswick*, eds Robert Tweedie, Fred Cogswell, W.S. MacNutt et al. (Fredericton: University Press of New Brunswick 1967) 34
18 Robert L. McDougall, 'The Dodo and the Cruising Auk: Class in Canadian Literature' in Eli Mandel, ed., *Contexts of Canadian Criticism* (Chicago: University of Chicago Press 1971) 217
19 Stanley Ryerson, *The Founding of Canada: Beginnings to 1815* (Toronto: Progress Books 1963) 289
20 MacNutt, *The Atlantic Provinces* 231
21 Alexander, 'New Notions of Happiness' 46–7
22 Forbes, *Maritime Rights Movement* vii
23 Thomas Chandler Haliburton, *The Clockmaker, or the Sayings and Doings of Samuel Slick of Slickville* (First Series) (1958; rpt, Toronto: McClelland & Stewart 1966) 71
24 Forbes, *Maritime Rights Movement* 108
25 Acorn's bumptious Marxism is well known; Nowlan's right-wing enthusiasms perhaps less so. A look at the 'Notebook' he wrote for the *Atlantic Monthly* reveals that Nowlan combined a passionate awareness of the punishing – not proud – poverty of the region with an intense admiration for the Right-to-Life movement, Barbara Amiel, and the Royal Family.
26 Quoted by Silver Donald Cameron in *Seasons in the Rain: An Expatriate's Notes on British Columbia* (Toronto: McClelland & Stewart 1978) 13
27 I would refer those who hold culture to be an autonomous realm to such works as *The Politics of Interpretation*, ed. W.J.T. Mitchell (Chicago: University of Chicago Press 1983); Edward W. Said's *The World, the Text, and the Critic* (Cambridge, MA: Harvard University Press 1983); Frederic Jameson's *The Political Unconscious: Narrative as a Socially Symbolic Act* (Ithaca, NY: Cornell University Press 1981); Terry Eagleton's *Literary Theory: An Introduction* (Oxford: Basil Blackwell 1983), and Robert Weimann's *Structure and Society in Literary History*, expanded edition (Baltimore: Johns Hopkins University Press 1984).
28 MacMechan, 'Spring in Ultima Thule,' *The Book of Ultima Thule* (Toronto: McClelland & Stewart 1927) 189–90
29 Kenneth J. Hughes, '*A Strange Manuscript*: Sources, Satire, a Positive Utopia'

and George Woodcock, 'De Mille and the Utopian Vision' in John Moss, ed., *The Canadian Novel: Beginnings, a Critical Anthology*, II, rev. ed. (Toronto: NC Press 1984) 123, 110, 108–9

30 *Ultima Thule* 281–6

31 Fraser Sutherland, 'Home Truths' in *Canadian Literature: Special Issue on the Maritimes* 105

32 James De Mille, *A Strange Manuscript Found in a Copper Cylinder* (1888; rpt, (Toronto: McClelland & Stewart 1969) 224. Subsequent quotations will be taken from this edition and incorporated into Chapter 5 using the abbreviation SM.

33 Kenneth J. Hughes states that the 'kin' at the end of 'Kosekin' 'suggests that they may be *our* kin.' Moss, *The Canadian Novel* 118

34 Adapted from a quotation in George A. Rawlyk's article 'J.M. Beck's Joseph Howe,' Hunt, *Joseph Howe Symposium*, 126

35 Ibid.

36 It is, of course, the writer's privilege to write of whatever and wherever she or he pleases. Yet since MacLennan is persistently held to be a Maritime as well as a Canadian writer, the extent of MacLennan's imaginative loyalty to his home region must be considered.

37 Hugh MacLennan, *Each Man's Son* (1951; rpt, Toronto: Macmillan 1971) 187. Subsequent quotations will be taken from this edition and incorporated into Chapter 5 using the abbreviation EMS.

38 Hugh MacLennan, *Barometer Rising* (Toronto: Macmillan 1948) 55. All subsequent quotations will be taken from this edition and incorporated into Chapter 5 using the abbreviation BR.

39 George Woodcock, *Hugh MacLennan* (Toronto: Copp Clark 1969) 29

40 See Frank W. Watt, 'Literature of Protest' in Carl F. Klinck, gen. ed., *Literary History of Canada: Canadian Literature in English* (Toronto: University of Toronto Press 1965; 2nd ed., 1976) I, 485

41 Woodcock, *Hugh MacLennan* 62

42 Jacques Brazeau, 'Perception du Canada français dans l'oeuvre de Hugh MacLennan' in Elspeth Cameron, ed., *Hugh MacLennan 1982: Proceedings of the MacLennan Conference at University College* (Canadian Studies Programme, University College, University of Toronto 1982)

43 Charles W. Dunn, *Highland Settler: A Portrait of the Scottish Gael in Nova Scotia* (Toronto: University of Toronto Press 1953, 1971) 107, 57

44 Peter Buitenhuis, *Canadian Writers and Their Works: Hugh MacLennan* (Toronto: Forum House 1969) 54; Paul Goetsch, ed., *Hugh MacLennan* (Toronto: McGraw-Hill 1973) 31; Warren Tallman, 'Wolf in the Snow' in Mandel, *Contexts of Canadian Criticism* 244. One exception to this rule is D.J. Dooley, who protests that while 'MacLennan is very convincing when he shows his main character ... as lying under an ancient curse ... of Calvinism, because that is what Ainslie senses most acutely in himself,' he fails to make a necessary dicrimination between Ainslie and 'the whole of Cape Breton island, even ... those who have never heard of Calvin ... Anyone who has ever seen

Cape Breton Highlanders on a spree,' he adds, 'will testify that the legacy of Calvinism did not seem particularly strong upon them.' *Moral Vision in the Canadian Novel* (Toronto: Clarke Irwin 1970) 80

45 Roy Daniells, 'Confederation to the First World War' in Klinck, I, 192

46 Forbes, *Maritime Rights Movement* 40

47 Irving Abella and David Millar, eds, *The Canadian Worker in the Twentieth Century* (Toronto: Oxford University Press 1978) 42

48 See William Hamilton, *Local History in Atlantic Canada* (Toronto: Macmillan 1974) 191–2. 'The cynical attitude of those in authority is best summarized in the words of J.E. McClurg, a vice-president of BESCO. Referring to the strike of 1925, he said, "We hold the cards, things are getting better every day they stay out. Let them stay out two months, or six months, it matters not, eventually they will come crawling to us. They can't stand the gaff."'

49 Abella and Millar, *The Canadian Worker* 138

50 Robert Cockburn, *The Novels of Hugh MacLennan* (Montreal: Harvest House 1969) 106

51 Woodcock, *Hugh MacLennan* 94. Woodcock omits from consideration the fact that the Highlanders did not own the mines in which they drudged for less than a living wage: Dominion Steel and Coal and BESCO did, and it was this that 'bred antagonism,' with the managers calling in the militia against the picketing miners.

52 Why, we might as well ask, did MacLennan make Jerome Martell in *The Watch that Ends the Night* a virtual clone of Norman Bethune only to turn him into a 'verray, parfit, gentil knyght' at the novel's end? Keiichi Hirano has argued that MacLennan's disavowal of the Martell-Bethune connection simply doesn't hold water, and demonstrates how, in Jerome Martell, MacLennan cuts Bethune down to size by making the idea of a commitment to radical political theory and praxis 'more a matter of temperament than of principle.' Practising a definite 'obscurantism' by his reluctance to allow characters to hold rational explanations for historical events, MacLennan turns his Jerome Martell into 'an easily digestible, absorbable and hygienically safe food for the public' ('Jerome Martell and Norman Bethune' in Goetsch, ed., *Hugh MacLennan* 133). In making Louis Camire a self-serving foreign radical who fights and works 'dirty,' MacLennan, it may be proposed, patches over a fact of Cape Breton history that is both unpalatable for an 'establishment' audience and embarrassing to MacLennan's Calvinist thesis in *Each Man's Son*. For, in the Cape Breton coal towns well before and after the period in which this novel is set, miners were being organized by 'foreigners' – not guitar-strumming draft-dodgers from the south of France, but radical Clydesiders for whom socialism, not Calvinism, was the *sine qua non*. By giving us a Louis Camire instead of a J.B. MacLachlan, the 'legendary leader of the Cape Breton miners' (Abella and Millar, *The Canadian Worker* 42) who was tried and arrested for 'seditious libel' – telling, quite truthfully, the story of the brutality with which the police and militia treated the miners and their families – by making the real villain of this novel not a doctor

arrogantly assuming the right to take a child away from his working-class parents, but a foreign spouter of 'socialist' propaganda, MacLennan passes the moral and aesthetic buck, rather as he does in *Barometer Rising*, by killing off all the inconvenient characters and the radical questions their lives had posed.

53 Cameron suggests that the company's multinational parent may have been siphoning off funds from the problem-ridden fish plants to other enterprises in order to bring about a convenient bankruptcy.

54 Milan Kundera, *The Unbearable Lightness of Being*, tr. Michael Henry Heim (New York: Harper & Row 1984) 248

55 Ibid. 251

56 Alexander, 'New Notions of Happiness' vii

CHAPTER SIX: READING THE REAL: MARITIME STRATEGIES

1 William French, review of *Will Ye Let the Mummers In?*, *Globe and Mail*, 18 Aug. 1984, 47

2 Alden Nowlan, 'Something to Write About' in *Canadian Literature: Special Issue on the Maritimes* 68–9 (Spring / Summer 1976) 8

3 William French, review of *Road to the Stilt House*, the *Globe and Mail* 13 July 1985, 13

4 Fraser Sutherland, 'A Lurking Devil,' *Canadian Literature* 60 (Spring 74) 120

5 For an example of this transvaluation of poverty, see Frank Kermode's *The Sense of an Ending: Studies in the Theory of Fiction* (New York: Oxford University Press 1969), in which he argues that our great human 'poverty' and 'need' derive from our lack of a 'supreme fiction' to plot and give meaning to our lives (155–64).

6 James Doyle, 'Shock: Recognition,' review of *Lives of Short Duration*, *Canadian Literature* 94 (Autumn 1982) 130

7 George Woodcock, 'Possessing the Land: Notes on Canadian Fiction' in David Staines, ed., *The Canadian Imagination: Dimensions of a Literary Culture* (Cambridge, MA: Harvard University Press 1977) 75

8 Georg Lukács, *Studies in European Realism* (New York: Grosset & Dunlap 1964) 83–4

9 Ernest Buckler, *Nova Scotia: Window on the Sea* (1973; rpt, Toronto: McClelland & Stewart 1978) 111

10 Kent Thompson, introduction to *Stories from Atlantic Canada* (Toronto: Macmillan 1973) x

11 Alden Nowlan, *Various Persons Named Kevin O'Brien: A Fictional Memoir* (Toronto: Clarke Irwin 1973) 101. Subsequent quotations will be taken from this edition and incorporated into the text of Chapter 6 using the abbreviation VP.

12 'Alden Nowlan's Notebook,' *The Atlantic Advocate* 72:1 (Sept. 1981) 78

13 J.M. Whalen and W.A. Oppen, 'Poor for Sale!' *The Atlantic Advocate* 67:1 (Sept. 1976) 50

14 George Woodcock, 'Views of Canadian Criticism' in *Odysseus Ever Returning: Essays on Canadian Writers and Writing* (Toronto: McClelland & Stewart 1970) 139

15 Bruce Hutchison, *The Unknown Country: Canada and Her People* (1942; rpt, Toronto: McClelland & Stewart 1965) 158

16 D.G. Jones, *Butterfly on Rock* (1970; rpt, Toronto: University of Toronto Press 1971) 166

17 Silver Donald Cameron, *Voices Down East: A Collection of New Writing from the Atlantic Provinces* (Halifax: Voices Down East, nd) 1; 'Letter from Halifax,' *Canadian Literature* 40 (Spring 1969) 60

18 Thomas Chandler Haliburton, *The Clockmaker, or The Sayings and Doings of Samuel Slick of Slickville* (First Series) (1958; rpt, Toronto: McClelland & Stewart 1966) 99

19 Fred Cogswell, 'The Development of Writing,' *Arts in New Brunswick* (Fredericton: University Press of New Brunswick 1967) 28–9

20 Thomas Raddall, *Tidefall* (Toronto: McClelland & Stewart 1953) 5

21 Douglas Barbour, 'Realism with a Vengeance,' review of *Blood Ties*, *Journal of Canadian Fiction* 19 (1977) 169–70

22 Ernest Buckler, *The Mountain and the Valley* (Toronto: McClelland & Stewart 1970) 299

23 David Adams Richards, *Lives of Short Duration* (Ottawa: Oberon 1981) 110. All subsequent quotations will be taken from this edition and incorporated into Chapter 6 using the abbreviation L.

24 Doyle, 'Shock, Recognition' 130

25 Antonine Maillet, *La Sagouine* (Montréal: Leméac 1974) 102. My translation. All subsequent quotations from this text will be my translations of passages taken from this edition and incorporated into the text of Chapter 6 using the abbreviation s.

26 Literary critics, particularly medievalists or those primarily interested in the origin and transmission of literary structures, have argued that Maillet has not so much chosen as been constrained to write epics rather than novels, given that Acadie has for so long been at an 'oral' rather than 'written' stage of cultural development. They argue that epics arise out of the desire of scattered communities to unite into one society; that the epic poem helps to realize that desire but is, paradoxically, destroyed by it, for once isolated communities become one society, other literary forms – in particular, the novel – are better suited to representing it. Thus Maillet would seem to have written herself into a corner – now that she has helped Acadie come to collective consciousness and become a society of readers, rather than isolated pockets of listeners, it badly needs other, more sophisticated literary forms in order to deal with present conflicts and the impinging future. See Hans R. Runte's 'L'Acadie des discours,' in Tessier and Vaillancourt, eds, *Les autres littératures d'expression française en Amérique du Nord* (Ottawa: Éditions de l'Université d'Ottawa 1987) 85–91. Yet despite Maillet's stated preference for chronicles, legends, even fortune-telling and genealogy over the novel as a

means to 'rebuild the world' (*Écrits du Canada français* 36 [1973] 23), it can be argued that many of her works owe as much to the novel and to realism as they do to more oral, popular forms. *Pélagie* and *Cent Ans dans les bois* are cases in point, and so is the earlier work *Mariaàgélas*, which James de Finney has shown to be a 'decomposition' of epic into, if not a novel, then what clearly should have been a novel. (See James de Finney's article '*Mariaàgélas* ou l'épopée impossible' in *Revue de l'Université de Moncton* 8:2 mai 1975 37–46, and Hans Runte's article 'L'Acadie entre l'épopée et le roman,' *Québec Studies* 4 [1986] 311–19.)

That Maillet is irresistibly attracted to the concerns and conventions of epic, fabulation and fairy tale is evident; so too is the fact that she writes with an irrepressible knowledge of her literary forebears, not only Rabelais but also Balzac, Flaubert, and other masters of that unavoidable genre, the novel.

27 See Marguerite Maillet's *Histoire de la littérature acadienne: De rêve en rêve* (Moncton: Éditions d'Acadie 1983) 183.
28 *Mariaàgélas* (Montréal: Leméac 1973) 236; my translation
29 Alistair MacLeod, *The Lost Salt Gift of Blood* (Toronto: McClelland & Stewart 1976) 25–6. All subsequent quotations will be taken from this edition and incorporated into the text of Chapter 6 using the abbreviation LSG.

CHAPTER SEVEN: PIGS IN THE PINEWOODS: SELF-DESTRUCTING REGIONAL IDYLLS

1 Lucy Maud Montgomery, *Emily's Quest* (Toronto: Macmillan 1927) 33
2 *Princeton Encyclopedia of Poetry and Poetics*, ed. Alex Preminger (Princeton, NJ: Princeton University Press 1974) 362
3 Desmond Pacey, 'Fiction 1920–1940' in Carl F. Klinck, gen. ed., *Literary History of Canada* (Toronto: University of Toronto Press 1965; 2nd ed., 1976) II, 177
4 Northrop Frye, 'Conclusion,' *Literary History of Canada* II, 357
5 Pacey, 'Fiction 1920–1940' II, 177–8
6 See John Sorfleet, ed., *Lucy Maud Montgomery: An Assessment* (Guelph: Children's Press 1976) for a sophisticated discussion of Montgomery's success in the field of children's literature.
7 George Woodcock, 'Possessing the Land: Notes on Canadian Fiction' in David Staines, ed., *The Canadian Imagination: Dimensions of a Literary Culture* (Cambridge, MA: Harvard University Press 1977) 76
8 Archibald MacMechan, *Headwaters of Canadian Literature* (1924; rpt, Toronto: McClelland & Stewart 1974) 211; E.K. Brown, 'The Problem of a Canadian Literature' in A.J.M. Smith, ed., *Masks of Fiction: Canadian Critics on Canadian Prose* (1961; rpt, Toronto: McClelland & Stewart 1969) 41 The injustice – and inaccuracy – of Brown's aspersions can be judged by a look at the biographical information and critical analysis to be found in Sorfleet's collection of essays on Montgomery.
9 Charles G.D. Roberts, *The Heart of the Ancient Wood* (1900; rpt, Toronto: Dent

1925) 168, 169. All subsequent quotations from this text will be taken from this edition and incorporated into Chapter 7 using the abbreviation HW.
10 Meat, of course, is used metonymically for sex, and vegetarianism for virginity / chastity in this text.
11 L.M. Montgomery, *Anne of Green Gables* (1908; rpt, Toronto: Ryerson 1962) 2. All subsequent quotations will be taken from this edition and incorporated into Chapter 7 using the abbreviation GG.
12 Muriel A. Whitaker, '"Queer Children": L.M. Montgomery's Heroines,' Sorfleet, *Lucy Maud Montgomery* 51–2
13 L.M. Montgomery, *The Alpine Path: The Story of My Career* (1917; rpt, Don Mills: Fitzhenry & Whiteside, nd) 78. Not only was Montgomery's earliest memory that of looking into the coffin of her dead mother; not only did she have to hide her feelings of abandonment by the beloved father who left her to the care of elderly, excessively strict grandparents, but her first truly painful encounter with the fact of death – that of a favourite cat – was brought about by the cat's having been poisoned. Not entirely tongue-in-cheek Montgomery writes: 'At that moment the curse of the race came upon me, death entered into my world and I turned my back on the Eden of my childhood where everything had seemed everlasting. I was barred out of it forevermore by the fiery sword of that keen and unforgettable pain' (pp 45–6).
14 Ibid. 47
15 Mollie Gillen, *The Wheel of Things: A Biography of Lucy Maud Montgomery, Author of Anne of Green Gables* (Don Mills: Fitzhenry & Whiteside 1975) 118
16 Ibid. 173
17 Given the overwhelming impression of rural tranquility, peace, and love with which *Anne* leaves most readers, it may be suggested that the corrective subtext I have alluded to is barely legible at all. A brief look at another of Montgomery's children's classics – *Jane of Lantern Hill* (Toronto: McClelland & Stewart 1937) – may clarify the issue.
*Jane* details the process whereby a passionately lonely eleven-year-old girl outgrows the tyranny of a hateful grandmother and patches up the breach between her loving but ineffectual parents, largely through the agency of a summer spent away from the prison of Toronto, on Prince Edward Island. The small Island community of Lantern Hill is utterly loving and accepting of her, and Jane lives out a 'fairy-tale come true,' with no need to escape into fantasy as she did in her grandmother's gloomy Toronto mansion. The world of Lantern Hill is unabashedly idyllic – that of Avonlea, by comparison, is as problematic as it is prosaic, requiring all of Anne's considerable imagination to make it liveable for anyone made 'of spirit and fire and dew.'
18 Jane Cowan Fredeman, 'The Land of Lost Content: The Use of Fantasy in L.M. Montgomery's Novels,' Sorfleet, *Lucy Maud Montgomery* 64
19 Mary Rubio, 'Satire, Realism, and Imagination in *Anne of Green Gables*,' Sorfleet, *Lucy Maud Montgomery* 34
20 As remarkable as Miranda Craig's eyesight or vision. After all, Anne, raised

by illiterate and often brutal foster parents, and having no other schooling than the most basic instruction in the asylum, manages, as one critic has it, to combine 'the sentimentality of an Alfred Austin with the vocabulary of a Bernard Shaw' (quoted in Douglas Daymond and Leslie Monkman, eds, *Canadian Novelists and the Novel* [Ottawa: Borealis 1981] 115).

21 Anne's passionate involvement with words is obviously reflective of Montgomery's own: one of her most vivid childhood memories is of the whipping a teacher gave her for using the expression, 'by the skin of my teeth' in one of her compositions. 'He said it was slang. If I had known then what I know now!!!' she wrote, some twenty-five years after the incident. 'It is in *Job*.' (Gillen, *The Wheel of Things* 10)

22 Elizabeth Waterston, 'Lucy Maud Montgomery: 1874–1942,' Sorfleet, *Lucy Maud Montgomery* 19

23 Gillen, *The Wheel of Things* 55

24 Gillian Thomas, 'The Decline of Anne: Matron vs Child,' Sorfleet, *Lucy Maud Montgomery* 38–9, 41

25 Gillen, *The Wheel of Things* 137, 175

26 Ernest Buckler, *Oxbells and Fireflies* (1968; rpt, Toronto: McClelland & Stewart 1974) 130. All subsequent quotations from this text will be taken from this edition and incorporated into Chapter 7 using the abbreviation OF.

27 The odd villager Syd Wright, whose story is told in Chapter 18, 'Another Man' is the exception to prove Buckler's rule. His loneliness comes not from the conditions and context of his life, as would a city-dweller's, but from his refusal to commit himself to the openhearted fellowship characteristic of Norstead. Even so, he is a member of the community, defining himself against its norms and, more importantly, accepted by it.

28 Thomas Chandler Haliburton, *The Clockmaker or The Sayings and Doings of Samuel Slick of Slickville* (First series) (1958; rpt, Toronto: McClelland & Stewart 1966) 123

29 Donna Smyth, *Quilt* (Toronto: Women's Press 1982) 17–18. All subsequent quotations will be taken from this edition and incorporated into Chapter 7 using the abbreviation Q.

30 Ernest Buckler, *Nova Scotia: Window on the Sea* (1973; rpt, Toronto: McClelland & Stewart 1978) 126

CHAPTER EIGHT: GOING OR STAYING: MARITIME PARADIGMS

1 Thomas Chandler Haliburton, *The Old Judge*, ed. R.E. Watters (Toronto: Clarke Irwin 1968) 202

2 Kent Thompson, *Stories from Atlantic Canada* (Toronto: Macmillan 1973) xii

3 D.C. Harvey, 'The Heritage of the Maritimes,' *Dalhousie Review* XIV (1934) 31

4 W.H. New, 'Maritime Cadences,' *Canadian Literature: Special Issue on the Maritimes* 68–9 (Spring / Summer 1976) 4

5 Fraser Sutherland, 'Home Truths,' *Canadian Literature: Special Issue on the Maritimes* 105

6 Ibid. 102

7 Ibid. 103

8 In an interview with Fraser Sutherland, MacLennan speaks approvingly of an English friend who commented that *Barometer Rising* was not Canadian but rather Nova Scotian literature, and that he would be well advised to set future novels in Quebec: 'It's the centre of Canada, if anything is.' Interview with Hugh MacLennan, *Canadian Literature: Special Issue on the Maritimes* 45.

9 Harvey, 'The Heritage of the Maritimes' 31

10 Hugh MacLennan, *On Being a Maritime Writer* (Sackville, NB, Centre for Canadian Studies, Mount Allison University 1983) 16

11 MacLennan has often expressed his admiration for Galsworthy's achievement in fiction. See 'The Writer *Engagé*' in Elspeth Cameron, ed., *The Other Side of Hugh MacLennan: Selected Essays Old and New* (Toronto: Macmillan 1978) 277 and *A Writer's Life* (Toronto: University of Toronto Press 1981) 168, in which Cameron describes MacLennan as having set out to create a Canadian *Forsyte Saga* in *Two Solitudes*.

12 Michael Nowlan, 'Atlantic Bookcase,' *Atlantic Advocate* 72:2 (Oct. 1981) 76

13 See Hugh MacLennan, *On Being a Maritime Writer* 19.

14 Emphasizing the thoroughness and ferocity of his religious upbringing, MacLennan has remarked, 'I don't believe that anybody who had ever been forced to memorize the shorter catechism was ever very comfortable for a long time afterwards.' Quoted in Donald Cameron, ed., *Conversations with Canadian Novelists* (Toronto: Macmillan 1973) 134

15 There are, of course, fine things in MacLennan's novels – the Galsworthian description of 'Dinner at the Methuens' in *Two Solitudes*, for example, or the terrifying encounter of Alan MacNeil with the hag-like Mrs MacCuish in *Each Man's Son*: were there much more of this kind of evocative writing in MacLennan's oeuvre, and much less ex cathedra pronouncement, he would be a fine novelist indeed.

16 *On Being a Maritime Writer* 27

17 *Other Side* 236

18 Ibid. 227

19 See MacLennan's essay 'Scotchman's Return' for an indication of the strength of his ties to the Scottish mystique.

20 See the opening chapters of Elspeth Cameron's *A Writer's Life*.

21 'French is a MUST for Canadians,' *Other Side* 164

22 Ibid. 262

23 See 'Reflections on Two Decades,' *Other Side* and Cameron, *A Writer's Life* 314–15.

24 T.D. MacLulich, *Hugh MacLennan* (Boston: Twayne 1983) 16

25 MacLennan's essay 'Confessions of a Wood-Chopping Man' reveals that the essence of his affection for the Quebec countryside lies in its very difference from the Maritime landscape: 'Along the Atlantic coast of Nova Scotia you grow up with the conviction that everything in nature here is as it is

forever, and that man, living with the unshifting immutability of granite rocks, can never dominate his fate, never play artist with nature, but must take life and the world as he finds them ... [T]he trees of my childhood helped the granite and the ocean to confirm me in the belief that nature can neither be altered nor improved.'

'It took me a good many years to respond to the soft luxuriance of the Eastern Townships, where the eye, the ear, and the sense of smell are played upon gently and with subtle variations. It took me no time at all, however, to learn that here landscape can and must be altered from time to time because it is continually altering itself to your disadvantage.' MacLennan concludes that 'A hardwood copse in the Eastern Townships of Quebec in Indian summer can be compared to nothing else on this earth, being itself an absolute' (pp 117, 116).

26 *The Return of the Sphinx* 307
27 MacLulich, *Hugh MacLennan* 120
28 Ernest Buckler, *The Mountain and the Valley* (1961; rpt, Toronto: McClelland & Stewart 1968) 226. All subsequent quotations will be taken from this edition and incorporated into Chapter 8 using the abbreviation MV.
29 'Ernest Buckler: A Conversation with an Irritated Oyster,' Cameron, *Conversations* 7-8
30 Douglas Daymond and Leslie Monkman, eds, *Canadian Novelists and the Novel* (Ottawa: Borealis 1981) 203
31 John Orange, 'On *Oxbells and Fireflies*' in Gregory Cook, ed., *Ernest Buckler* (Toronto: McGraw-Hill 1972) 140
32 Cameron, *Conversations* 8
33 Ibid. 5-6
34 Ibid. 5
35 Alden Nowlan, 'All the Layers of Meaning' in Cook, *Ernest Buckler* 116
36 *New York Times Book Review* quoted in Cook, ibid. 29
37 Orange, 'On *Oxbells and Fireflies*,' Cook, ibid. 142
38 'Various Kinds of Love,' Cook, ibid. 85
39 'Creed and Craft Expounded,' Cook, ibid. 91-2
40 John Orange, 'Ernest Buckler' in Jeffrey M. Heath, ed., *Profiles in Canadian Literature 2* (Toronto: Dundurn Press 1980) 18
41 D.J. Dooley, *Moral Vision in the Canadian Novel* (Toronto: Clarke Irwin 1979) 50
42 Dooley, *Moral Vision* 53
43 Ibid. 55
44 Ibid. 58-9
45 See Alan R. Young's reference in *Ernest Buckler* to a letter in which Buckler described David's death as 'the crowning point of the whole dramatic irony' and his plans to be 'the greatest writer in the whole world' a 'final transport of self-deception.' *Ernest Buckler* (Toronto: Macmillan 1976) 35
46 'My First Novel,' *Canadian Novelists and the Novel* 201
47 Dooley, *Moral Vision* 53

48 Robert Harlow, 'Sound and Fury,' *Canadian Literature* 19 (Winter 1964) 58
49 D.O. Spettigue, 'The Way It Was,' Cook, *Ernest Buckler* 109
50 Ibid. 107–8
51 To be able to make such judgments – grounded in what the text reveals to us of a certain character's consciousness and actions, and in our own experience of human behaviour outside the novel – is, of course, the privilege of the Transparent as opposed to the Opaque critic. See A.D. Nuttall's *A New Mimesis: Shakespeare and the Representation of Reality* (London: Methuen 1983) 82–4.
52 Percy Lubbock, ed. *The Letters of Henry James* II (1920; rpt, New York: Octagon Books 1970) 361
53 D.G. Jones, *Butterfly on Rock* (1970; rpt, Toronto: University of Toronto Press 1971) 37
54 Dooley, *Moral Vision* 49
55 Alistair MacLeod, *As Birds Bring Forth the Sun, and Other Stories* (Toronto: McClelland & Stewart 1986) 12. Subsequent quotations from this text will be incorporated into Chapter 8 using the abbreviation BBS.

CHAPTER NINE: WORDS AND WOMEN

1 Lucy Maud Montgomery, *Emily's Quest* (Toronto: McClelland & Stewart 1927) 3–4. Subsequent quotations will be taken from this edition and incorporated into the text of Chapter 9 using the abbreviation EQ.
2 Of course there are other female writers to be found outside the canon: Julia Beckwith Hart (*St Ursula's Convent*, 1824) and, as revealed by Gwendolyn Davies's article 'Belles and the Backwoods: A Study of Fiction in Nineteenth-Century Maritime Periodicals,' *Atlantic Provinces Literature Colloquium Papers* (Saint John: Atlantic Canada Institute 1977), Mrs F. Beavan (*Life in the Backwoods*, 1845), and Mary Eliza Herbert (*Belinda Dalton*, 1859). Among Lucy Maud Montgomery's *consoeurs* were such writers as Alice Jones (*Bubbles We Buy*, 1903), Margaret Marshall Saunders (*Rose à Charlitte*, 1898), as well as such phenomenally popular and prolific writers as May Agnes Fleming (*Estella's Husband; or, Thrice Lost, Thrice Won*, 1891). As with almost all Maritime works outside the canon constituted by the New Canadian Library series, these novels are virtually unobtainable, except for the highly motivated reader living close to large university libraries or else to second-hand bookshops. Some of these works may be excruciatingly bad, but it would be desirable to have at least a critical survey of women's writing in the Maritimes, to know which texts reward reading, and what these women writers can tell us about the literary and social contexts in which they produced their prose.
3 'According to one eulogist, Miss Tonge was "the highly-gifted songstress of Acadia ... [who] has left behind her a few imperishable specimens of heaven-born genius ..."' (*Acadian Magazine*, May 1827). Footnote by M.G. Parks to p 66 of Howe's *Western and Eastern Rambles*

4 Archibald MacMechan, *The Book of Ultima Thule* (Toronto: McClelland &
   Stewart 1927) 86
5 Thomas Chandler Haliburton, *The Clockmaker, or The Sayings and Doings of
   Samuel Slick of Slickville* First Series (1958; rpt, Toronto: McClelland &
   Stewart 1966) 14
6 Ann S. Cowan writes that 'Anne does give up her writing. When Gilbert
   suggests that she has sacrificed, Anne replies that her family is more important than the 'few children's stories' she wrote, an attitude Montgomery
   certainly never shared.' Cowan goes on to conclude that 'Montgomery, in
   the *Emily* trilogy, has successfully expanded the themes of her novels for girls
   to create a work of literature that sensitively explores the problems and
   conflicts facing the young Canadian female novelist in a society which places
   a literary career second to the role of wife and mother' ('Canadian Writers:
   Lucy Maud and Emily Byrd' in John R. Sorfleet, ed., *Lucy Maud Montgomery:
   An Assessment* [Guelph: Canadian Children's Press 1976] 46, 48).
7 Alden Nowlan, 'Something to Write About' in *Canadian Literature: Special
   Issue on the Maritimes* 68–9 (Spring / Summer 1976) 8
8 Nowlan, ibid., and 'Ernest Buckler: A Conversation with an Irritated Oyster' in Silver Donald Cameron, ed., *Conversations with Canadian Novelists*
   (Toronto: Macmillan 1973) 5. Too many writers, explains Buckler, 'rub themselves off against each other' and talk themselves out, whereas 'you have
   to conserve your orgasm for the thing itself.'
9 Lucy Maud Montgomery, *Emily of New Moon* (1925; rpt, Toronto: McClelland
   & Stewart 1981) 49. All subsequent quotations will be taken from this
   edition and incorporated into the text of Chapter 9 using the abbreviation
   ENM.
10 It is interesting that there is no question of any legal, as opposed to symbolic
   marriage between Paul and Letty – though Paul does intend to make his
   house over to Letty in his will. Obsessed as Buckler was with relations between parents and children, brothers and sisters, grandparents and grandchildren, he shied away from committing himself or his fictional alter-egos –
   David Canaan and Paul Creed – to being either husband or father. The
   reason Buckler gave to Claude Bissell for having never married any of the
   country women who lived with him as housekeepers and sexual partners,
   was that a writer should never marry: the wife would always be there in the
   kitchen, telling you to come away from your typewriter to supper – just at
   a crucial moment in your manuscript – because if you didn't, the carrots
   would burn (paraphrased from a radio interview with Claude Bissell aired
   on CBC radio shortly after Buckler's death).
11 Tortuous language such as the following: 'He caught himself, close to the
   wispily elegiac plaintiveness that unconsciously poeticizes itself, frighteningly close to rehearsing his deprivation with that toxic "lingering" regard of
   the self-commiserative' (CM 66).
12 Of course I am taking what may be enormous licence in reading 'Lucy Maud'
   for 'Emily Byrd,' yet Montgomery's own descriptions and her biographers'

accounts of her childhood and her writing would seem to make it no great trespass to see Emily as Montgomery's fictional alter-ego.

13 See Vladimir Nabokov's *Speak, Memory: An Autobiography Revisited* rev. ed. (New York: Putnam's 1966) 34–9. The relevant passage from *Emily of New Moon* reads as following:

> How pretty the wallpaper was, with the garland of roses inside the gilt diamond! Emily wondered if she could 'see it in the air.' She tried – yes she could – there it hung, a yard from her eyes, a little fairy pattern, suspended in mid-air like a screen. Emily had discovered that she possessed this odd knack when she was six. By a certain movement of the muscles of her eyes, which she could never describe, she could produce a tiny replica of the wallpaper in the air before her – could hold it there and look at it as long as she liked – could shift it back and forth, to any distance she chose, making it larger or smaller as it went farther away or came nearer. It was one of her secret joys when she went into a new room to 'see the paper in the air.' (ENM 57).

14 L.M. Montgomery, *Emily Climbs* (Toronto: McClelland & Stewart 1975) 214
15 Virginia Woolf, *To the Lighthouse* (Penguin 1968) 57. If Lily Briscoe is an inverted image of Woolf – a successful artist's creation of an unrecognized, persistent but only mildly gifted painter – then the opposite is true of Montgomery's Emily, who is the legitimate, successful artist that Montgomery – a popularly successful author but a severly flawed novelist and a failed poet – never was. (*To The Lighthouse* and the *Emily* trilogy are virtually contemporaneous.)
16 Nancy Bauer, *Wise-Ears* (Ottawa: Oberon 1984) 81
17 Susan Kerslake, *Middlewatch* (Ottawa: Oberon 1976) 7. Subsequent quotations will be taken from this edition and incorporated into Chapter 9 using the abbreviation M.
18 Susan Kerslake, *Penumbra* (Toronto: Aya 1984) 54. Subsequent quotations will be taken from this edition and incorporated into Chapter 9 using the abbreviation P.

# Selected Bibliography

PRINCIPAL AUTHORS

Acorn, Milton *The Island Means Minago* Toronto: NC Press 1975
– 'An Afternoon with Milton Acorn' *New Maritimes* (4 May 1984) 4–8
Bauer, Nancy *Flora, Write this Down* Fredericton: Goose Lane 1982
– *Wise-Ears* Ottawa: Oberon 1985
Bruce, Charles *The Channel Shore*. New Canadian Library series 178. Toronto: McClelland & Stewart 1984
– *The Township of Time*. Toronto: McClelland & Stewart 1959
Bruce, Harry *Nova Scotia* Toronto: Hounslow 1975
Buckler, Ernest *The Mountain and the Valley*. New Canadian Library series 23. 1952. Toronto: McClelland & Stewart 1968
– *The Cruelest Month* Toronto: McClelland & Stewart 1963
– *Oxbells and Fireflies: A Memoir* New Canadian Library series 99. 1968. Toronto: McClelland & Stewart 1983
– *Nova Scotia: Window on the Sea* 1973. Toronto: McClelland & Stewart 1978
– *The Rebellion of Young David and Other Stories* Toronto: McClelland & Stewart 1975
– *Whirligig: Selected Prose and Verse* Toronto: McClelland & Stewart 1977
– 'Ernest Buckler: A Conversation with an Irritated Oyster' *Conversations with Canadian Novelists*. Ed. Donald Cameron. Toronto: Macmillan 1973, pp 3–12
Cook, Gregory M., ed. *Ernest Buckler* Toronto: McGraw-Hill Ryerson 1972
Heath, Jeffrey M., ed. 'Ernest Buckler' *Profiles in Canadian Literature* 2 Toronto: Dundurn Press 1980
Noonan, Gerald 'Egoism and Style in *The Mountain and the Valley*. *Atlantic Provinces Literature Colloquium Papers*. Saint John: Atlantic Canada Institute 1977, pp 68–78
Young, Alan R. *Ernest Buckler* Toronto: McClelland & Stewart 1976

Cameron, Silver Donald [Donald Cameron] *Conversations with Canadian Novelists* Toronto: Macmillan 1973
- *The Education of Everett Richardson: The Nova Scotia Fishermen's Strike 1970–1971* Toronto: McClelland & Stewart 1977
- *Seasons in the Rain: An Expatriate's Notes on British Columbia* Toronto: McClelland & Stewart 1978
- *Voices Down East: A Collection of New Writing from the Atlantic Provinces* Halifax: Voices Down East, nd
- 'Letter from Halifax' *Canadian Literature* 40 (Spring 1969) 55–60
Day, Frank Parker *Rockbound*. 1928. Toronto: University of Toronto Press 1973
De Mille, James *A Strange Manuscript Found in a Copper Cylinder*. New Canadian Library series 68. 1888. Toronto: McClelland & Stewart 1969
Haliburton, Thomas C. *The Clockmaker, or The Sayings and Doings of Samuel Slick of Slickville* First series. New Canadian Library series 6. 1871. 1958. Toronto: McClelland & Stewart 1966.
- *The Old Judge, or Life in a Colony* 1849. Ottawa: Tecumseh 1978
- *The Old Judge* Introd. R.E. Watters. Toronto: Clarke Irwin 1968
- *The Sam Slick Anthology* Ed. and introd. R.E. Watters. Toronto: Clarke Irwin 1969
    Harvey, D.C. "The Centenary of Sam Slick' *Dalhousie Review* XVI (1936–7) 429–40
    Morrison, Katherine 'In Haliburton's Nova Scotia: *The Old Judge or Life in a Colony' Canadian Literature* 101 (Summer 1984) 58–68
Howe, Joseph *Western and Eastern Rambles: Travel Sketches of Nova Scotia*. 1828–31. Ed. M.G. Parks. Toronto: University of Toronto Press 1973
- *Poems and Essays* Montreal: Lovell 1874
- *Joseph Howe: Voice of Nova Scotia* Ed. J. Murray Beck. Toronto: McClelland & Stewart 1964
    Hunt, Wayne, ed. *The Proceedings of the Joseph Howe Symposium, Mount Allison University* Halifax: Nimbus 1984
Huyghue, Samuel Douglas Smith ('Eugene') *Arigmou: A Legend of the Micmac*. 1847. Sackville, NB: R.P. Bell Library, Mount Allison University 1977
Kerslake, Susan *Middlewatch*. Ottawa: Oberon 1976
- *Penumbra* Toronto: Aya Press 1984
MacLennan, Hugh *Barometer Rising* 1941. Toronto: Macmillan 1948
- *Two Solitudes* Toronto: Collins 1945
- *The Precipice* Toronto: Collins 1948
- *Each Man's Son* Laurentian Library 11. 1951. Toronto: Macmillan 1971
- *The Watch that Ends the Night* 1959. New York: Signet 1964
- *The Return of the Sphinx* Laurentian Library 10. 1967. Toronto: Macmillan 1970
- *Voices in Time* Toronto: Macmillan 1980
- *The Other Side of Hugh MacLennan: Selected Essays Old and New* Ed. Elspeth Cameron. Toronto: Macmillan 1978
- *On Being a Maritime Writer*. Sackville, NB: Centre for Canadian Studies, Mount Allison University 1983

- 'Hugh MacLennan: The Tennis Racket Is an Antelope Bone' Donald Cameron, ed. *Conversations with Canadian Novelists*. Toronto: Macmillan 1973, pp 130–48
  Buitenhuis, Peter *Canadian Writers and Their Works: Hugh MacLennan* Toronto: Forum House 1969
  Cameron, Elspeth. *Hugh MacLennan: A Writer's Life*. Toronto: University of Toronto Press 1981
  - ed. *Hugh MacLennan: 1982. Proceedings of the MacLennan Conference at University College* Toronto: Canadian Studies Programme, University of Toronto 1982
  Cockburn, Robert H. *The Novels of Hugh MacLennan* Montreal: Harvest House 1969
  Goetsch, Paul, ed. *Hugh MacLennan* Critical Views on Canadian Writers series 8. Toronto: McGraw-Hill 1973
  MacLulich, T.D. *Hugh MacLennan* Boston: Twayne 1983
  Woodcock, George *Hugh MacLennan* Studies in Canadian Literature series. Toronto: Copp Clark 1969
MacLeod, Alistair *The Lost Salt Gift of Blood*. New Canadian Library series 157. Toronto: McClelland & Stewart 1976
- *As Birds Bring Forth the Sun and Other Stories*. Toronto: McClelland & Stewart 1986
Macphail, Sir Andrew *The Master's Wife*. New Canadian Library series 138, 1939. Toronto: McClelland & Stewart 1977
Maillet, Antonine *Mariaàgélas*. Montreal: Leméac 1973
- *La Sagouine* Montreal: Leméac 1974
- *Pélagie* Trans. Philip Stratford. Toronto: General Publishing 1983
- *Cents Ans dans les bois* Montreal: Leméac 1981
  de Finney, James *Mariaàgélas ou l'épopée impossible' Revue de l'Université de Moncton* 8:2 (mai 1975) 37–46
  Quinlan, James *'Pélagie-la-charrette: Spoken History in the Lyrical Novel' Revue de l'Université Sainte-Anne* (1984-5) 26–32
  Runte, Hans R. *'L'Acadie entre l'épopée et le roman' Québec Studies* 4 (1986) 311–19.
McCulloch, Thomas *The Stepsure Letters* New Canadian Library series 16. Toronto: McClelland & Stewart 1960
Montgomery, Lucy M. *Anne of Green Gables* 1908. Toronto: Ryerson 1962
- *Anne of Avonlea* 1909. New York: Grosset 1936
- *The Story Girl* 1910. Toronto: Ryerson 1944
- *The Golden Road* 1910. Toronto: McGraw-Hill, nd
- *Anne of the Island* 1915. Bantam 1976
- *Emily of New Moon* 1925. Toronto: McClelland & Stewart 1981
- *The Blue Castle* 1926. Toronto: McClelland & Stewart 1974
- *Emily Climbs* 1924. Toronto: McClelland & Stewart 1975
- *Emily's Quest* Toronto: McClelland & Stewart 1927
- *Jane of Lantern Hill* Toronto: McClelland & Stewart 1937

- *The Alpine Path: The Story of My Career* 1917. Don Mills: Fitzhenry, nd
  Bolger, Francis W.P. *The Years before 'Anne'* Prince Edward Island Heritage
  Foundation 1974
  Gillen, Mollie *The Wheel of Things: A Biography of L.M. Montgomery, Author of
  Anne of Green Gables* Don Mills: Fitzhenry & Whiteside 1975
  Sorfleet, John R., ed. *L.M. Montgomery: An Assessment* Guelph: Canadian
  Children's Press 1976
Nowlan, Alden *Miracle at Indian River* Toronto: Clarke Irwin 1968
- *Various Persons Named Kevin O'Brien: A fictional memoir* Toronto: Clarke Irwin
  1973
- *Will Ye Let the Mummers In?* Toronto: Clarke Irwin 1984
- 'My Canada' *Maclean's* 84:6 (June 1971) 17–40
- 'Something to Write About' *Canadian Literature: Special Issue on the Maritimes*
  68–9 (Spring / summer 1976) 7–12
- 'The National Whipping Boy' *The Atlantic Advocate* 67:11 (July 1977) 71
- 'For a Confederation of Equals' *The Atlantic Advocate* 71:7 (Mar. 1981) 86
- 'No Naughtier than in the Past' *The Atlantic Advocate* 72:1 (Sept. 81) 78
Raddall, Thomas H. *His Majesty's Yankees* 1942. New York: Popular Library, nd
- *Roger Sudden* Toronto: McClelland & Stewart 1944
- *The Nymph and the Lamp* New Canadian Library Series 38. 1950. Toronto:
  McClelland & Stewart 1968
- *Tidefall* Toronto: McClelland & Stewart 1953
- *The Wings of Night* New York: Doubleday 1956
- *At the Tide's Turn* New Canadian Library series 9. 1959. Toronto: McClelland &
  Stewart 1971
- *Hangman's Beach* 1966. Toronto: McClelland & Stewart 1979
- *Halifax: Warden of the North* Toronto: McClelland & Stewart 1971
- *In My Time: A Memoir* Toronto: McClelland & Stewart 1976
  Cameron, Donald 'Thomas Raddall: The Art of Historical Fiction' *The Dal-
  housie Review* 49:4 (Winter 1969–70) 540–8
Richards, David Adams *The Coming of Winter* New Canadian Library series 174.
  1974. Toronto: McClelland & Stewart 1982
- *Blood Ties* Ottawa: Oberon 1976
- *Dancers at Night* Ottawa: Oberon 1978
- *Lives of Short Duration* Ottawa: Oberon 1981
Roberts, Sir Charles G.D., Trans. and Introd. *Canadians of Old* by Philippe
  Aubert de Gaspé. 1890. New Canadian Library series 106. Introd. Clara
  Thomas. Toronto: McClelland & Stewart 1974
- *The Forge in the Forest* Boston: Lamson Wolffe 1896
- *A Sister to Evangeline* London: John Lane 1900
- *The Heart of the Ancient Wood* 1900. Toronto: Dent 1925
- *The Kindred of the Wild* London: Duckworth 1903
- *The Prisoner of Mademoiselle* New York: Grosset & Dunlap 1904
- *The Heart that Knows* Toronto: Copp Clark 1906
- *The Backwoodsmen* London: Ward Lock 1909

- *In the Morning of Time* London: Hutchison 1919
- *The Last Barrier and Other Stories* New Canadian Library series 7. Toronto: McClelland & Stewart 1970
- *Selected Poetry and Critical Prose* Ed. W.J. Keith. Toronto: University of Toronto Press 1974
    Keith, W.J. *Charles G.D. Roberts* Toronto: Copp Clark 1969
    Clever, Glenn, ed. *The Sir Charles G.D. Roberts Symposium* Ottawa: University of Ottawa Press 1983
Smyth, Donna E. *Quilt* Toronto: The Women's Press 1982

SECONDARY SOURCES

*Atlantic Literature Colloquium Papers* Saint John: Atlantic Canada Institute 1977
Abella, Irving and Millar, David, eds *The Canadian Worker in the Twentieth Century* Toronto: Oxford University Press 1978
Alexander, David *Atlantic Canada and Confederation: Essays on Canadian Political Economy* Toronto: University of Toronto Press in association with Memorial University of Newfoundland 1983
Arsenault, Bona *History of the Acadians* Québec: Le Conseil de la vie française en Amérique 1966
Barclay, Patricia 'Regionalism and the Writer: A Talk with W.O. Mitchell' *Canadian Literature* 14 (Autumn 1962) 53–6
Baglole, Harry, ed. *Exploring Island History: A Guide to the Historical Resources of Prince Edward Island* Belfast: Ragweed 1977
Bird, Will R., and Lucas, Alec, eds *Atlantic Anthology* Toronto: McClelland & Stewart 1959
*Canadian Literature: Special Issue on the Maritimes* 68–9 (Spring / summer 1976)
Cockburn, R., and Gibbs, R., eds *Ninety Seasons: Modern Poems from the Maritimes* Toronto: McClelland & Stewart 1974
Daymond, Douglas, and Leslie Monkman, eds *Canadian Novelists and the Novel* Ottawa: Borealis 1981
Denham, Paul, and Mary Jane Edwards, eds *Canadian Literature in the 70's* Toronto: Holt Rinehart 1980
Dooley, D.J. *Moral Vision in the Canadian Novel* Toronto: Clarke Irwin 1979
Dunn, Charles W. *Highland Settler: A Portrait of the Scottish Gael in Nova Scotia* 1953. Toronto: University of Toronto Press 1971
Forbes, Ernest R. *The Maritime Rights Movement, 1919–1927: A Study in Canadian Regionalism* Montreal: McGill-Queen's University Press 1979
Frank, David 'Regional Disparities Reviewed' Review of *Regional Disparities* by Paul Phillips *Atlantic Provinces Book Review* 10:2 (Sept.–Oct. 1983) 2
Frye, Northrop *The Bush Garden: Essays on the Canadian Imagination* Toronto: Anansi 1971
- *Divisions on a Ground: Essays on Canadian Culture* Ed. James Polk. Toronto: Anansi 1982
- 'From Nationalism to Regionalism: The Maturing of Canadian Culture. Robert

Fulford talks with Northrop Frye' *Aurora: New Canadian Writing 1980* Ed.
Morris Wolfe. Toronto: Doubleday 1980, pp 5–15
Fulford, Robert, Dave Godfrey, Abraham Rotstein, eds *Read Canadian: A Book
about Canadian Books* Toronto: James Lewis & Samuel 1972
Grant, George *Lament for a Nation: The Defeat of Canadian Nationalism* 1965.
Toronto: McClelland & Stewart 1971
Hamilton, William B. *Local History in Atlantic Canada* Toronto: Macmillan 1974
Harvey, D.C. 'The Heritage of the Maritimes' *Dalhousie Review* xiv (1934) 28–32
Hinz, Evelyn J., ed. *Beyond Nationalism: The Canadian Literary Scene in Global
Perspective* Winnipeg: University of Manitoba Press 1981
Hutchison, Bruce *The Unknown Country: Canada and Her People* 1942. Toronto:
McClelland & Stewart 1965
Jones, D.G. *Butterfly on Rock* 1970. Toronto: University of Toronto Press 1971
Klinck, Carl F., gen. ed. *Literary History of Canada: Canadian Literature in English.*
Toronto: University of Toronto Press 1965; 2nd ed., 1976
Lawrence, D.H. 'Why the Novel Matters' *A Selection from Phoenix*, ed. A.A.H.
Inglis. Harmondsworth: Penguin 1979
– 'The Spirit of Place' *Studies in Classic American Literature.* Harmondsworth:
Penguin 1977
Lower, Arthur R.M. *History of Canada: Colony to Nation.* 4th ed., Don Mills:
Longmans 1964
MacMechan, Archibald *The Book of Ultima Thule* Toronto: McClelland & Stewart
1927
– *Headwaters of Canadian Literature* 1924. Toronto: McClelland & Stewart 1974
MacNutt, W.S. *The Atlantic Provinces: The Emergence of Colonial Society 1712–1857.*
1965. Toronto: McClelland & Stewart 1968
Maillet, Marguerite *Histoire de la littérature acadienne: De rêve en rêve* Moncton:
Éditions d'Acadie 1983
Mandel, Eli, ed. *Contexts of Canadian Criticism* Chicago: University of Chicago
Press 1971
Matthews, Robin *Canadian Literature: Surrender or Revolution?* Toronto: Steel Rail
1978
McInnis, Edgar *Canada: A Political and Social History* 1947. Toronto: Clarke Irwin
1959
Metcalf, John *Kicking Against the Pricks* Toronto: ECW 1982
Moody, Barry *The Acadians* Toronto: Grolier 1981
Moss, John *Patterns of Isolation in English-Canadian Fiction* Toronto: McClelland &
Stewart 1974
– *The Canadian Novel: Beginnings. A Critical Anthology* Rev. ed. Toronto: NC Press
1984
New, W.H. *Articulating West: Essays on Purpose and Form in Modern Canadian
Literature* Toronto: New Press 1972
O'Flaherty, Patrick *The Rock Observed: Studies in the Literature of Newfoundland*
Toronto: University of Toronto Press 1979

Rawlyk, George ed. *Historical Essays on the Atlantic Provinces* 1967. Toronto: McClelland & Stewart 1971.

Ricou, Laurence *Vertical Man / Horizontal World: Man and Landscape in Canadian Prairie Fiction* Vancouver: University of British Columbia Press 1973

Roy, Michel *L'Acadie des origines à nos jours: Essai de synthèse historique* Montréal: Québec / Amérique 1981

Ryerson, Stanley B. *The Founding of Canada: Beginnings to 1815* 2nd ed. Toronto: Progress 1963

– *Unequal Union: Confederation and the Roots of Conflict in the Canadas, 1815–1873* Toronto: Progress 1968

Smith, A.J.M., ed. *Masks of Fiction: Canadian Critics on Canadian Prose* 1961. Toronto: McClelland & Stewart 1969

Staines, David, ed. *The Canadian Imagination: Dimensions of a Literary Culture* Cambridge, MA: Harvard University Press 1977

Stephens, Donald 'From the Maritimes' Review of Will Bird's *Atlantic Anthology. Canadian Literature* 3 (Winter 1960) 83–4

Sutherland, Ronald 'The Mainstream' *Canadian Literature* 53 (Summer 1972) 30–41

Thompson, Kent, ed. *Stories from Atlantic Canada* Toronto: Macmillan 1973

Tierney, Frank, ed. and introd. *The Thomas Chandler Haliburton Symposium* Reappraisals: Canadian Writers 11. Ottawa: University of Ottawa Press 1985

Tweedie, Robert A. ed. *Arts in New Brunswick* Fredericton: University Press of New Brunswick 1967

Whalen, J.M. and W.A. Oppen. 'Poor for Sale!' *The Atlantic Advocate* 67:1 (Sept. 1976) 50–1

Whalen, Terry, ed. *The Atlantic Anthology* Vol. III. *Critical Essays* Charlottetown: ECW / Ragweed 1985

– 'Atlantic Possibilities' *Essays on Canadian Writing* 20 (Winter 1980–1) 32–60

Woodcock, George *Odysseus Ever Returning: Essays on Canadian Writers and Writing* Toronto: McClelland & Stewart 1970

– *The Canadian Novel in the Twentieth Century: Essays from 'Canadian Literature'* Toronto: McClelland & Stewart 1975

# Index